NOT JUST ANOTHER
SWEETHEART DEAL

A COLLECTION OF ROSE IS ROSE® COMICS
CREATED BY PAT BRADY, BY DON WIMMER

Andrews McMeel
Publishing, LLC
Kansas City • Sydney • London

Rose is Rose® is distributed internationally by United Feature Syndicate, Inc.

Not Just Another Sweetheart Deal copyright © 2010 by United Feature Syndicate, Inc. All rights reserved. Printed in China. No part of this book may be used or reproduced in any manner whatsoever without written permission except in the case of reprints in the context of reviews. For information, write Andrews McMeel Publishing, LLC, an Andrews McMeel Universal company, 1130 Walnut Street, Kansas City, Missouri 64106.

10 11 12 13 14 TEN 10 9 8 7 6 5 4 3 2 1

ISBN-13: 978-0-7407-9777-4
ISBN-10: 0-7407-9777-8

Library of Congress Control Number: 2010921943

www.andrewsmcmeel.com

Cover design, cover art, and flip book by Pat Brady.

ATTENTION: SCHOOLS AND BUSINESSES

Andrews McMeel books are available at quantity discounts with bulk
purchase for educational, business, or sales promotional use.
For information, please write to: Special Sales Department,
Andrews McMeel Publishing, LLC, 1130 Walnut Street,
Kansas City, Missouri 64106.

Other *Rose is Rose*® Books

She's a Momma, Not a Movie Star

License to Dream

Rose is Rose 15th Anniversary Collection

The Irresistible Rose is Rose

High-Spirited Rose is Rose

Rose is Rose Right on the Lips

Rose is Rose Running on Alter Ego

Red Carpet Rose

The Enchanting Rose

100% Whole Grin Rose is Rose

Peekaboo Planet

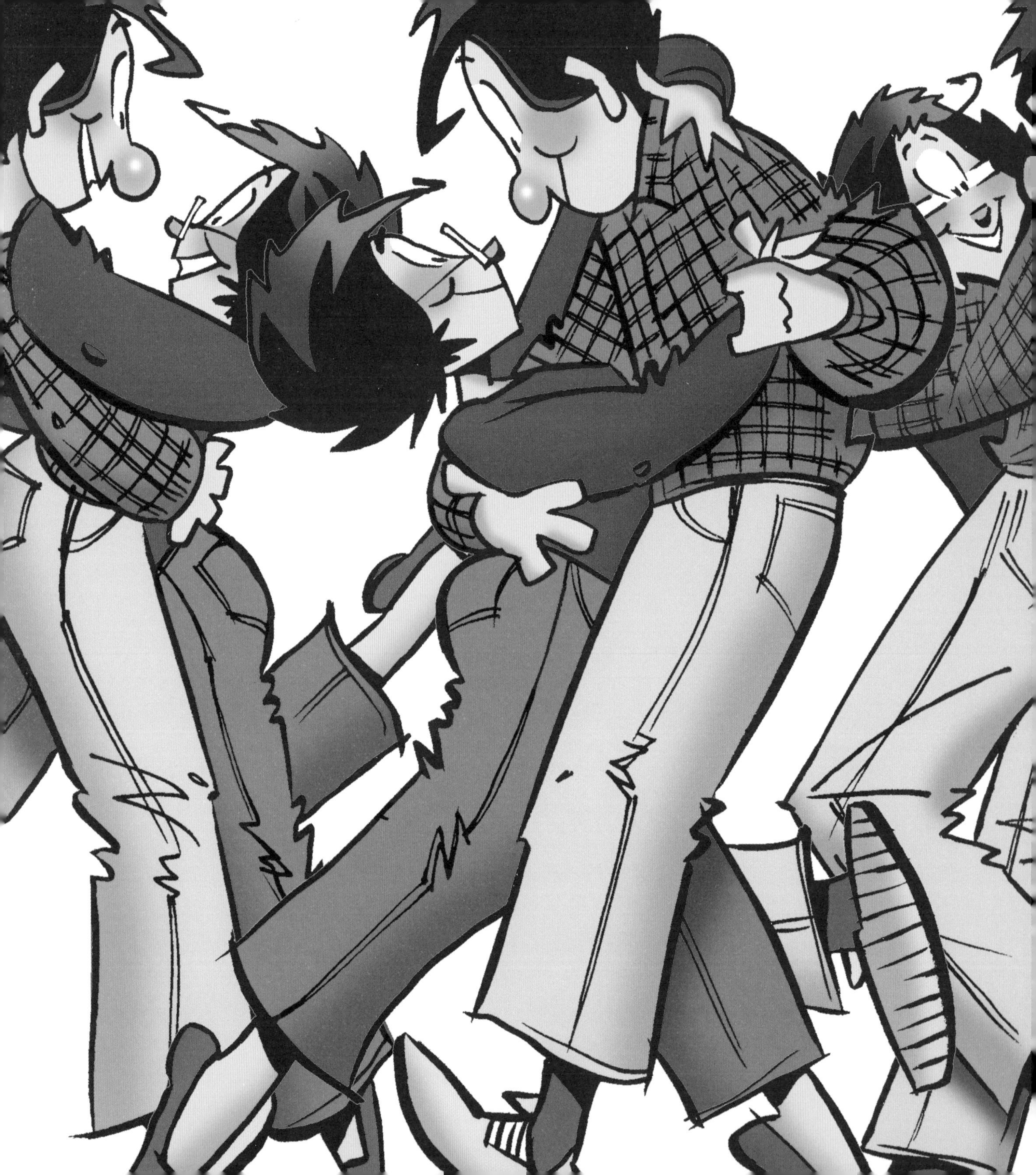

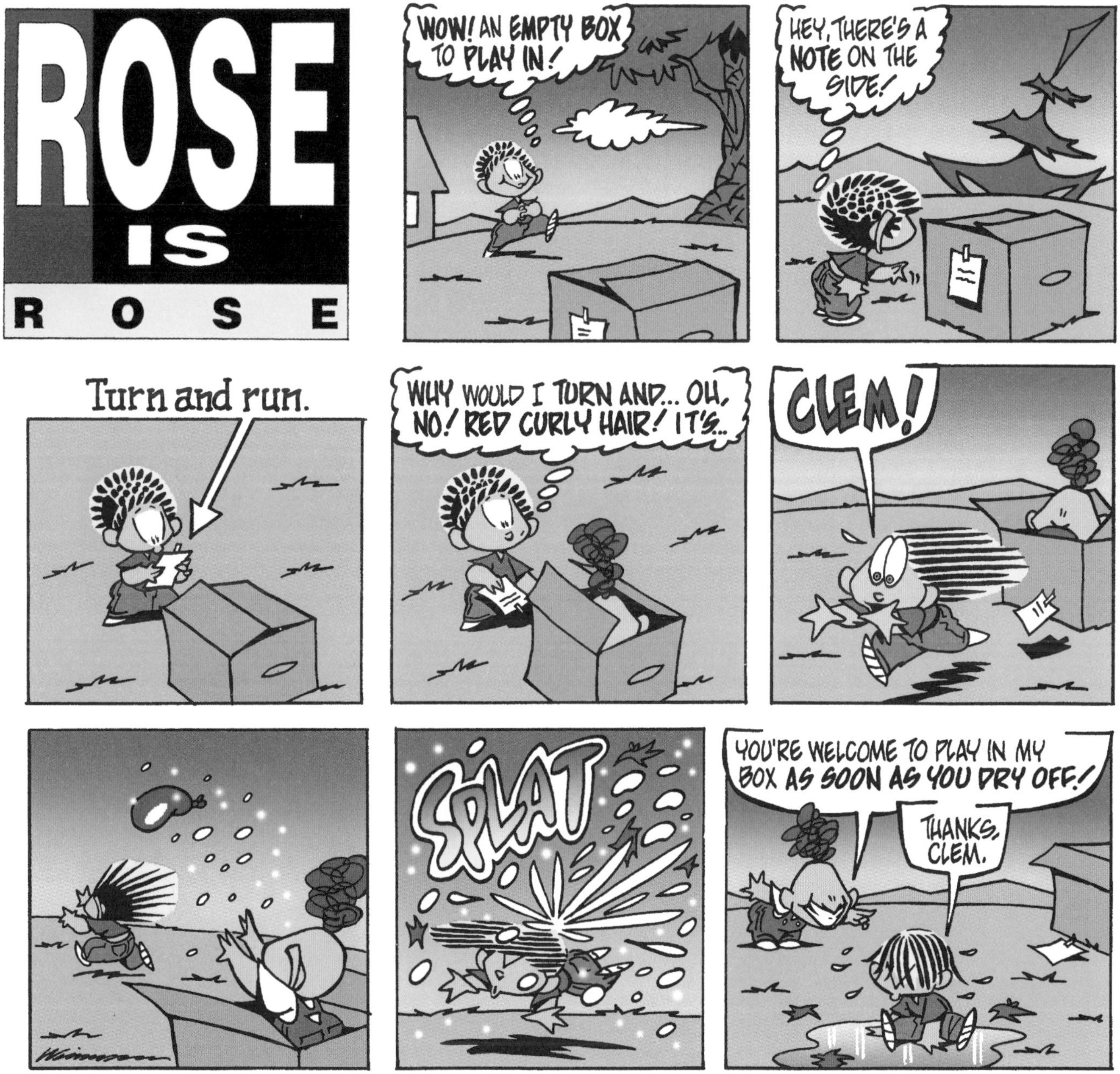
ROSE IS ROSE
WOW! AN EMPTY BOX TO PLAY IN!
HEY, THERE'S A NOTE ON THE SIDE!
Turn and run.
WHY WOULD I TURN AND... OH, NO! RED CURLY HAIR! IT'S...
CLEM!
SPLAT
YOU'RE WELCOME TO PLAY IN MY BOX AS SOON AS YOU DRY OFF!
THANKS, CLEM.

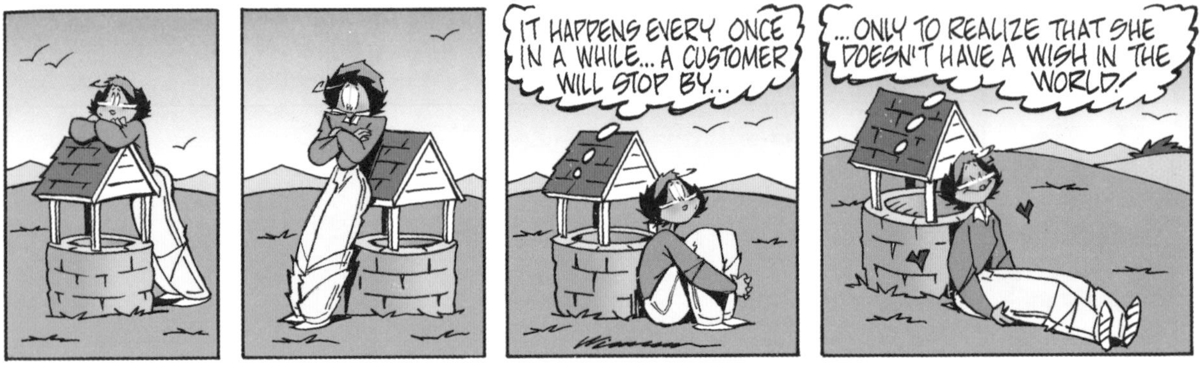
IT HAPPENS EVERY ONCE IN A WHILE... A CUSTOMER WILL STOP BY...
...ONLY TO REALIZE THAT SHE DOESN'T HAVE A WISH IN THE WORLD!

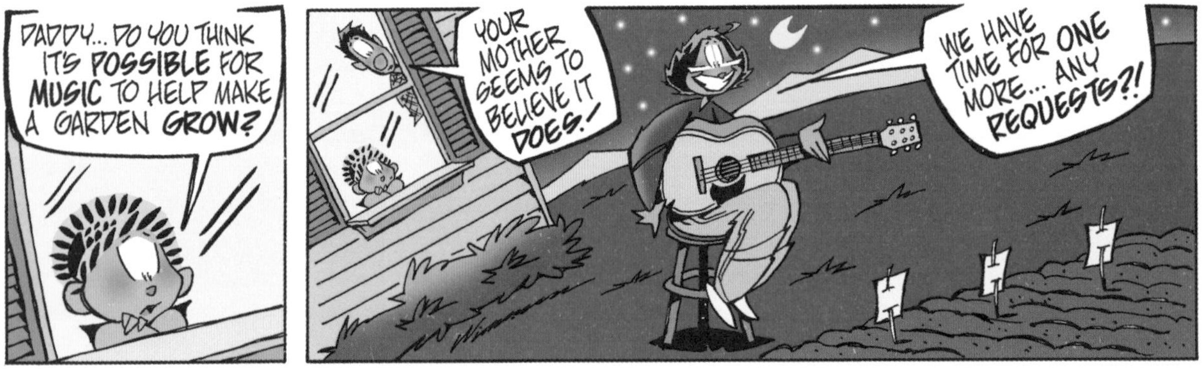
DADDY... DO YOU THINK IT'S **POSSIBLE** FOR **MUSIC** TO HELP MAKE A GARDEN **GROW?**
YOUR MOTHER SEEMS TO BELIEVE IT **DOES!**
WE HAVE TIME FOR **ONE** MORE... ANY **REQUESTS?!**

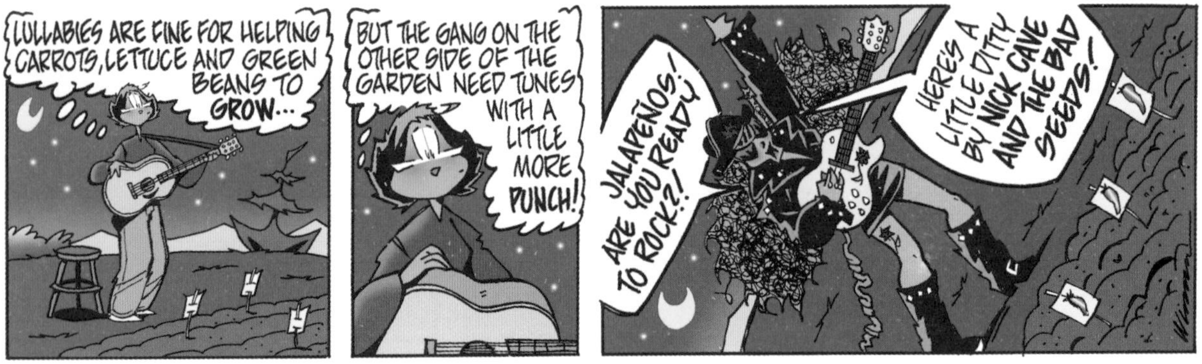
LULLABIES ARE FINE FOR HELPING CARROTS, LETTUCE AND GREEN BEANS TO **GROW...**
BUT THE GANG ON THE OTHER SIDE OF THE GARDEN NEED TUNES WITH A LITTLE MORE **PUNCH!**
JALAPEÑOS! ARE YOU READY TO ROCK?!
HERE'S A LITTLE DITTY BY **NICK CAVE AND THE BAD SEEDS!**

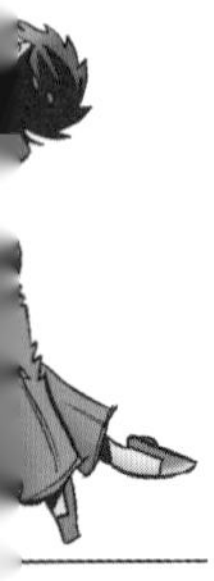

FLIP THE PAGE CORNERS TO SEE ROSE AND JIMBO DANCE.

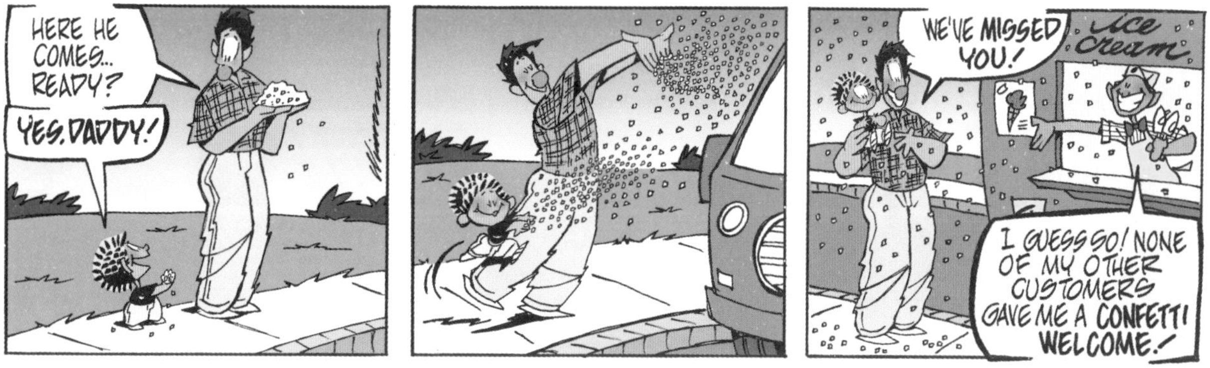
HERE HE COMES... READY?
YES, DADDY!
WE'VE MISSED YOU!
Ice Cream
I GUESS SO! NONE OF MY OTHER CUSTOMERS GAVE ME A CONFETTI WELCOME!

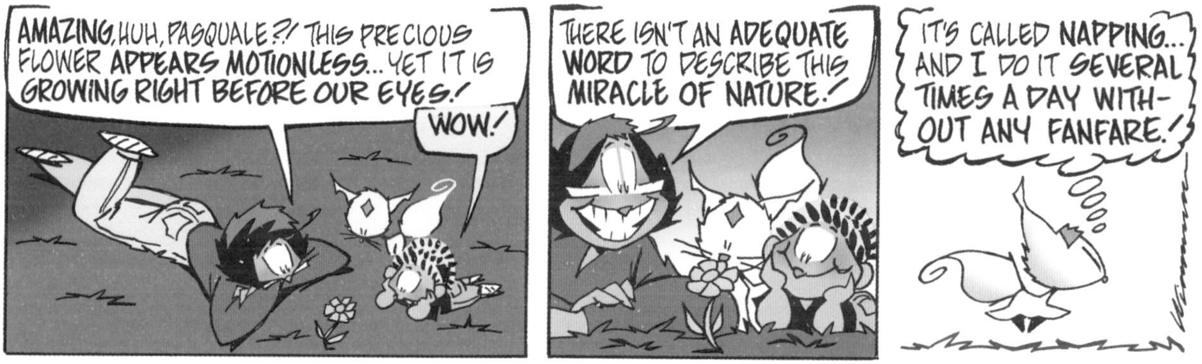
AMAZING, HUH, PASQUALE?! THIS PRECIOUS FLOWER APPEARS MOTIONLESS... YET IT IS GROWING RIGHT BEFORE OUR EYES!
WOW!
THERE ISN'T AN ADEQUATE WORD TO DESCRIBE THIS MIRACLE OF NATURE!
IT'S CALLED NAPPING... AND I DO IT SEVERAL TIMES A DAY WITHOUT ANY FANFARE!

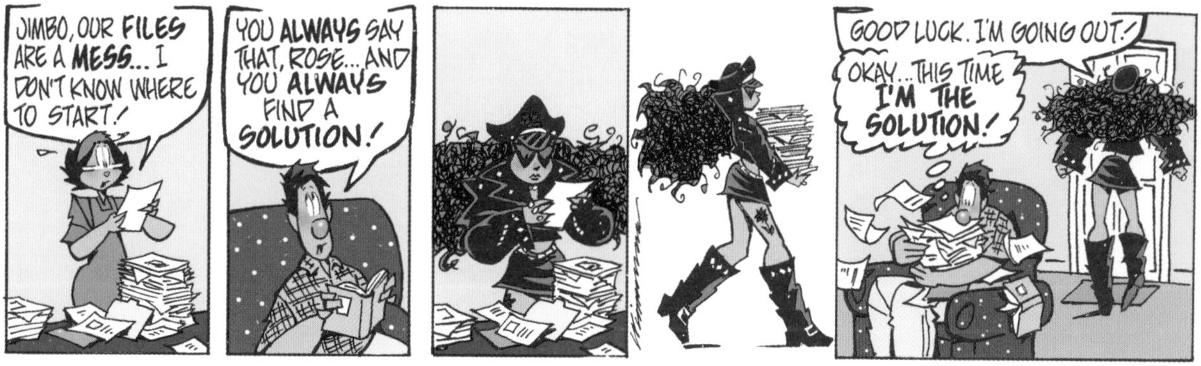
JIMBO, OUR FILES ARE A MESS... I DON'T KNOW WHERE TO START!
YOU ALWAYS SAY THAT, ROSE... AND YOU ALWAYS FIND A SOLUTION!
GOOD LUCK. I'M GOING OUT!
OKAY... THIS TIME I'M THE SOLUTION!

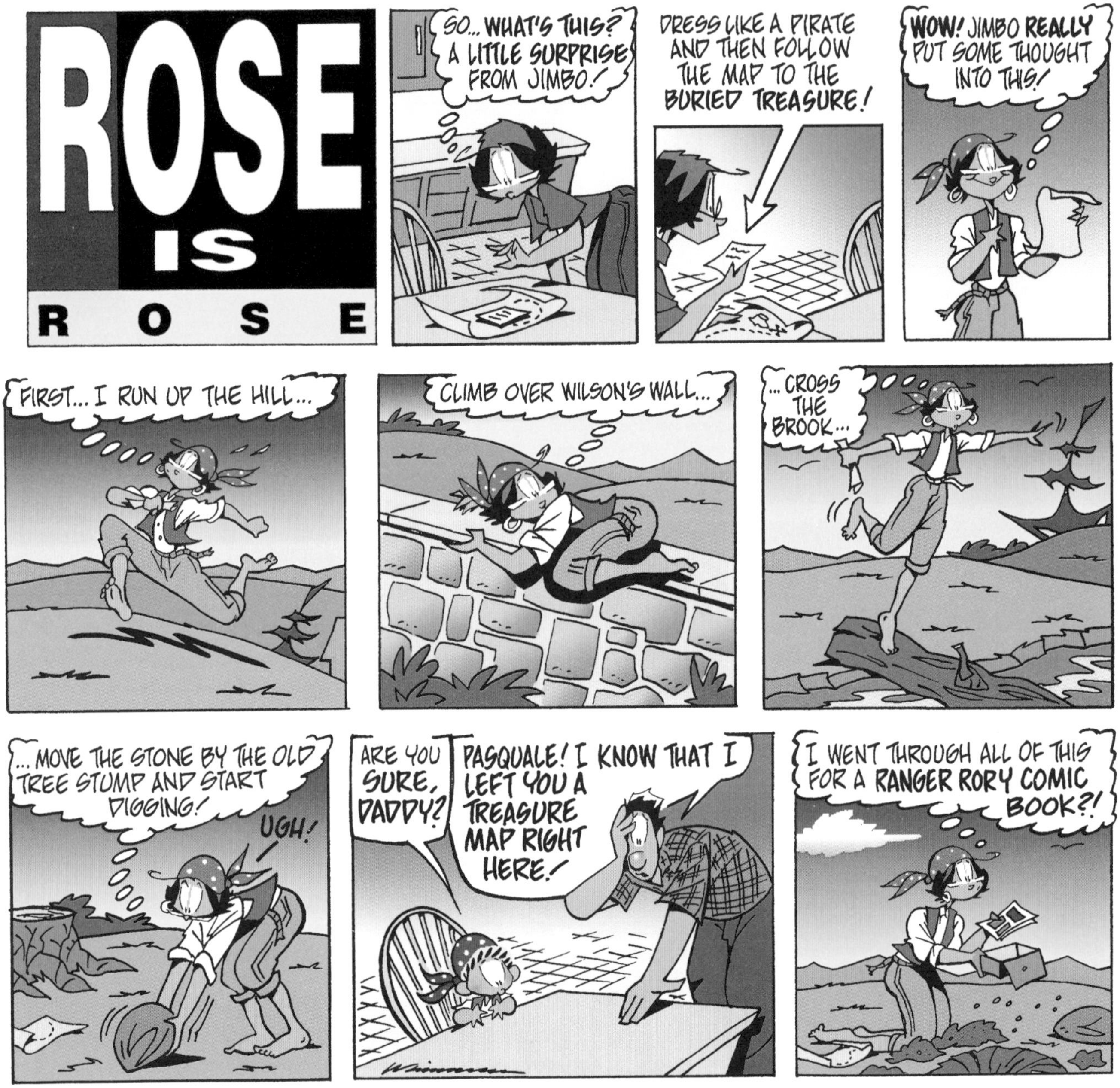
ROSE IS ROSE
SO... WHAT'S THIS? A LITTLE SURPRISE FROM JIMBO!
DRESS LIKE A PIRATE AND THEN FOLLOW THE MAP TO THE BURIED TREASURE!
WOW! JIMBO REALLY PUT SOME THOUGHT INTO THIS!
FIRST... I RUN UP THE HILL...
CLIMB OVER WILSON'S WALL...
... CROSS THE BROOK...
... MOVE THE STONE BY THE OLD TREE STUMP AND START DIGGING!
UGH!
ARE YOU SURE, DADDY?
PASQUALE! I KNOW THAT I LEFT YOU A TREASURE MAP RIGHT HERE!
I WENT THROUGH ALL OF THIS FOR A RANGER RORY COMIC BOOK?!

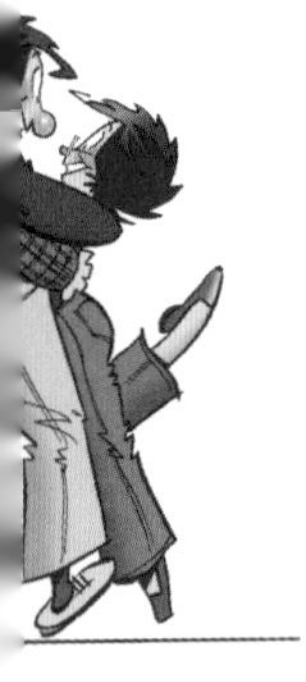

SOME WELCOME SPRING WITH A SERIES OF GRACEFUL PIROUETTES...
OTHERS SHOULD BE STRONGLY CAUTIONED TO AVOID ALL VARIETIES OF CELEBRATORY DANCE!
LEAP
TRIP
FLIP
THUMP!
OOOF!

NOT LONG AGO YOU WERE TINY SEEDS BURIED BENEATH THE SOIL! BUT WITH DRIVE, DETERMINATION...
AND AN UNYIELDING ZEST FOR LIFE... YOU BROKE THROUGH! YOU HAVE MADE THIS GARDENER VERY PROUD!
I THOUGHT HER SPEECH WOULD NEVER END!
YOU HAVE TO ADMIT... THEY WERE INSPIRING WORDS!
INSPIRATION MAKES ME HUNGRY!
SAVE ME SOME RADISH SPROUTS!

SHURIZZA LOTTA ZAND!
YOU'RE RIGHT, MIMI... I MAY HAVE GONE OVERBOARD ON THE SAND!
SAND
SAN

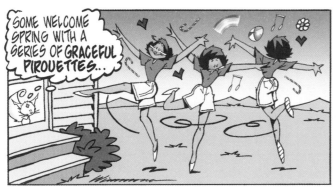

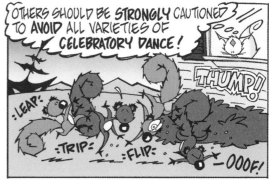

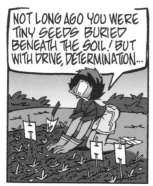

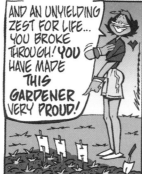

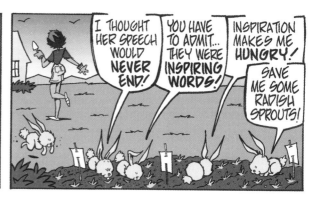

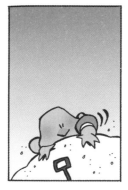

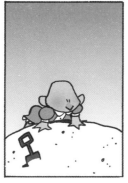

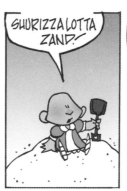

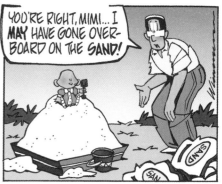

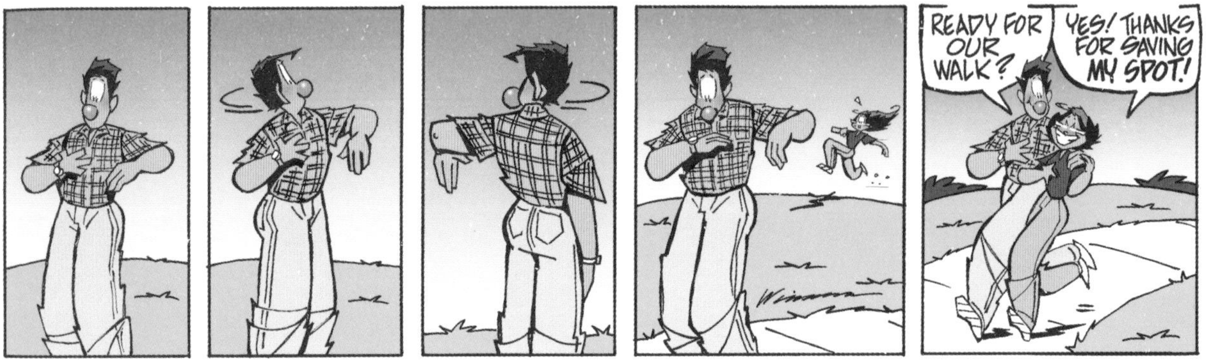
READY FOR OUR WALK?
YES! THANKS FOR SAVING MY SPOT!

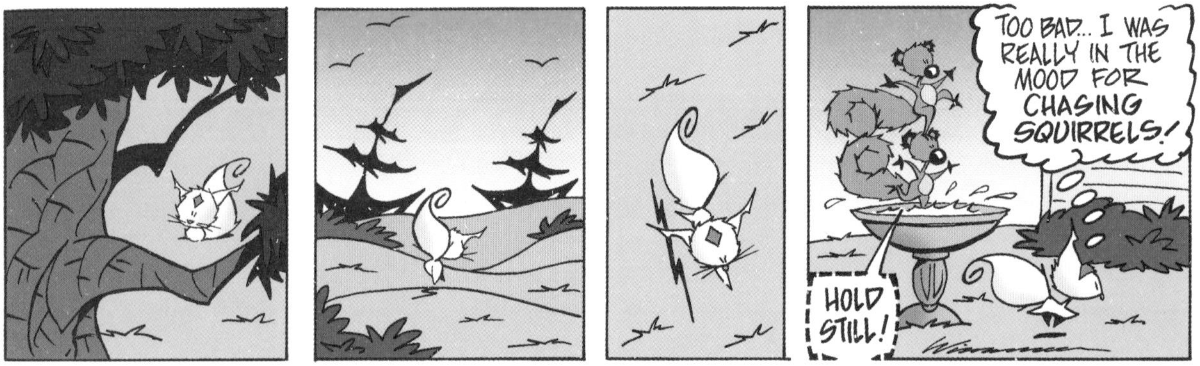
TOO BAD... I WAS REALLY IN THE MOOD FOR CHASING SQUIRRELS!
HOLD STILL!

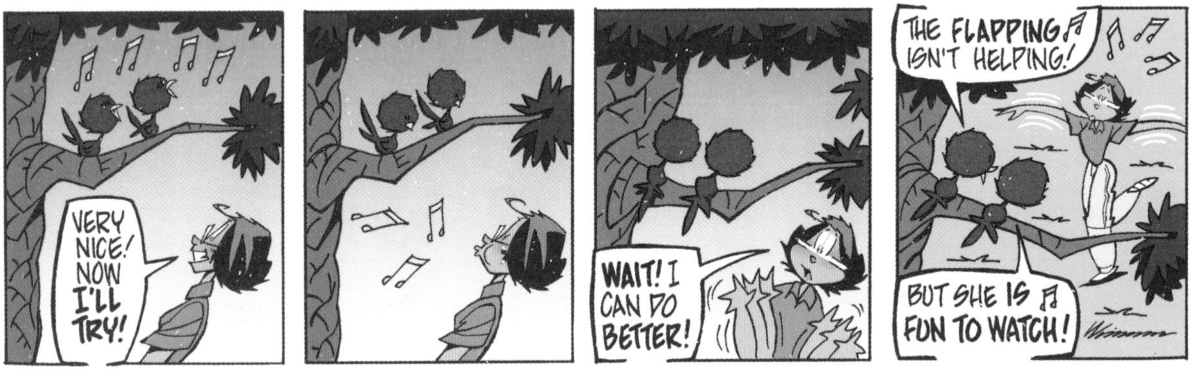
VERY NICE! NOW I'LL TRY!
WAIT! I CAN DO BETTER!
THE FLAPPING ISN'T HELPING!
BUT SHE IS FUN TO WATCH!

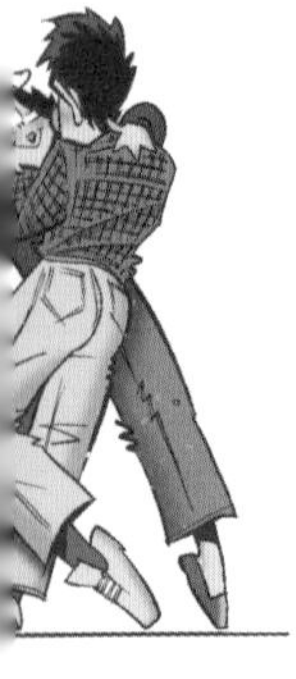

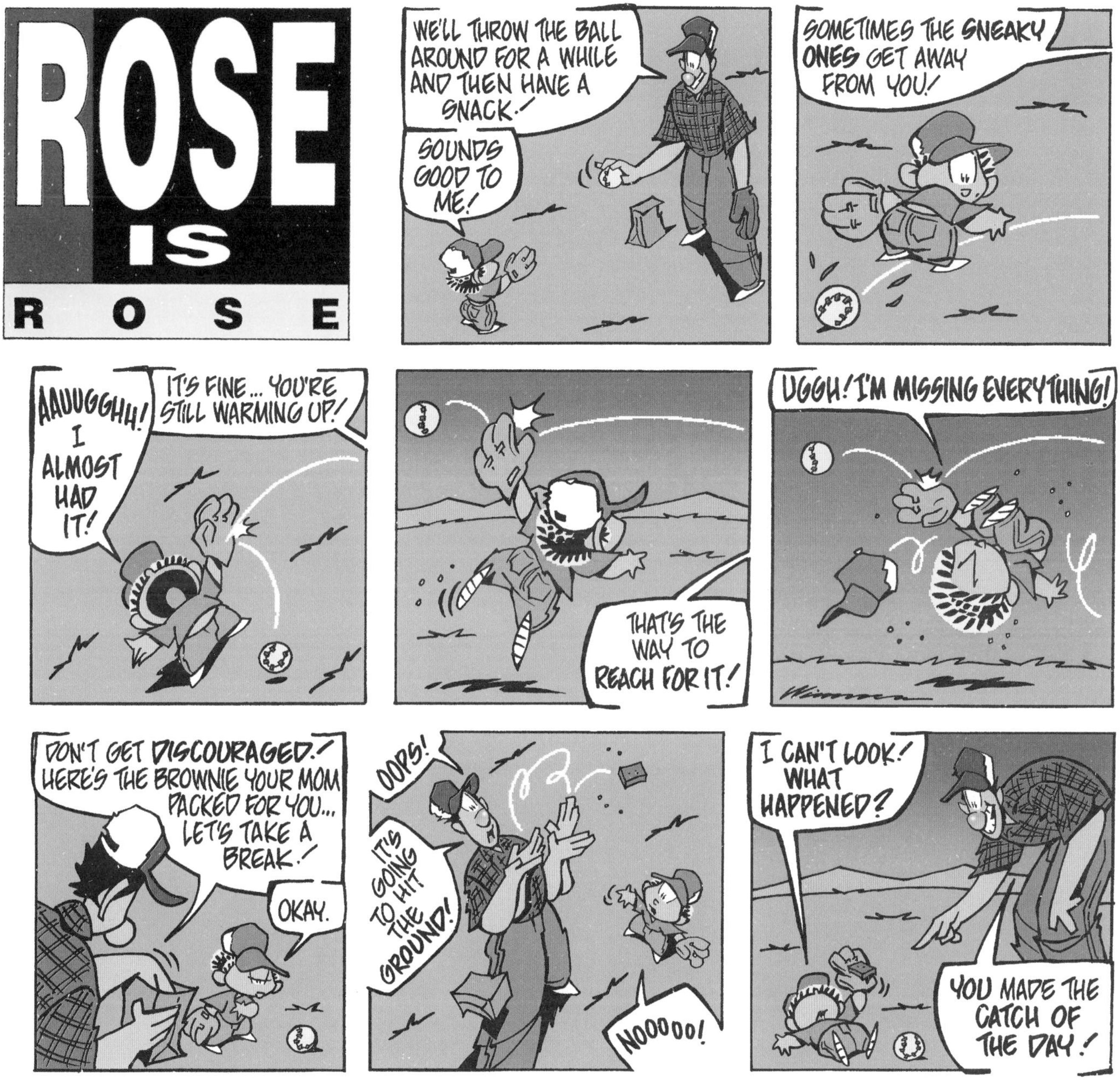
ROSE IS ROSE
WE'LL THROW THE BALL AROUND FOR A WHILE AND THEN HAVE A SNACK!
SOUNDS GOOD TO ME!
SOMETIMES THE SNEAKY ONES GET AWAY FROM YOU!
AAUUGGHH! I ALMOST HAD IT!
IT'S FINE... YOU'RE STILL WARMING UP!
THAT'S THE WAY TO REACH FOR IT!
UGGH! I'M MISSING EVERYTHING!
DON'T GET DISCOURAGED! HERE'S THE BROWNIE YOUR MOM PACKED FOR YOU... LET'S TAKE A BREAK!
OKAY.
OOPS!
IT'S GOING TO HIT THE GROUND!
NOOOOO!
I CAN'T LOOK! WHAT HAPPENED?
YOU MADE THE CATCH OF THE DAY!

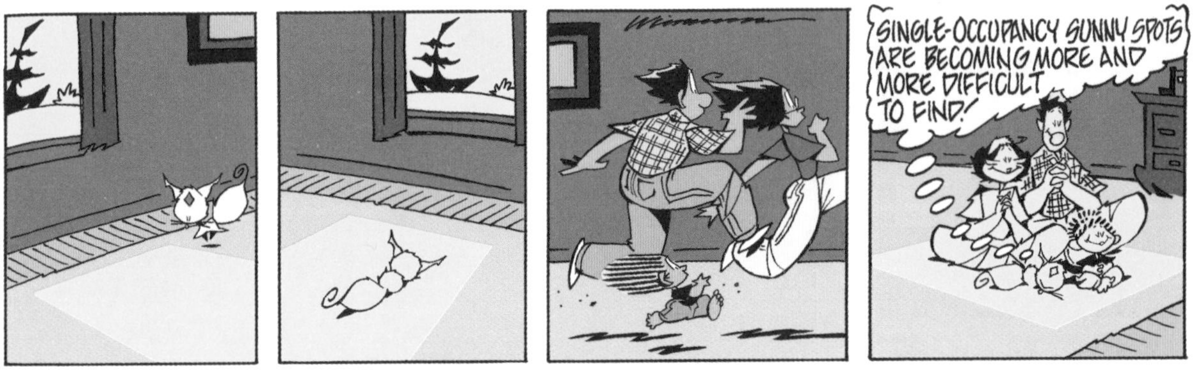
SINGLE-OCCUPANCY SUNNY SPOTS ARE BECOMING MORE AND MORE DIFFICULT TO FIND!

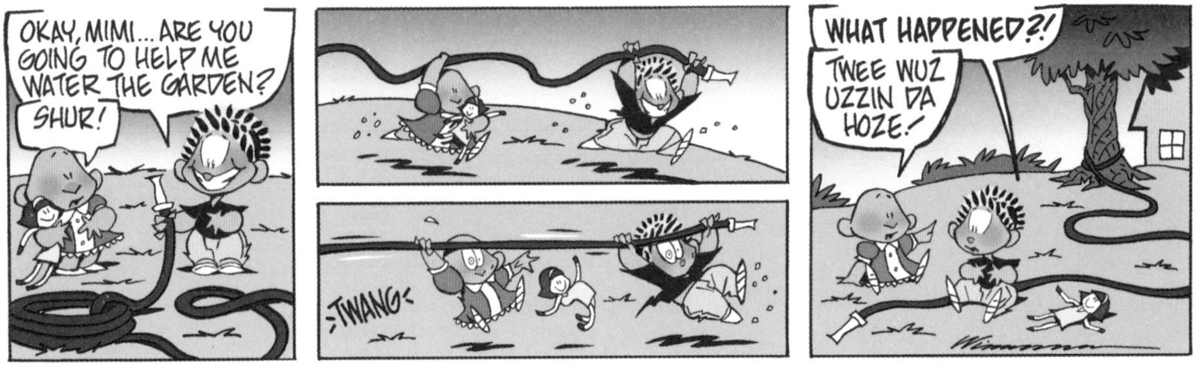
OKAY, MIMI... ARE YOU GOING TO HELP ME WATER THE GARDEN?
SHUR!
TWANG
WHAT HAPPENED?!
TWEE WUZ UZZIN DA HOZE!

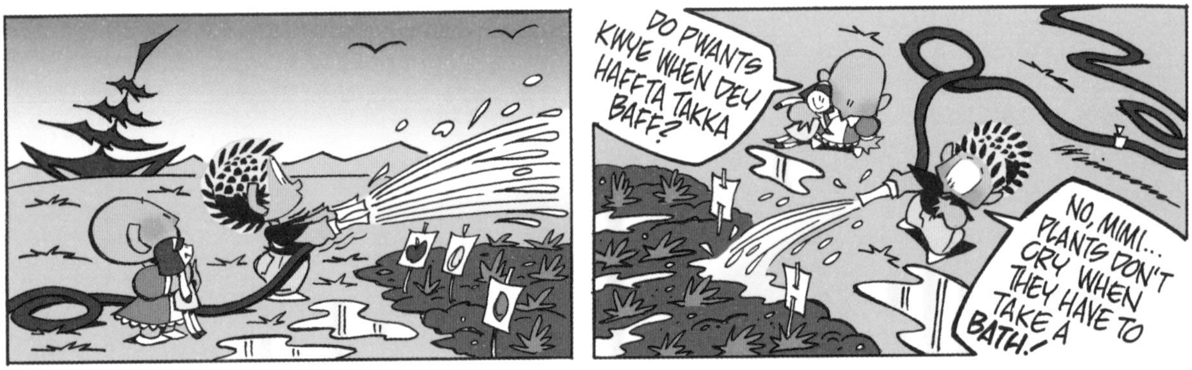
DO PWANTS KWYE WHEN DEY HAFFTA TAKKA BAFF?
NO, MIMI... PLANTS DON'T CRY WHEN THEY HAVE TO TAKE A BATH!

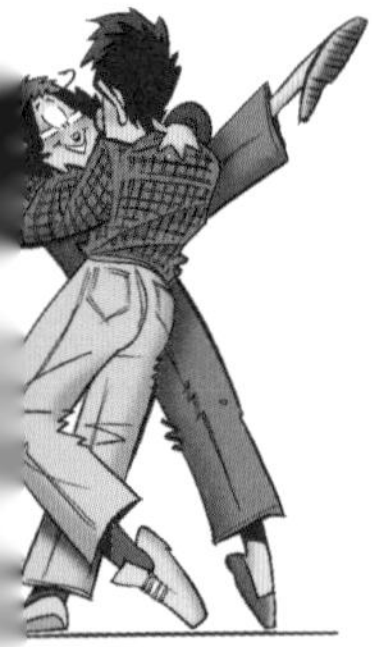

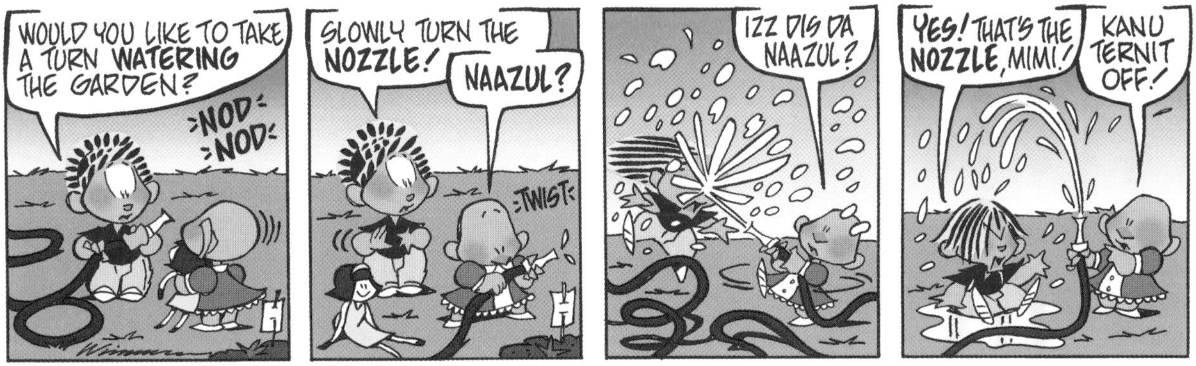

WOULD YOU LIKE TO TAKE A TURN **WATERING** THE GARDEN?
NOD NOD
SLOWLY TURN THE **NOZZLE!**
NAAZUL?
TWIST
IZZ DIS DA NAAZUL?
YES! THAT'S THE **NOZZLE,** MIMI!
KANU TERNIT OFF!

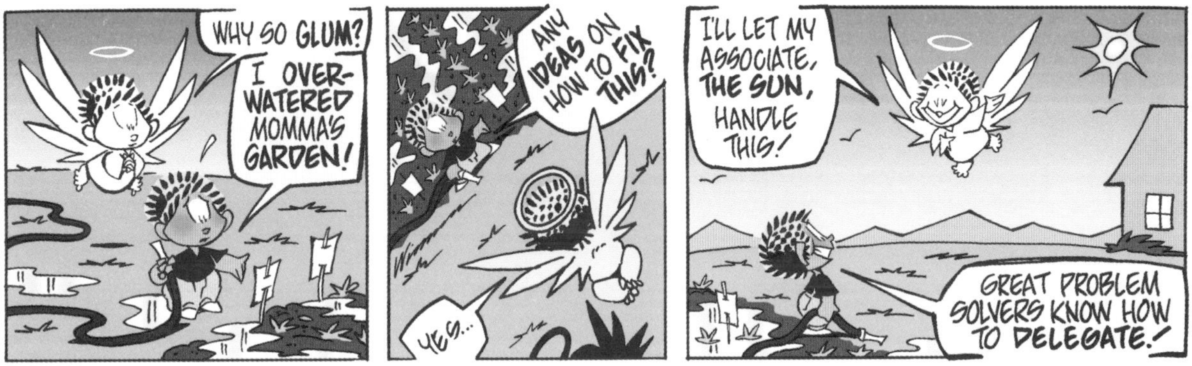

WHY SO **GLUM?**
I **OVER-WATERED** MOMMA'S **GARDEN!**
ANY **IDEAS** ON HOW TO **FIX THIS?**
YES...
I'LL LET MY ASSOCIATE, **THE SUN,** HANDLE THIS!
GREAT PROBLEM SOLVERS KNOW HOW TO **DELEGATE!**

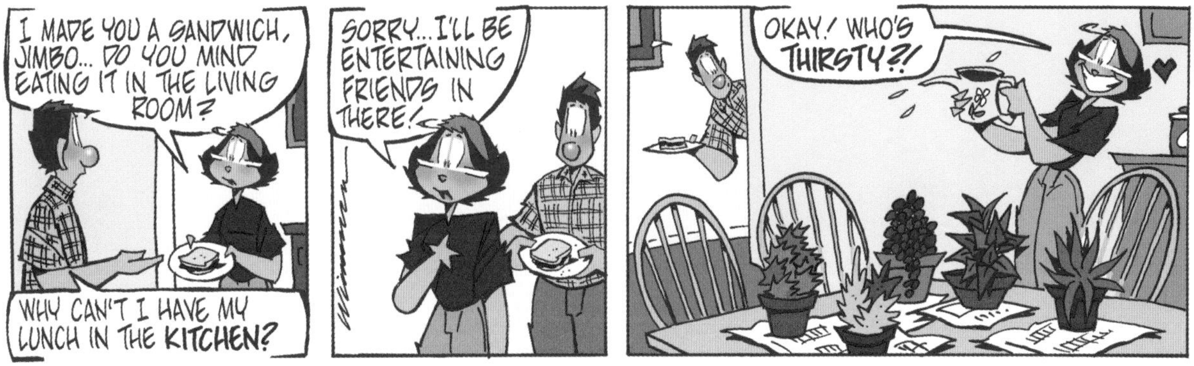

I MADE YOU A SANDWICH, JIMBO... DO YOU MIND EATING IT IN THE LIVING ROOM?
WHY CAN'T I HAVE MY LUNCH IN THE **KITCHEN?**
SORRY... I'LL BE ENTERTAINING FRIENDS IN THERE!
OKAY! WHO'S **THIRSTY?!**

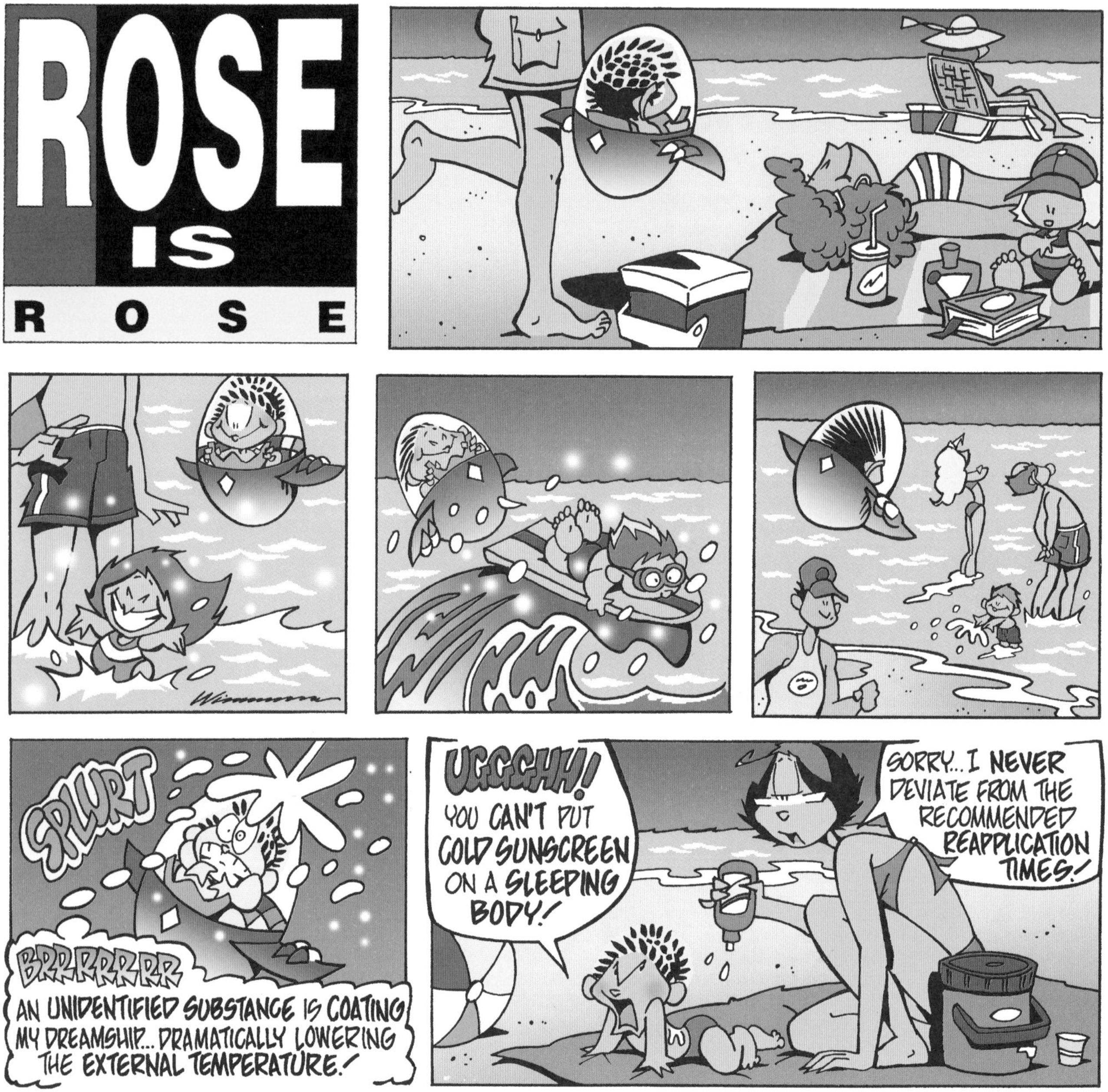
ROSE IS ROSE
SPLURT
BRRRRRRR
AN UNIDENTIFIED SUBSTANCE IS COATING MY DREAMSHIP... DRAMATICALLY LOWERING THE EXTERNAL TEMPERATURE!
UGGGHH! YOU CAN'T PUT COLD SUNSCREEN ON A SLEEPING BODY!
SORRY... I NEVER DEVIATE FROM THE RECOMMENDED REAPPLICATION TIMES!

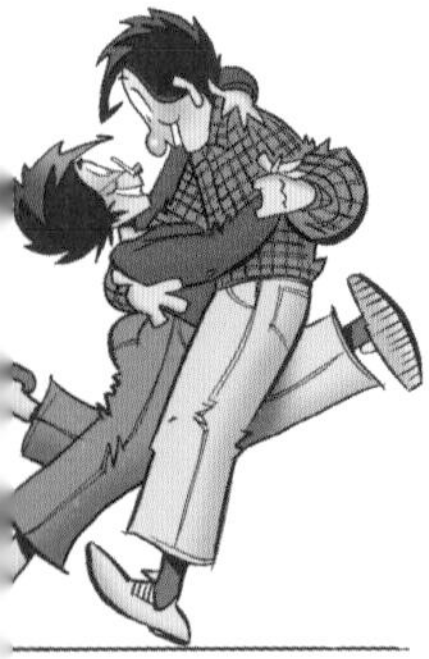

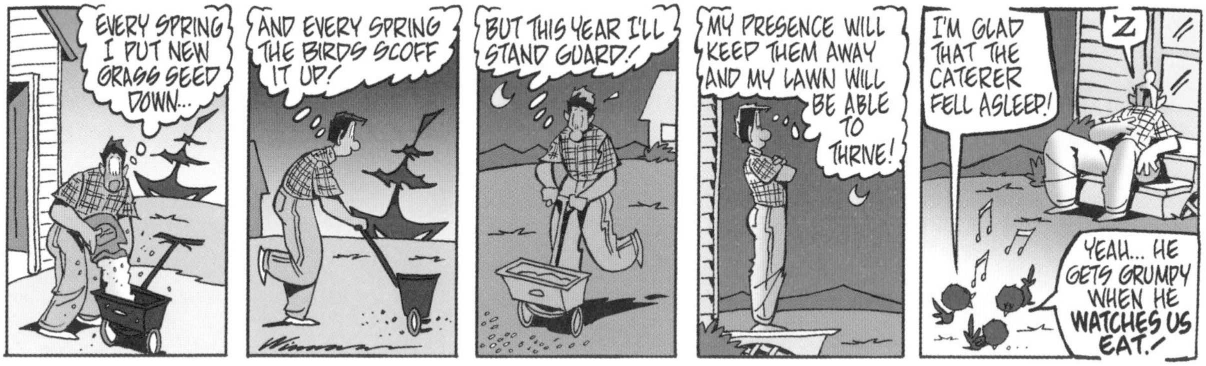
EVERY SPRING I PUT NEW GRASS SEED DOWN...
AND EVERY SPRING THE BIRDS SCOFF IT UP!
BUT THIS YEAR I'LL STAND GUARD!
MY PRESENCE WILL KEEP THEM AWAY AND MY LAWN WILL BE ABLE TO THRIVE!
Z
I'M GLAD THAT THE CATERER FELL ASLEEP!
YEAH... HE GETS GRUMPY WHEN HE **WATCHES US EAT.**!

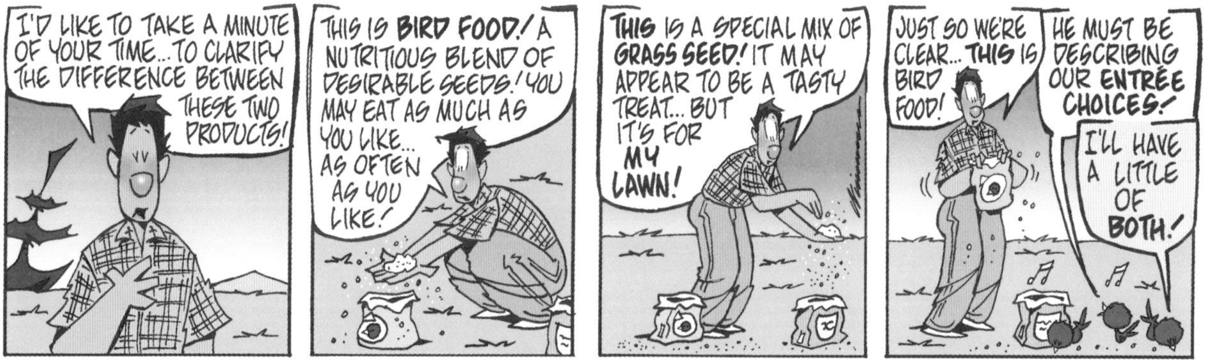
I'D LIKE TO TAKE A MINUTE OF YOUR TIME... TO CLARIFY THE DIFFERENCE BETWEEN THESE TWO PRODUCTS!
THIS IS **BIRD FOOD!** A NUTRITIOUS BLEND OF DESIRABLE SEEDS! YOU MAY EAT AS MUCH AS YOU LIKE... AS OFTEN AS YOU LIKE!
THIS IS A SPECIAL MIX OF **GRASS SEED!** IT MAY APPEAR TO BE A TASTY TREAT... BUT IT'S FOR **MY LAWN!**
JUST SO WE'RE CLEAR... **THIS** IS BIRD FOOD!
HE MUST BE DESCRIBING OUR **ENTRÉE CHOICES!**
I'LL HAVE A LITTLE OF **BOTH!**

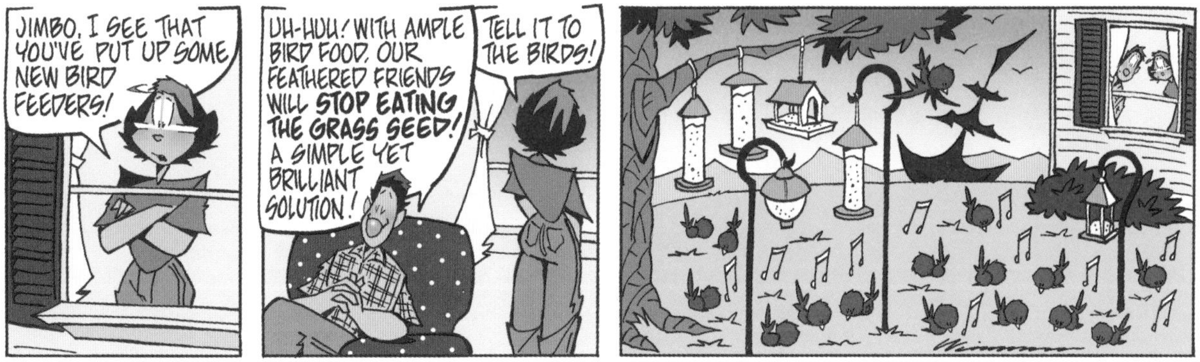
JIMBO, I SEE THAT YOU'VE PUT UP SOME NEW BIRD FEEDERS!
UH-HUH! WITH AMPLE BIRD FOOD, OUR FEATHERED FRIENDS WILL **STOP EATING THE GRASS SEED!** A SIMPLE YET BRILLIANT SOLUTION!
TELL IT TO THE BIRDS!

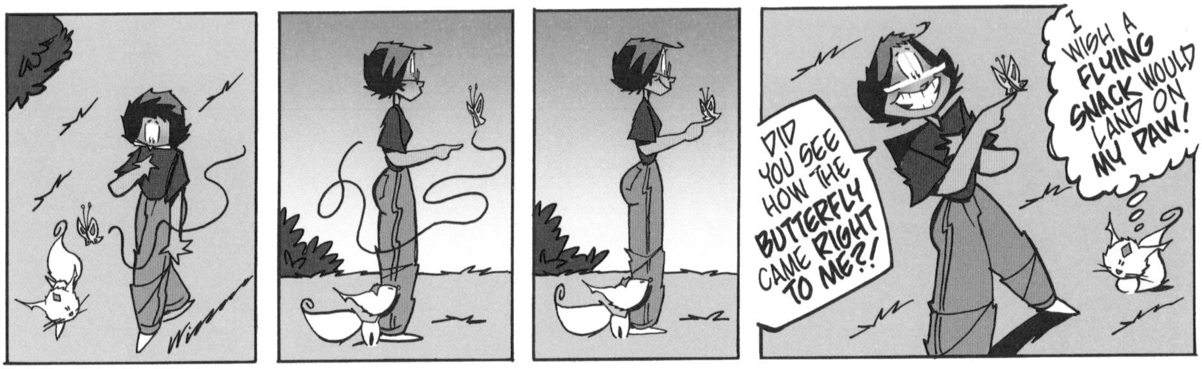
DID YOU SEE HOW THE BUTTERFLY CAME RIGHT TO ME?!
I WISH A FLYING SNACK WOULD LAND ON MY PAW!

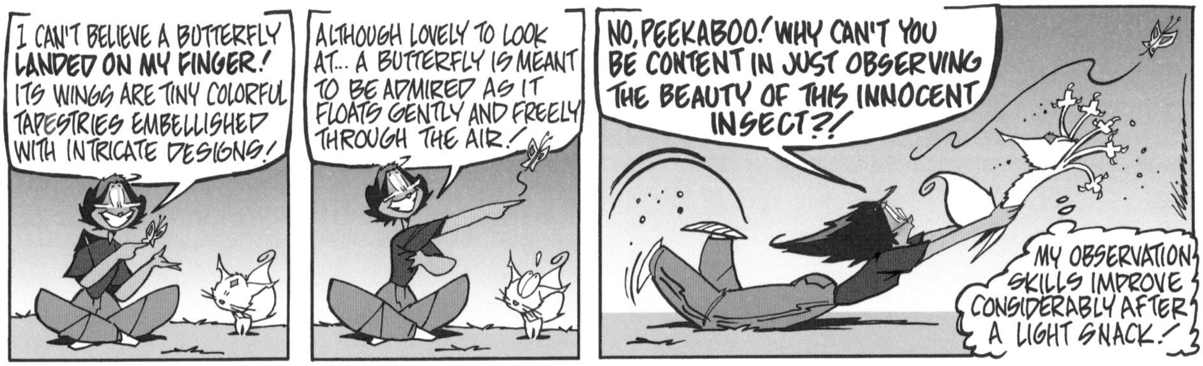
I CAN'T BELIEVE A BUTTERFLY LANDED ON MY FINGER! ITS WINGS ARE TINY COLORFUL TAPESTRIES EMBELLISHED WITH INTRICATE DESIGNS!
ALTHOUGH LOVELY TO LOOK AT... A BUTTERFLY IS MEANT TO BE ADMIRED AS IT FLOATS GENTLY AND FREELY THROUGH THE AIR!
NO, PEEKABOO! WHY CAN'T YOU BE CONTENT IN JUST OBSERVING THE BEAUTY OF THIS INNOCENT INSECT?!
MY OBSERVATION SKILLS IMPROVE CONSIDERABLY AFTER A LIGHT SNACK!

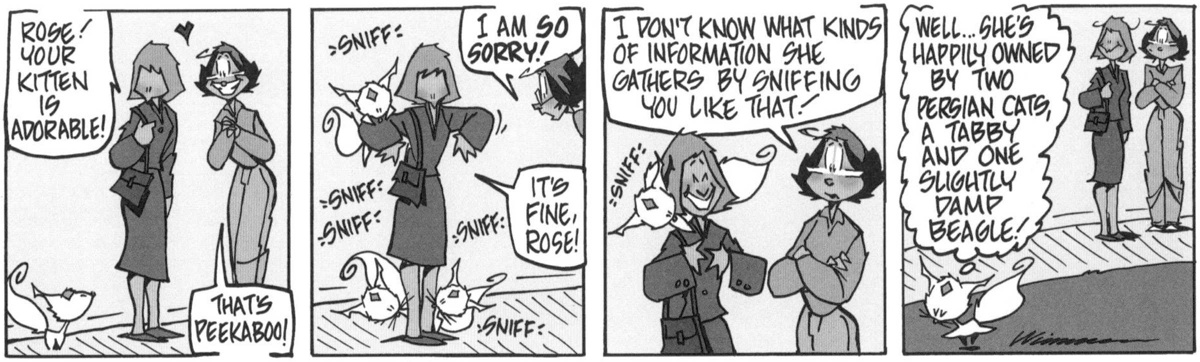
ROSE! YOUR KITTEN IS ADORABLE!
THAT'S PEEKABOO!
:SNIFF:
I AM SO SORRY!
:SNIFF:
:SNIFF:
:SNIFF:
IT'S FINE, ROSE!
:SNIFF:
I DON'T KNOW WHAT KINDS OF INFORMATION SHE GATHERS BY SNIFFING YOU LIKE THAT!
:SNIFF:
WELL... SHE'S HAPPILY OWNED BY TWO PERSIAN CATS, A TABBY AND ONE SLIGHTLY DAMP BEAGLE!

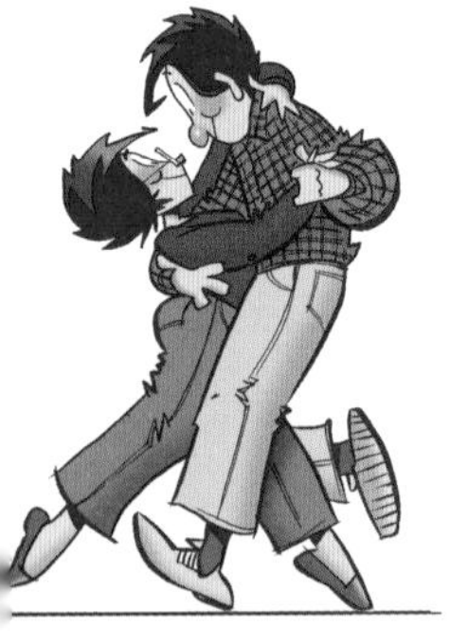

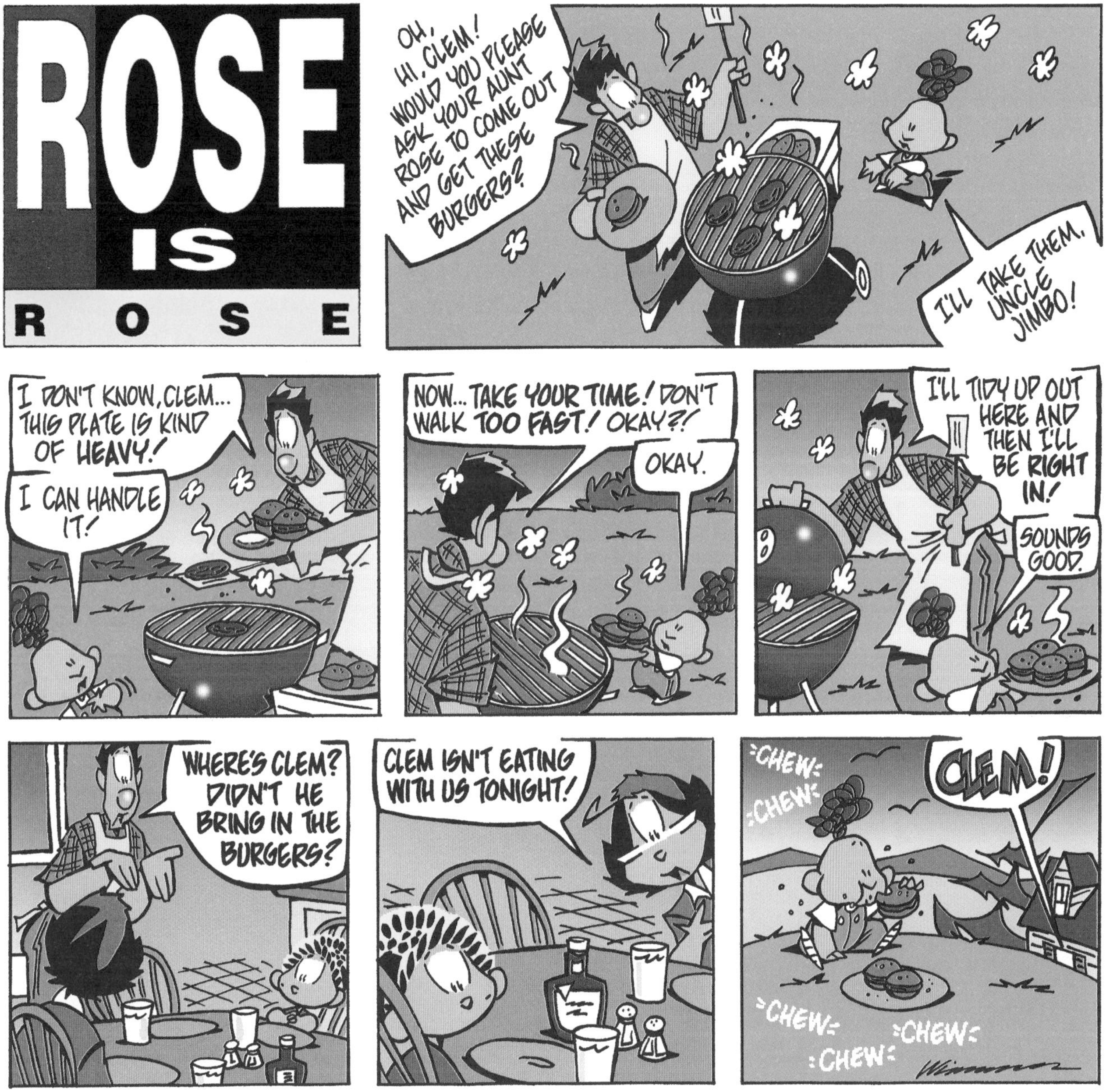
ROSE IS ROSE
OH, HI, CLEM! WOULD YOU PLEASE ASK YOUR AUNT ROSE TO COME OUT AND GET THESE BURGERS?
I'LL TAKE THEM, UNCLE JIMBO!
I DON'T KNOW, CLEM... THIS PLATE IS KIND OF HEAVY!
I CAN HANDLE IT!
NOW... TAKE YOUR TIME! DON'T WALK TOO FAST! OKAY?!
OKAY.
I'LL TIDY UP OUT HERE AND THEN I'LL BE RIGHT IN!
SOUNDS GOOD.
WHERE'S CLEM? DIDN'T HE BRING IN THE BURGERS?
CLEM ISN'T EATING WITH US TONIGHT!
CHEW
CHEW
CLEM!
CHEW
CHEW
CHEW

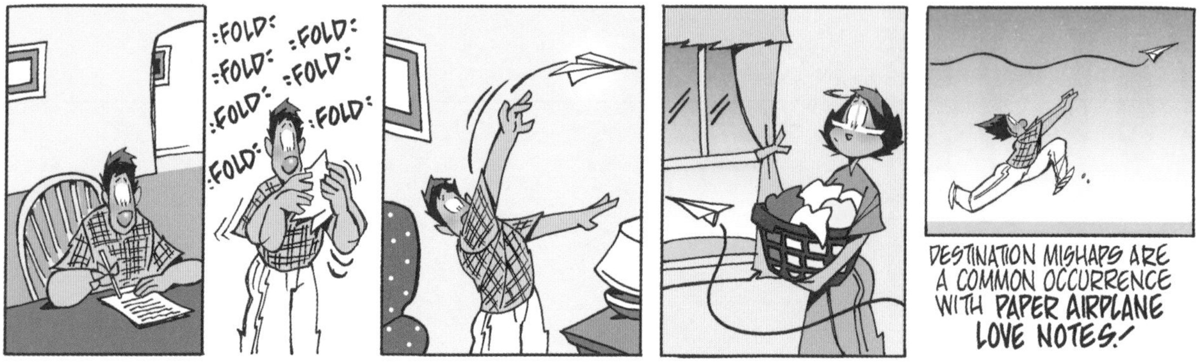
:FOLD: :FOLD: :FOLD: :FOLD: :FOLD: :FOLD: :FOLD:
DESTINATION MISHAPS ARE A COMMON OCCURRENCE WITH PAPER AIRPLANE LOVE NOTES!

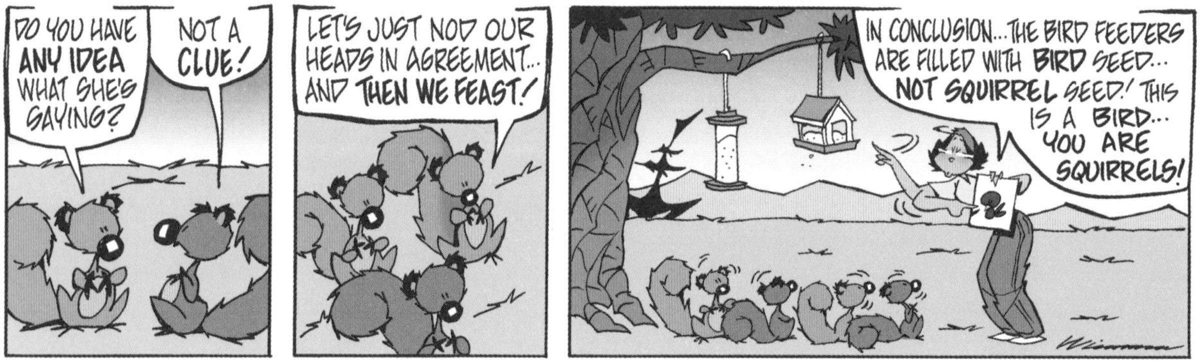
DO YOU HAVE ANY IDEA WHAT SHE'S SAYING?
NOT A CLUE!
LET'S JUST NOD OUR HEADS IN AGREEMENT... AND THEN WE FEAST!
IN CONCLUSION... THE BIRD FEEDERS ARE FILLED WITH BIRD SEED... NOT SQUIRREL SEED! THIS IS A BIRD... YOU ARE SQUIRRELS!

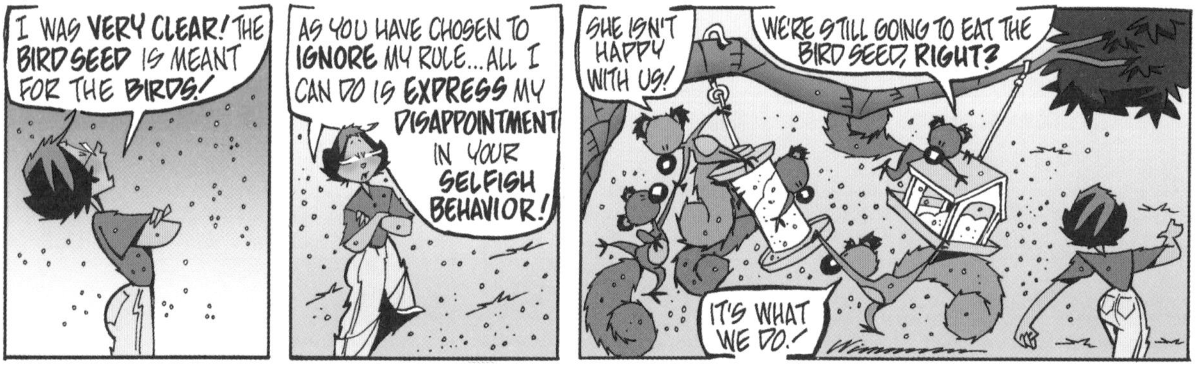
I WAS VERY CLEAR! THE BIRD SEED IS MEANT FOR THE BIRDS!
AS YOU HAVE CHOSEN TO IGNORE MY RULE... ALL I CAN DO IS EXPRESS MY DISAPPOINTMENT IN YOUR SELFISH BEHAVIOR!
SHE ISN'T HAPPY WITH US!
WE'RE STILL GOING TO EAT THE BIRD SEED, RIGHT?
IT'S WHAT WE DO!

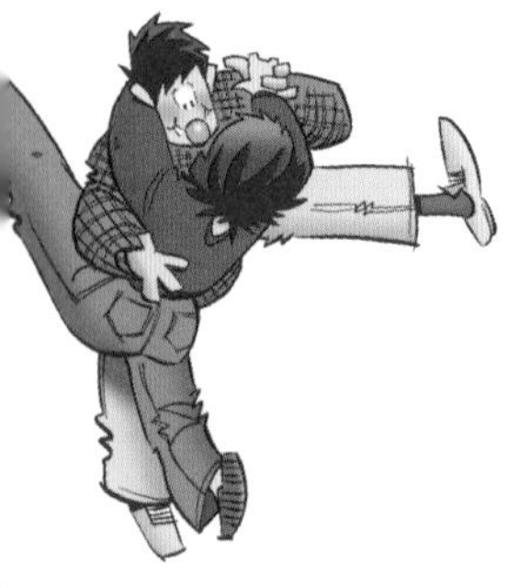

SINCE YOU'RE HERE... YOU MIGHT AS WELL JOIN ME! I'M DOING YOGA EXERCISES!
I'D APPRECIATE IT IF YOU'D SHOW SOME SIGN OF EXERTION, PEEKAPOO!
SORRY, MAKING IT ALL LOOK SO EASY IS ONE OF MY GREATEST JOYS!

PWWITT
A STRAW WRAPPER LOVE NOTE REQUIRES A STEADY HAND, GOOD LUNG CAPACITY AND A RECIPIENT WITHIN RANGE!

MOMMA SAID IT WOULD BE OKAY FOR ME TO DO ABSOLUTELY NOTHING TODAY!
SPLASH
CLEM! WHY DID YOU HAVE TO THROW A WATER BALLOON AT ME?
I DON'T HAVE THE LUXURY OF TAKING TIME OFF FROM MY DAILY OBLIGATIONS!

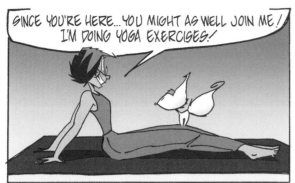

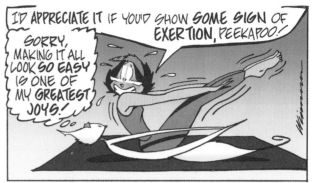

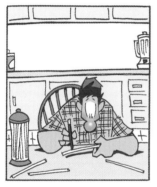

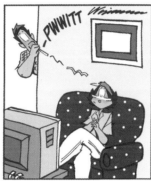

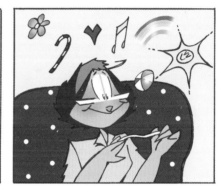

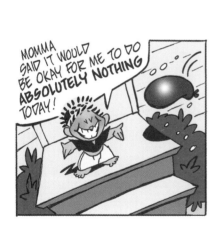

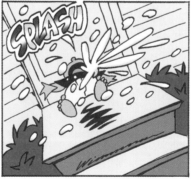

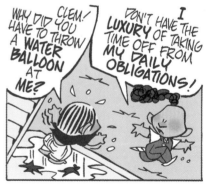

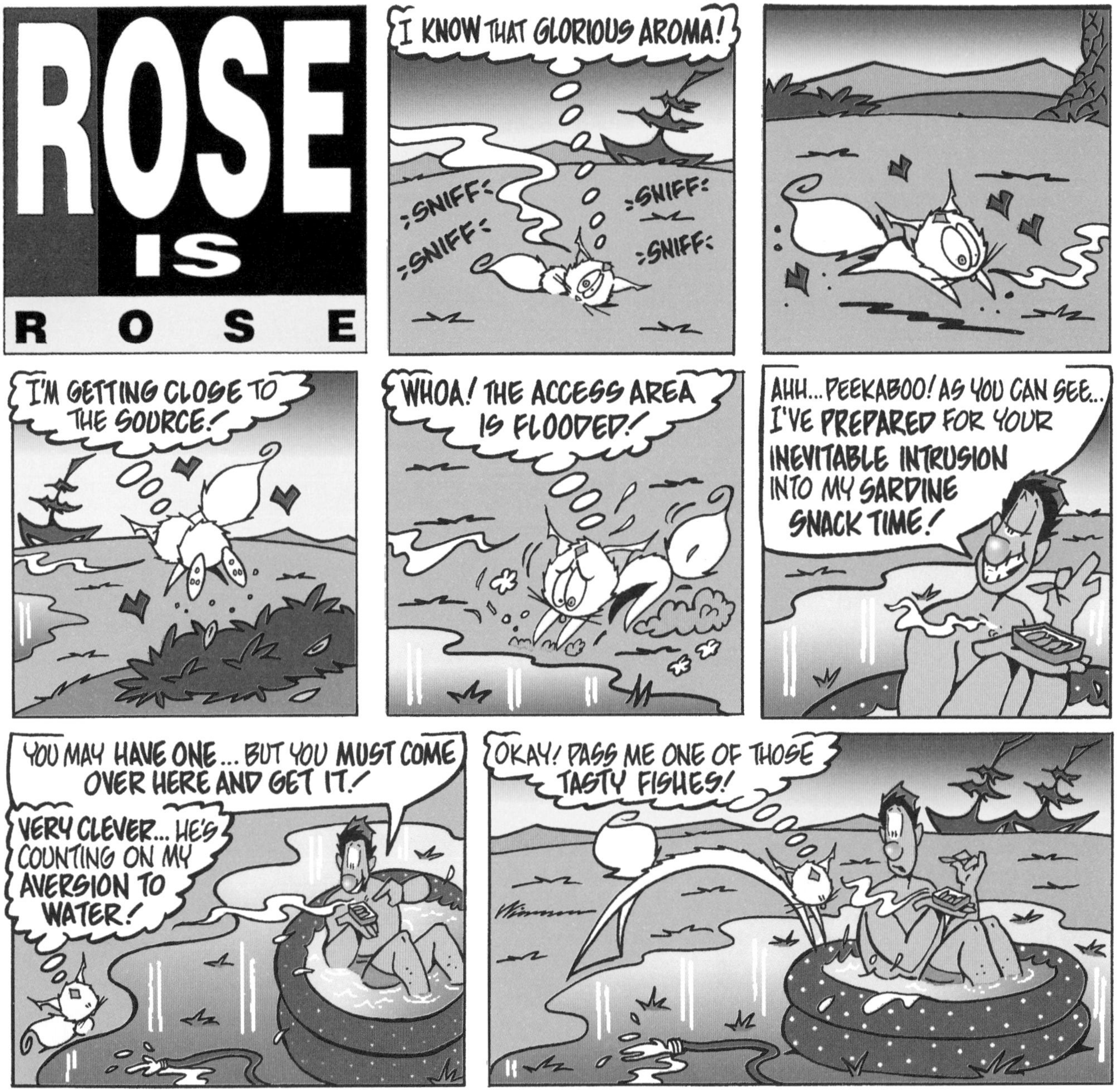
ROSE IS ROSE
I KNOW THAT GLORIOUS AROMA!
SNIFF
SNIFF
SNIFF
SNIFF
I'M GETTING CLOSE TO THE SOURCE!
WHOA! THE ACCESS AREA IS FLOODED!
AHH...PEEKABOO! AS YOU CAN SEE... I'VE PREPARED FOR YOUR INEVITABLE INTRUSION INTO MY SARDINE SNACK TIME!
YOU MAY HAVE ONE... BUT YOU MUST COME OVER HERE AND GET IT!
VERY CLEVER... HE'S COUNTING ON MY AVERSION TO WATER!
OKAY! PASS ME ONE OF THOSE TASTY FISHES!

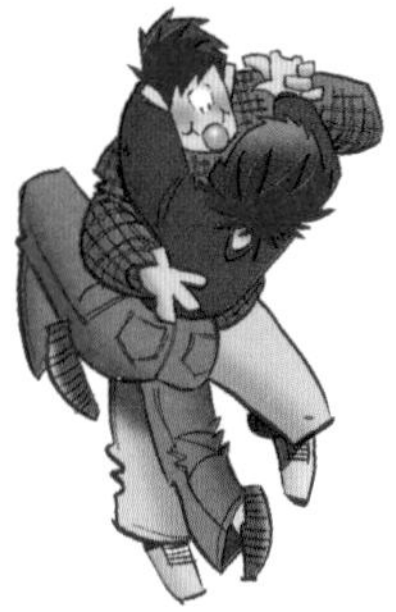

OH! THIS WILL NEVER DO!
USE YESTERDAY'S AGAIN... YOU LIKED THAT ONE!
CAN I? IS THAT ALLOWED?
THERE'S NO HARM DOING IT THIS ONE TIME!
MORE PEOPLE SHOULD BE GIVEN PERMISSION TO REUSE A GREAT HOROSCOPE!

THIS IS THE SONG I TOLD YOU ABOUT! DO YOU THINK YOU CAN LEARN IT?
THE HARMONIES ARE DOABLE!
THE DRUM SOLO MAY BE A PROBLEM!

DO YOU THINK THAT THEY'RE HAVING A GOOD TIME, MOMMA?
EVEN INDOOR PLANTS ENJOY A FIELD TRIP NOW AND THEN!

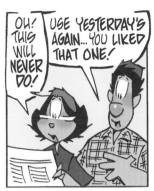

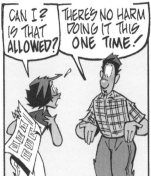

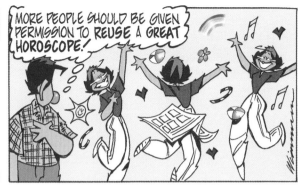

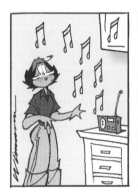

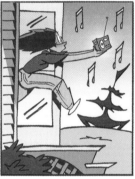

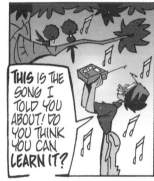

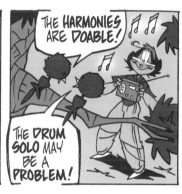

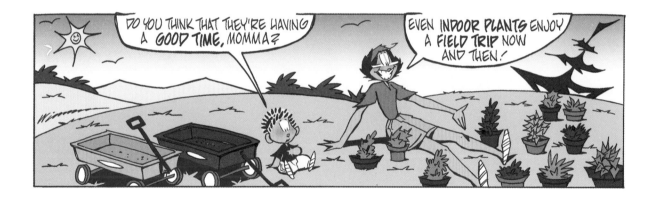

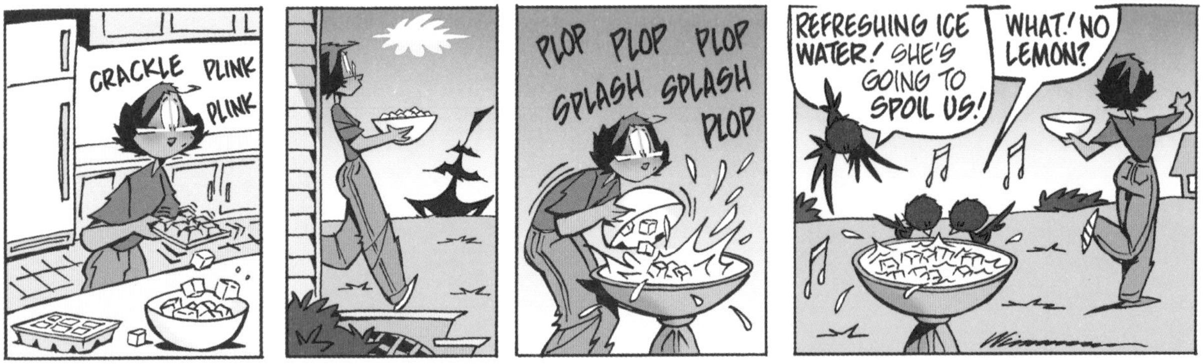
CRACKLE PLINK
PLINK
PLOP PLOP PLOP
SPLASH SPLASH
PLOP
REFRESHING ICE WATER! SHE'S GOING TO SPOIL US!
WHAT! NO LEMON?

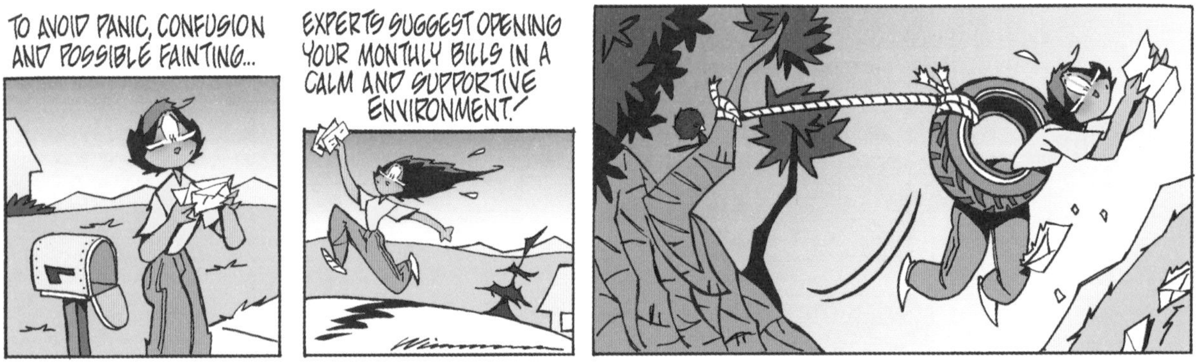
TO AVOID PANIC, CONFUSION AND POSSIBLE FAINTING...
EXPERTS SUGGEST OPENING YOUR MONTHLY BILLS IN A CALM AND SUPPORTIVE ENVIRONMENT!

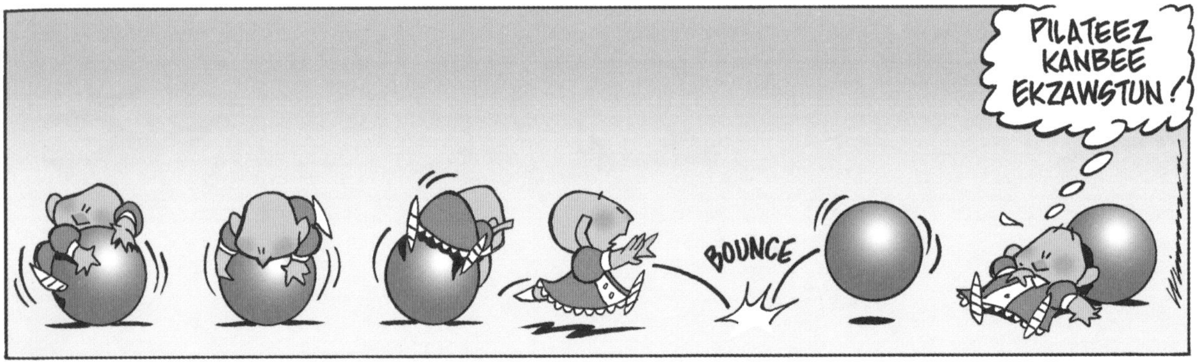
PILATEEZ KANBEE EKZAWSTUN!
BOUNCE

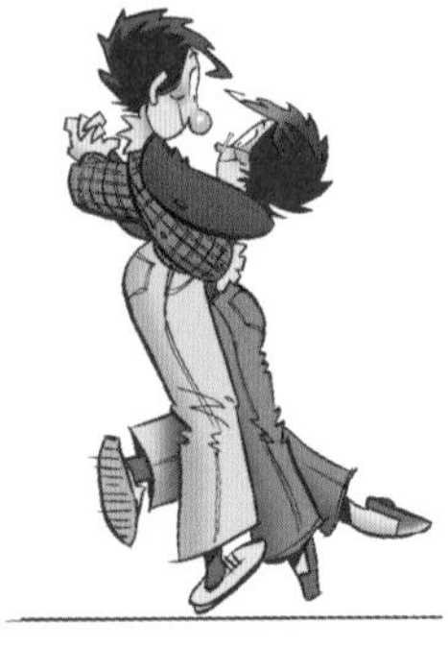

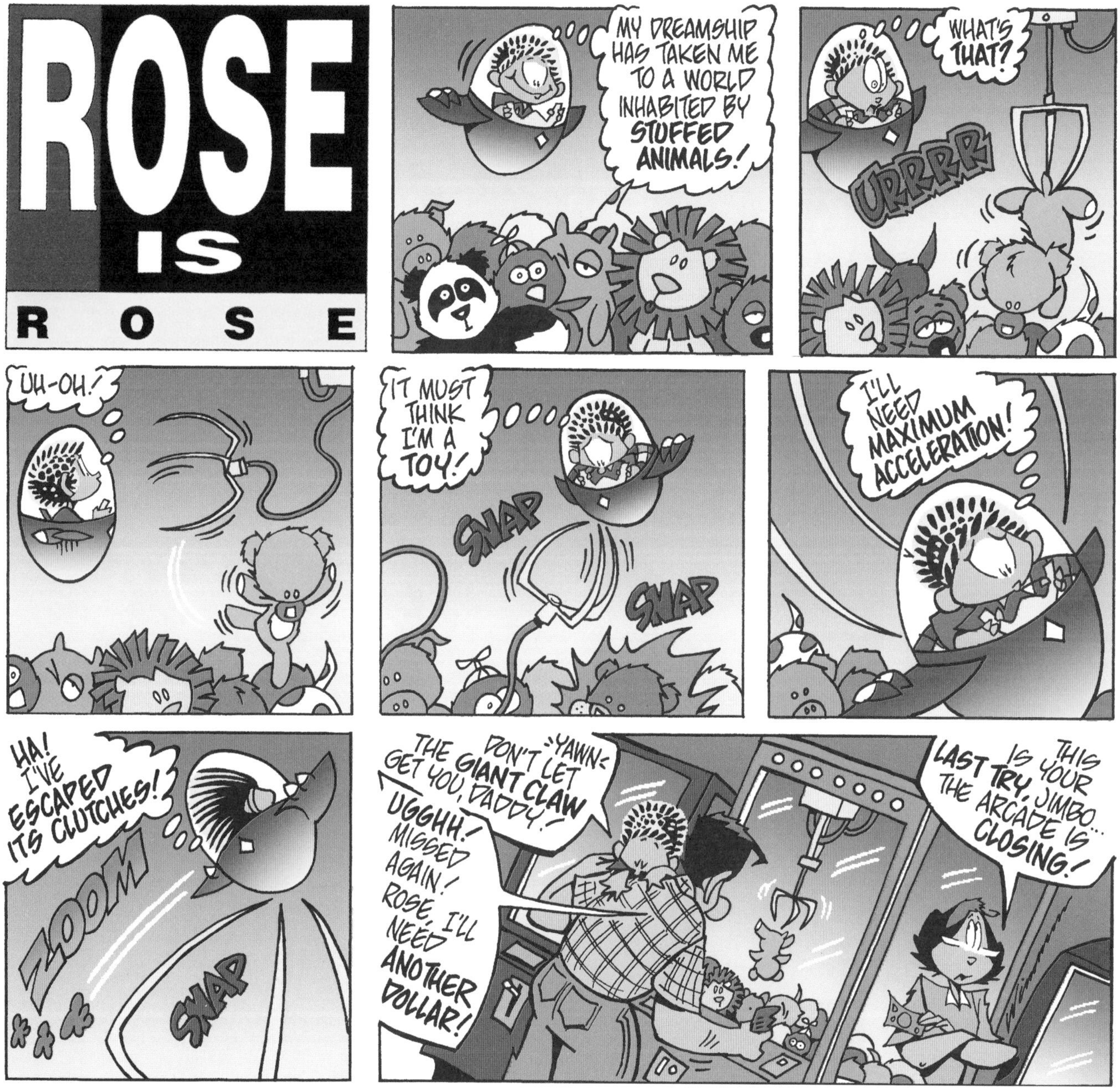
ROSE IS ROSE
MY DREAMSHIP HAS TAKEN ME TO A WORLD INHABITED BY STUFFED ANIMALS!
WHAT'S THAT?
URRRR
UH-OH!
IT MUST THINK I'M A TOY!
SNAP
SNAP
I'LL NEED MAXIMUM ACCELERATION!
HA! I'VE ESCAPED ITS CLUTCHES!
ZOOM
SNAP
=YAWN=
DON'T LET THE GIANT CLAW GET YOU, DADDY.
IS THIS YOUR LAST TRY, JIMBO... THE ARCADE IS CLOSING!
UGGHH! MISSED AGAIN! ROSE, I'LL NEED ANOTHER DOLLAR!

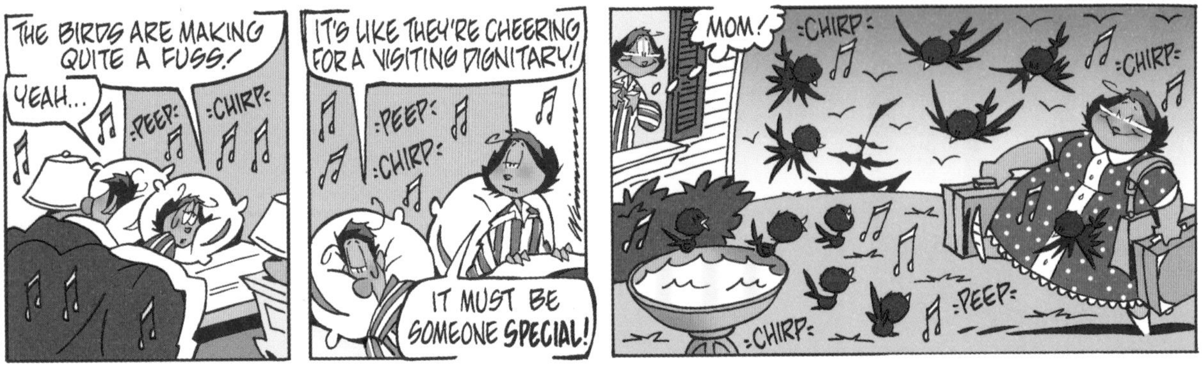
THE BIRDS ARE MAKING QUITE A FUSS!
YEAH...
PEEP
CHIRP
IT'S LIKE THEY'RE CHEERING FOR A VISITING DIGNITARY!
PEEP
CHIRP
IT MUST BE SOMEONE **SPECIAL**!
MOM!
CHIRP
CHIRP
CHIRP
PEEP

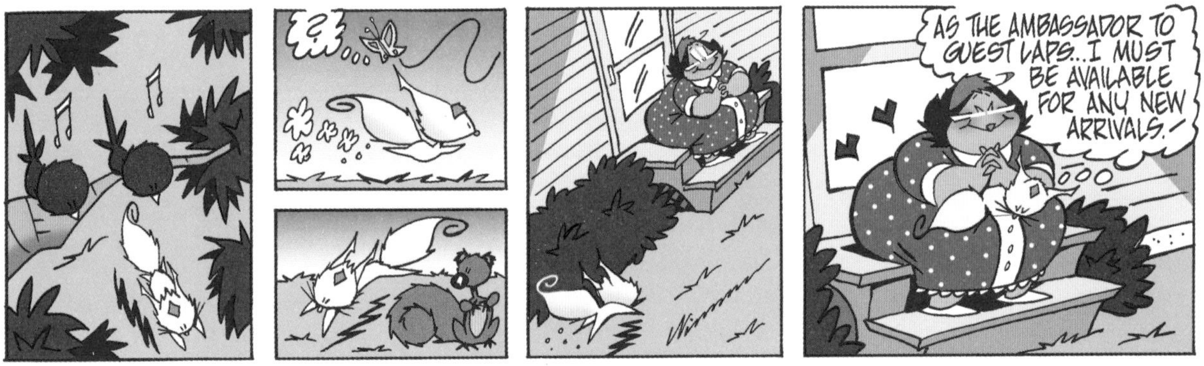
?
AS THE AMBASSADOR TO GUEST LAPS...I MUST BE AVAILABLE FOR ANY NEW ARRIVALS!

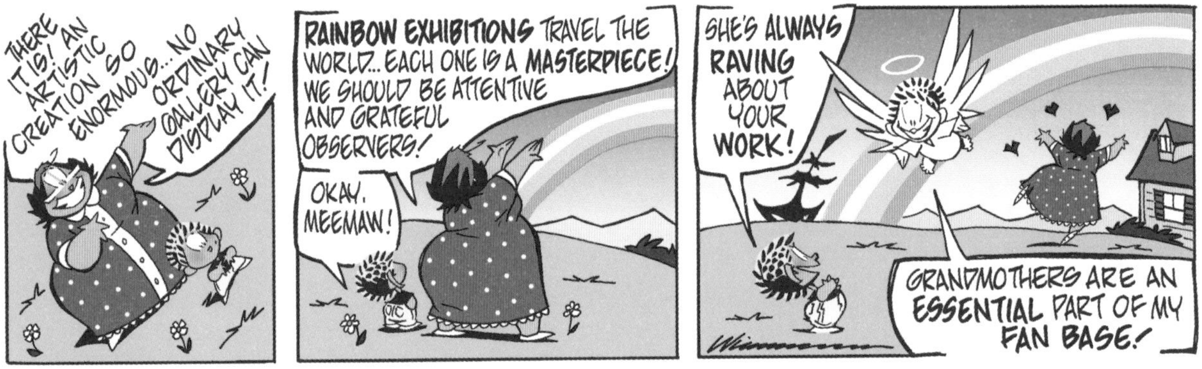
THERE IT IS! AN ARTISTIC CREATION SO ENORMOUS...NO ORDINARY GALLERY CAN DISPLAY IT!
RAINBOW EXHIBITIONS TRAVEL THE WORLD... EACH ONE IS A **MASTERPIECE**! WE SHOULD BE ATTENTIVE AND GRATEFUL OBSERVERS!
OKAY, MEEMAW!
SHE'S **ALWAYS RAVING** ABOUT YOUR **WORK**!
GRANDMOTHERS ARE AN **ESSENTIAL** PART OF MY **FAN BASE**!

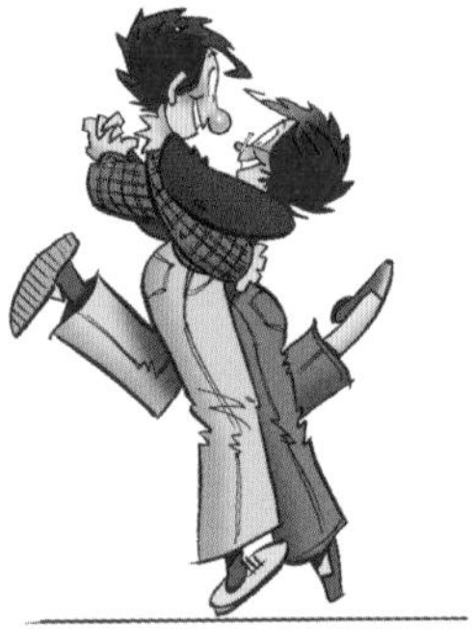

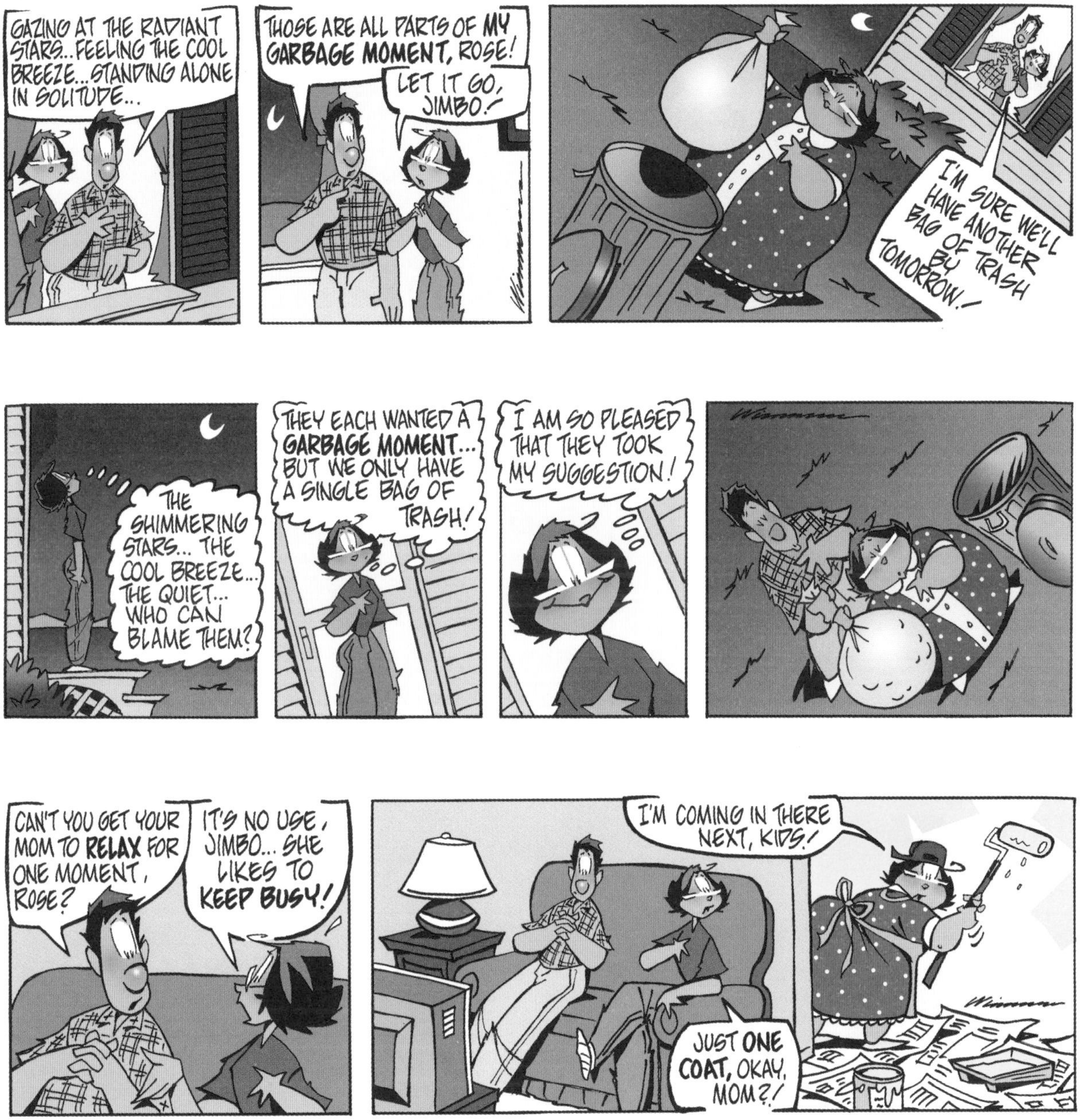
GAZING AT THE RADIANT STARS... FEELING THE COOL BREEZE... STANDING ALONE IN SOLITUDE...
THOSE ARE ALL PARTS OF MY GARBAGE MOMENT, ROSE!
LET IT GO, JIMBO!
I'M SURE WE'LL HAVE ANOTHER BAG OF TRASH BY TOMORROW!
THE SHIMMERING STARS... THE COOL BREEZE... THE QUIET... WHO CAN BLAME THEM?
THEY EACH WANTED A GARBAGE MOMENT... BUT WE ONLY HAVE A SINGLE BAG OF TRASH!
I AM SO PLEASED THAT THEY TOOK MY SUGGESTION!
CAN'T YOU GET YOUR MOM TO RELAX FOR ONE MOMENT, ROSE?
IT'S NO USE, JIMBO... SHE LIKES TO KEEP BUSY!
I'M COMING IN THERE NEXT, KIDS!
JUST ONE COAT, OKAY, MOM?!

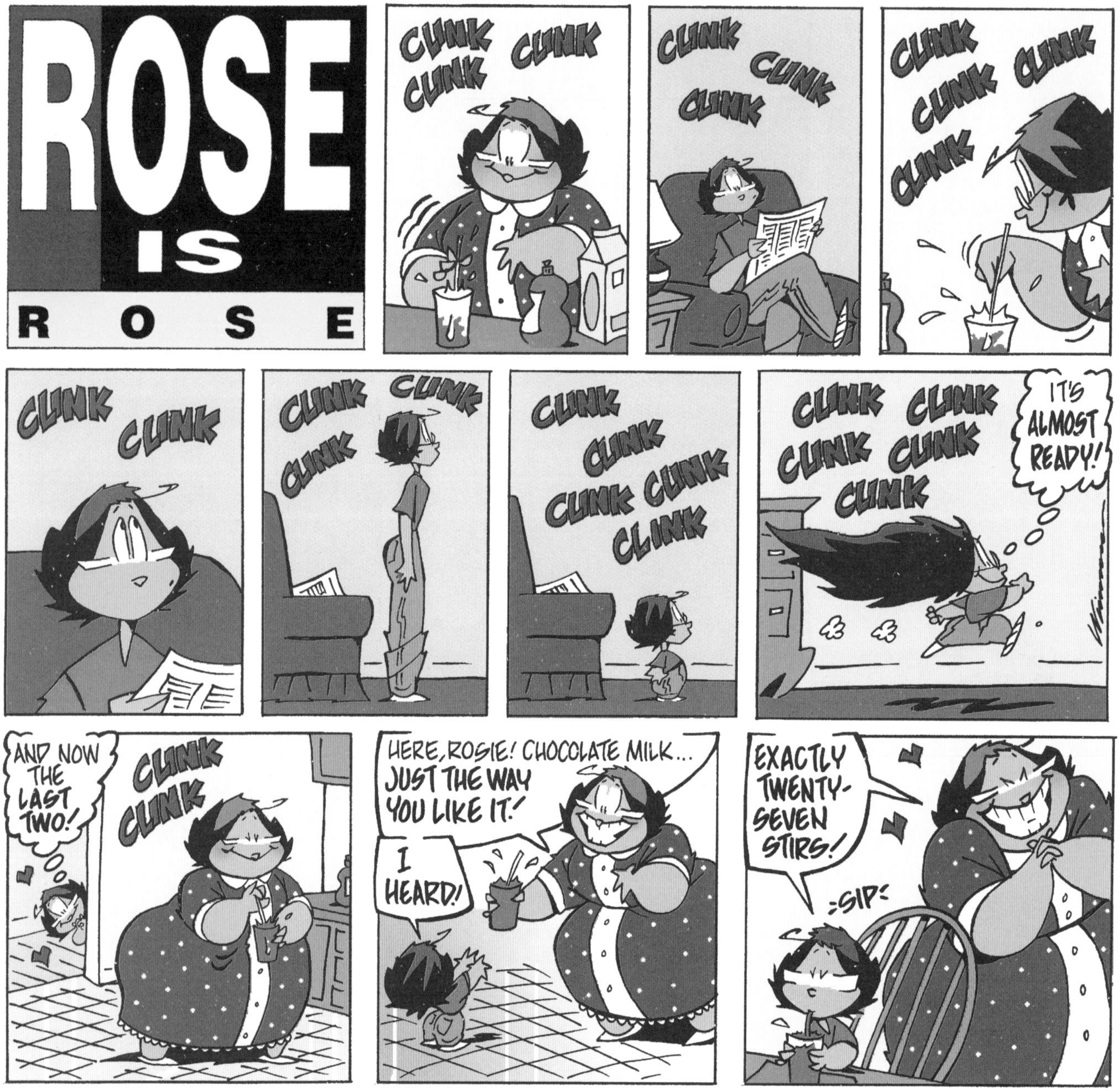
ROSE IS ROSE
CLINK CLINK CLINK
CLINK CLINK CLINK
CLINK CLINK CLINK CLINK
CLINK CLINK
CLINK CLINK CLINK
CLINK CLINK CLINK CLINK CLINK
CLINK CLINK CLINK CLINK CLINK
IT'S ALMOST READY!
AND NOW THE LAST TWO!
CLINK CLINK
HERE, ROSIE! CHOCOLATE MILK... JUST THE WAY YOU LIKE IT!
I HEARD!
EXACTLY TWENTY-SEVEN STIRS!
SIP

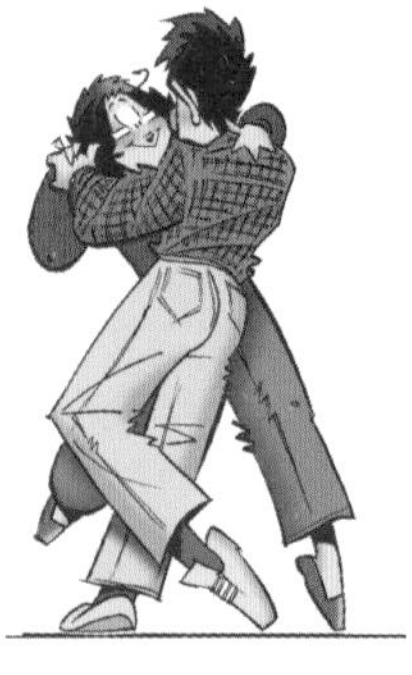

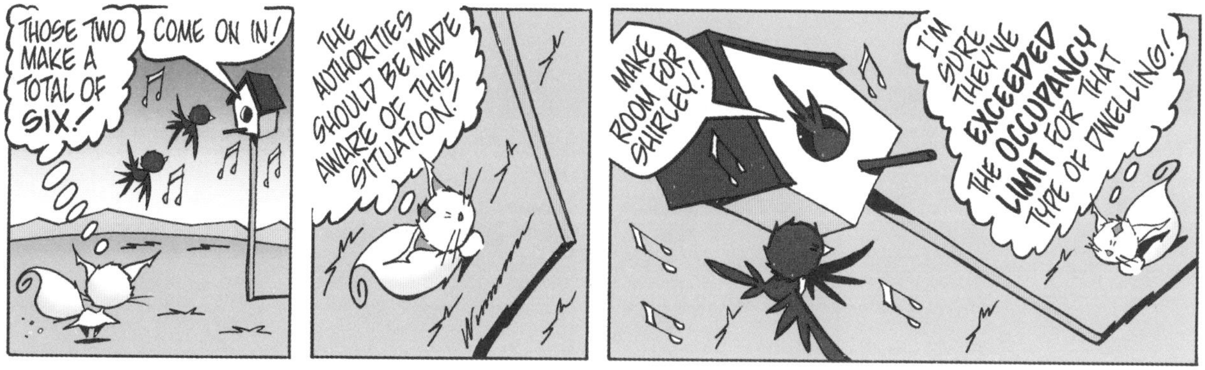
THOSE TWO MAKE A TOTAL OF SIX!
COME ON IN!
THE AUTHORITIES SHOULD BE MADE AWARE OF THIS SITUATION!
MAKE ROOM FOR SHIRLEY!
I'M SURE THEY'VE EXCEEDED THE OCCUPANCY LIMIT FOR THAT TYPE OF DWELLING!

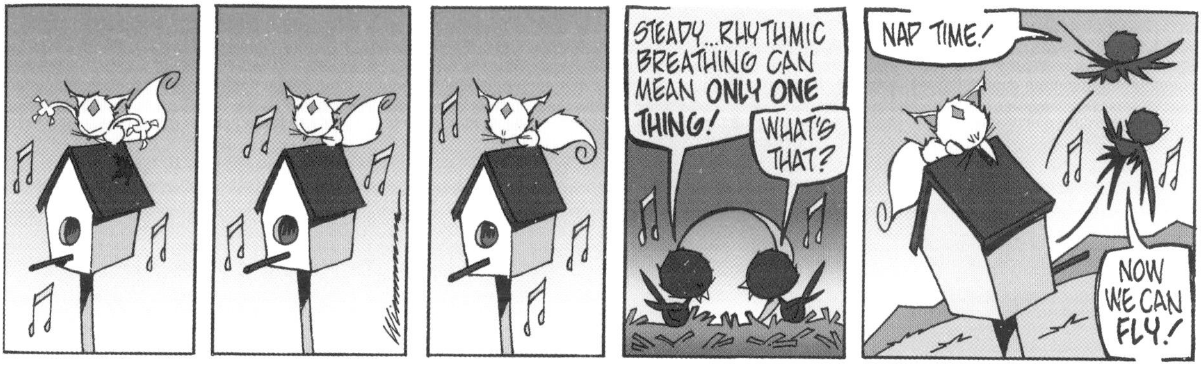
STEADY...RHYTHMIC BREATHING CAN MEAN ONLY ONE THING!
WHAT'S THAT?
NAP TIME!
NOW WE CAN FLY!

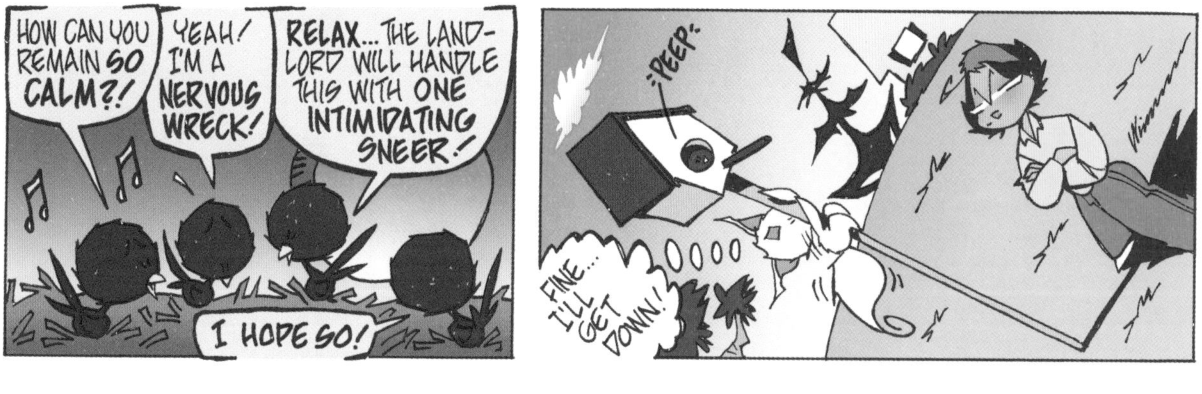
HOW CAN YOU REMAIN SO CALM?!
YEAH! I'M A NERVOUS WRECK!
RELAX... THE LAND-LORD WILL HANDLE THIS WITH ONE INTIMIDATING SNEER!
I HOPE SO!
PEEP
FINE... I'LL GET DOWN!

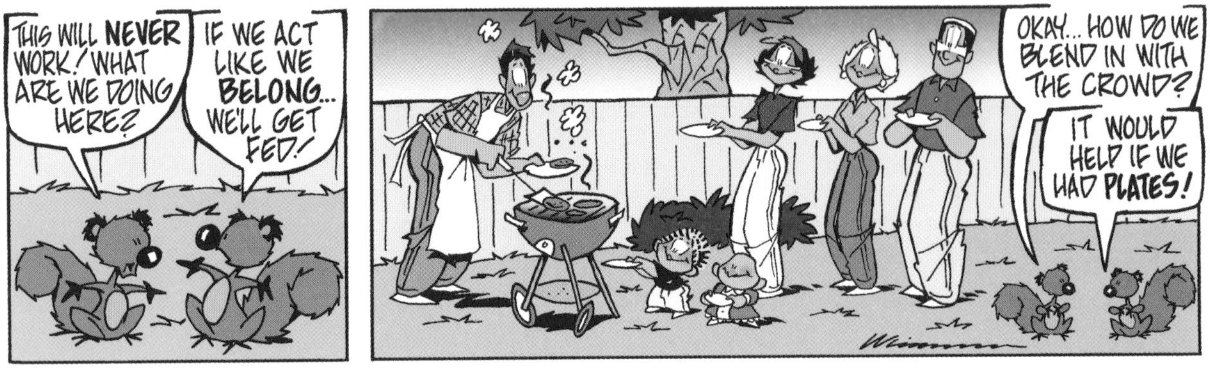
THIS WILL NEVER WORK! WHAT ARE WE DOING HERE?
IF WE ACT LIKE WE BELONG... WE'LL GET FED!
OKAY... HOW DO WE BLEND IN WITH THE CROWD?
IT WOULD HELP IF WE HAD PLATES!

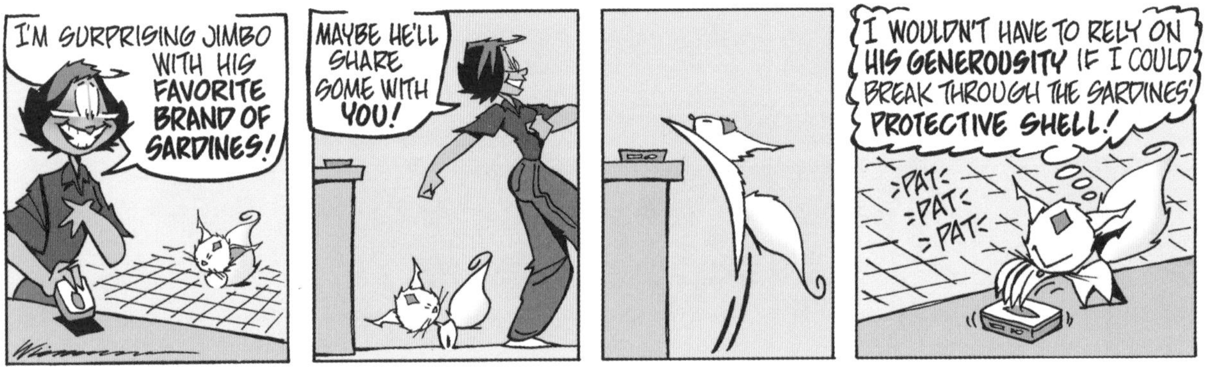
I'M SURPRISING JIMBO WITH HIS FAVORITE BRAND OF SARDINES!
MAYBE HE'LL SHARE SOME WITH YOU!
I WOULDN'T HAVE TO RELY ON HIS GENEROUSITY IF I COULD BREAK THROUGH THE SARDINES' PROTECTIVE SHELL!
PAT PAT PAT

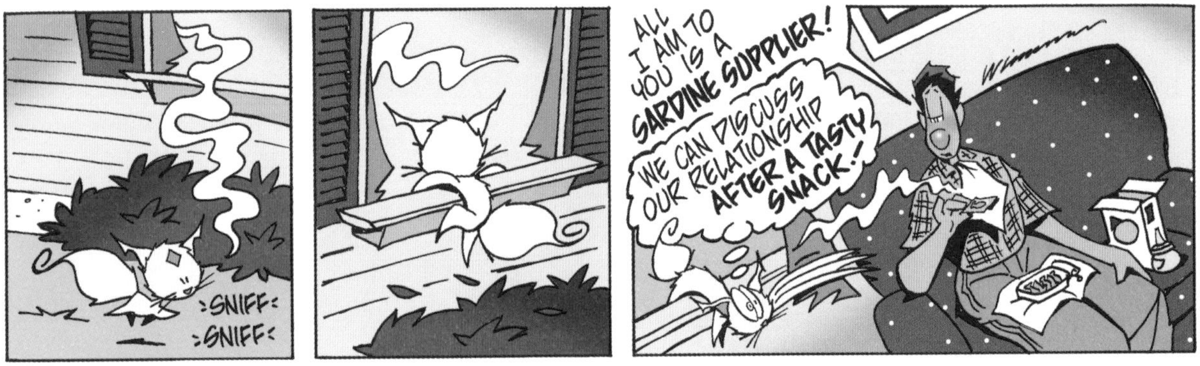
SNIFF SNIFF
ALL I AM TO YOU IS A SARDINE SUPPLIER!
WE CAN DISCUSS OUR RELATIONSHIP AFTER A TASTY SNACK!

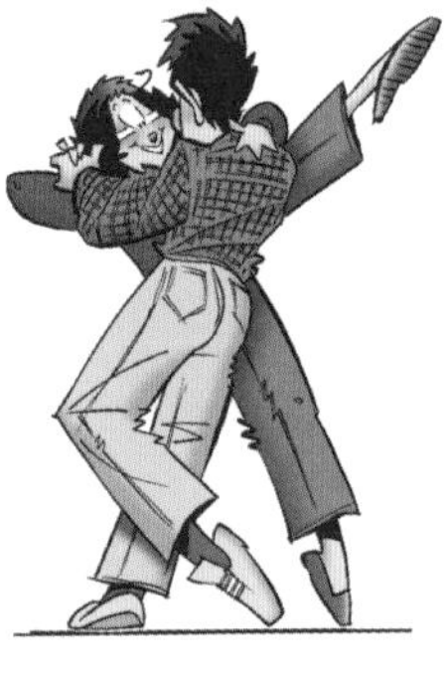

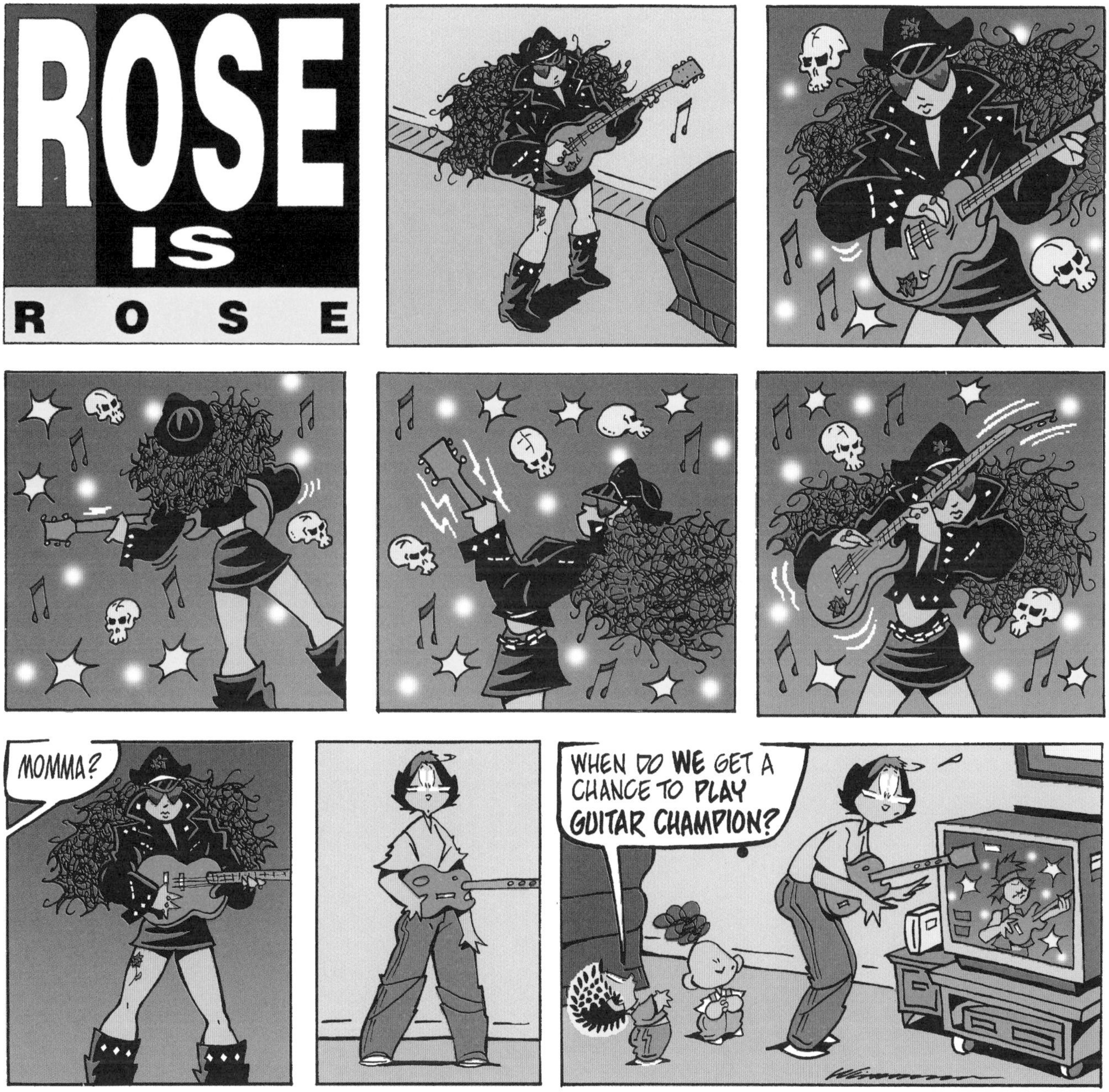
ROSE IS ROSE
MOMMA?
WHEN DO WE GET A CHANCE TO PLAY GUITAR CHAMPION?

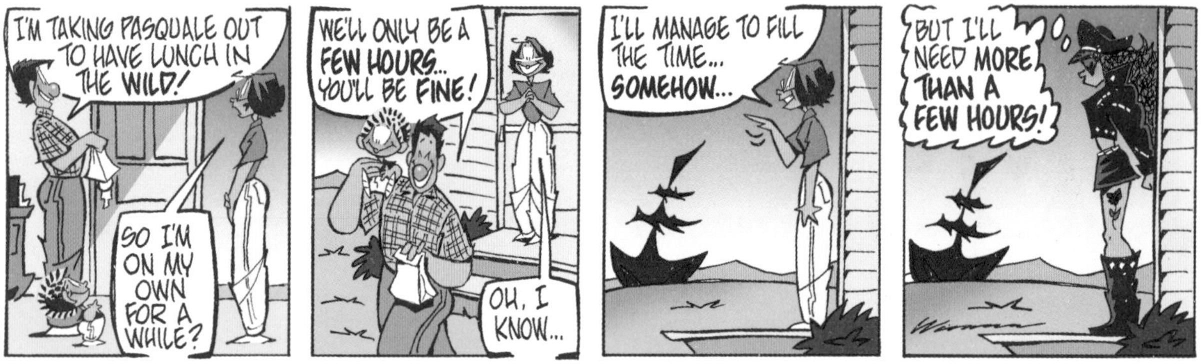
I'M TAKING PASQUALE OUT TO HAVE LUNCH IN THE WILD!
SO I'M ON MY OWN FOR A WHILE?
WE'LL ONLY BE A FEW HOURS... YOU'LL BE FINE!
OH, I KNOW...
I'LL MANAGE TO FILL THE TIME... SOMEHOW...
BUT I'LL NEED MORE THAN A FEW HOURS!

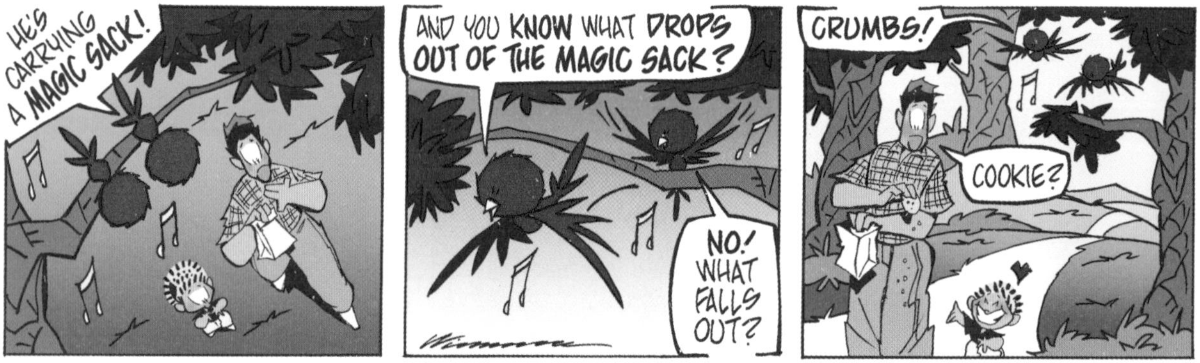
HE'S CARRYING A MAGIC SACK!
AND YOU KNOW WHAT DROPS OUT OF THE MAGIC SACK?
NO! WHAT FALLS OUT?
CRUMBS!
COOKIE?

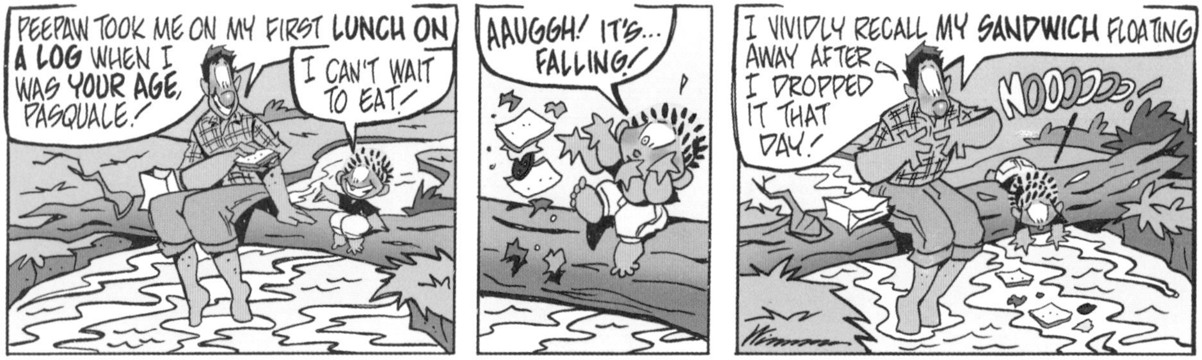
PEEPAW TOOK ME ON MY FIRST LUNCH ON A LOG WHEN I WAS YOUR AGE, PASQUALE!
I CAN'T WAIT TO EAT!
AAUGGH! IT'S... FALLING!
I VIVIDLY RECALL MY SANDWICH FLOATING AWAY AFTER I DROPPED IT THAT DAY!
NOOOOOO!

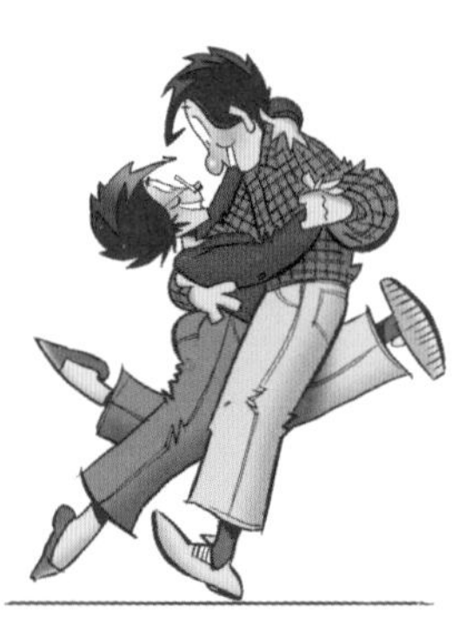

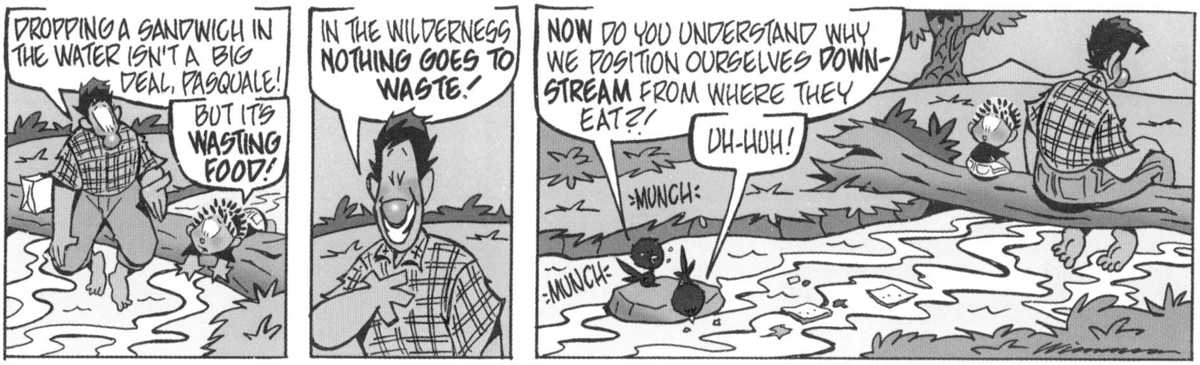
DROPPING A SANDWICH IN THE WATER ISN'T A BIG DEAL, PASQUALE!
BUT IT'S WASTING FOOD!
IN THE WILDERNESS NOTHING GOES TO WASTE!
NOW DO YOU UNDERSTAND WHY WE POSITION OURSELVES DOWN-STREAM FROM WHERE THEY EAT?!
UH-HUH!
MUNCH
MUNCH

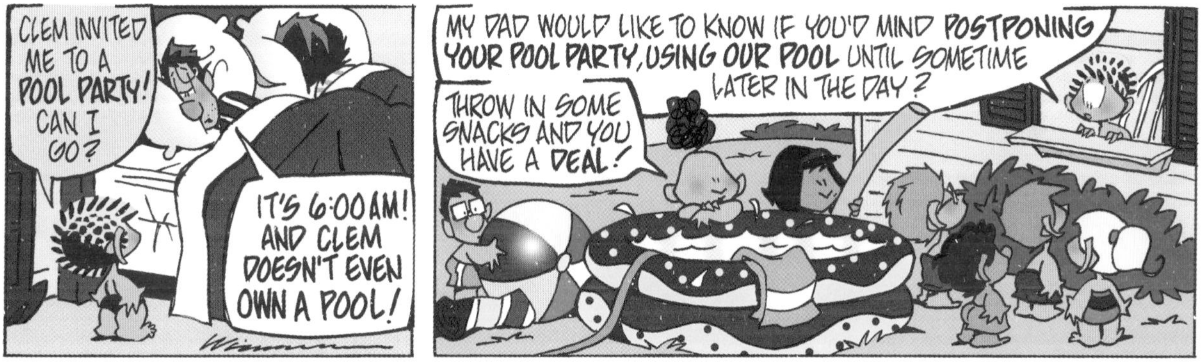
CLEM INVITED ME TO A POOL PARTY! CAN I GO?
IT'S 6:00 AM! AND CLEM DOESN'T EVEN OWN A POOL!
MY DAD WOULD LIKE TO KNOW IF YOU'D MIND POSTPONING YOUR POOL PARTY, USING OUR POOL UNTIL SOMETIME LATER IN THE DAY?
THROW IN SOME SNACKS AND YOU HAVE A DEAL!

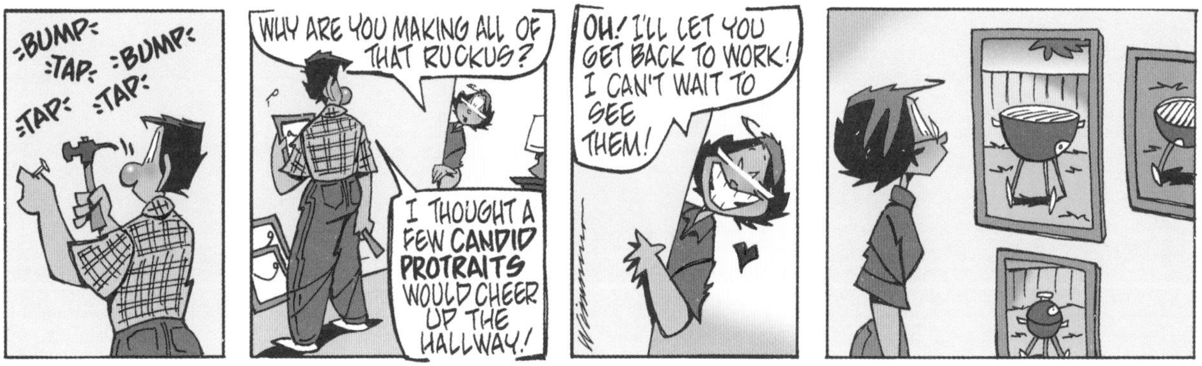
BUMP
TAP
BUMP
TAP
TAP
WHY ARE YOU MAKING ALL OF THAT RUCKUS?
I THOUGHT A FEW CANDID PROTRAITS WOULD CHEER UP THE HALLWAY!
OH! I'LL LET YOU GET BACK TO WORK! I CAN'T WAIT TO SEE THEM!

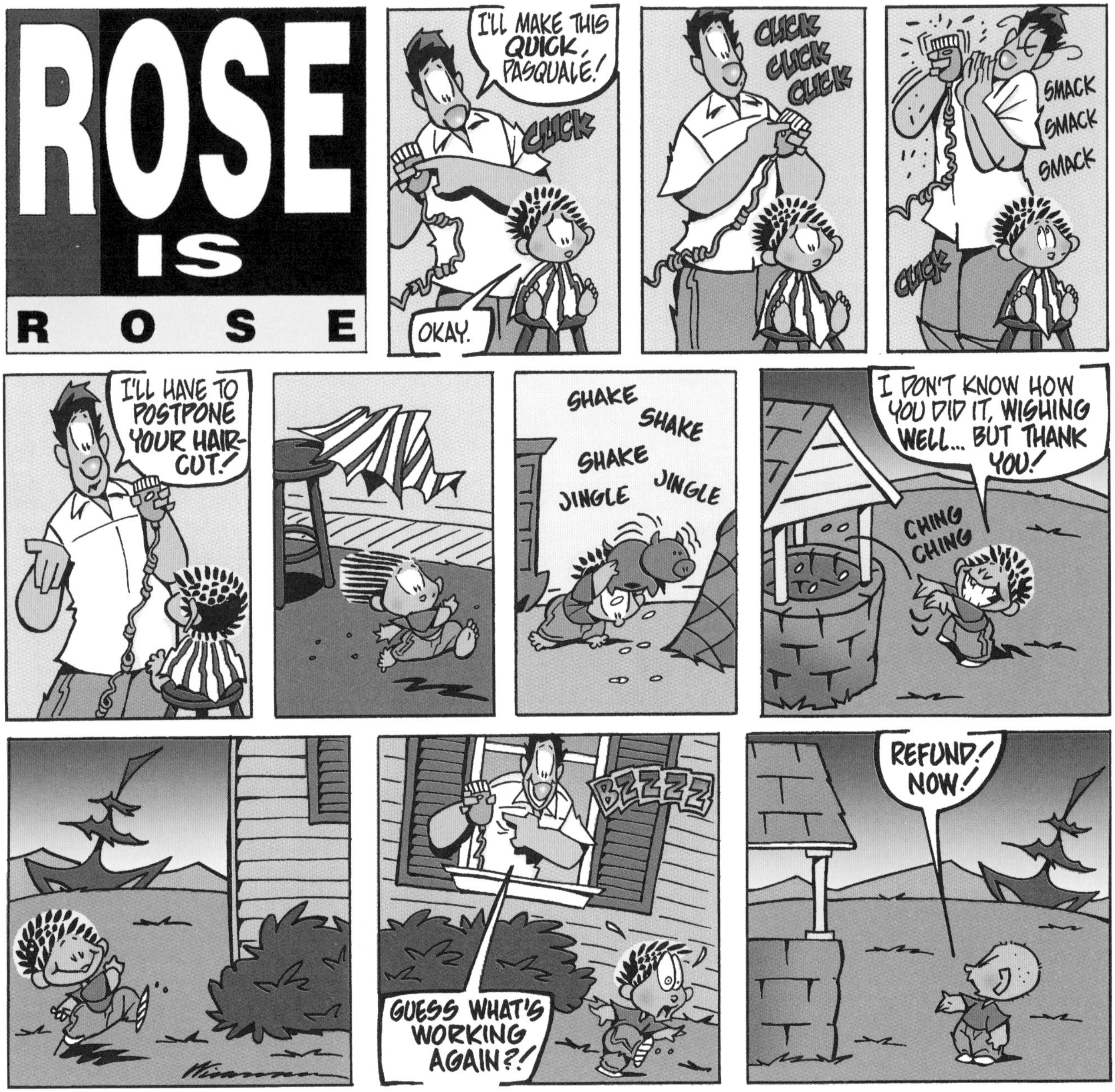
ROSE IS ROSE
I'LL MAKE THIS QUICK, PASQUALE!
CLICK
OKAY.
CLICK CLICK CLICK
SMACK SMACK SMACK
CLICK
I'LL HAVE TO POSTPONE YOUR HAIR-CUT!
SHAKE SHAKE SHAKE
JINGLE JINGLE
I DON'T KNOW HOW YOU DID IT, WISHING WELL... BUT THANK YOU!
CHING CHING
BZZZZ
GUESS WHAT'S WORKING AGAIN?!
REFUND! NOW!

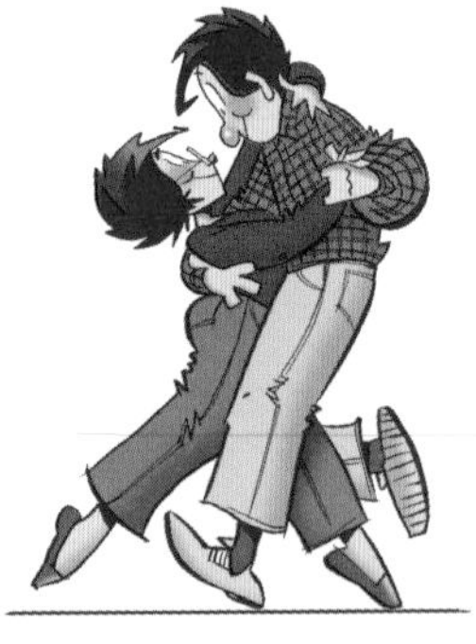

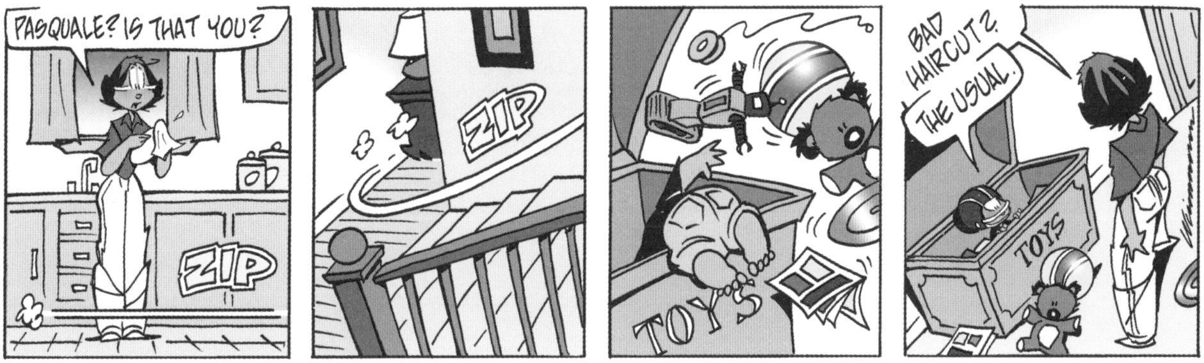
PASQUALE? IS THAT YOU?
ZIP
ZIP
TOYS
BAD HAIRCUT?
THE USUAL.
TOYS

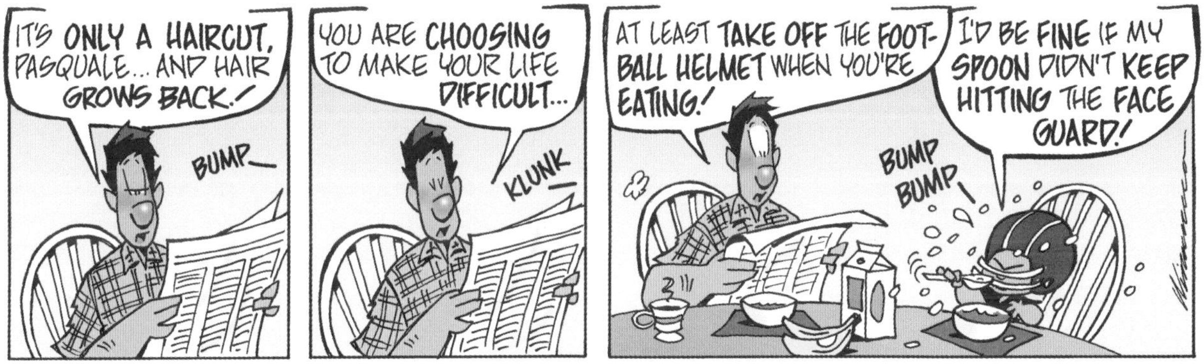
IT'S ONLY A HAIRCUT, PASQUALE... AND HAIR GROWS BACK!
BUMP
YOU ARE CHOOSING TO MAKE YOUR LIFE DIFFICULT...
KLUNK
AT LEAST TAKE OFF THE FOOTBALL HELMET WHEN YOU'RE EATING!
I'D BE FINE IF MY SPOON DIDN'T KEEP HITTING THE FACE GUARD!
BUMP BUMP

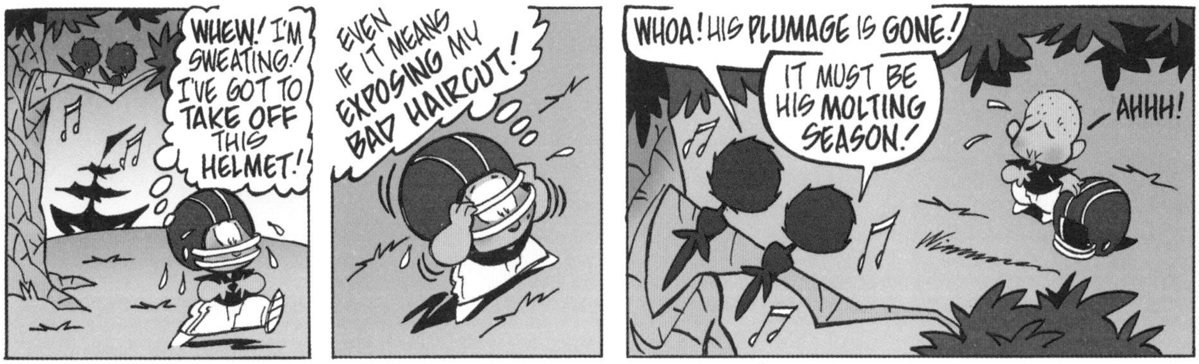
WHEW! I'M SWEATING! I'VE GOT TO TAKE OFF THIS HELMET!
EVEN IF IT MEANS EXPOSING MY BAD HAIRCUT!
WHOA! HIS PLUMAGE IS GONE!
IT MUST BE HIS MOLTING SEASON!
AHHH!

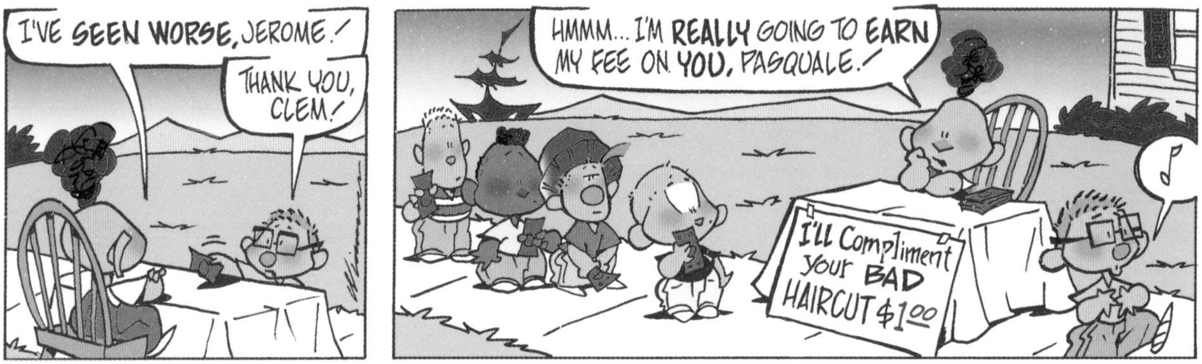
I'VE SEEN WORSE, JEROME!
THANK YOU, CLEM!
HMMM... I'M REALLY GOING TO EARN MY FEE ON YOU, PASQUALE!
I'LL Compliment your BAD HAIRCUT $1.00

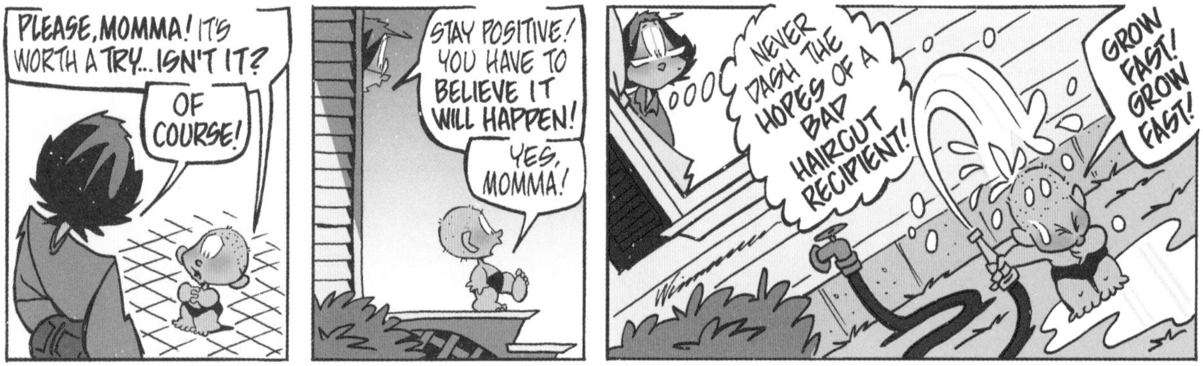
PLEASE, MOMMA! IT'S WORTH A TRY... ISN'T IT?
OF COURSE!
STAY POSITIVE! YOU HAVE TO BELIEVE IT WILL HAPPEN!
YES, MOMMA!
NEVER DASH THE HOPES OF A BAD HAIRCUT RECIPIENT!
GROW FAST! GROW FAST!

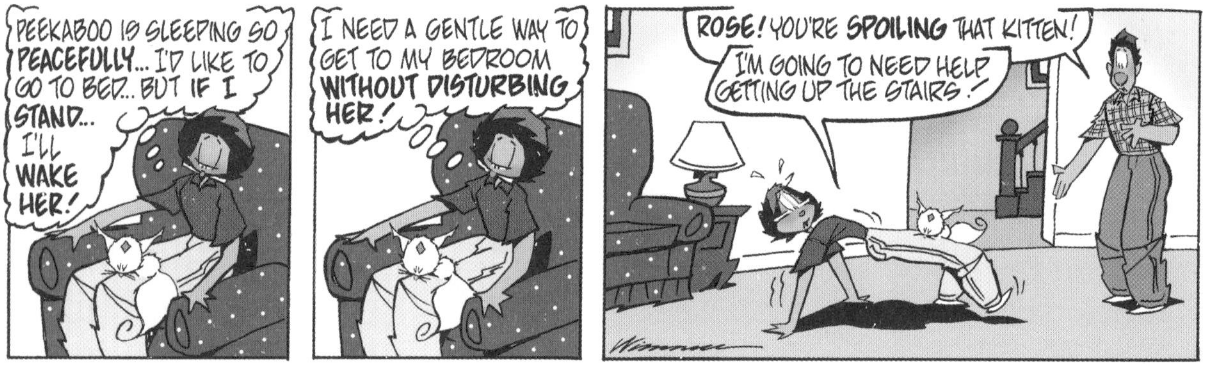
PEEKABOO IS SLEEPING SO PEACEFULLY... I'D LIKE TO GO TO BED... BUT IF I STAND... I'LL WAKE HER!
I NEED A GENTLE WAY TO GET TO MY BEDROOM WITHOUT DISTURBING HER!
ROSE! YOU'RE SPOILING THAT KITTEN!
I'M GOING TO NEED HELP GETTING UP THE STAIRS!

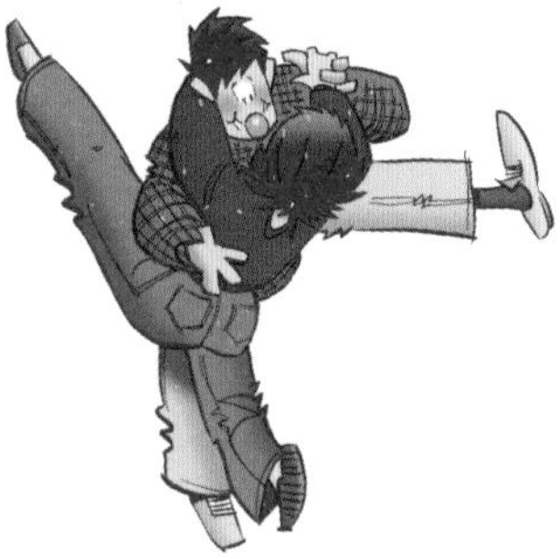

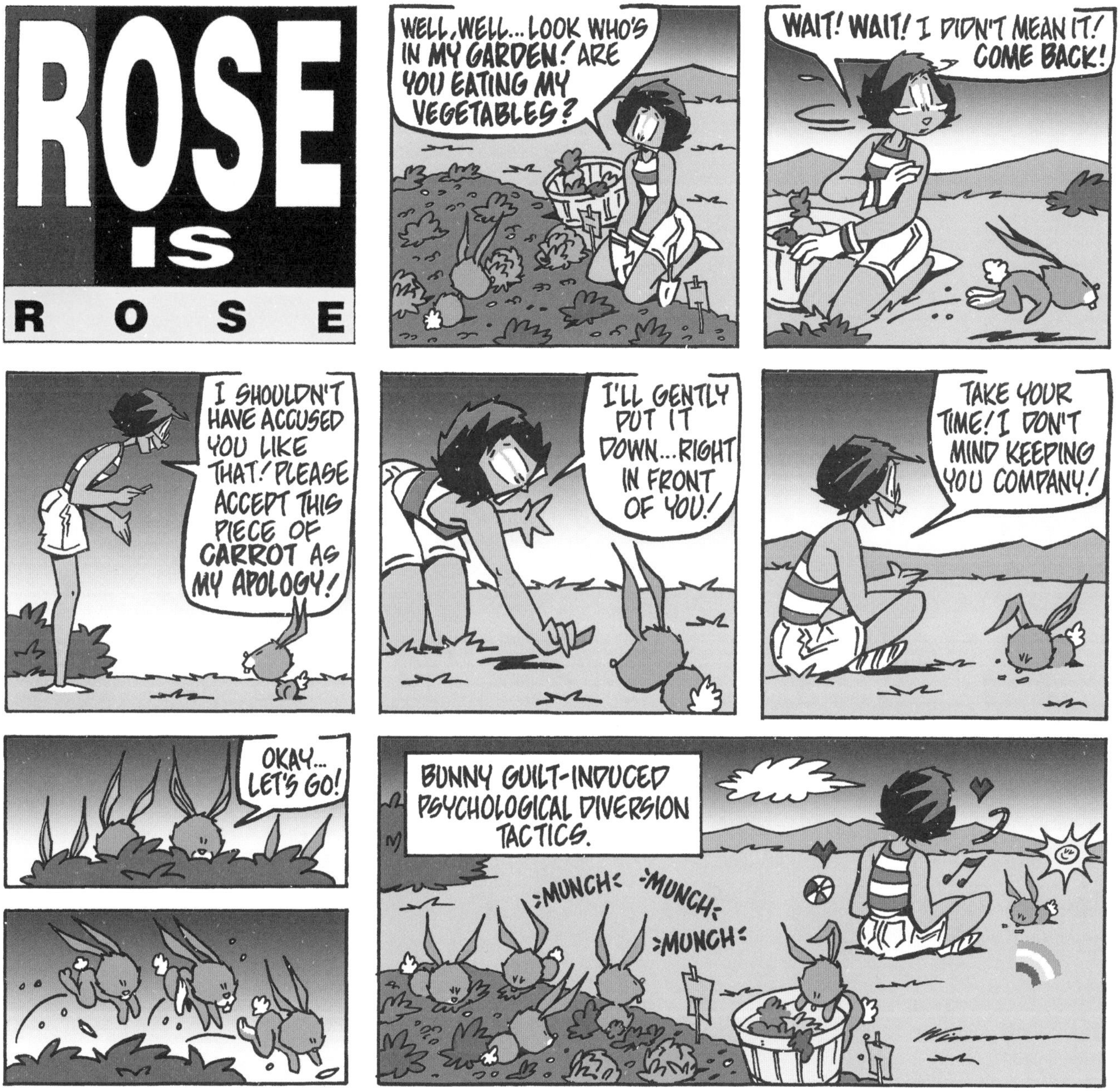
ROSE IS ROSE
WELL, WELL... LOOK WHO'S IN MY GARDEN! ARE YOU EATING MY VEGETABLES?
WAIT! WAIT! I DIDN'T MEAN IT! COME BACK!
I SHOULDN'T HAVE ACCUSED YOU LIKE THAT! PLEASE ACCEPT THIS PIECE OF CARROT AS MY APOLOGY!
I'LL GENTLY PUT IT DOWN... RIGHT IN FRONT OF YOU!
TAKE YOUR TIME! I DON'T MIND KEEPING YOU COMPANY!
OKAY... LET'S GO!
BUNNY GUILT-INDUCED PSYCHOLOGICAL DIVERSION TACTICS.
MUNCH
MUNCH
MUNCH

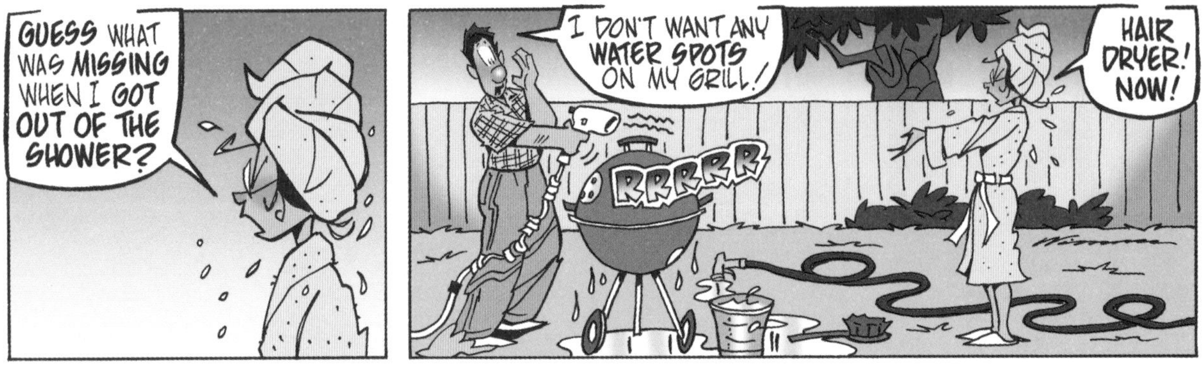
GUESS WHAT WAS MISSING WHEN I GOT OUT OF THE SHOWER?
I DON'T WANT ANY WATER SPOTS ON MY GRILL!
RRRRR
HAIR DRYER! NOW!

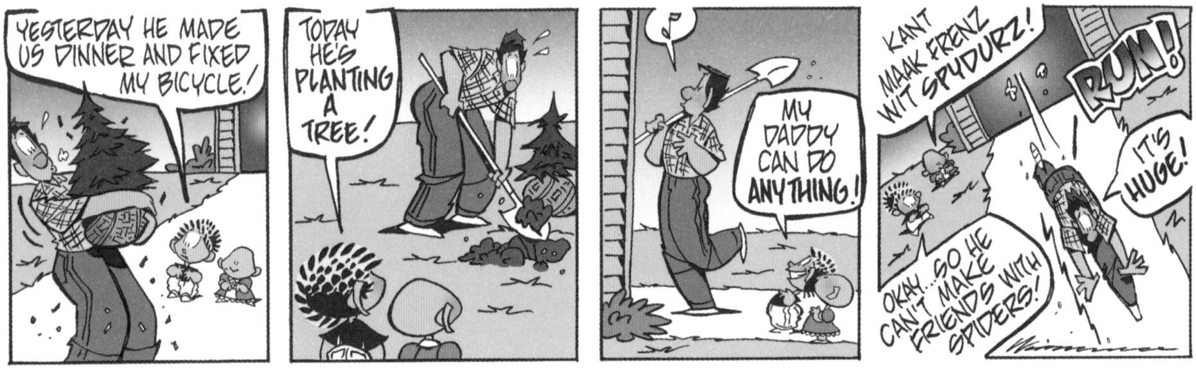
YESTERDAY HE MADE US DINNER AND FIXED MY BICYCLE!
TODAY HE'S PLANTING A TREE!
MY DADDY CAN DO ANYTHING!
KANT MAAK FRENZ WIT SPYDURZ!
RUN!
IT'S HUGE!
OKAY...SO HE CAN'T MAKE FRIENDS WITH SPIDERS!

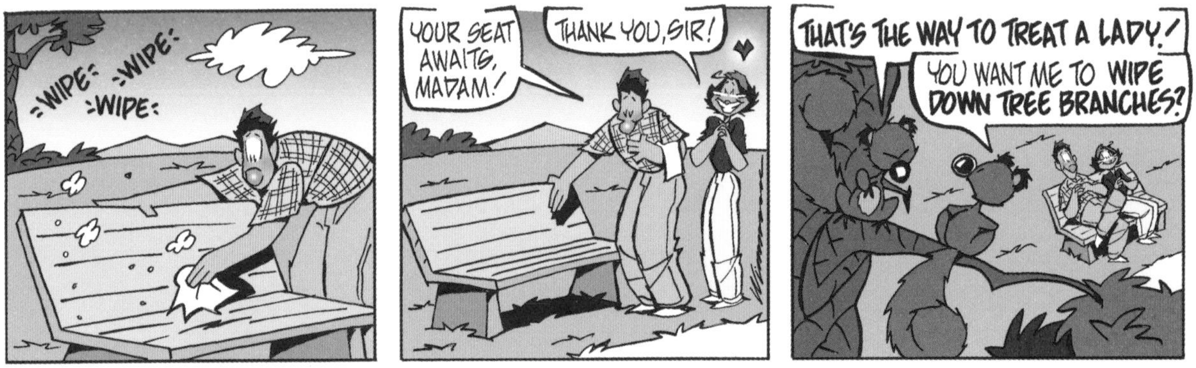
WIPE
WIPE
WIPE
YOUR SEAT AWAITS, MADAM!
THANK YOU, SIR!
THAT'S THE WAY TO TREAT A LADY!
YOU WANT ME TO WIPE DOWN TREE BRANCHES?

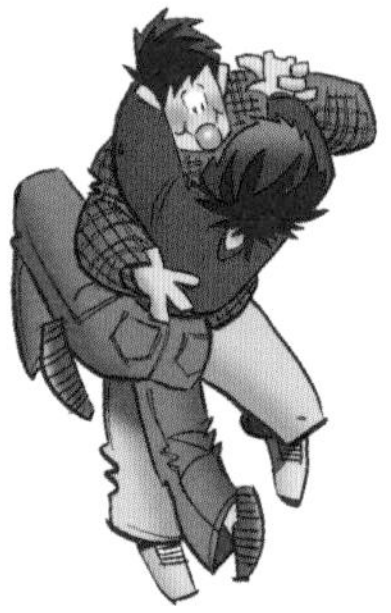

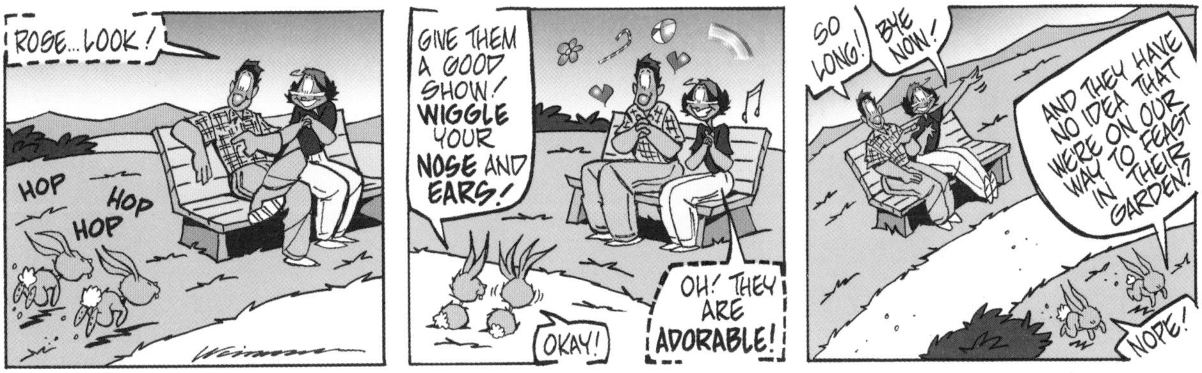
ROSE... LOOK!
HOP
HOP
HOP
GIVE THEM A GOOD SHOW! WIGGLE YOUR NOSE AND EARS!
OKAY!
OH! THEY ARE ADORABLE!
SO LONG!
BYE NOW!
AND THEY HAVE NO IDEA THAT WE'RE ON OUR WAY TO FEAST IN THEIR GARDEN?
NOPE!

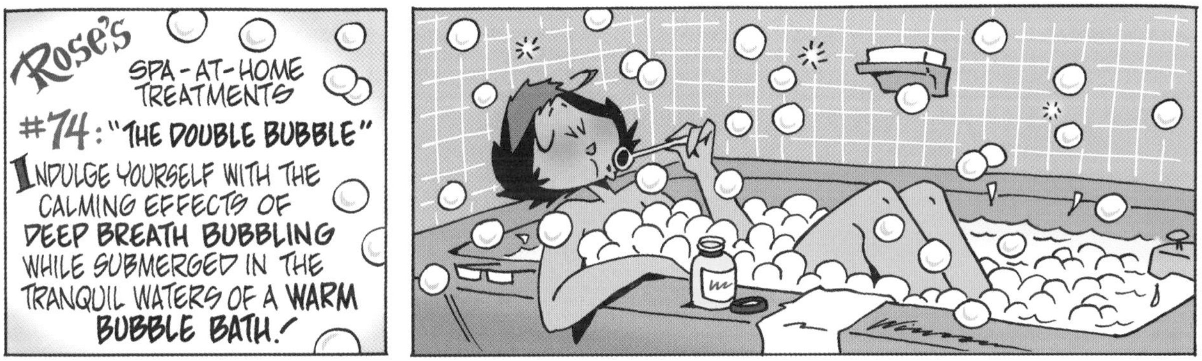
Rose's
SPA-AT-HOME TREATMENTS
#74: "THE DOUBLE BUBBLE"
INDULGE YOURSELF WITH THE CALMING EFFECTS OF DEEP BREATH BUBBLING WHILE SUBMERGED IN THE TRANQUIL WATERS OF A WARM BUBBLE BATH!

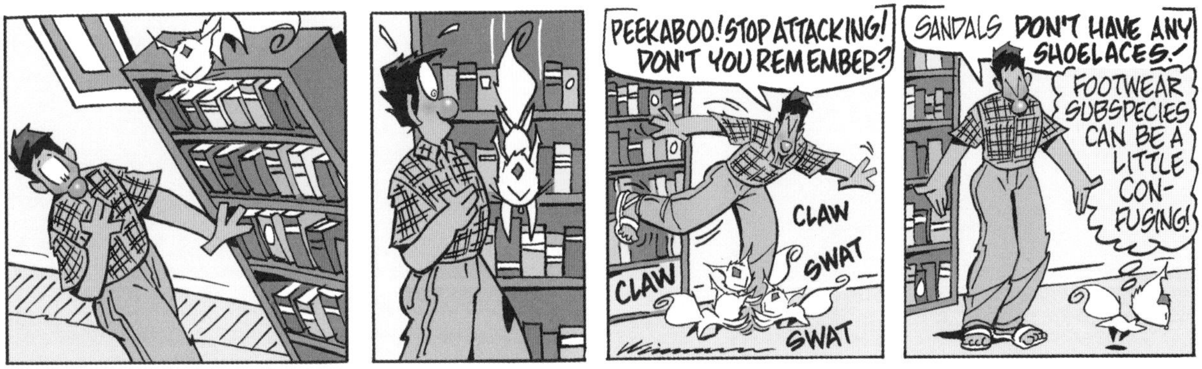
PEEKABOO! STOP ATTACKING! DON'T YOU REMEMBER?
CLAW
CLAW
SWAT
SWAT
SANDALS DON'T HAVE ANY SHOELACES!
FOOTWEAR SUBSPECIES CAN BE A LITTLE CON-FUSING!

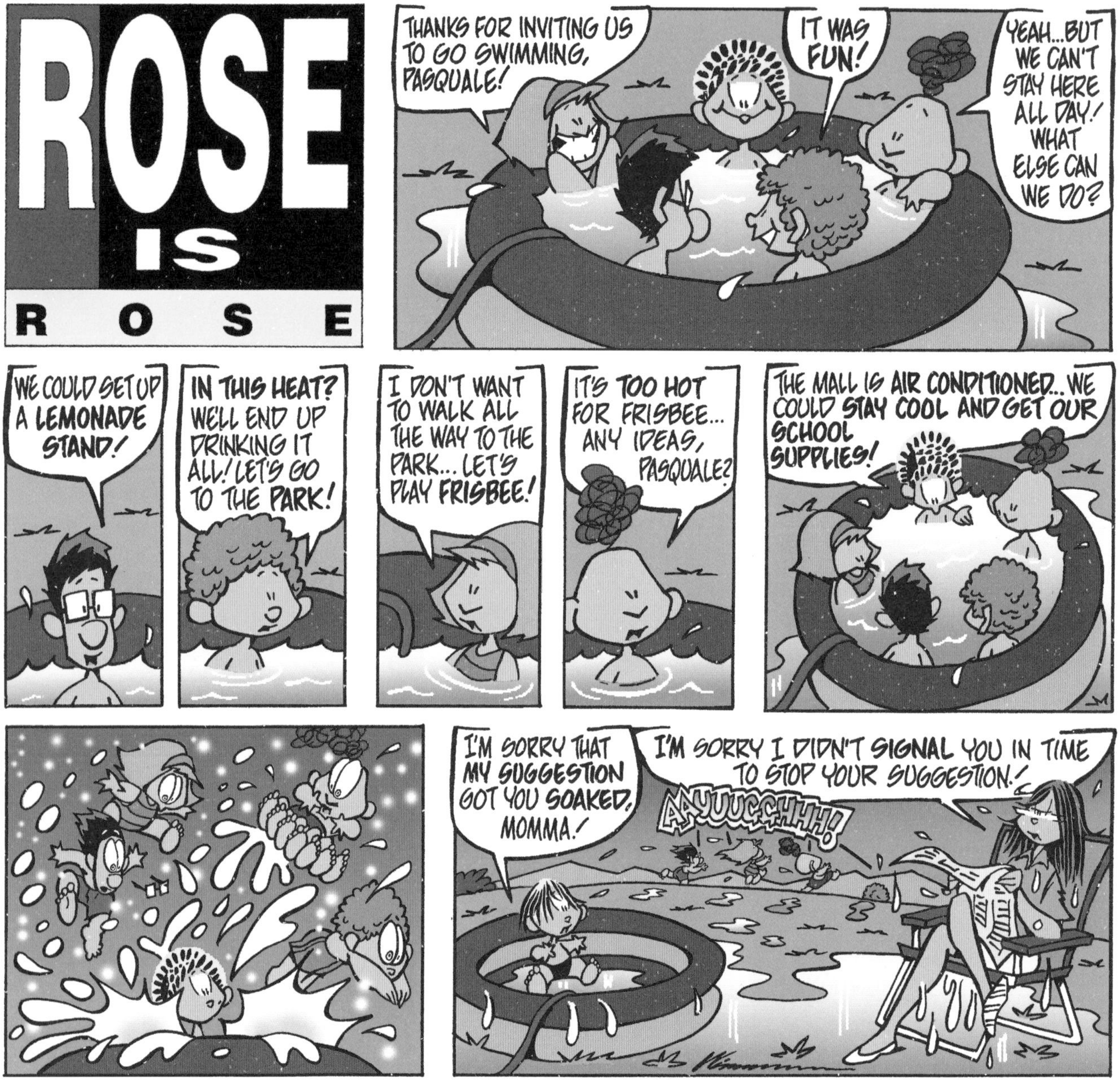
ROSE IS ROSE
THANKS FOR INVITING US TO GO SWIMMING, PASQUALE!
IT WAS FUN!
YEAH...BUT WE CAN'T STAY HERE ALL DAY! WHAT ELSE CAN WE DO?
WE COULD SET UP A LEMONADE STAND!
IN THIS HEAT? WE'LL END UP DRINKING IT ALL! LET'S GO TO THE PARK!
I DON'T WANT TO WALK ALL THE WAY TO THE PARK... LET'S PLAY FRISBEE!
IT'S TOO HOT FOR FRISBEE... ANY IDEAS, PASQUALE?
THE MALL IS AIR CONDITIONED...WE COULD STAY COOL AND GET OUR SCHOOL SUPPLIES!
I'M SORRY THAT MY SUGGESTION GOT YOU SOAKED, MOMMA!
I'M SORRY I DIDN'T SIGNAL YOU IN TIME TO STOP YOUR SUGGESTION!
AAYUUGGHHH!

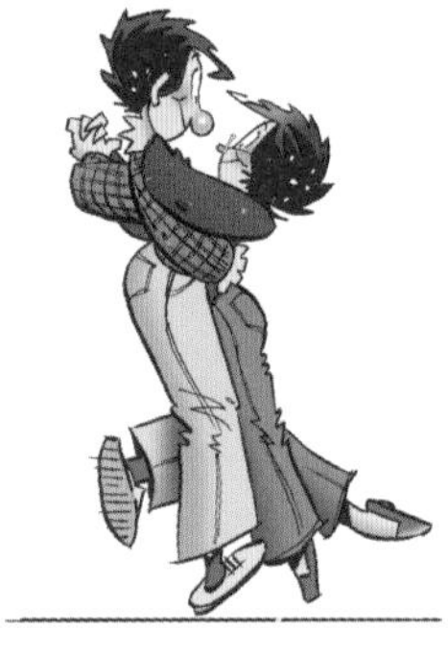

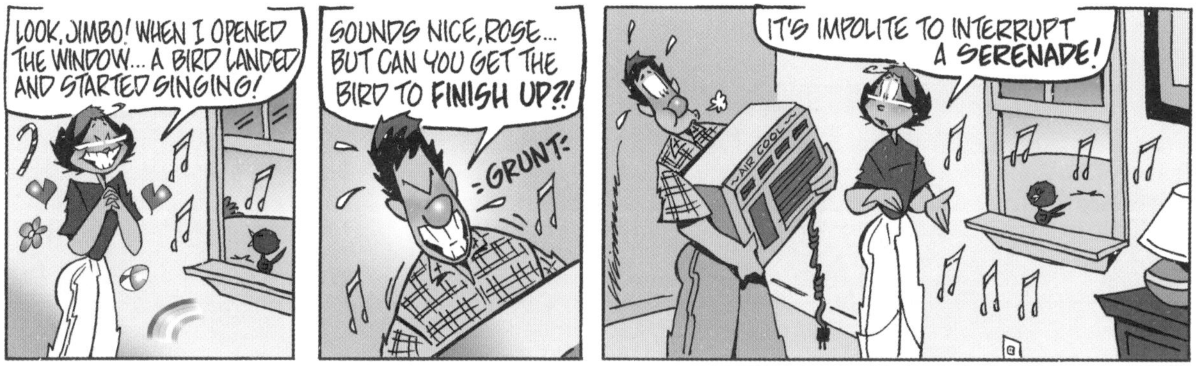
LOOK, JIMBO! WHEN I OPENED THE WINDOW... A BIRD LANDED AND STARTED SINGING!
SOUNDS NICE, ROSE... BUT CAN YOU GET THE BIRD TO FINISH UP?!
GRUNT
IT'S IMPOLITE TO INTERRUPT A SERENADE!
AIR COOL

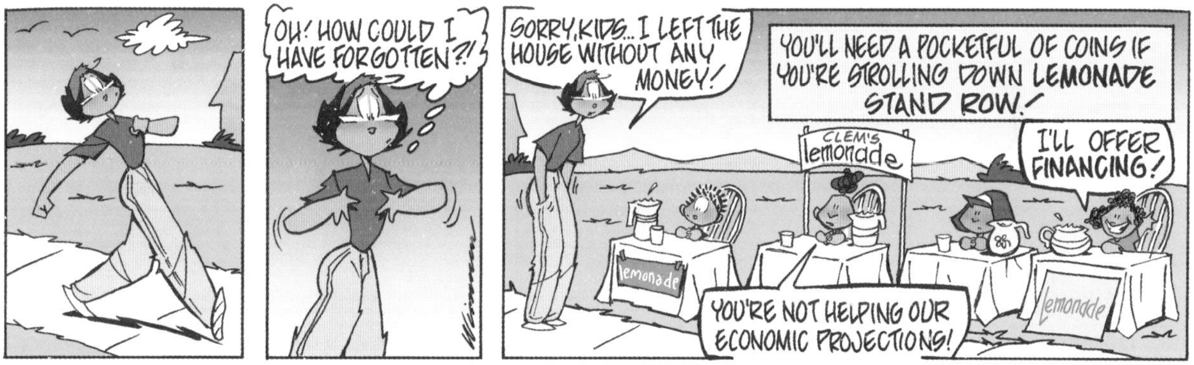
OH! HOW COULD I HAVE FORGOTTEN?!
SORRY, KIDS... I LEFT THE HOUSE WITHOUT ANY MONEY!
YOU'LL NEED A POCKETFUL OF COINS IF YOU'RE STROLLING DOWN LEMONADE STAND ROW!
CLEM'S lemonade
I'LL OFFER FINANCING!
lemonade
lemonade
YOU'RE NOT HELPING OUR ECONOMIC PROJECTIONS!

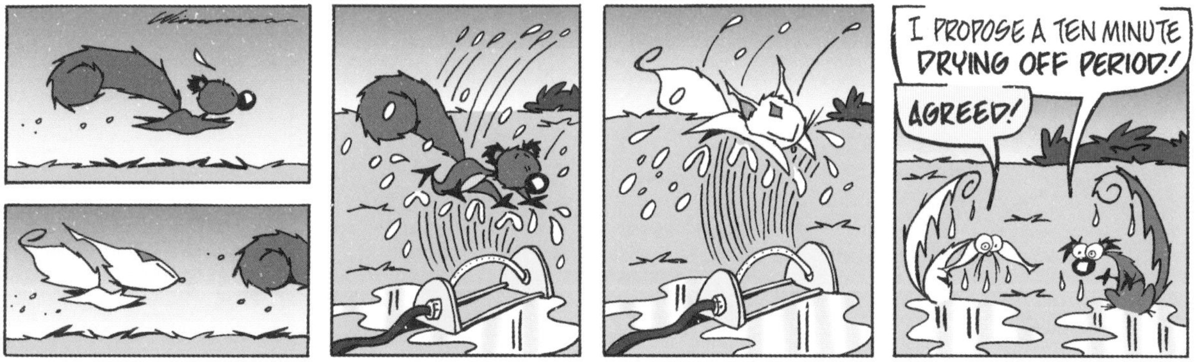
I PROPOSE A TEN MINUTE DRYING OFF PERIOD!
AGREED!

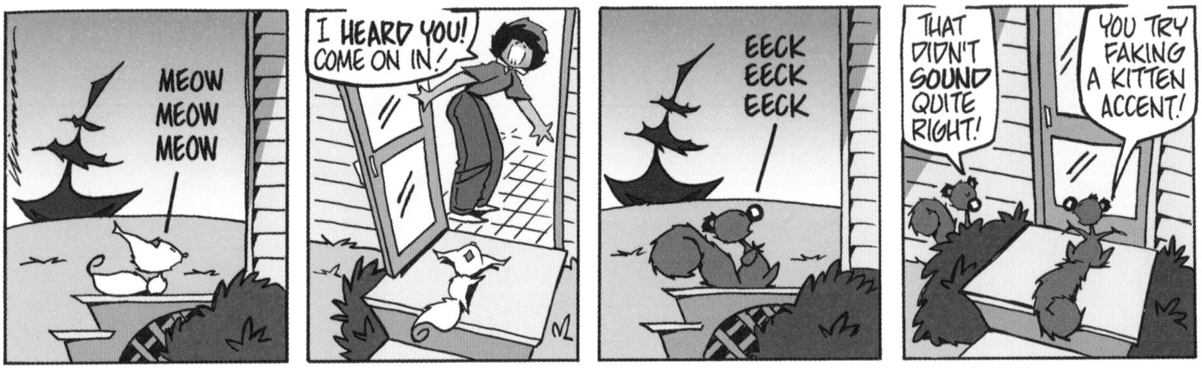
MEOW
MEOW
MEOW
I HEARD YOU! COME ON IN!
EECK
EECK
EECK
THAT DIDN'T SOUND QUITE RIGHT!
YOU TRY FAKING A KITTEN ACCENT!

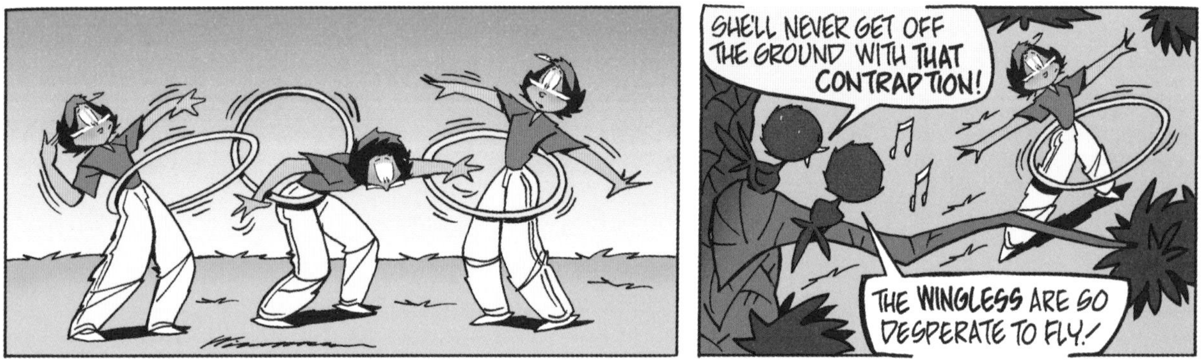
SHE'LL NEVER GET OFF THE GROUND WITH THAT CONTRAPTION!
THE WINGLESS ARE SO DESPERATE TO FLY!

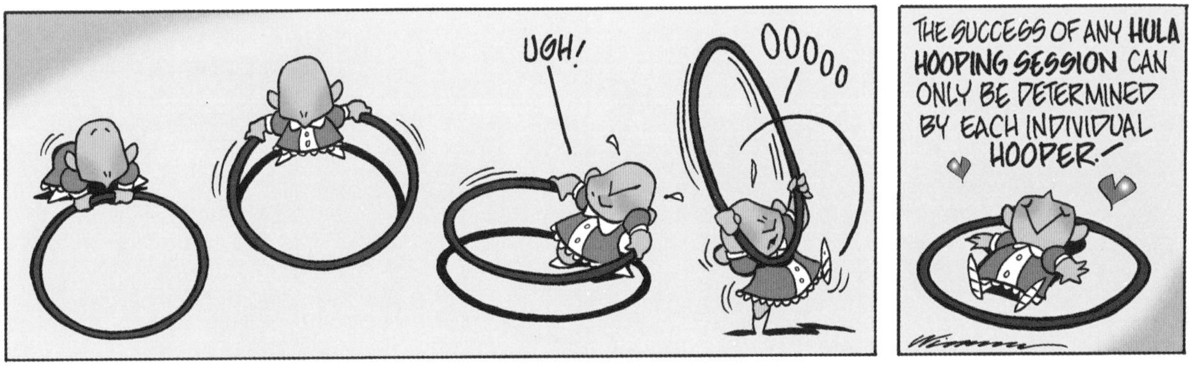
UGH!
OOOOO
THE SUCCESS OF ANY HULA HOOPING SESSION CAN ONLY BE DETERMINED BY EACH INDIVIDUAL HOOPER!

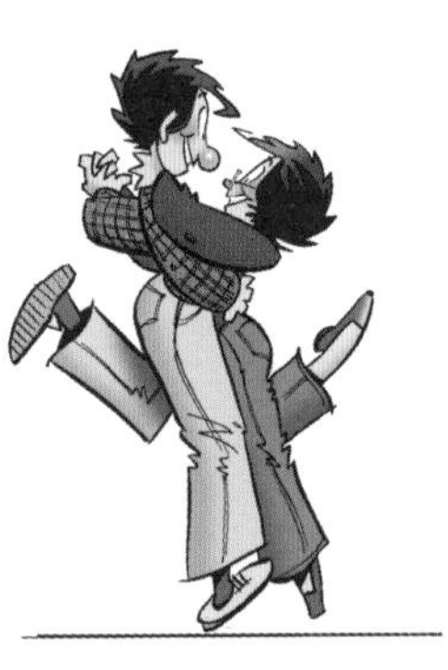

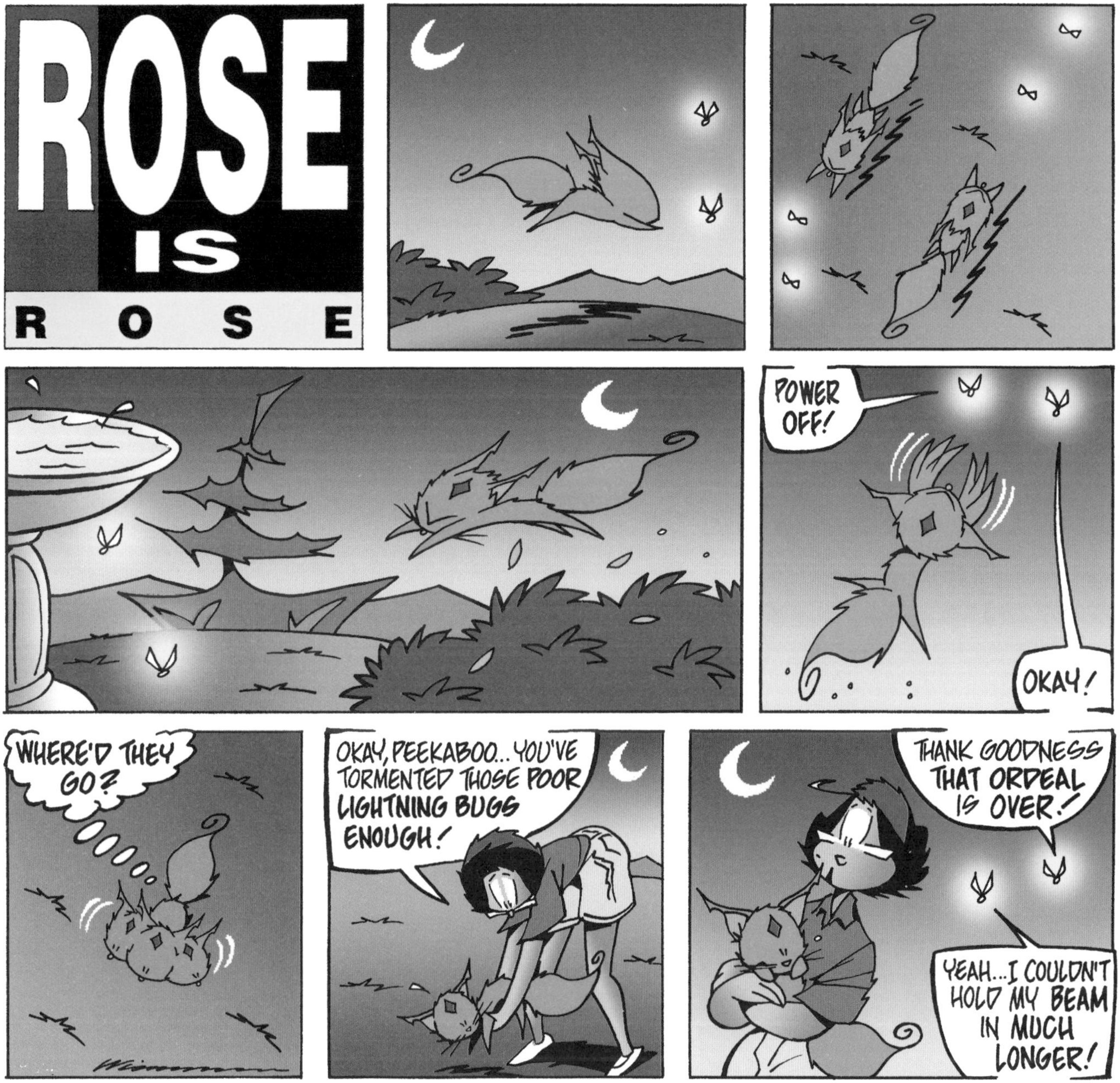
ROSE IS ROSE
POWER OFF!
OKAY!
WHERE'D THEY GO?
OKAY, PEEKABOO... YOU'VE TORMENTED THOSE POOR LIGHTNING BUGS ENOUGH!
THANK GOODNESS THAT ORDEAL IS OVER!
YEAH... I COULDN'T HOLD MY BEAM IN MUCH LONGER!

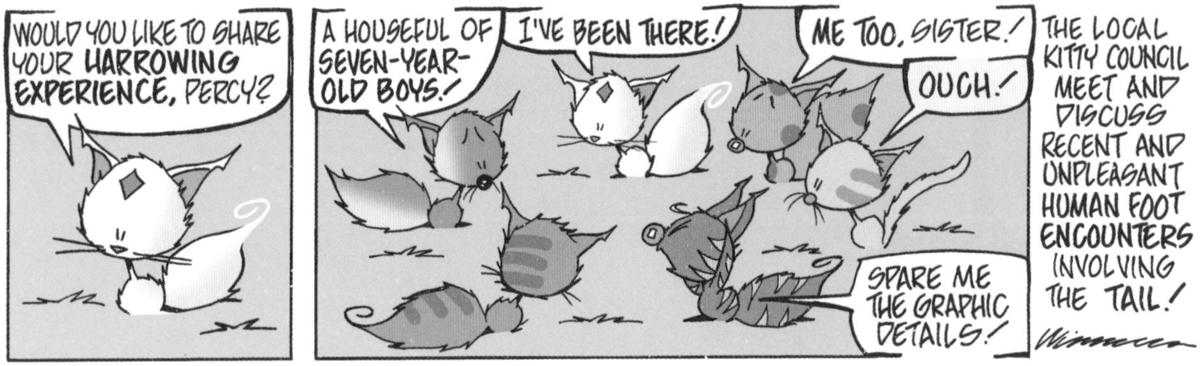
WOULD YOU LIKE TO SHARE YOUR HARROWING EXPERIENCE, PERCY?
A HOUSEFUL OF SEVEN-YEAR-OLD BOYS!
I'VE BEEN THERE!
ME TOO, SISTER!
OUCH!
SPARE ME THE GRAPHIC DETAILS!
THE LOCAL KITTY COUNCIL MEET AND DISCUSS RECENT AND UNPLEASANT HUMAN FOOT ENCOUNTERS INVOLVING THE TAIL!

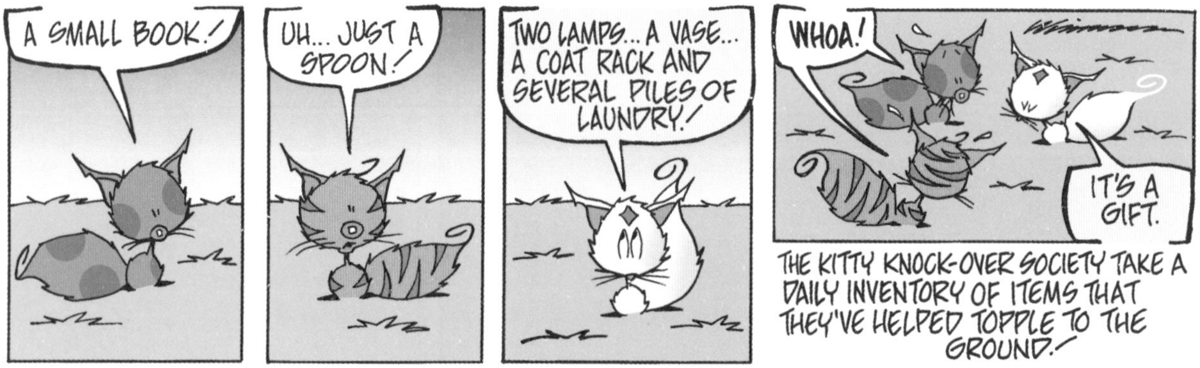
A SMALL BOOK!
UH... JUST A SPOON!
TWO LAMPS... A VASE... A COAT RACK AND SEVERAL PILES OF LAUNDRY!
WHOA!
IT'S A GIFT.
THE KITTY KNOCK-OVER SOCIETY TAKE A DAILY INVENTORY OF ITEMS THAT THEY'VE HELPED TOPPLE TO THE GROUND!

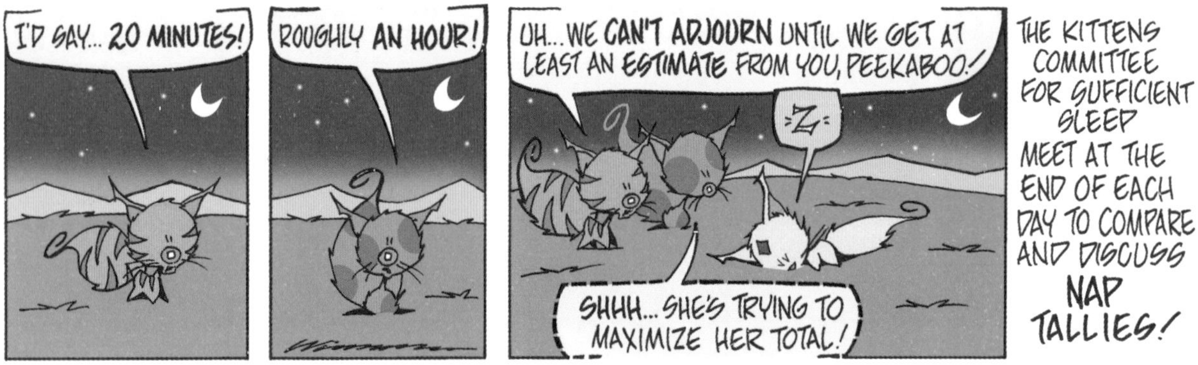
I'D SAY... 20 MINUTES!
ROUGHLY AN HOUR!
UH... WE CAN'T ADJOURN UNTIL WE GET AT LEAST AN ESTIMATE FROM YOU, PEEKABOO!
Z
SHHH... SHE'S TRYING TO MAXIMIZE HER TOTAL!
THE KITTENS COMMITTEE FOR SUFFICIENT SLEEP MEET AT THE END OF EACH DAY TO COMPARE AND DISCUSS NAP TALLIES!

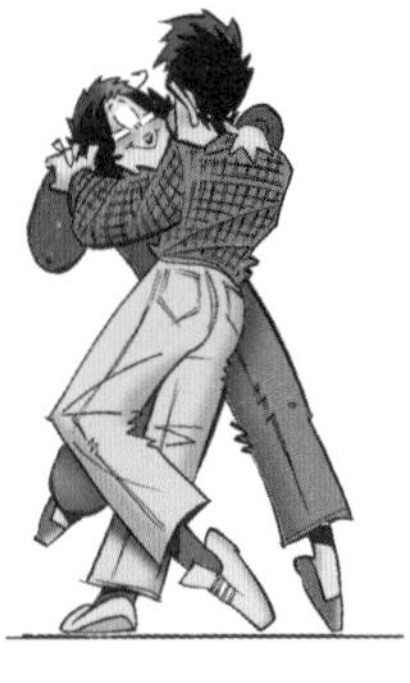

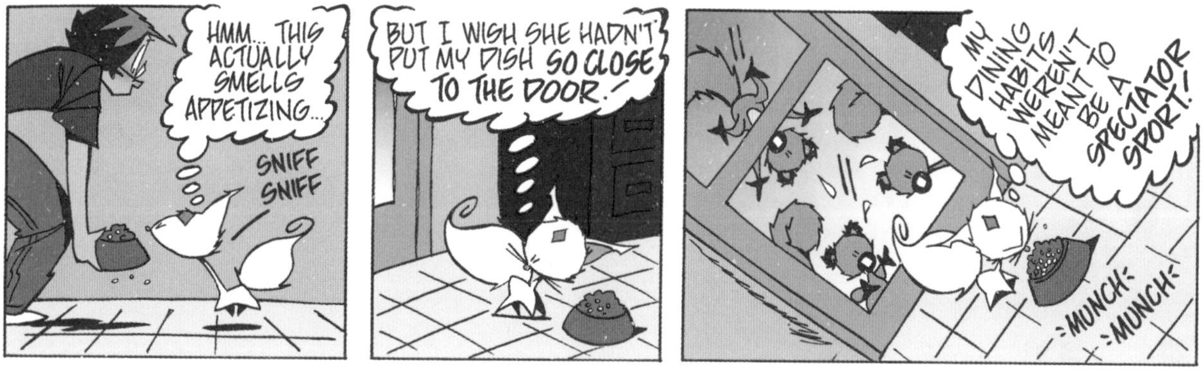
HMM... THIS ACTUALLY SMELLS APPETIZING...
SNIFF SNIFF
BUT I WISH SHE HADN'T PUT MY DISH **SO CLOSE TO THE DOOR**!
MY DINING HABITS WEREN'T MEANT TO BE A **SPECTATOR SPORT**!
MUNCH MUNCH

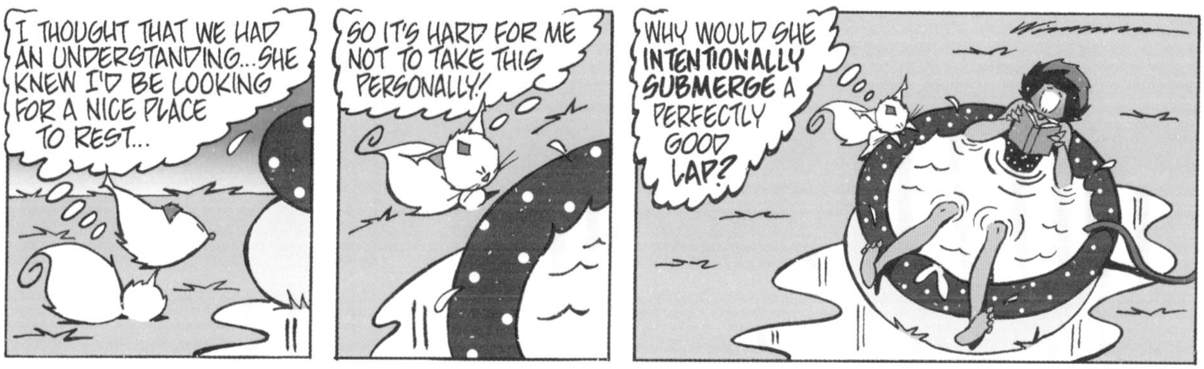
I THOUGHT THAT WE HAD AN UNDERSTANDING...SHE KNEW I'D BE LOOKING FOR A NICE PLACE TO REST...
SO IT'S HARD FOR ME NOT TO TAKE THIS PERSONALLY!
WHY WOULD SHE **INTENTIONALLY SUBMERGE** A PERFECTLY GOOD **LAP**?

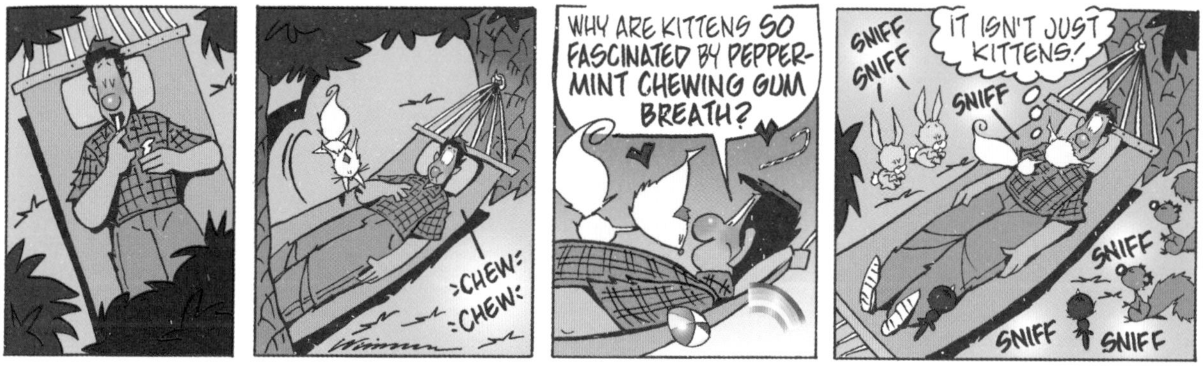
CHEW CHEW
WHY ARE KITTENS SO FASCINATED BY PEPPERMINT CHEWING GUM BREATH?
SNIFF SNIFF
IT ISN'T JUST KITTENS!
SNIFF
SNIFF
SNIFF
SNIFF

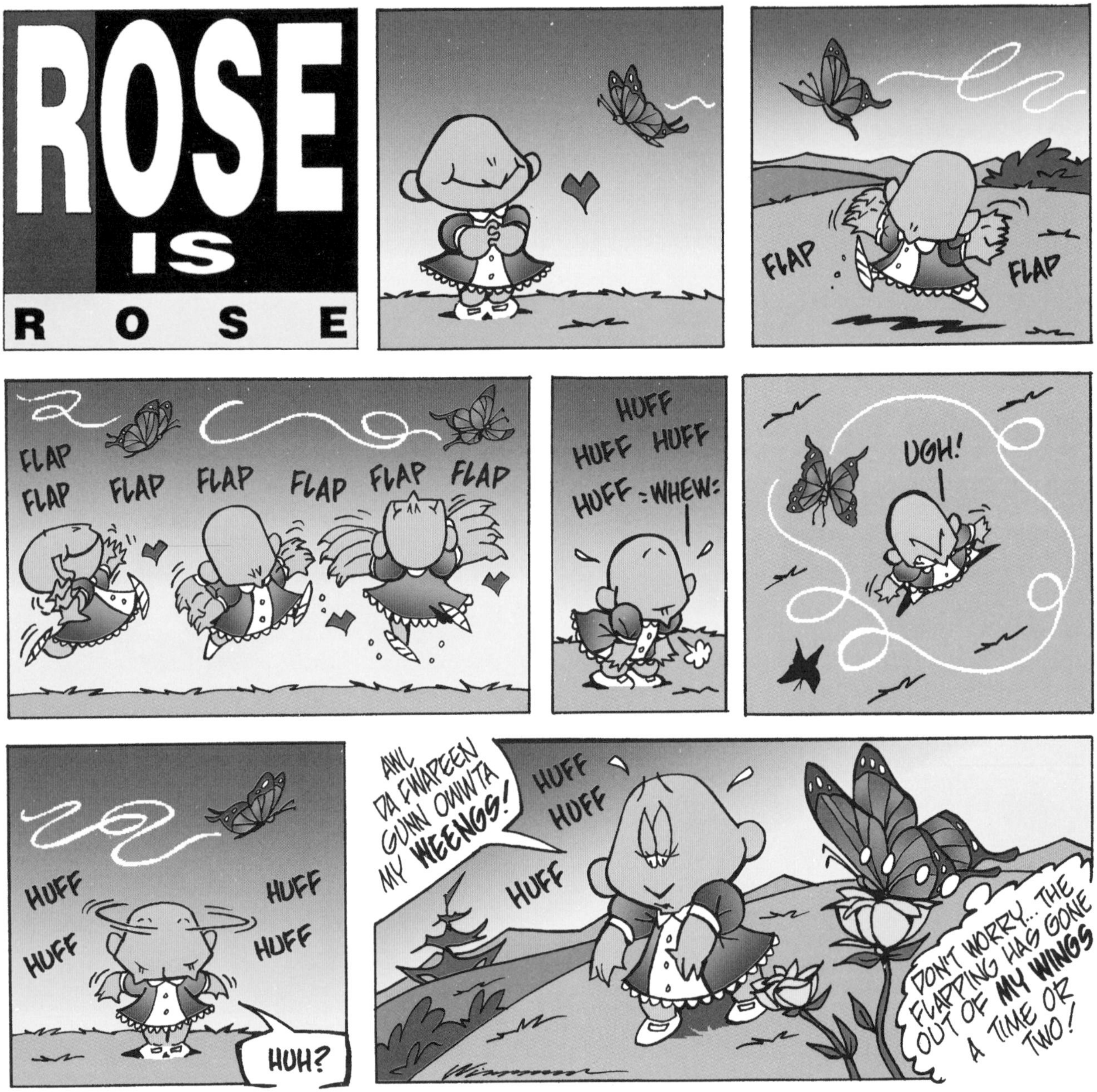
ROSE IS ROSE
FLAP
FLAP
FLAP
FLAP
FLAP
FLAP
FLAP
FLAP
FLAP
HUFF
HUFF HUFF
HUFF :WHEW:
UGH!
HUFF
HUFF
HUFF
HUFF
HUH?
AWL DA FWAPEEN GUNN OWWTA MY **WEENGS**!
HUFF
HUFF
HUFF
DON'T WORRY... THE FLAPPING HAS GONE OUT OF **MY WINGS** A TIME OR TWO!

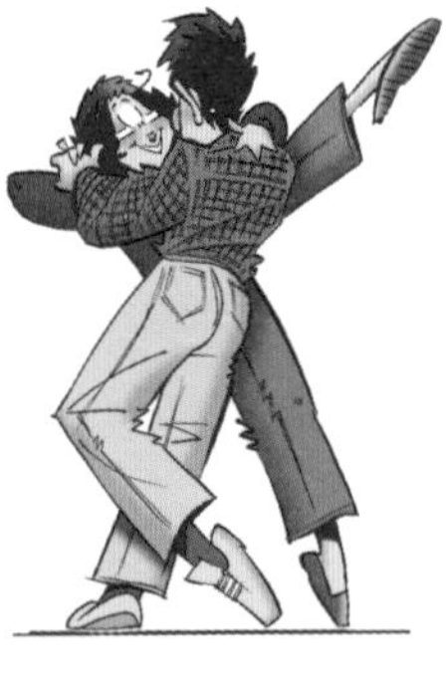

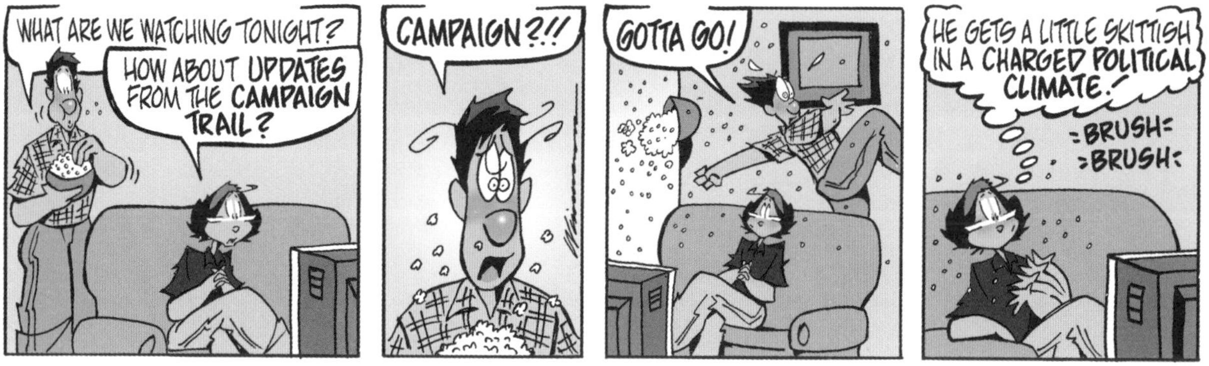
WHAT ARE WE WATCHING TONIGHT?
HOW ABOUT UPDATES FROM THE CAMPAIGN TRAIL?
CAMPAIGN?!!
GOTTA GO!
HE GETS A LITTLE SKITTISH IN A CHARGED POLITICAL CLIMATE.!
=BRUSH=
=BRUSH=

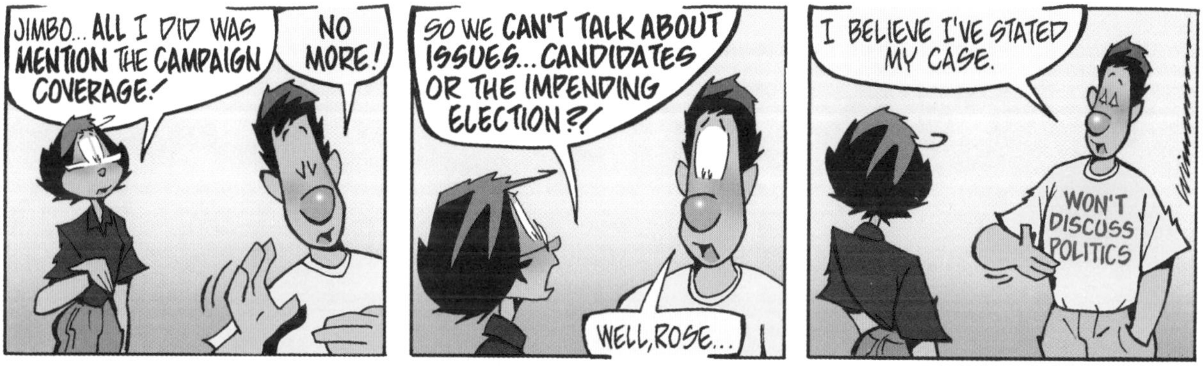
JIMBO... ALL I DID WAS MENTION THE CAMPAIGN COVERAGE.!
NO MORE!
SO WE CAN'T TALK ABOUT ISSUES... CANDIDATES OR THE IMPENDING ELECTION?!
WELL, ROSE...
I BELIEVE I'VE STATED MY CASE.
WON'T DISCUSS POLITICS

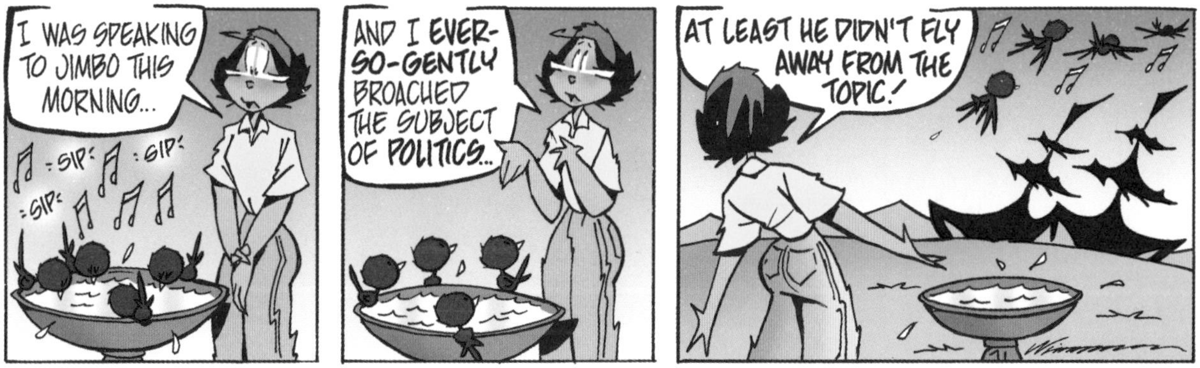
I WAS SPEAKING TO JIMBO THIS MORNING...
=SIP=
=SIP=
=SIP=
AND I EVER-SO-GENTLY BROACHED THE SUBJECT OF POLITICS...
AT LEAST HE DIDN'T FLY AWAY FROM THE TOPIC.!

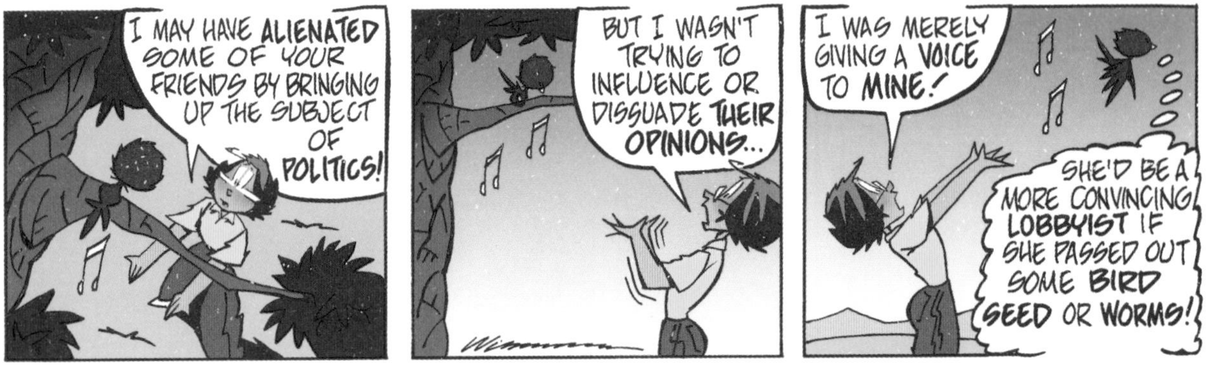
I MAY HAVE ALIENATED SOME OF YOUR FRIENDS BY BRINGING UP THE SUBJECT OF POLITICS!
BUT I WASN'T TRYING TO INFLUENCE OR DISSUADE THEIR OPINIONS...
I WAS MERELY GIVING A VOICE TO MINE!
SHE'D BE A MORE CONVINCING LOBBYIST IF SHE PASSED OUT SOME BIRD SEED OR WORMS!

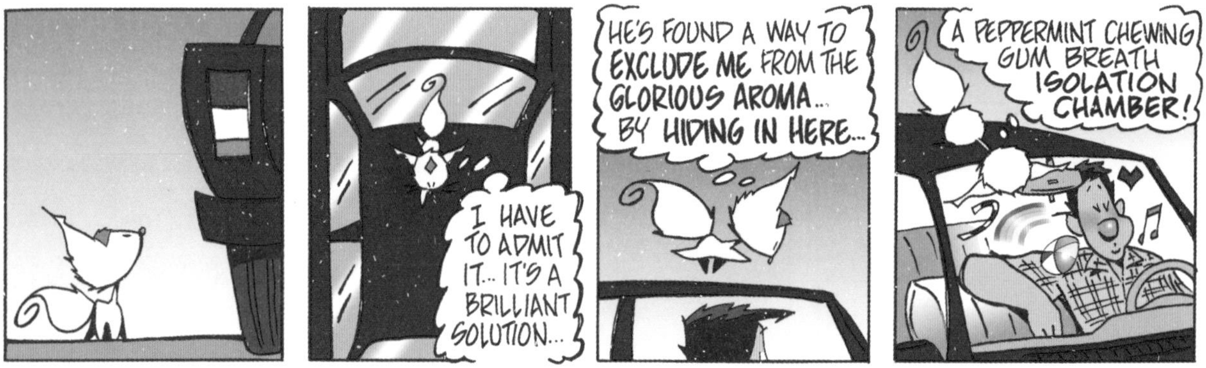
I HAVE TO ADMIT IT... IT'S A BRILLIANT SOLUTION...
HE'S FOUND A WAY TO EXCLUDE ME FROM THE GLORIOUS AROMA... BY HIDING IN HERE...
A PEPPERMINT CHEWING GUM BREATH ISOLATION CHAMBER!

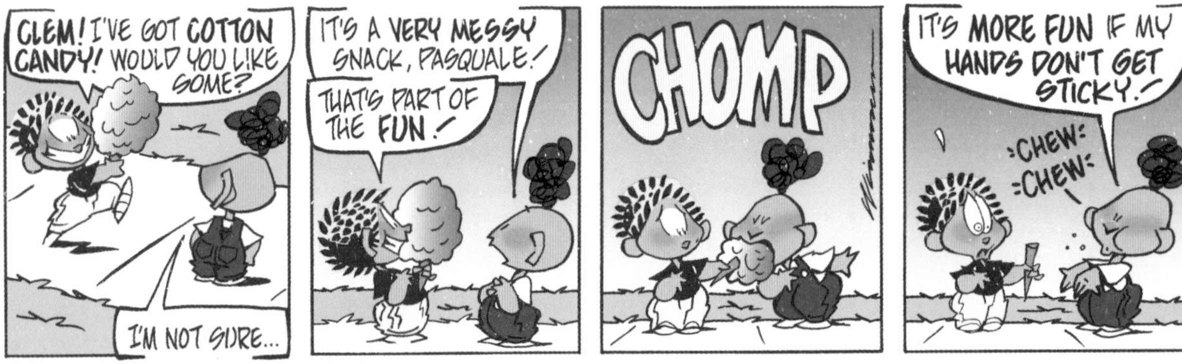
CLEM! I'VE GOT COTTON CANDY! WOULD YOU LIKE SOME?
I'M NOT SURE...
IT'S A VERY MESSY SNACK, PASQUALE!
THAT'S PART OF THE FUN!
CHOMP
CHEW
CHEW
IT'S MORE FUN IF MY HANDS DON'T GET STICKY!

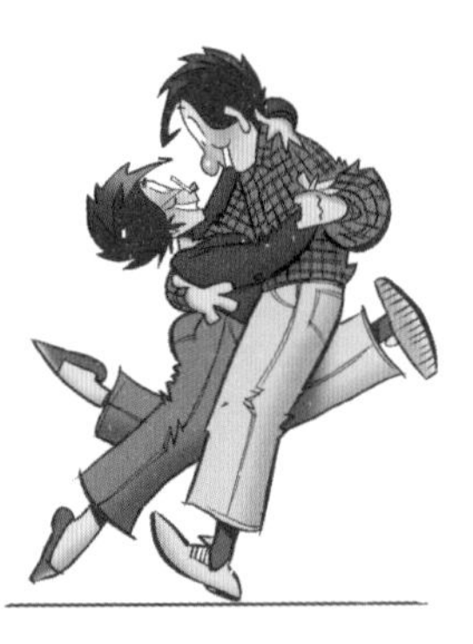

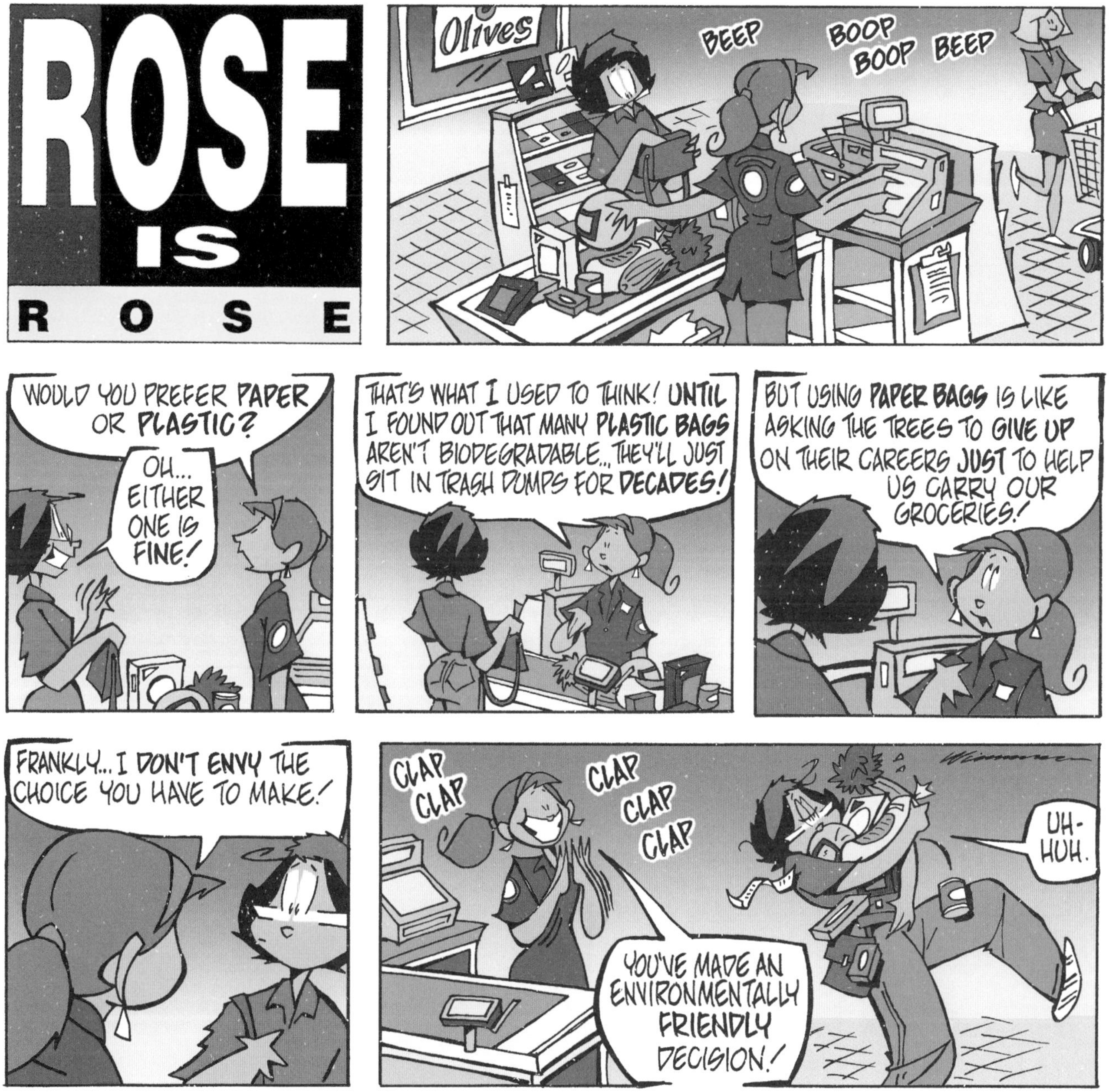
ROSE IS ROSE
Olives
BEEP
BOOP
BOOP BEEP
WOULD YOU PREFER PAPER OR PLASTIC?
OH... EITHER ONE IS FINE!
THAT'S WHAT I USED TO THINK! UNTIL I FOUND OUT THAT MANY PLASTIC BAGS AREN'T BIODEGRADABLE... THEY'LL JUST SIT IN TRASH DUMPS FOR DECADES!
BUT USING PAPER BAGS IS LIKE ASKING THE TREES TO GIVE UP ON THEIR CAREERS JUST TO HELP US CARRY OUR GROCERIES!
FRANKLY... I DON'T ENVY THE CHOICE YOU HAVE TO MAKE!
CLAP CLAP
CLAP CLAP CLAP
UH-HUH.
YOU'VE MADE AN ENVIRONMENTALLY FRIENDLY DECISION!

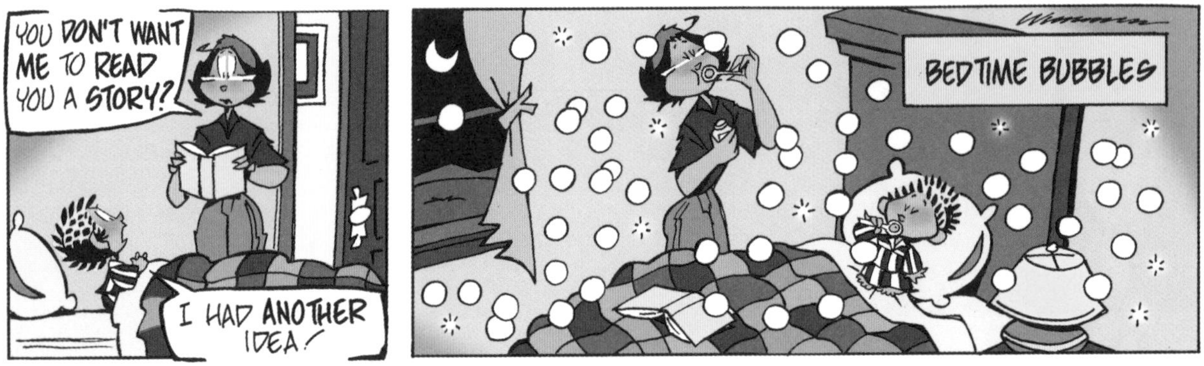
YOU DON'T WANT ME TO READ YOU A STORY?
I HAD ANOTHER IDEA!
BEDTIME BUBBLES

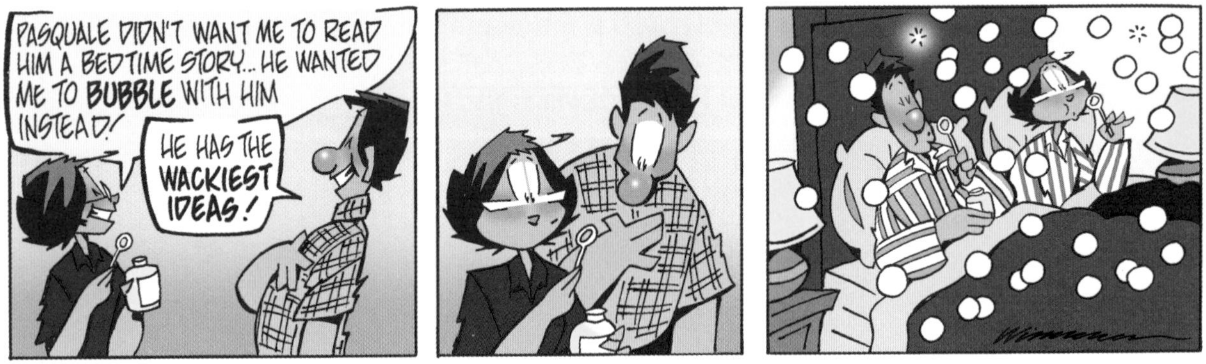
PASQUALE DIDN'T WANT ME TO READ HIM A BEDTIME STORY... HE WANTED ME TO BUBBLE WITH HIM INSTEAD!
HE HAS THE WACKIEST IDEAS!

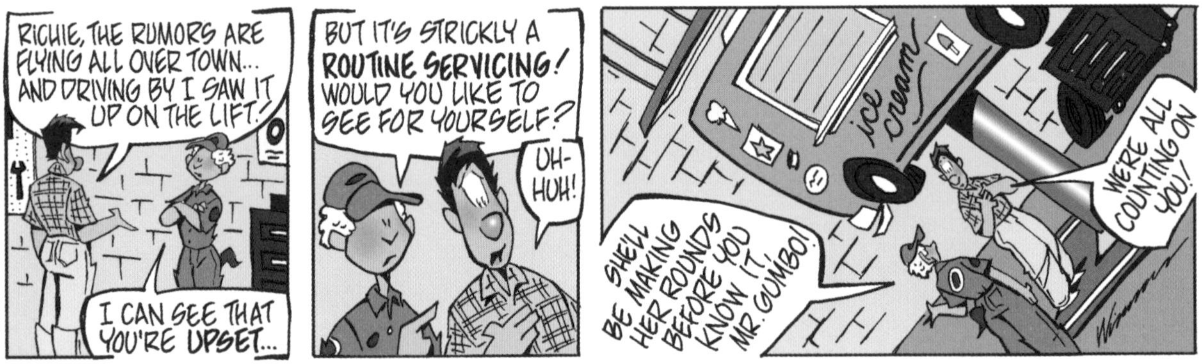
RICHIE, THE RUMORS ARE FLYING ALL OVER TOWN... AND DRIVING BY I SAW IT UP ON THE LIFT!
I CAN SEE THAT YOU'RE UPSET...
BUT IT'S STRICKLY A ROUTINE SERVICING! WOULD YOU LIKE TO SEE FOR YOURSELF?
UH-HUH!
ice cream
WE'RE ALL COUNTING ON YOU!
SHE'LL BE MAKING HER ROUNDS BEFORE YOU KNOW IT, MR. GUMBO!

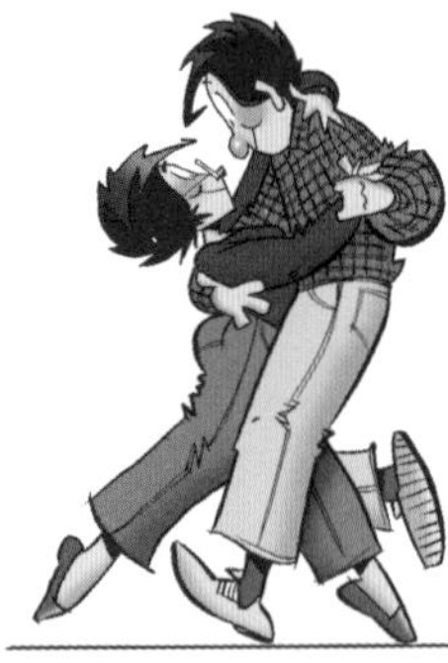

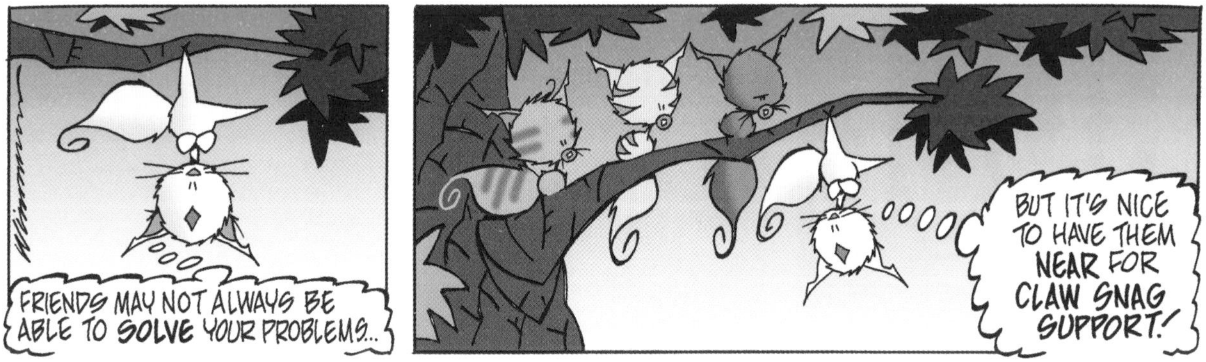
FRIENDS MAY NOT ALWAYS BE ABLE TO SOLVE YOUR PROBLEMS...
BUT IT'S NICE TO HAVE THEM NEAR FOR CLAW SNAG SUPPORT!

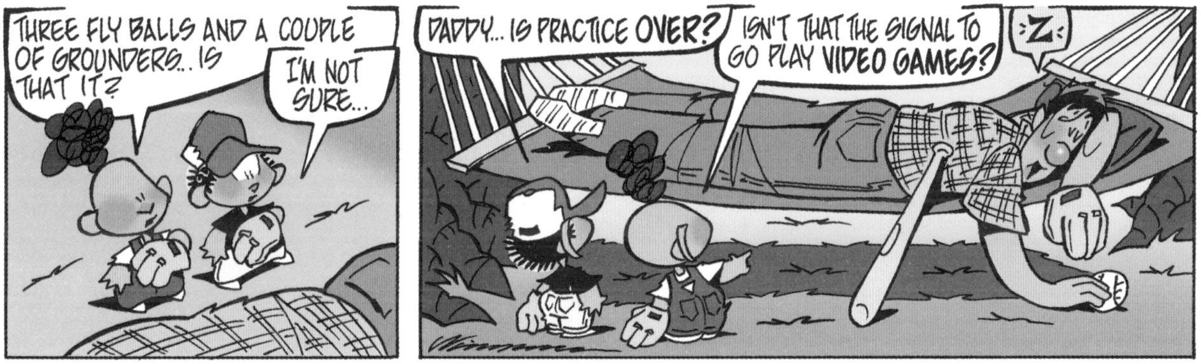
THREE FLY BALLS AND A COUPLE OF GROUNDERS... IS THAT IT?
I'M NOT SURE...
DADDY... IS PRACTICE OVER?
ISN'T THAT THE SIGNAL TO GO PLAY VIDEO GAMES?
Z

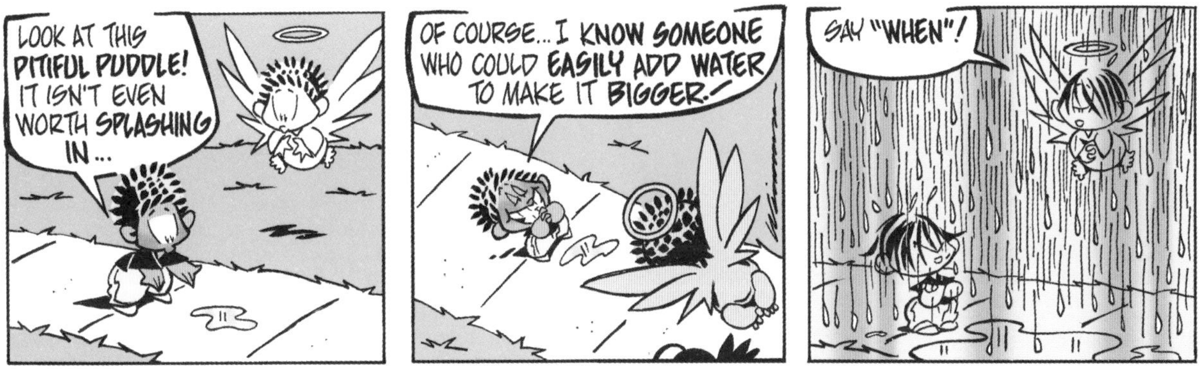
LOOK AT THIS PITIFUL PUDDLE! IT ISN'T EVEN WORTH SPLASHING IN...
OF COURSE... I KNOW SOMEONE WHO COULD EASILY ADD WATER TO MAKE IT BIGGER!
SAY "WHEN"!

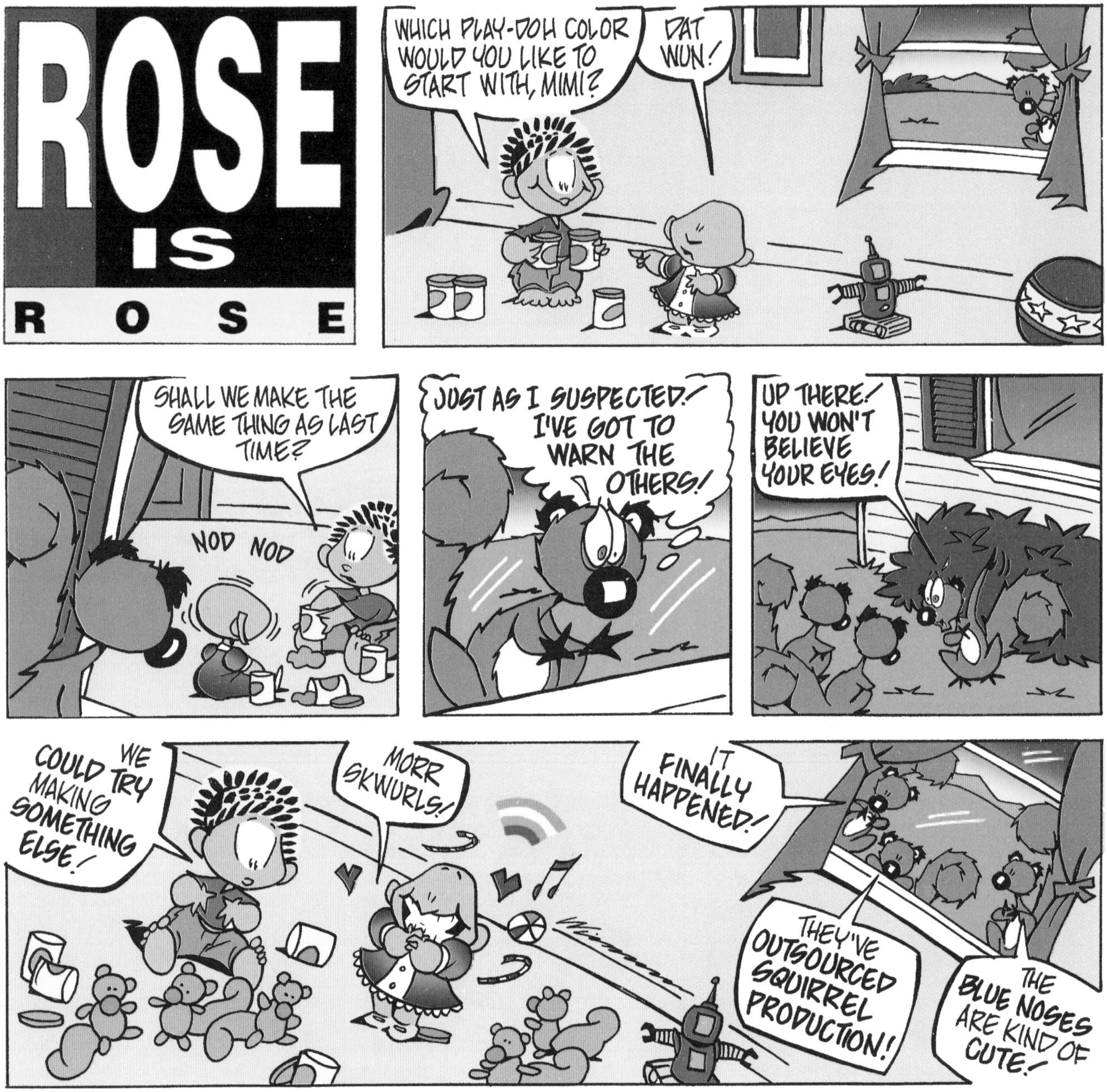
ROSE IS ROSE
WHICH PLAY-DOH COLOR WOULD YOU LIKE TO START WITH, MIMI?
DAT WUN!
SHALL WE MAKE THE SAME THING AS LAST TIME?
NOD NOD
JUST AS I SUSPECTED! I'VE GOT TO WARN THE OTHERS!
UP THERE! YOU WON'T BELIEVE YOUR EYES!
WE COULD TRY MAKING SOMETHING ELSE!
MORR SKWURLS!
IT FINALLY HAPPENED!
THEY'VE OUTSOURCED SQUIRREL PRODUCTION!
THE BLUE NOSES ARE KIND OF CUTE!

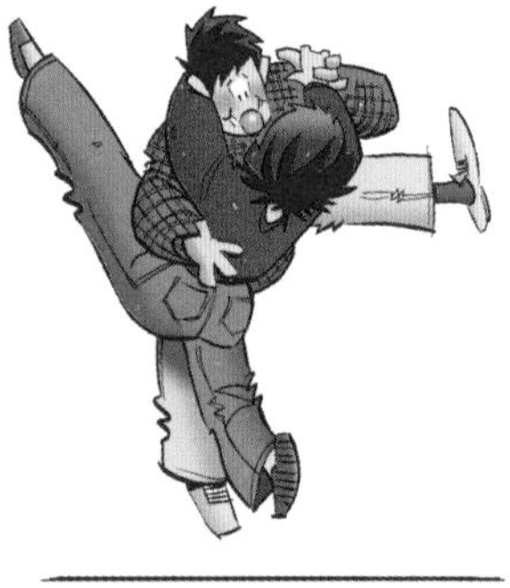

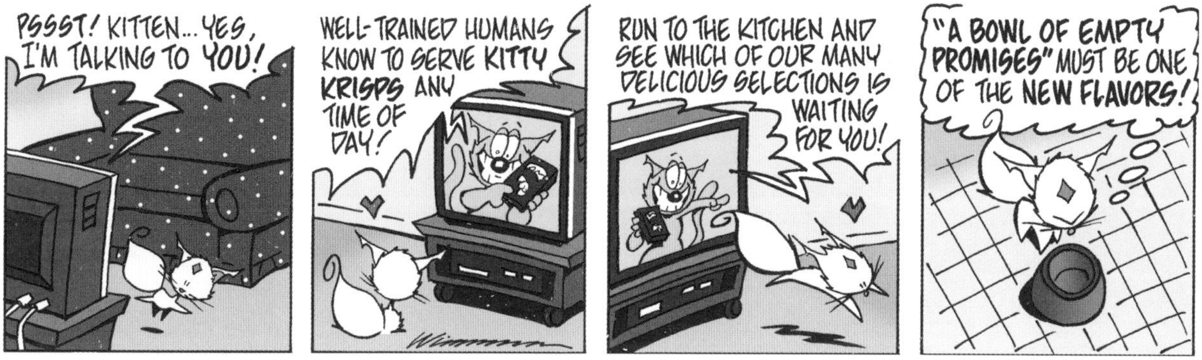
PSSST! KITTEN... YES, I'M TALKING TO YOU!
WELL-TRAINED HUMANS KNOW TO SERVE KITTY KRISPS ANY TIME OF DAY!
RUN TO THE KITCHEN AND SEE WHICH OF OUR MANY DELICIOUS SELECTIONS IS WAITING FOR YOU!
"A BOWL OF EMPTY PROMISES" MUST BE ONE OF THE NEW FLAVORS!

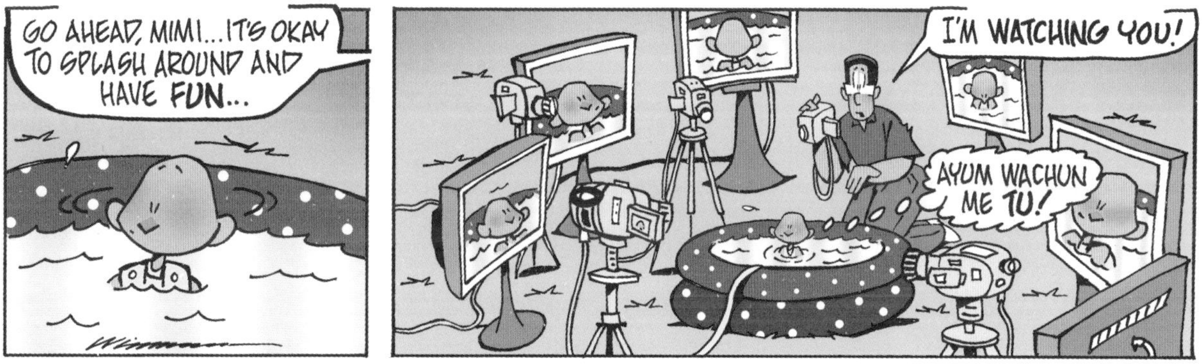
GO AHEAD, MIMI... IT'S OKAY TO SPLASH AROUND AND HAVE FUN...
I'M WATCHING YOU!
AYUM WACHUN ME TU!

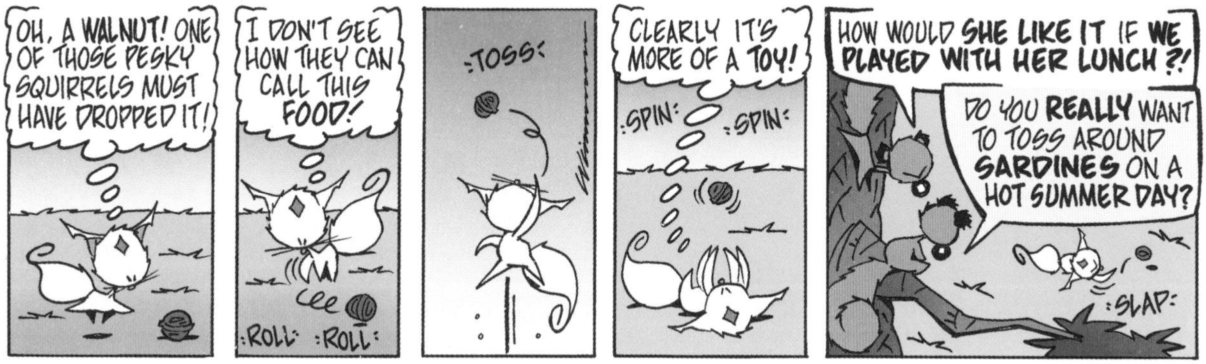
OH, A WALNUT! ONE OF THOSE PESKY SQUIRRELS MUST HAVE DROPPED IT!
I DON'T SEE HOW THEY CAN CALL THIS FOOD!
:ROLL: :ROLL:
:TOSS:
CLEARLY IT'S MORE OF A TOY!
:SPIN: :SPIN:
HOW WOULD SHE LIKE IT IF WE PLAYED WITH HER LUNCH?!
DO YOU REALLY WANT TO TOSS AROUND SARDINES ON A HOT SUMMER DAY?
:SLAP:

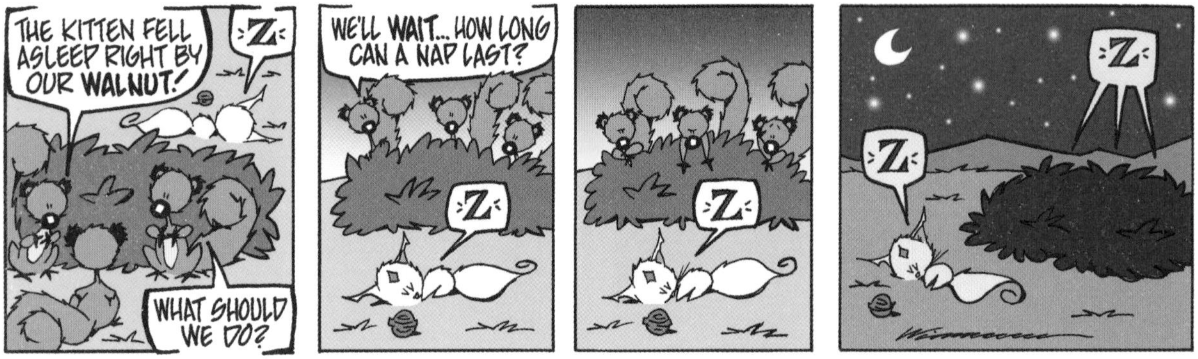
THE KITTEN FELL ASLEEP RIGHT BY OUR **WALNUT!**
Z
WHAT SHOULD WE DO?
WE'LL **WAIT**... HOW LONG CAN A NAP LAST?
Z
Z
Z
Z

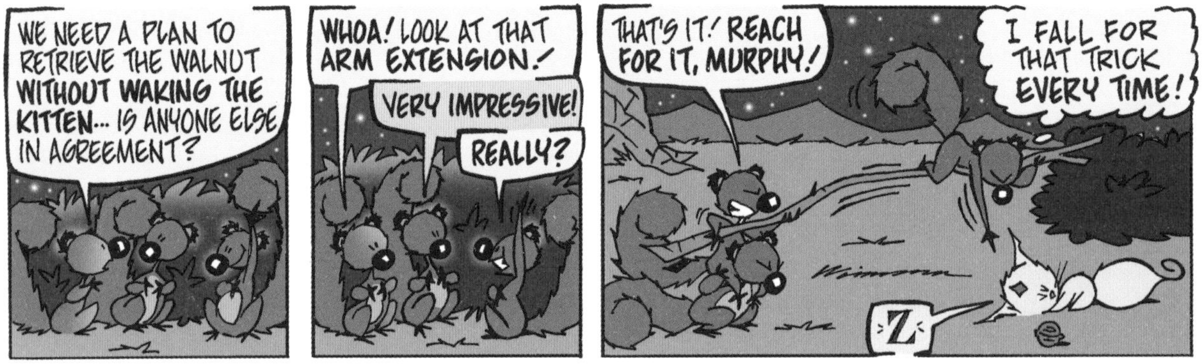
WE NEED A PLAN TO RETRIEVE THE WALNUT **WITHOUT WAKING THE KITTEN**... IS ANYONE ELSE IN AGREEMENT?
WHOA! LOOK AT THAT **ARM EXTENSION!**
VERY IMPRESSIVE!
REALLY?
THAT'S IT! **REACH FOR IT, MURPHY!**
I FALL FOR THAT TRICK **EVERY TIME!**
Z

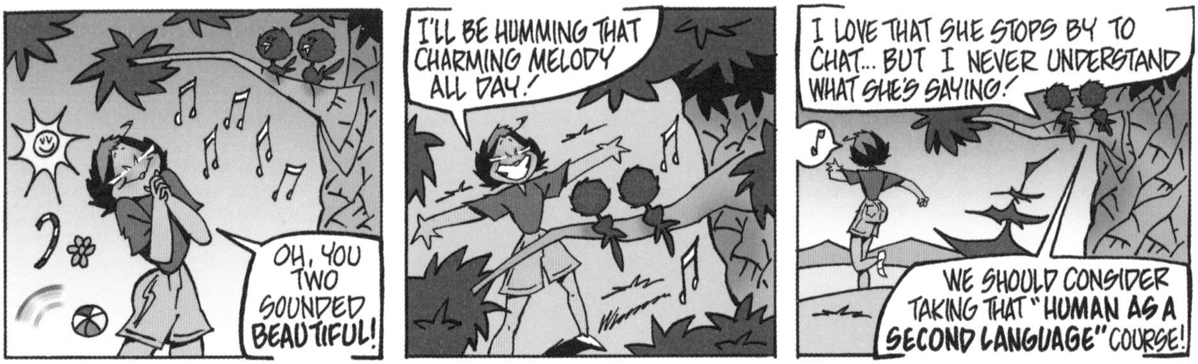
OH, YOU TWO SOUNDED **BEAUTIFUL!**
I'LL BE HUMMING THAT CHARMING MELODY ALL DAY!
I LOVE THAT SHE STOPS BY TO CHAT... BUT I NEVER UNDERSTAND WHAT SHE'S SAYING!
WE SHOULD CONSIDER TAKING THAT **"HUMAN AS A SECOND LANGUAGE"** COURSE!

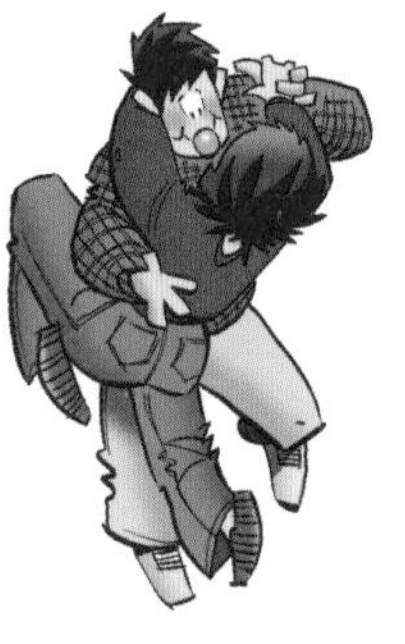

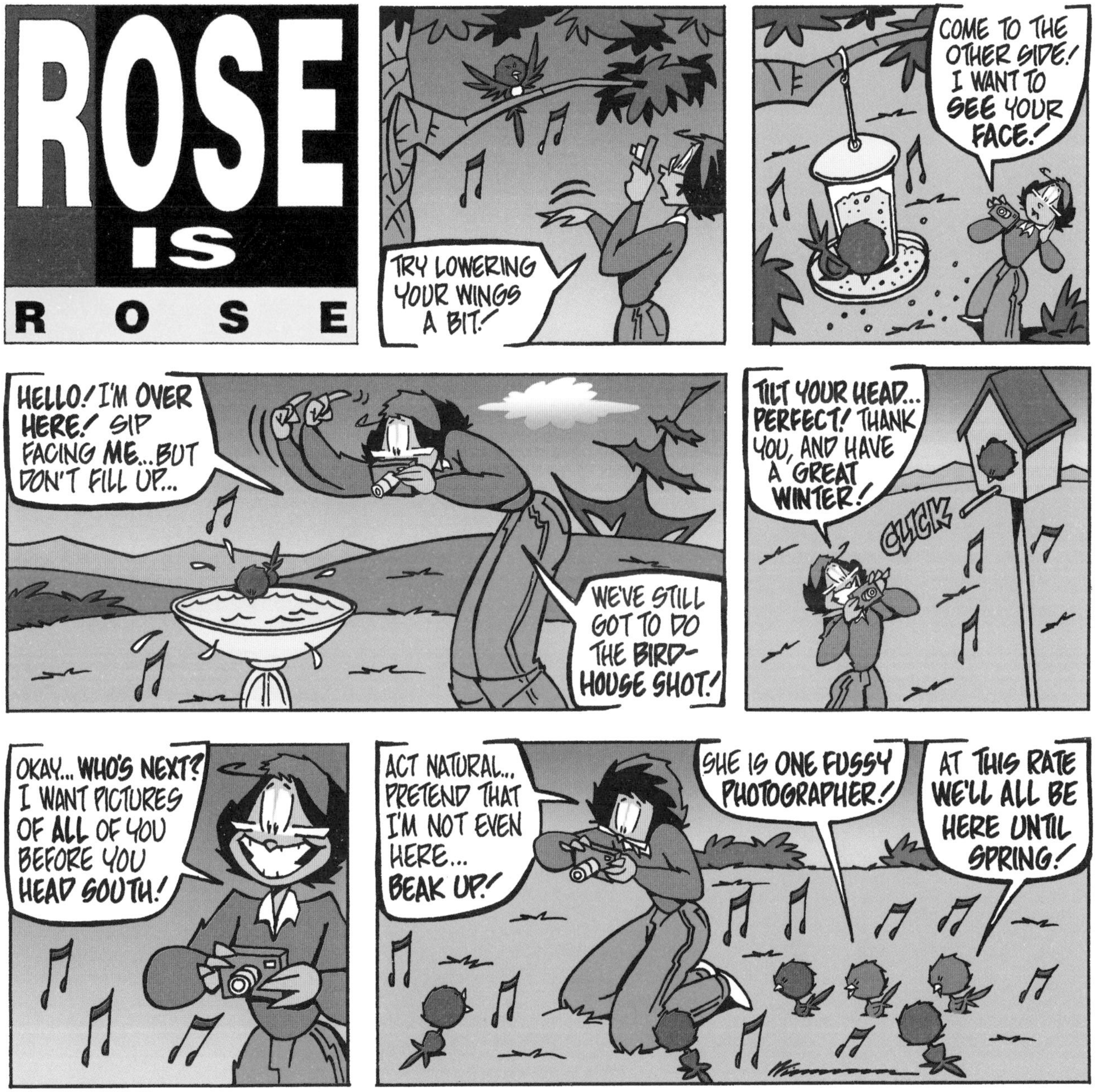
ROSE IS ROSE
TRY LOWERING YOUR WINGS A BIT!
COME TO THE OTHER SIDE! I WANT TO SEE YOUR FACE!
HELLO! I'M OVER HERE! SIP FACING ME...BUT DON'T FILL UP...
WE'VE STILL GOT TO DO THE BIRD-HOUSE SHOT!
TILT YOUR HEAD... PERFECT! THANK YOU, AND HAVE A GREAT WINTER!
CLICK
OKAY... WHO'S NEXT? I WANT PICTURES OF ALL OF YOU BEFORE YOU HEAD SOUTH!
ACT NATURAL... PRETEND THAT I'M NOT EVEN HERE... BEAK UP!
SHE IS ONE FUSSY PHOTOGRAPHER!
AT THIS RATE WE'LL ALL BE HERE UNTIL SPRING!

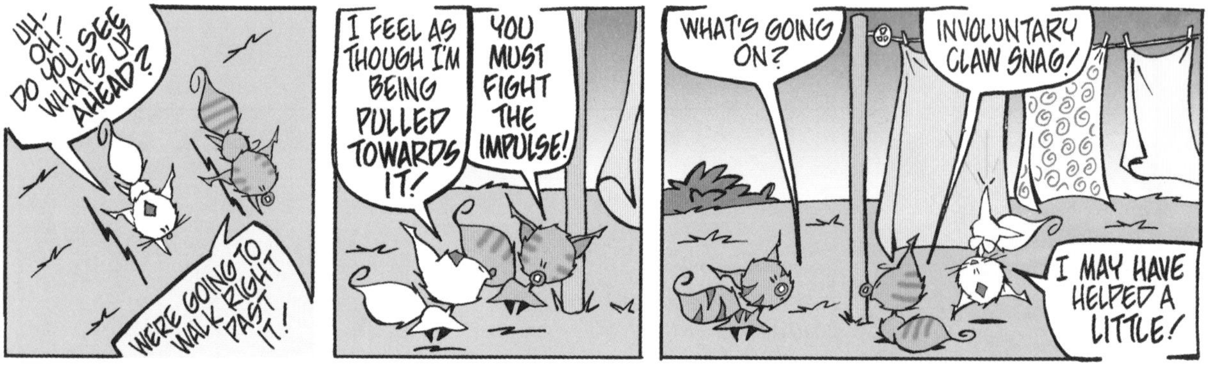
UH-OH! DO YOU SEE WHAT'S UP AHEAD?
WE'RE GOING TO WALK RIGHT PAST IT!
I FEEL AS THOUGH I'M BEING PULLED TOWARDS IT!
YOU MUST FIGHT THE IMPULSE!
WHAT'S GOING ON?
INVOLUNTARY CLAW SNAG!
I MAY HAVE HELPED A LITTLE!

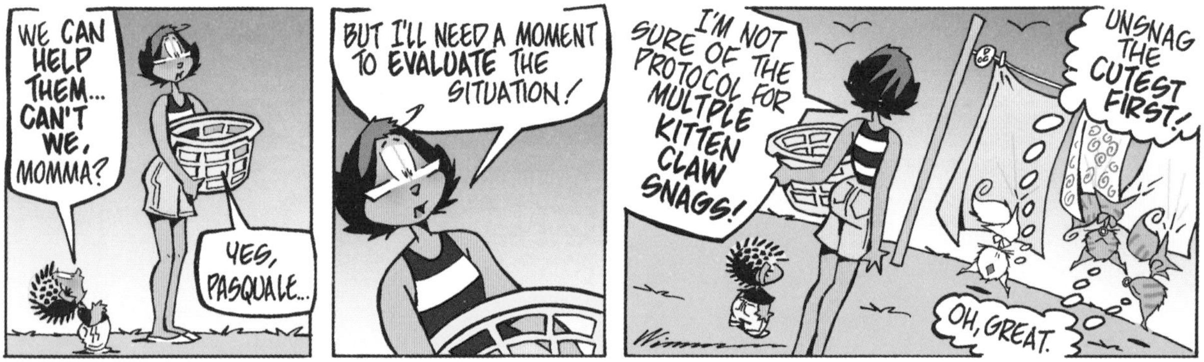
WE CAN HELP THEM... CAN'T WE, MOMMA?
YES, PASQUALE...
BUT I'LL NEED A MOMENT TO EVALUATE THE SITUATION!
I'M NOT SURE OF THE PROTOCOL FOR MULTPLE KITTEN CLAW SNAGS!
UNSNAG THE CUTEST FIRST!
OH, GREAT.

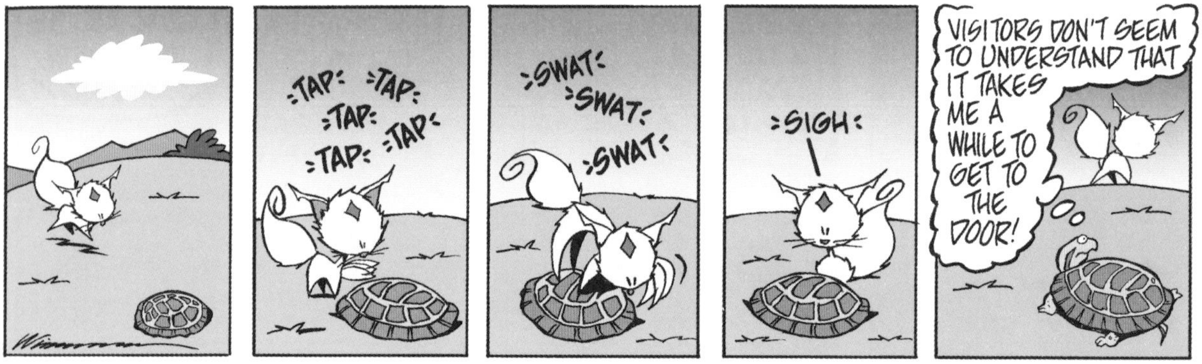
TAP TAP
TAP
TAP TAP
SWAT
SWAT
SWAT
SIGH
VISITORS DON'T SEEM TO UNDERSTAND THAT IT TAKES ME A WHILE TO GET TO THE DOOR!

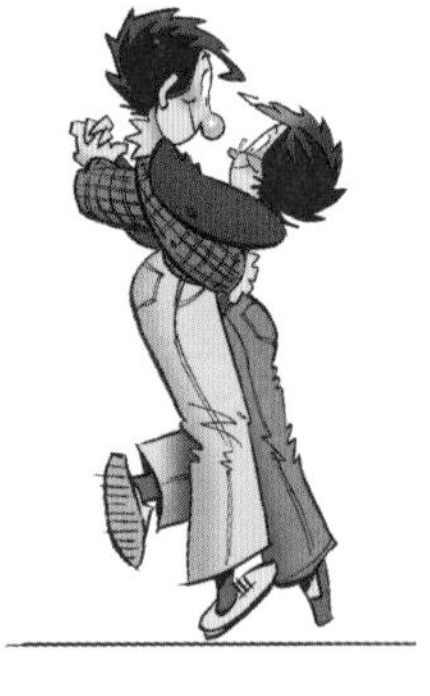

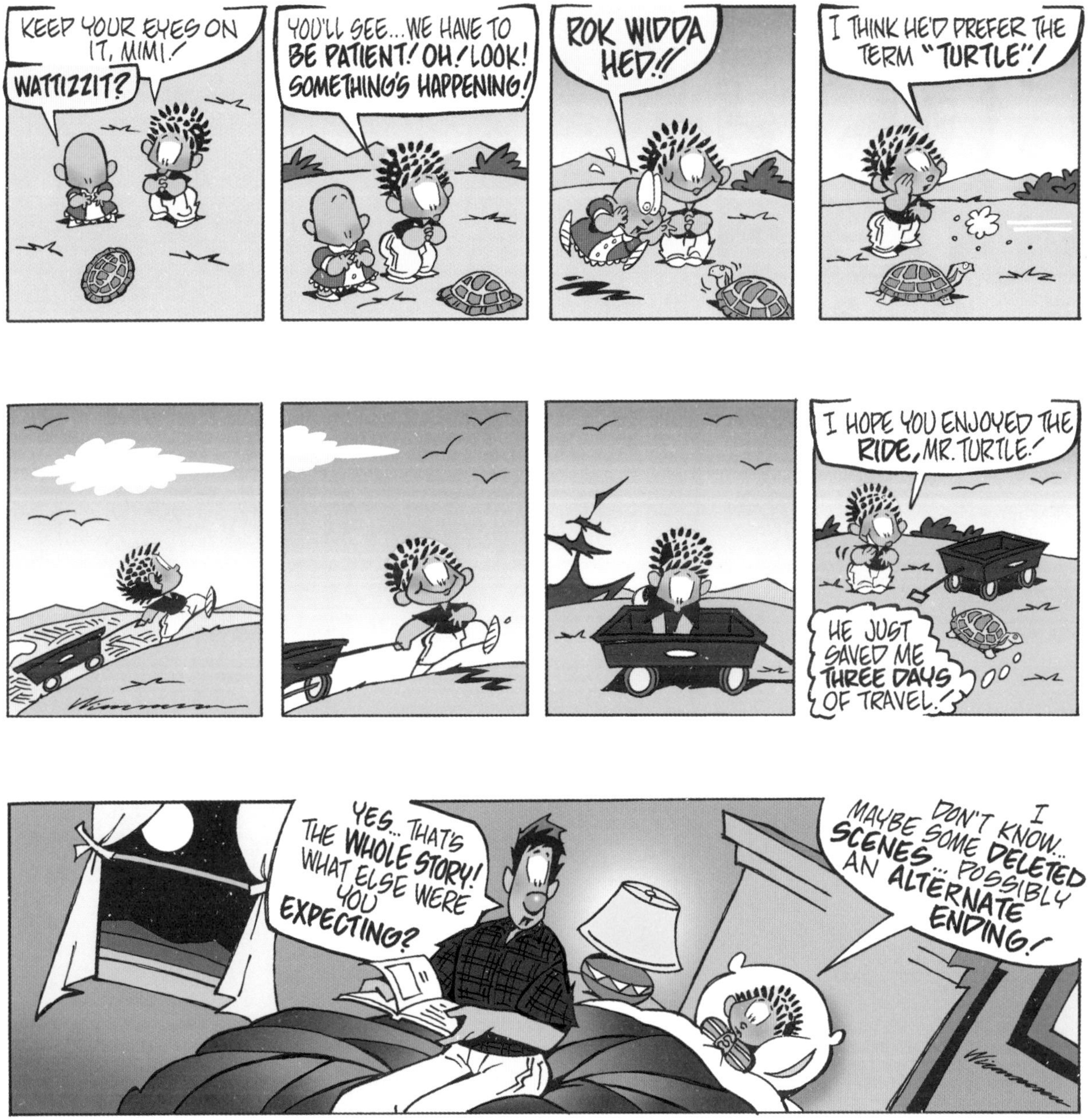
KEEP YOUR EYES ON IT, MIMI!
WATTIZZIT?
YOU'LL SEE... WE HAVE TO BE PATIENT! OH! LOOK! SOMETHING'S HAPPENING!
ROK WIDDA HED!!
I THINK HE'D PREFER THE TERM "TURTLE"!
I HOPE YOU ENJOYED THE RIDE, MR. TURTLE!
HE JUST SAVED ME THREE DAYS OF TRAVEL!
YES... THAT'S THE WHOLE STORY! WHAT ELSE WERE YOU EXPECTING?
I DON'T KNOW... MAYBE SOME DELETED SCENES... POSSIBLY AN ALTERNATE ENDING!

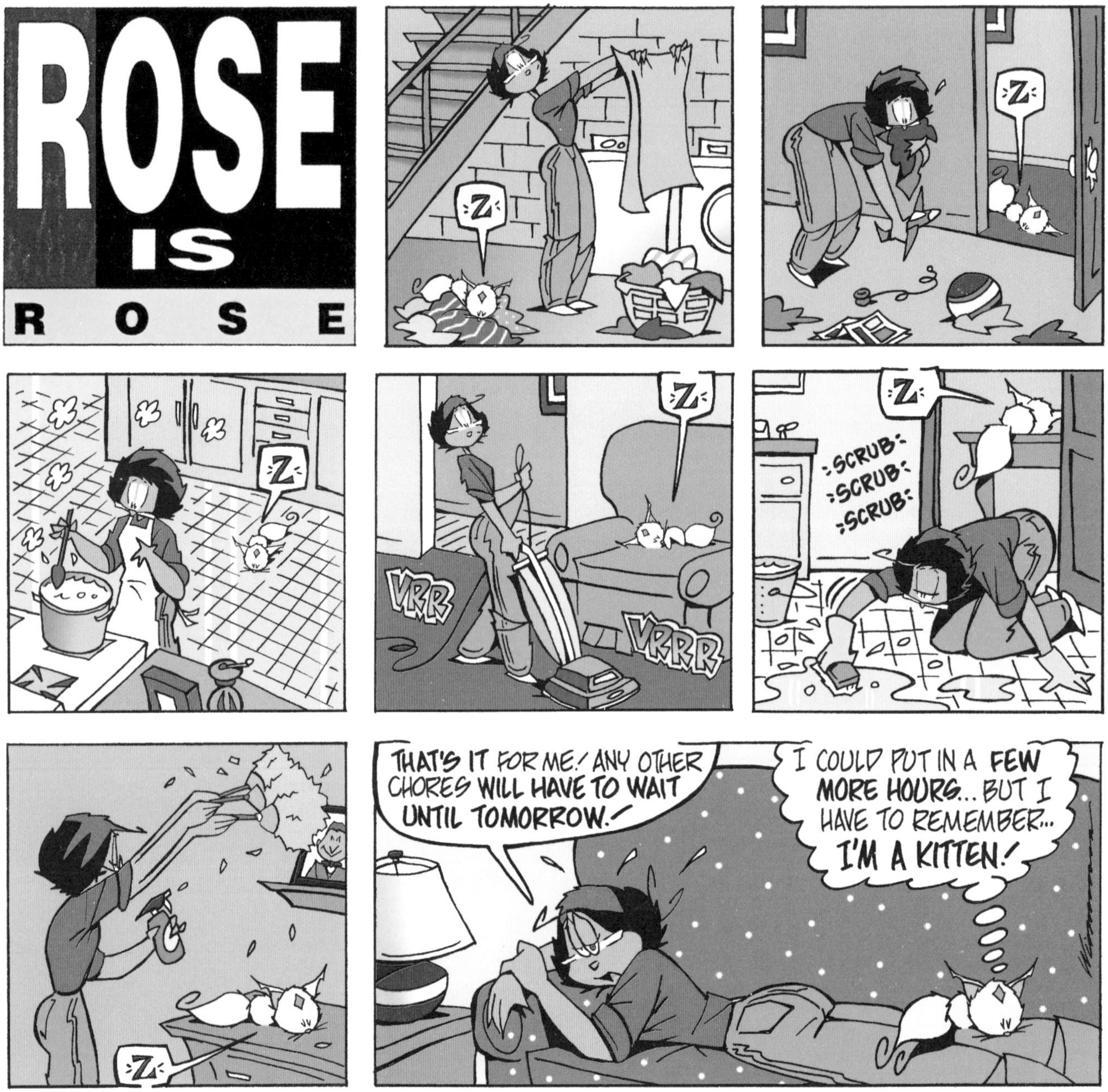
ROSE IS ROSE
Z
Z
Z
Z
SCRUB
SCRUB
SCRUB
Z
VRR
VRRR
Z
THAT'S IT FOR ME! ANY OTHER CHORES WILL HAVE TO WAIT UNTIL TOMORROW!
I COULD PUT IN A FEW MORE HOURS... BUT I HAVE TO REMEMBER... I'M A KITTEN!

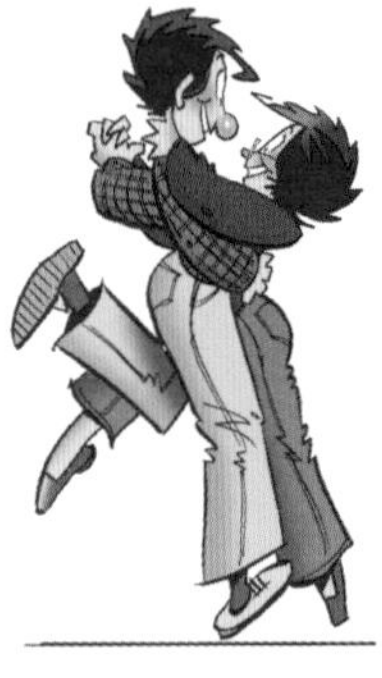

IS THAT ONE OVER THERE, MIMI?
AYE DUN ZEE ENEETHIN!
WATCH THIS!
=LEAP=
YU KAWTAA WAINBO!
YOU HAVE TO KNOW WHERE THEY HIDE!

HOZ KEN KATCHA WAINBO?
WELL...THE HOSE CAN HELP CATCH A RAINBOW...
IF YOU AIM IT TOWARDS THE SKY AND TURN THE NOZZLE...YOU MAY BE LUCKY ENOUGH TO NAB A BIG ONE...
=TWIST=
=TWIST=
...OR A LOT OF TINY ONES!

IT'S FINE TO OBSERVE THESE MAGNIFICENT CREATURES... BUT LET'S NOT GET TOO CLOSE...
WE DON'T WANT TO SCARE THEM AWAY!

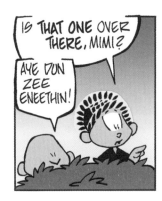

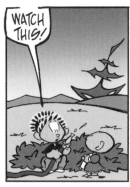

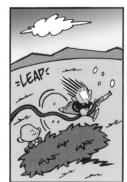

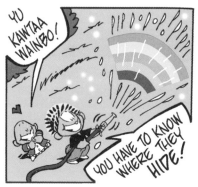

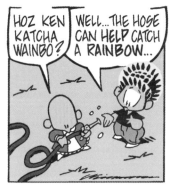

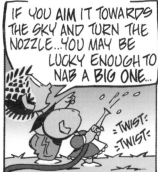

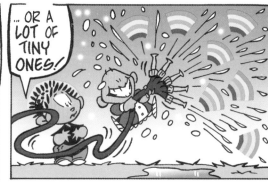

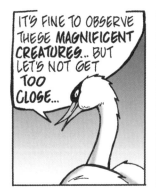

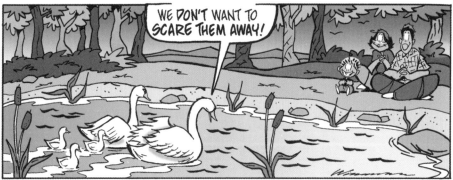

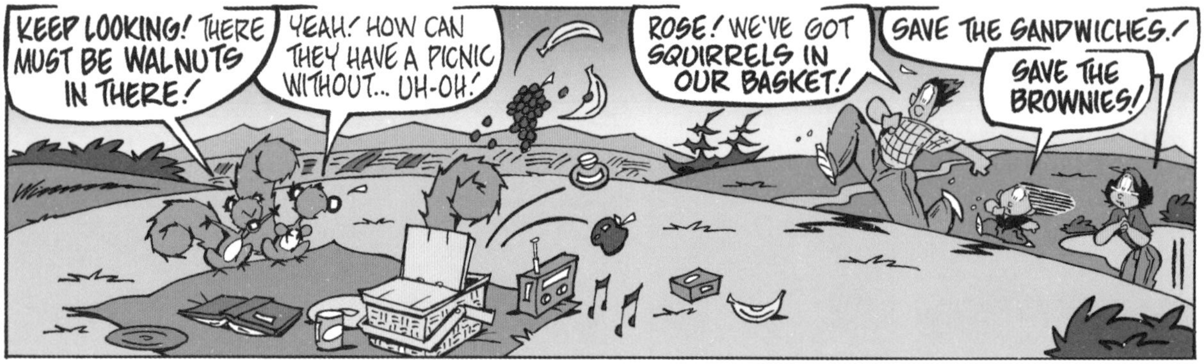
KEEP LOOKING! THERE MUST BE WALNUTS IN THERE!
YEAH! HOW CAN THEY HAVE A PICNIC WITHOUT... UH-OH!
ROSE! WE'VE GOT SQUIRRELS IN OUR BASKET!
SAVE THE SANDWICHES!
SAVE THE BROWNIES!

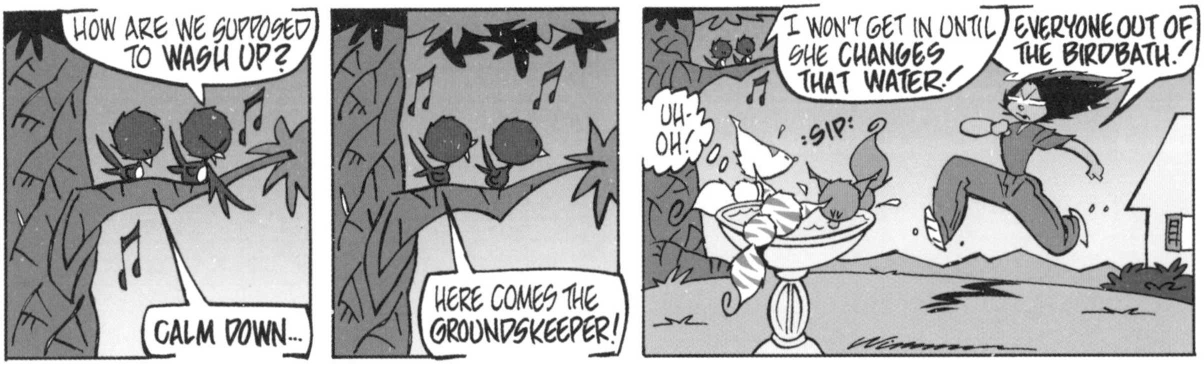
HOW ARE WE SUPPOSED TO WASH UP?
CALM DOWN...
HERE COMES THE GROUNDSKEEPER!
I WON'T GET IN UNTIL SHE CHANGES THAT WATER!
EVERYONE OUT OF THE BIRDBATH!
UH-OH!
:SIP:

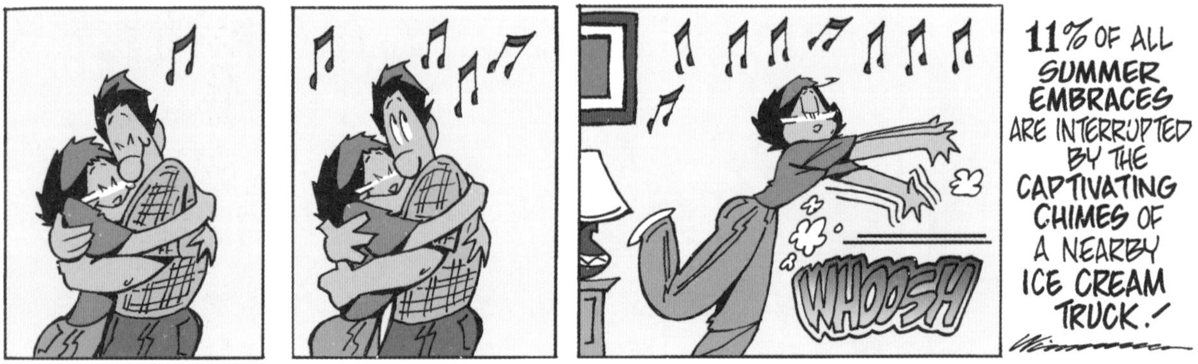
WHOOSH
11% OF ALL SUMMER EMBRACES ARE INTERRUPTED BY THE CAPTIVATING CHIMES OF A NEARBY ICE CREAM TRUCK!

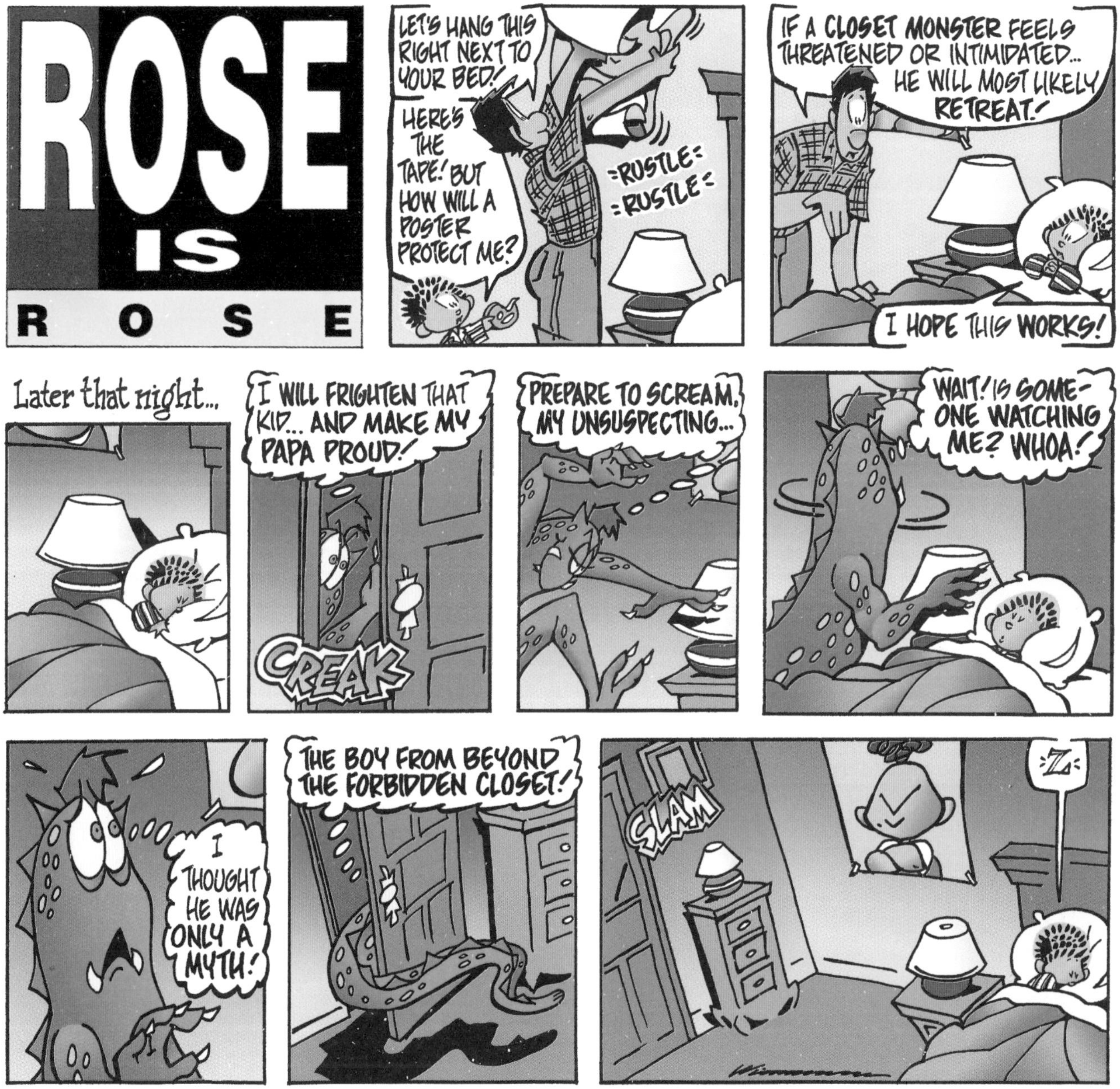
ROSE IS ROSE
LET'S HANG THIS RIGHT NEXT TO YOUR BED!
HERE'S THE TAPE! BUT HOW WILL A POSTER PROTECT ME?
=RUSTLE=
=RUSTLE=
IF A CLOSET MONSTER FEELS THREATENED OR INTIMIDATED... HE WILL MOST LIKELY RETREAT!
I HOPE THIS WORKS!
Later that night...
I WILL FRIGHTEN THAT KID... AND MAKE MY PAPA PROUD!
CREAK
PREPARE TO SCREAM, MY UNSUSPECTING...
WAIT! IS SOME-ONE WATCHING ME? WHOA!
I THOUGHT HE WAS ONLY A MYTH!
THE BOY FROM BEYOND THE FORBIDDEN CLOSET!
SLAM
Z

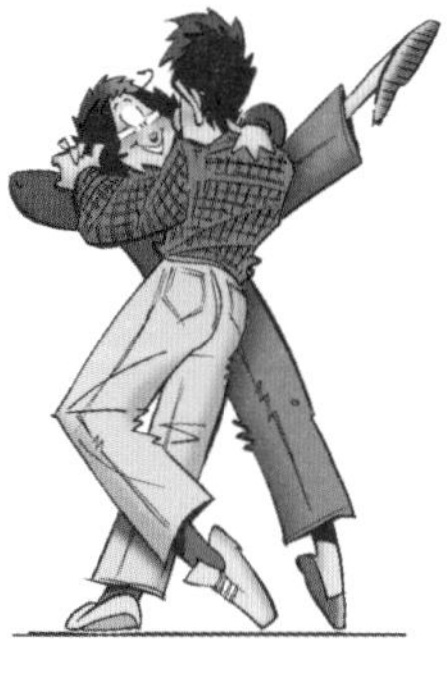

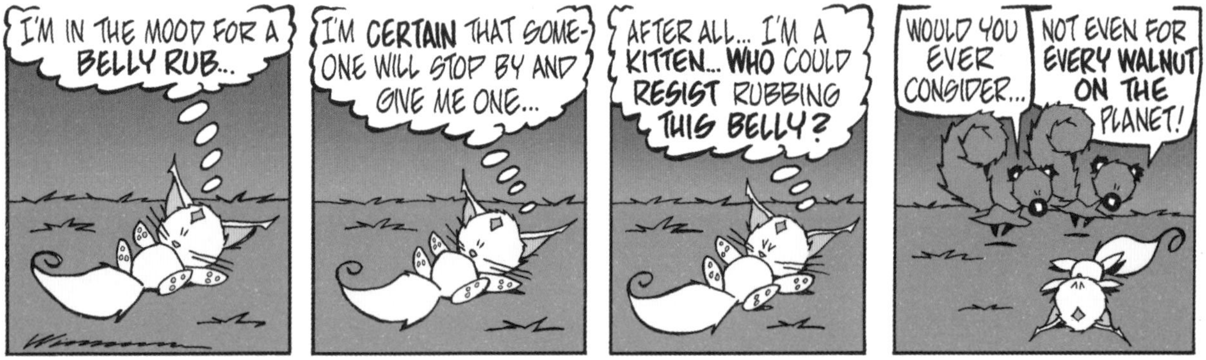
I'M IN THE MOOD FOR A BELLY RUB...
I'M CERTAIN THAT SOMEONE WILL STOP BY AND GIVE ME ONE...
AFTER ALL... I'M A KITTEN... WHO COULD RESIST RUBBING THIS BELLY?
WOULD YOU EVER CONSIDER...
NOT EVEN FOR EVERY WALNUT ON THE PLANET!

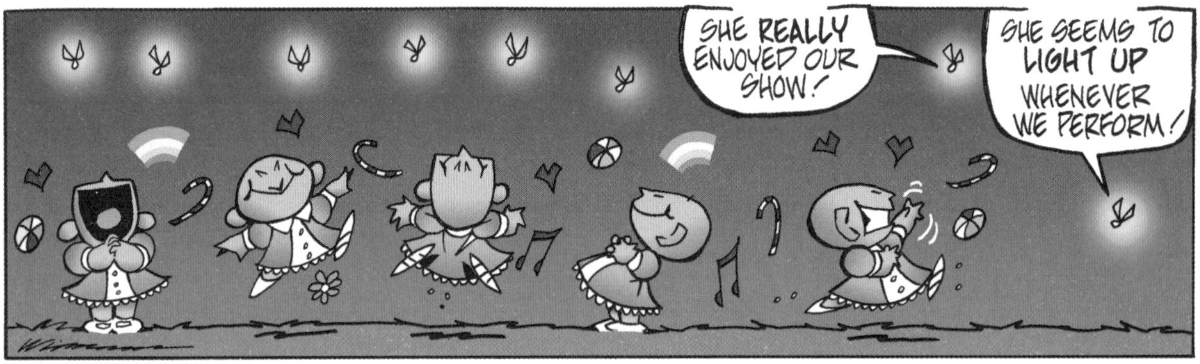
SHE REALLY ENJOYED OUR SHOW!
SHE SEEMS TO LIGHT UP WHENEVER WE PERFORM!

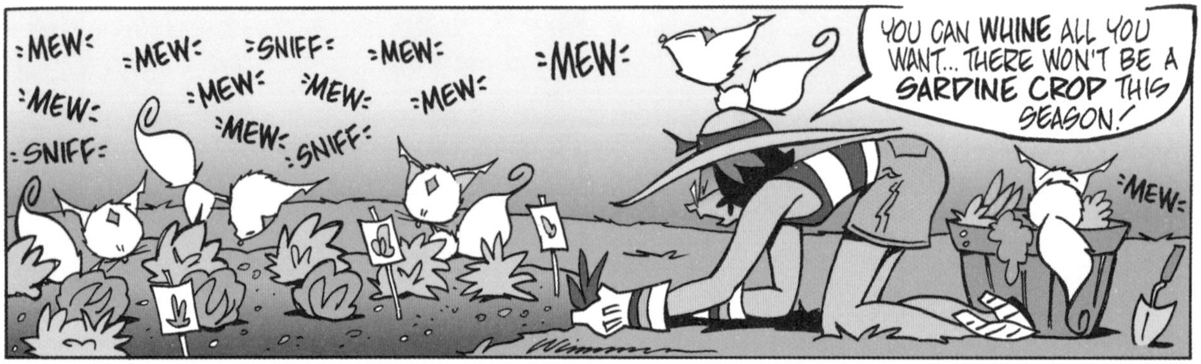
MEW MEW SNIFF MEW MEW
MEW MEW MEW MEW
MEW SNIFF
SNIFF
YOU CAN WHINE ALL YOU WANT... THERE WON'T BE A SARDINE CROP THIS SEASON!
MEW

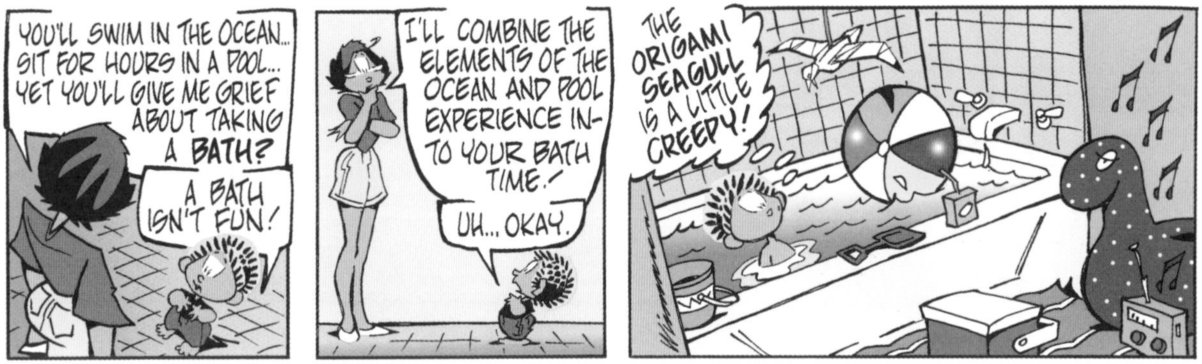
YOU'LL SWIM IN THE OCEAN... SIT FOR HOURS IN A POOL... YET YOU'LL GIVE ME GRIEF ABOUT TAKING A BATH?
A BATH ISN'T FUN!
I'LL COMBINE THE ELEMENTS OF THE OCEAN AND POOL EXPERIENCE IN-TO YOUR BATH TIME!
UH... OKAY.
THE ORIGAMI SEAGULL IS A LITTLE CREEPY!

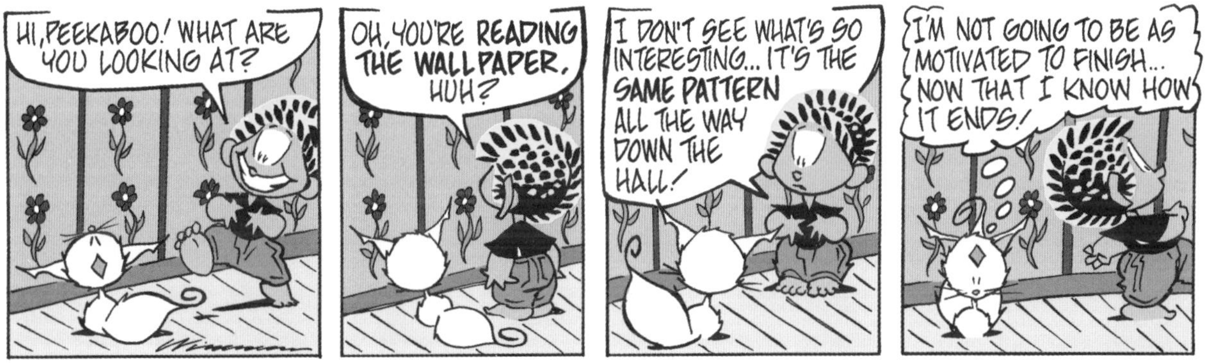
HI, PEEKABOO! WHAT ARE YOU LOOKING AT?
OH, YOU'RE READING THE WALLPAPER, HUH?
I DON'T SEE WHAT'S SO INTERESTING... IT'S THE SAME PATTERN ALL THE WAY DOWN THE HALL!
I'M NOT GOING TO BE AS MOTIVATED TO FINISH... NOW THAT I KNOW HOW IT ENDS!

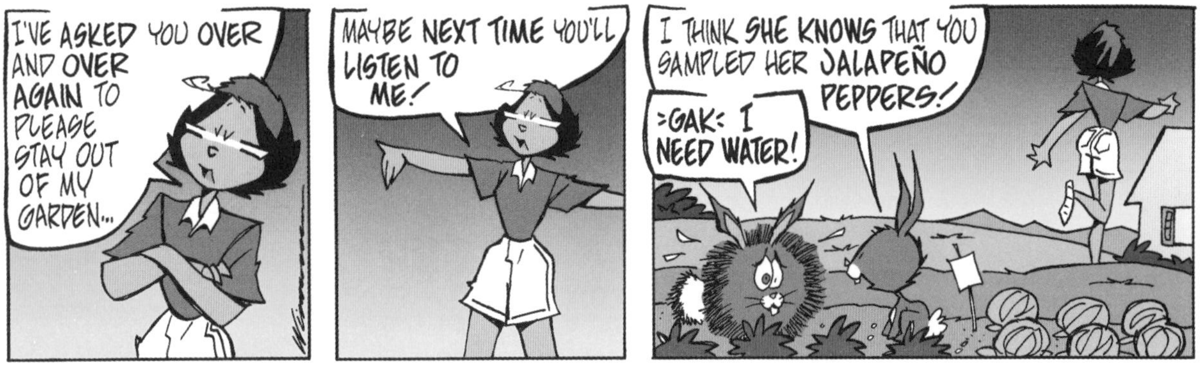
I'VE ASKED YOU OVER AND OVER AGAIN TO PLEASE STAY OUT OF MY GARDEN...
MAYBE NEXT TIME YOU'LL LISTEN TO ME!
I THINK SHE KNOWS THAT YOU SAMPLED HER JALAPEÑO PEPPERS!
>GAK< I NEED WATER!

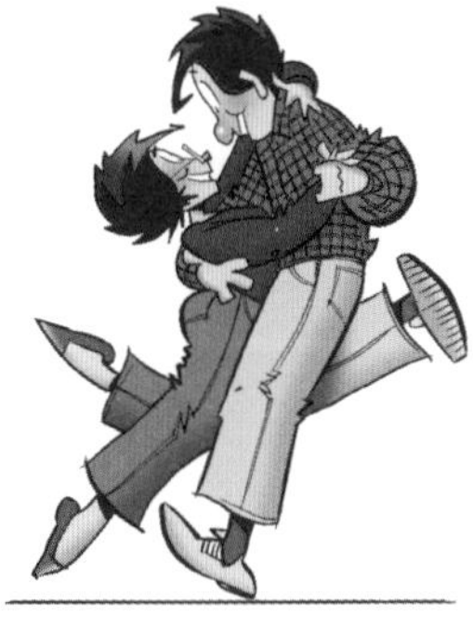

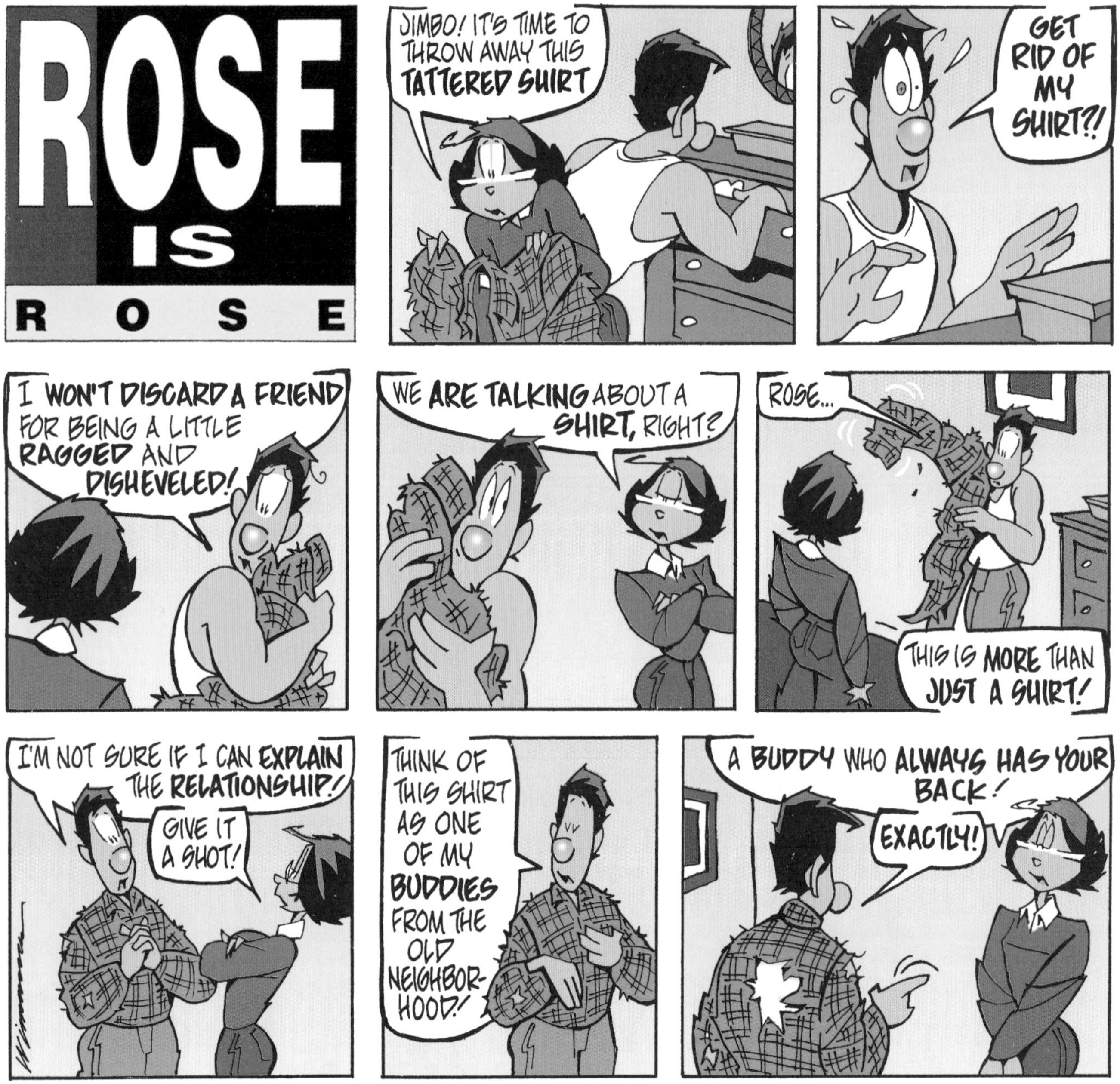
ROSE IS ROSE
JIMBO! IT'S TIME TO THROW AWAY THIS TATTERED SHIRT
GET RID OF MY SHIRT?!
I WON'T DISCARD A FRIEND FOR BEING A LITTLE RAGGED AND DISHEVELED!
WE ARE TALKING ABOUT A SHIRT, RIGHT?
ROSE...
THIS IS MORE THAN JUST A SHIRT!
I'M NOT SURE IF I CAN EXPLAIN THE RELATIONSHIP!
GIVE IT A SHOT!
THINK OF THIS SHIRT AS ONE OF MY BUDDIES FROM THE OLD NEIGHBOR-HOOD!
A BUDDY WHO ALWAYS HAS YOUR BACK!
EXACTLY!

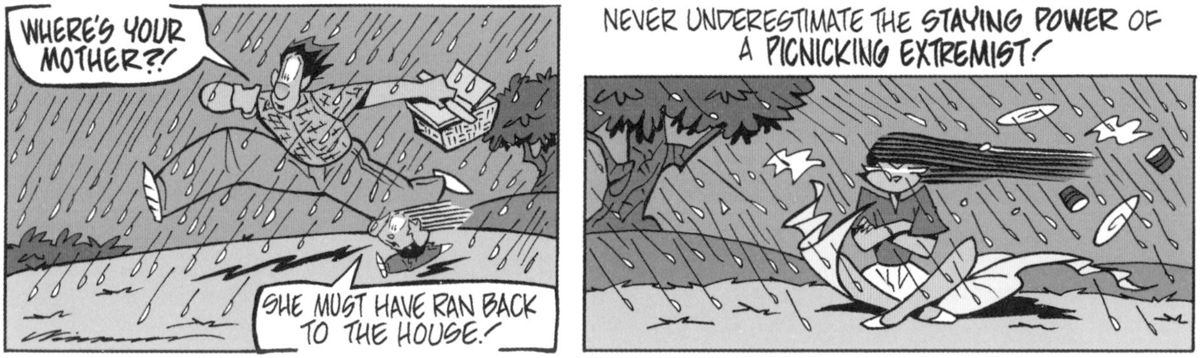
WHERE'S YOUR MOTHER?!
SHE MUST HAVE RAN BACK TO THE HOUSE!
NEVER UNDERESTIMATE THE STAYING POWER OF A PICNICKING EXTREMIST!

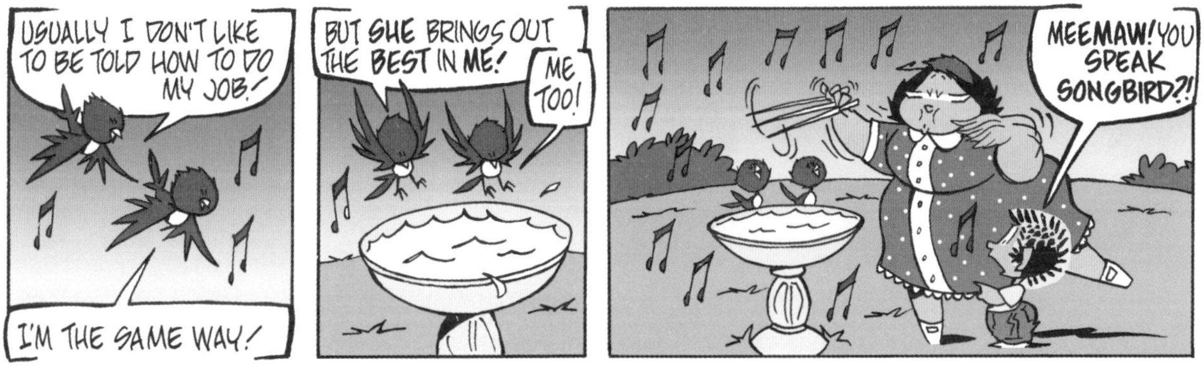
USUALLY I DON'T LIKE TO BE TOLD HOW TO DO MY JOB!
I'M THE SAME WAY!
BUT SHE BRINGS OUT THE BEST IN ME!
ME TOO!
MEEMAW! YOU SPEAK SONGBIRD?!

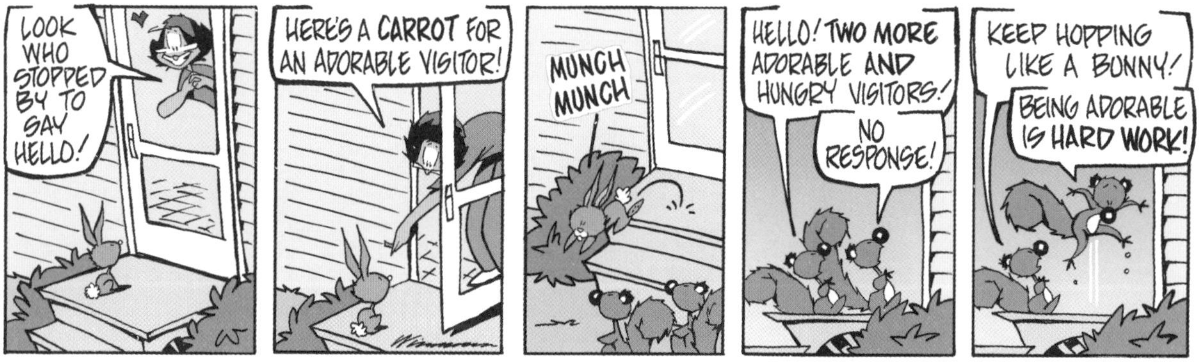
LOOK WHO STOPPED BY TO SAY HELLO!
HERE'S A CARROT FOR AN ADORABLE VISITOR!
MUNCH MUNCH
HELLO! TWO MORE ADORABLE AND HUNGRY VISITORS!
NO RESPONSE!
KEEP HOPPING LIKE A BUNNY!
BEING ADORABLE IS HARD WORK!

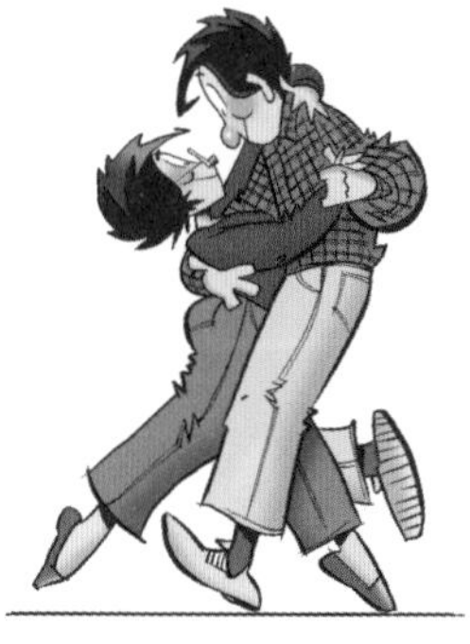

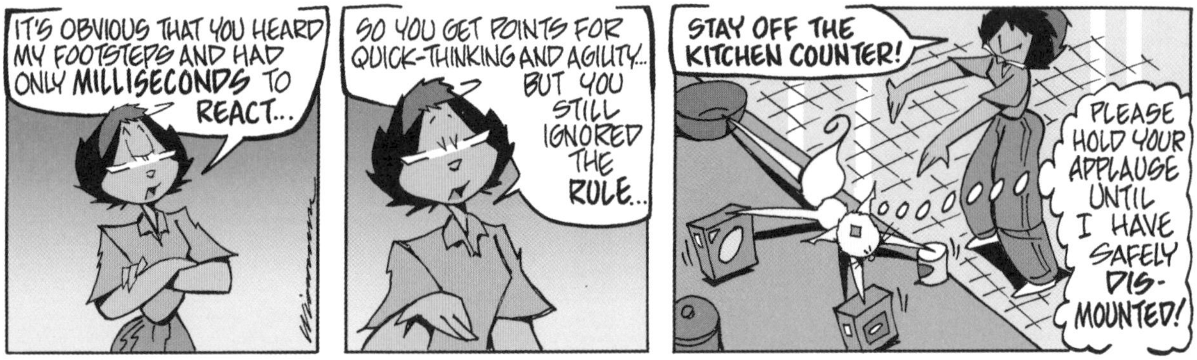
IT'S OBVIOUS THAT YOU HEARD MY FOOTSTEPS AND HAD ONLY MILLISECONDS TO REACT...
SO YOU GET POINTS FOR QUICK-THINKING AND AGILITY... BUT YOU STILL IGNORED THE RULE...
STAY OFF THE KITCHEN COUNTER!
PLEASE HOLD YOUR APPLAUSE UNTIL I HAVE SAFELY DIS-MOUNTED!

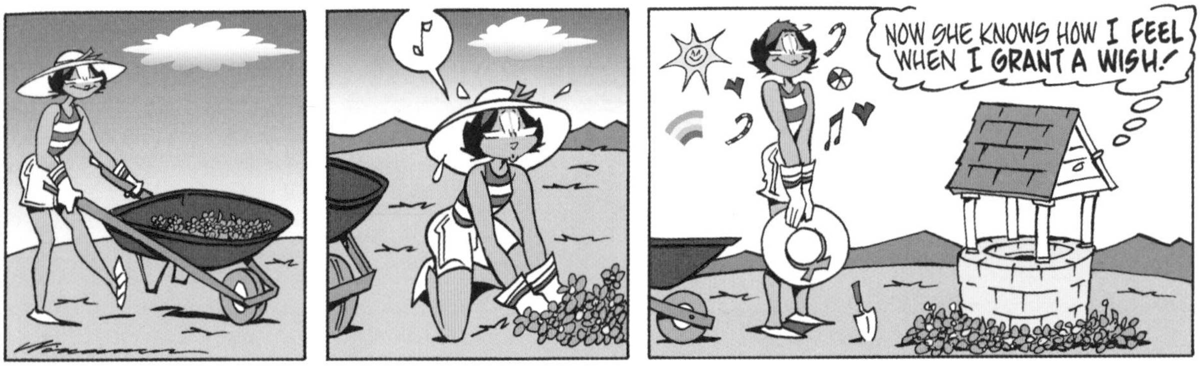
NOW SHE KNOWS HOW I FEEL WHEN I GRANT A WISH!

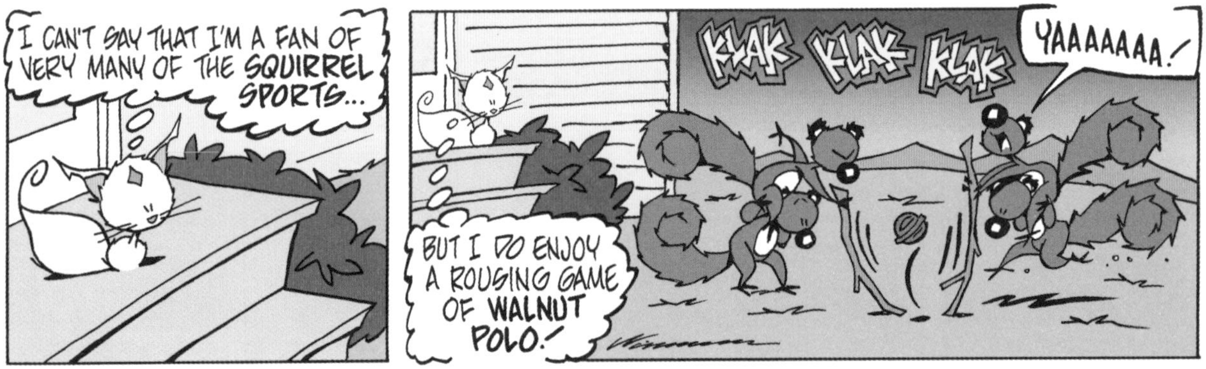
I CAN'T SAY THAT I'M A FAN OF VERY MANY OF THE SQUIRREL SPORTS...
BUT I DO ENJOY A ROUSING GAME OF WALNUT POLO!
KLAK KLAK KLAK
YAAAAAAA!

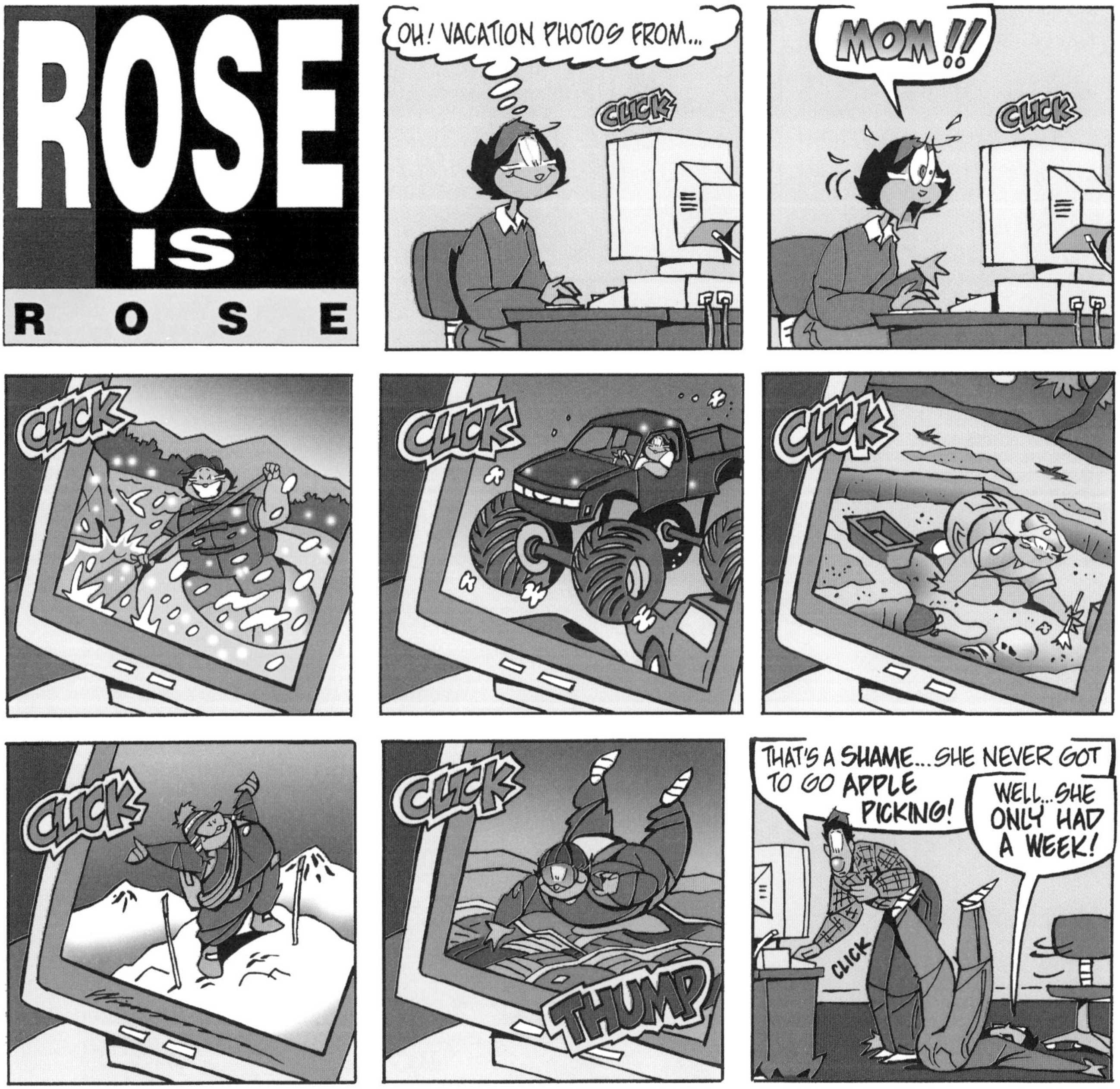
ROSE IS ROSE
OH! VACATION PHOTOS FROM...
CLICK
MOM!!
CLICK
CLICK
CLICK
CLICK
CLICK
CLICK
THUMP
THAT'S A SHAME...SHE NEVER GOT TO GO APPLE PICKING!
WELL...SHE ONLY HAD A WEEK!
CLICK

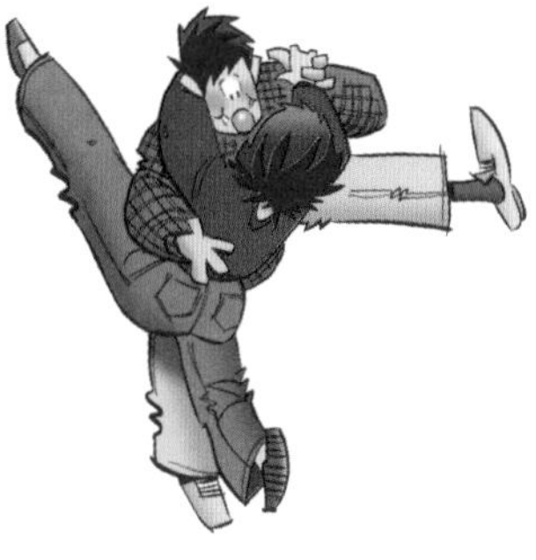

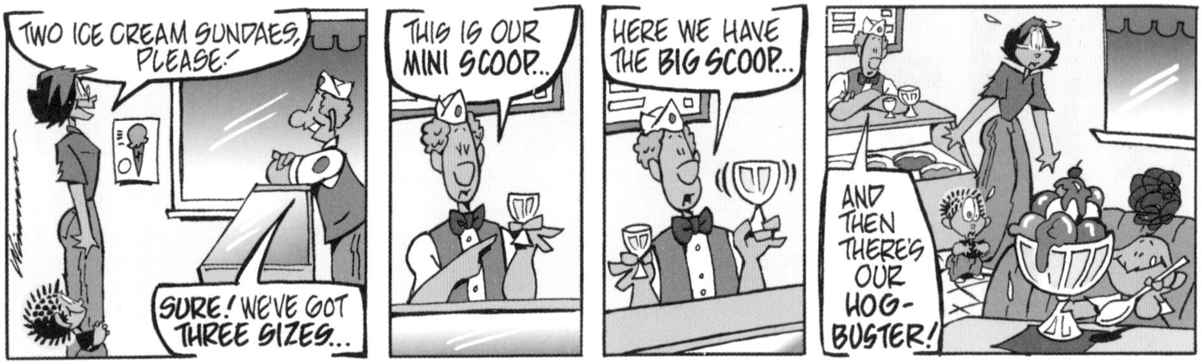

TWO ICE CREAM SUNDAES, PLEASE!
SURE! WE'VE GOT THREE SIZES...
THIS IS OUR MINI SCOOP...
HERE WE HAVE THE BIG SCOOP...
AND THEN THERE'S OUR HOG-BUSTER!

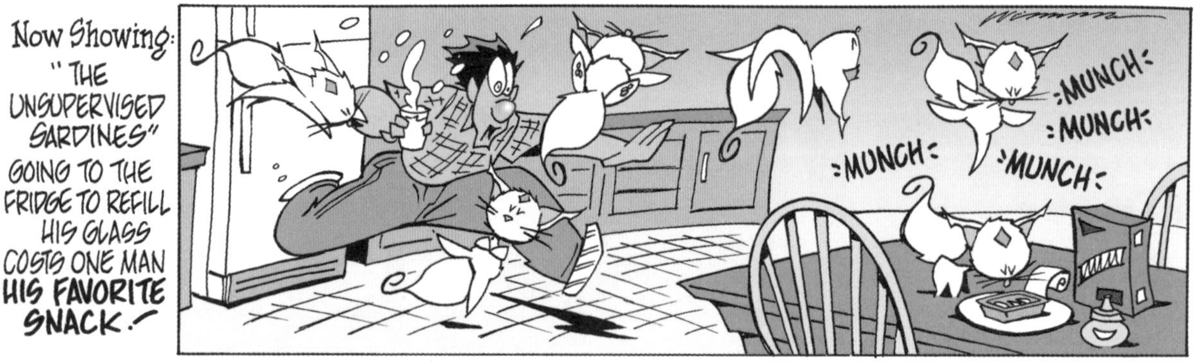

Now Showing: "THE UNSUPERVISED SARDINES"
GOING TO THE FRIDGE TO REFILL HIS GLASS COSTS ONE MAN HIS FAVORITE SNACK!
MUNCH
MUNCH
MUNCH
MUNCH

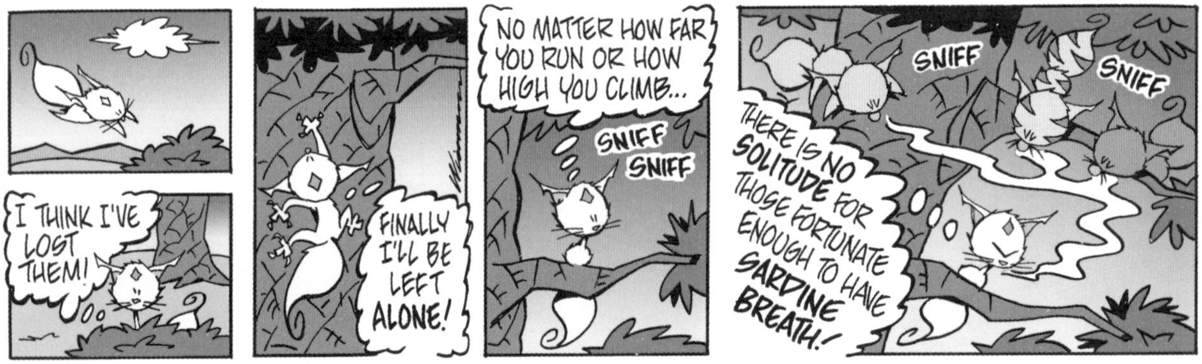

I THINK I'VE LOST THEM!
FINALLY I'LL BE LEFT ALONE!
NO MATTER HOW FAR YOU RUN OR HOW HIGH YOU CLIMB...
SNIFF
SNIFF
THERE IS NO SOLITUDE FOR THOSE FORTUNATE ENOUGH TO HAVE SARDINE BREATH!
SNIFF
SNIFF

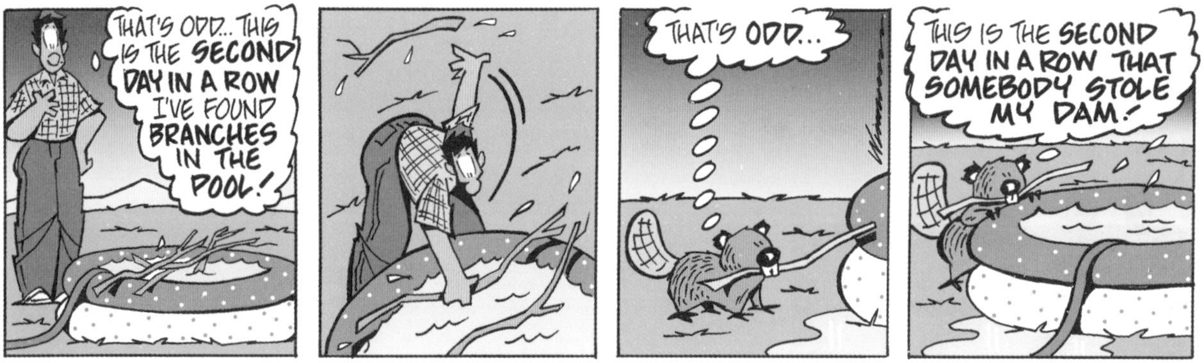
THAT'S ODD... THIS IS THE SECOND DAY IN A ROW I'VE FOUND BRANCHES IN THE POOL!
THAT'S ODD...
THIS IS THE SECOND DAY IN A ROW THAT SOMEBODY STOLE MY DAM!

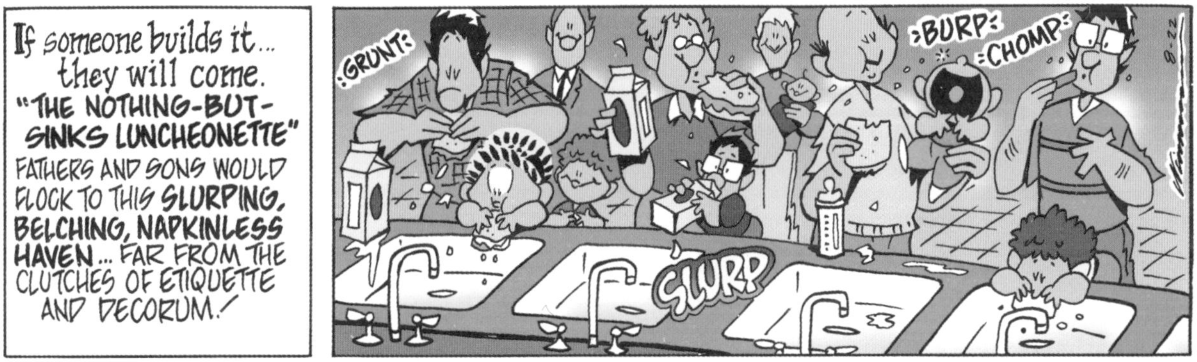
If someone builds it... they will come.
"THE NOTHING-BUT-SINKS LUNCHEONETTE"
FATHERS AND SONS WOULD FLOCK TO THIS SLURPING, BELCHING, NAPKINLESS HAVEN... FAR FROM THE CLUTCHES OF ETIQUETTE AND DECORUM!
:GRUNT:
:BURP:
:CHOMP:
SLURP

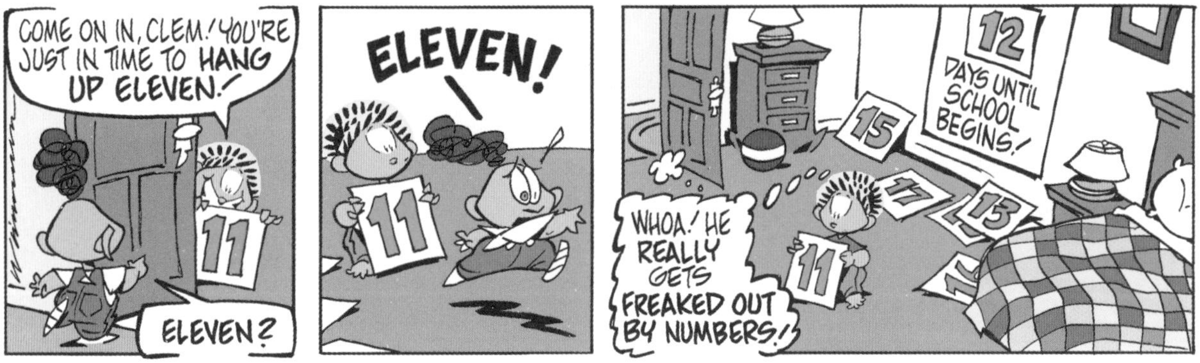
COME ON IN, CLEM! YOU'RE JUST IN TIME TO HANG UP ELEVEN!
11
ELEVEN?
ELEVEN!
11
12
DAYS UNTIL SCHOOL BEGINS!
15
17
13
11
WHOA! HE REALLY GETS FREAKED OUT BY NUMBERS!

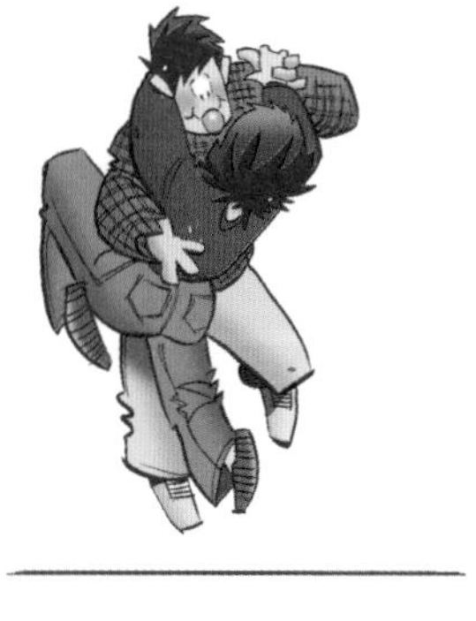

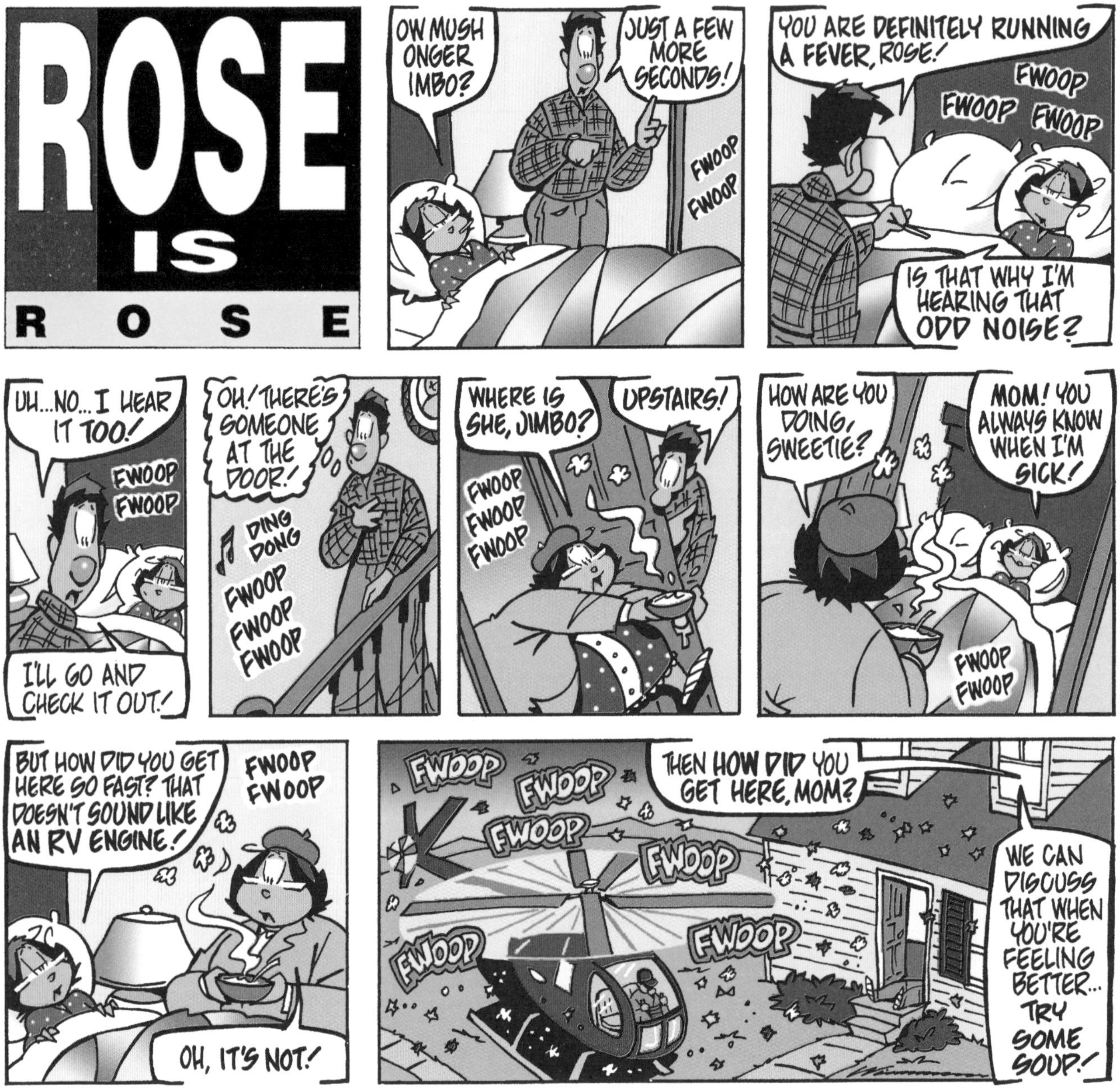
ROSE IS ROSE
OW MUSH ONGER IMBO?
JUST A FEW MORE SECONDS!
FWOOP FWOOP
YOU ARE DEFINITELY RUNNING A FEVER, ROSE!
FWOOP FWOOP FWOOP
IS THAT WHY I'M HEARING THAT ODD NOISE?
UH...NO...I HEAR IT TOO!
FWOOP FWOOP
I'LL GO AND CHECK IT OUT!
OH! THERE'S SOMEONE AT THE DOOR!
DING DONG
FWOOP FWOOP FWOOP
WHERE IS SHE, JIMBO?
UPSTAIRS!
FWOOP FWOOP FWOOP
HOW ARE YOU DOING, SWEETIE?
MOM! YOU ALWAYS KNOW WHEN I'M SICK!
FWOOP FWOOP
BUT HOW DID YOU GET HERE SO FAST? THAT DOESN'T SOUND LIKE AN RV ENGINE!
FWOOP FWOOP
OH, IT'S NOT!
FWOOP FWOOP FWOOP FWOOP FWOOP FWOOP
THEN HOW DID YOU GET HERE, MOM?
WE CAN DISCUSS THAT WHEN YOU'RE FEELING BETTER... TRY SOME SOUP!

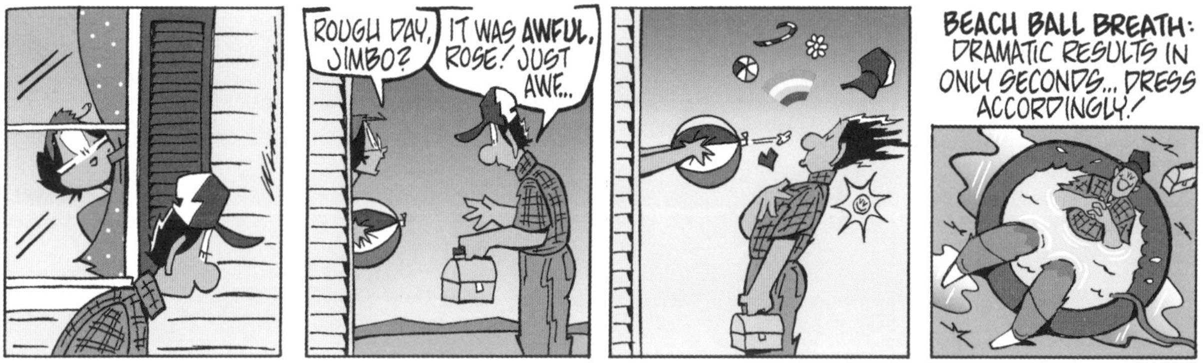
ROUGH DAY, JIMBO?
IT WAS AWFUL, ROSE! JUST AWF...
BEACH BALL BREATH: DRAMATIC RESULTS IN ONLY SECONDS... DRESS ACCORDINGLY!

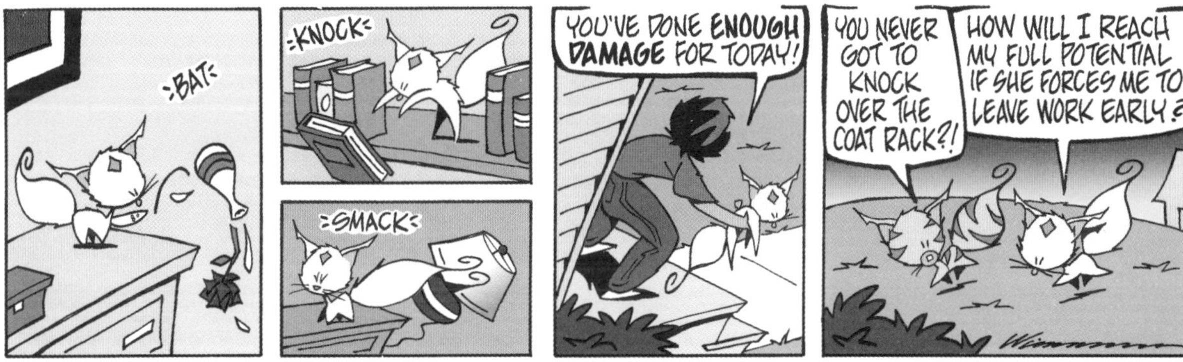
BAT
KNOCK
SMACK
YOU'VE DONE ENOUGH DAMAGE FOR TODAY!
YOU NEVER GOT TO KNOCK OVER THE COAT RACK?!
HOW WILL I REACH MY FULL POTENTIAL IF SHE FORCES ME TO LEAVE WORK EARLY?

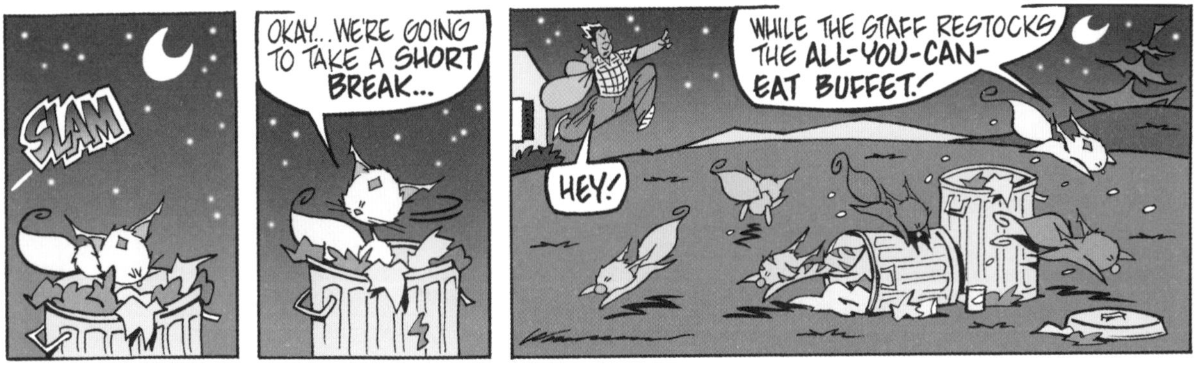
SLAM
OKAY...WE'RE GOING TO TAKE A SHORT BREAK...
WHILE THE STAFF RESTOCKS THE ALL-YOU-CAN-EAT BUFFET!
HEY!

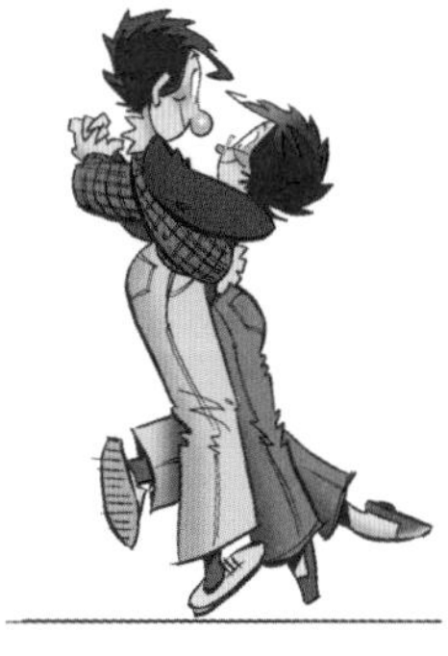

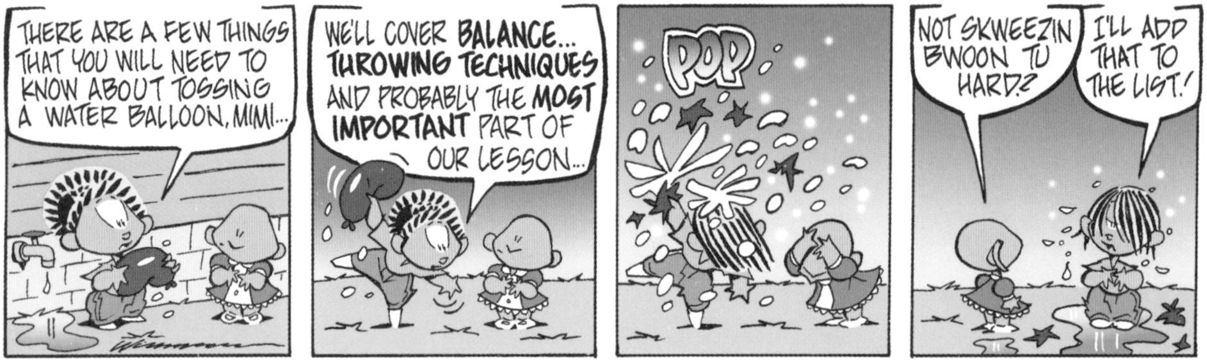
THERE ARE A FEW THINGS THAT YOU WILL NEED TO KNOW ABOUT TOSSING A WATER BALLOON, MIMI...
WE'LL COVER BALANCE... THROWING TECHNIQUES AND PROBABLY THE MOST IMPORTANT PART OF OUR LESSON...
POP
NOT SKWEEZIN BWOON TU HARD?
I'LL ADD THAT TO THE LIST!

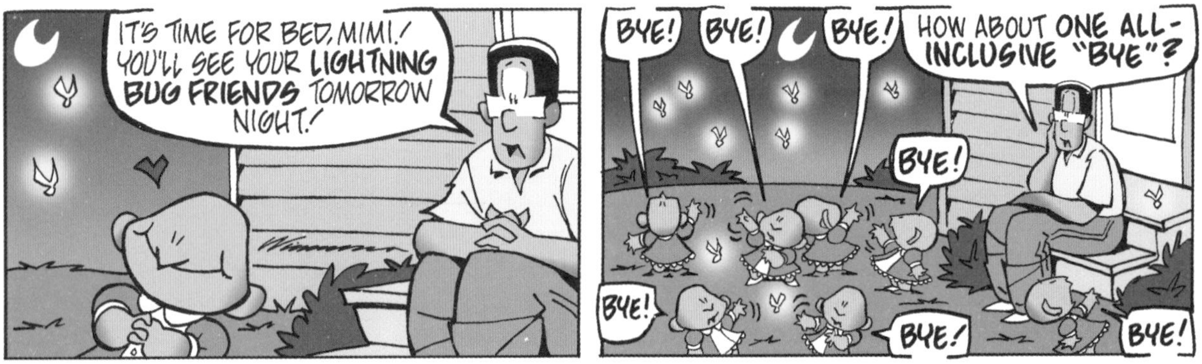
IT'S TIME FOR BED, MIMI! YOU'LL SEE YOUR LIGHTNING BUG FRIENDS TOMORROW NIGHT!
BYE!
BYE!
BYE!
HOW ABOUT ONE ALL-INCLUSIVE "BYE"?
BYE!
BYE!
BYE!
BYE!

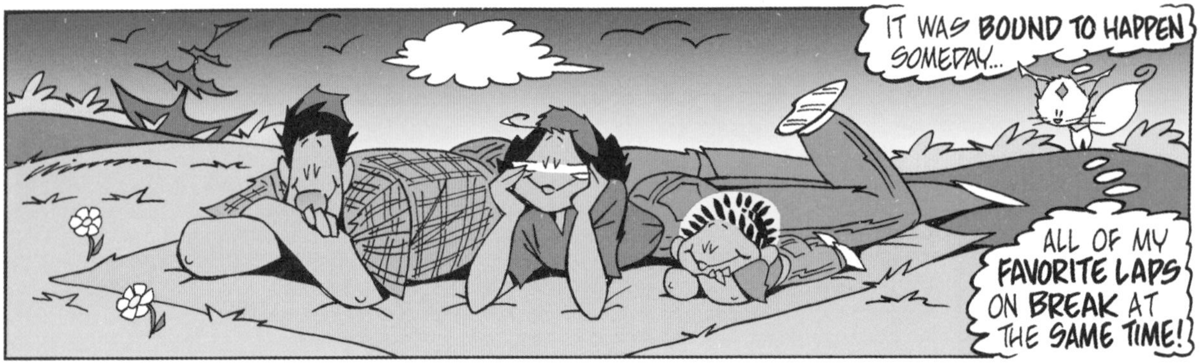
IT WAS BOUND TO HAPPEN SOMEDAY...
ALL OF MY FAVORITE LAPS ON BREAK AT THE SAME TIME!

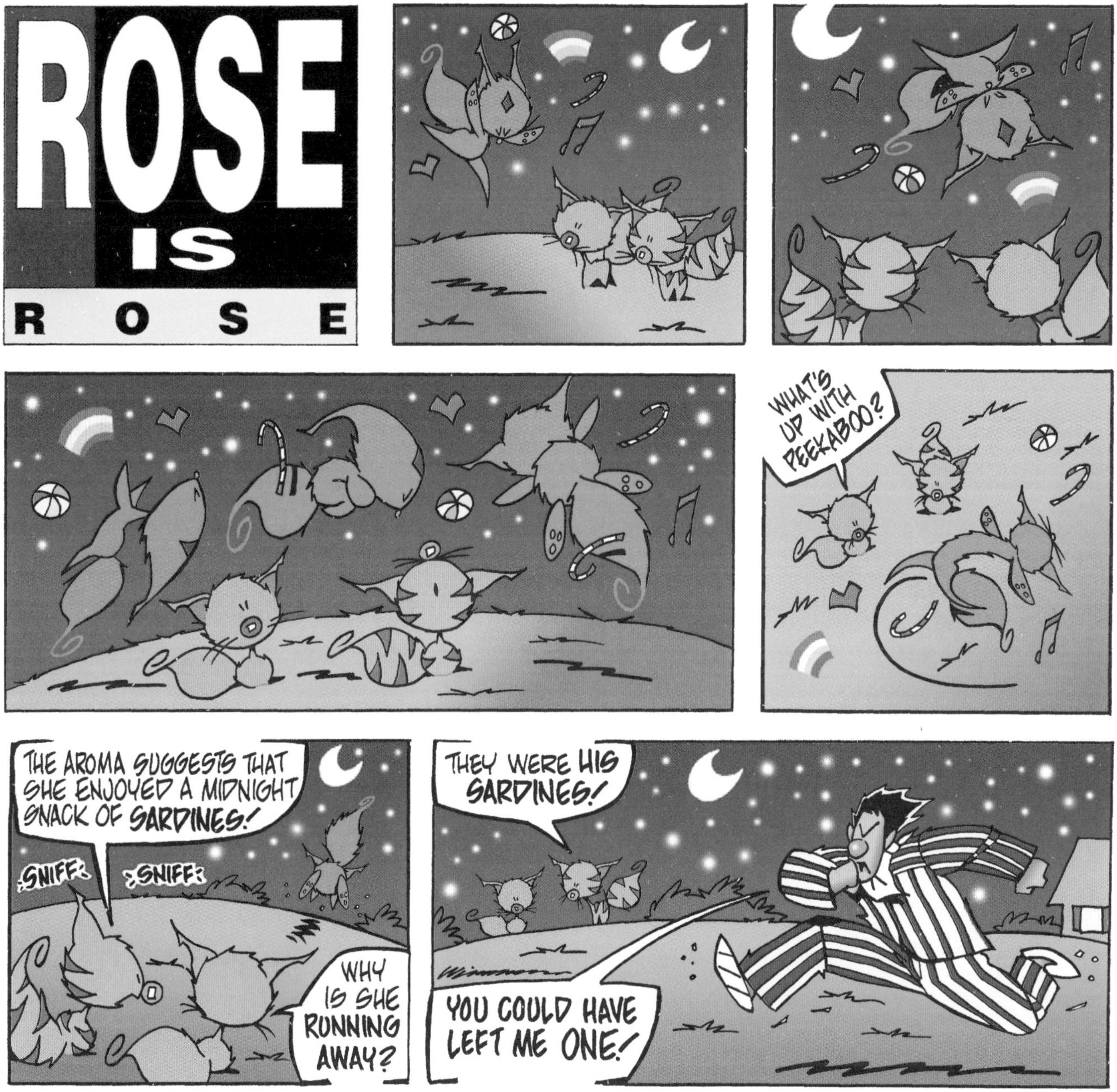
ROSE IS ROSE
WHAT'S UP WITH PEEKABOO?
THE AROMA SUGGESTS THAT SHE ENJOYED A MIDNIGHT SNACK OF SARDINES!
SNIFF
SNIFF
WHY IS SHE RUNNING AWAY?
THEY WERE HIS SARDINES!
YOU COULD HAVE LEFT ME ONE!

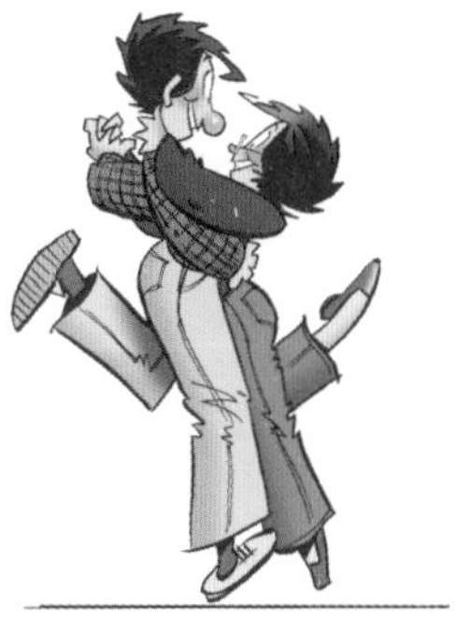

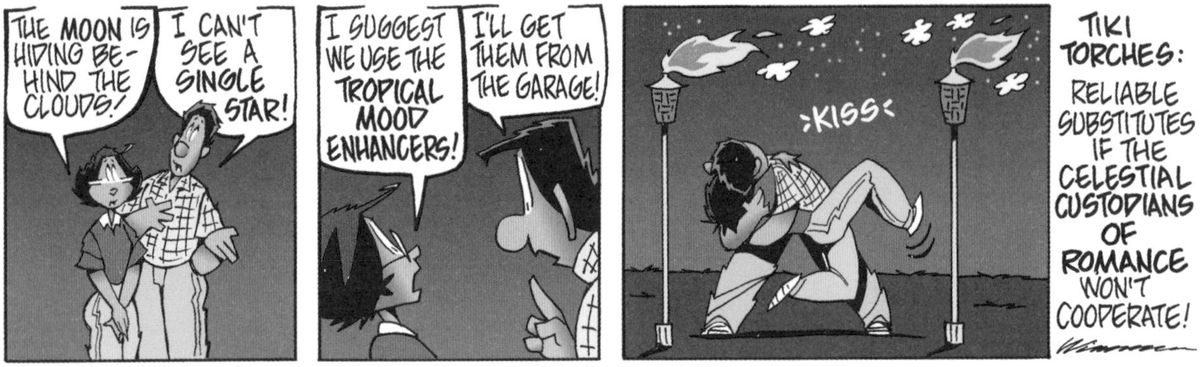
THE MOON IS HIDING BEHIND THE CLOUDS!
I CAN'T SEE A SINGLE STAR!
I SUGGEST WE USE THE TROPICAL MOOD ENHANCERS!
I'LL GET THEM FROM THE GARAGE!
>KISS<
TIKI TORCHES: RELIABLE SUBSTITUTES IF THE CELESTIAL CUSTODIANS OF ROMANCE WON'T COOPERATE!

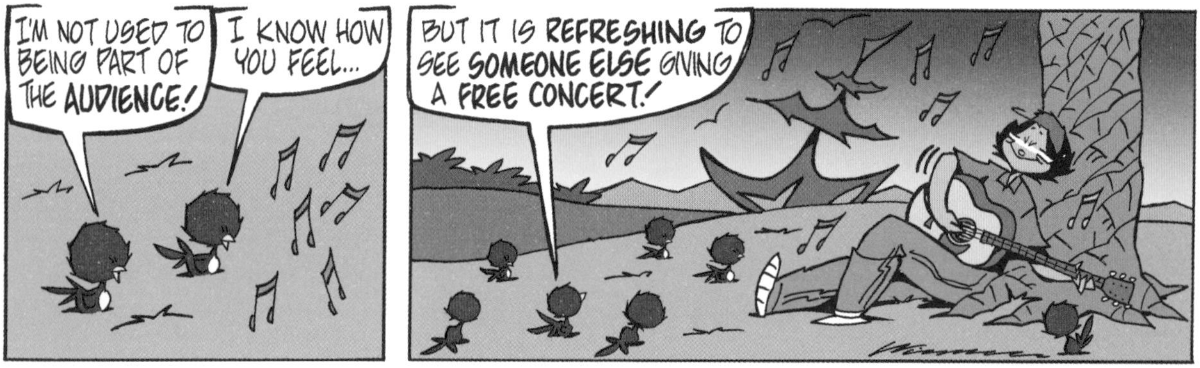
I'M NOT USED TO BEING PART OF THE AUDIENCE!
I KNOW HOW YOU FEEL...
BUT IT IS REFRESHING TO SEE SOMEONE ELSE GIVING A FREE CONCERT!

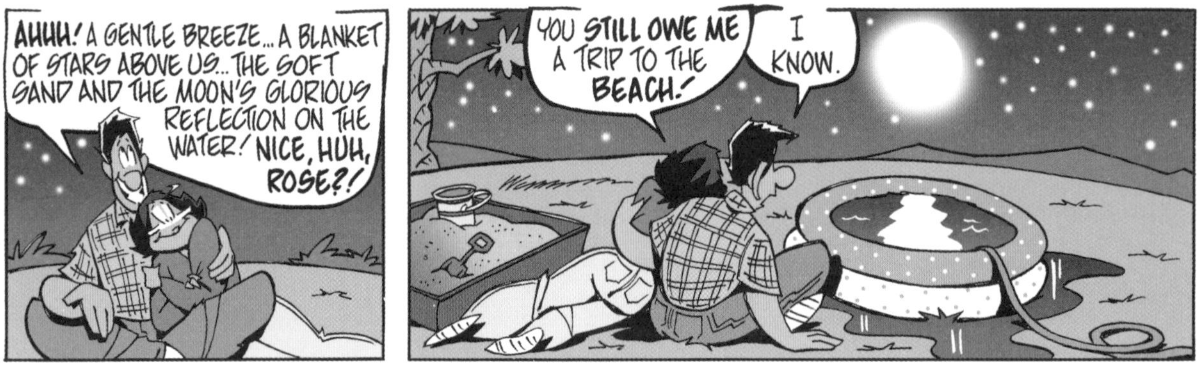
AHHH! A GENTLE BREEZE... A BLANKET OF STARS ABOVE US... THE SOFT SAND AND THE MOON'S GLORIOUS REFLECTION ON THE WATER! NICE, HUH, ROSE?!
YOU STILL OWE ME A TRIP TO THE BEACH!
I KNOW.

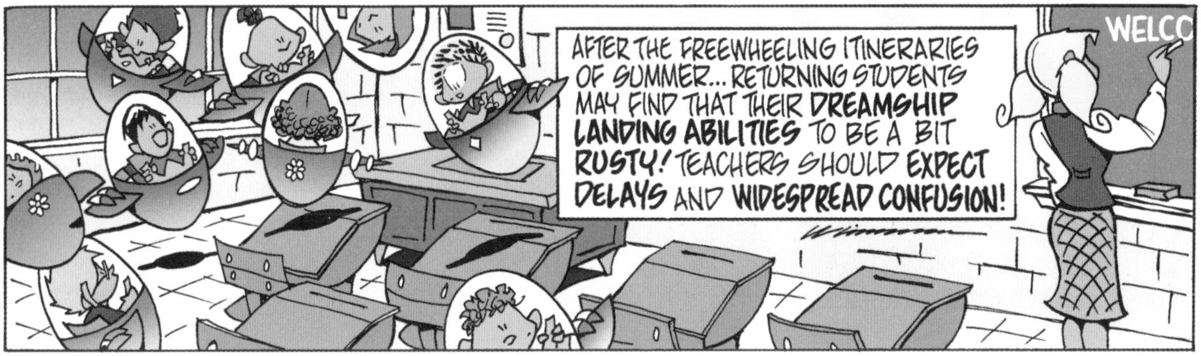
WELC
AFTER THE FREEWHEELING ITINERARIES OF SUMMER... RETURNING STUDENTS MAY FIND THAT THEIR **DREAMSHIP LANDING ABILITIES** TO BE A BIT **RUSTY!** TEACHERS SHOULD **EXPECT DELAYS** AND **WIDESPREAD CONFUSION!**

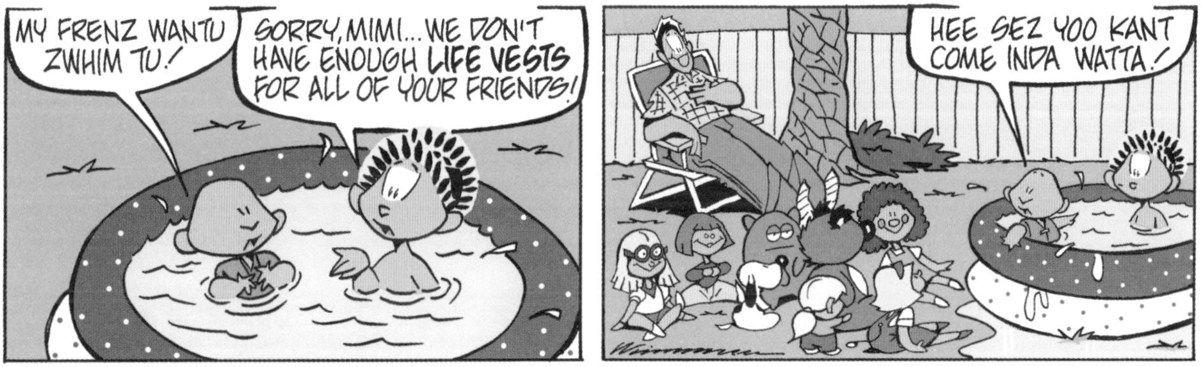
MY FRENZ WANTU ZWHIM TU!
SORRY, MIMI... WE DON'T HAVE ENOUGH **LIFE VESTS** FOR ALL OF YOUR FRIENDS!
HEE SEZ YOO KANT COME INDA WATTA!

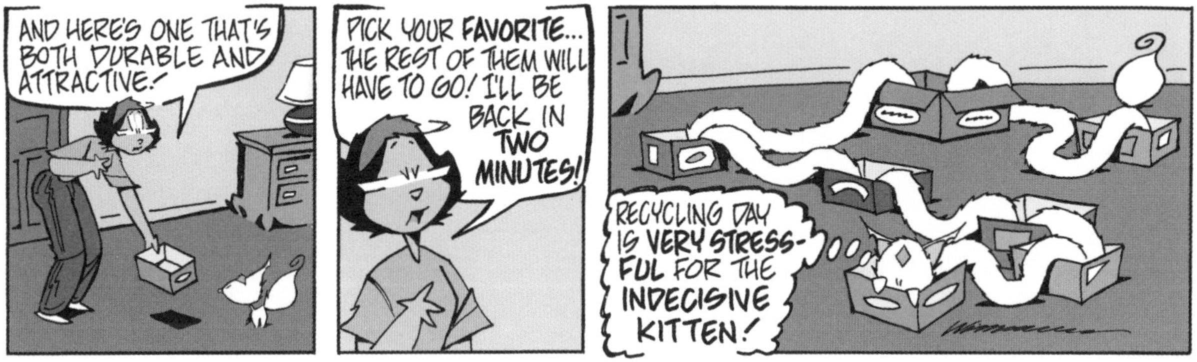
AND HERE'S ONE THAT'S BOTH DURABLE AND ATTRACTIVE!
PICK YOUR **FAVORITE**... THE REST OF THEM WILL HAVE TO GO! I'LL BE BACK IN **TWO MINUTES!**
RECYCLING DAY IS **VERY STRESSFUL** FOR THE **INDECISIVE KITTEN!**

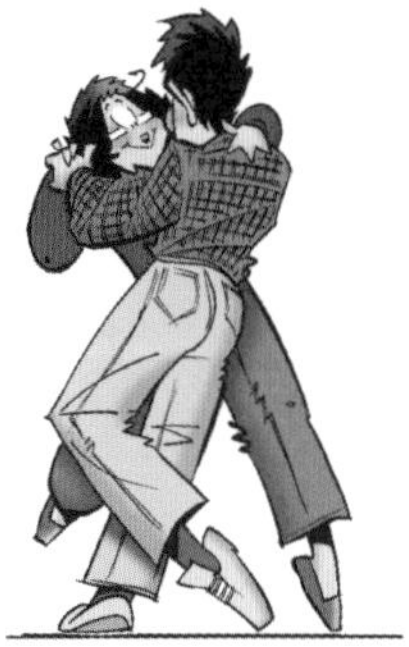

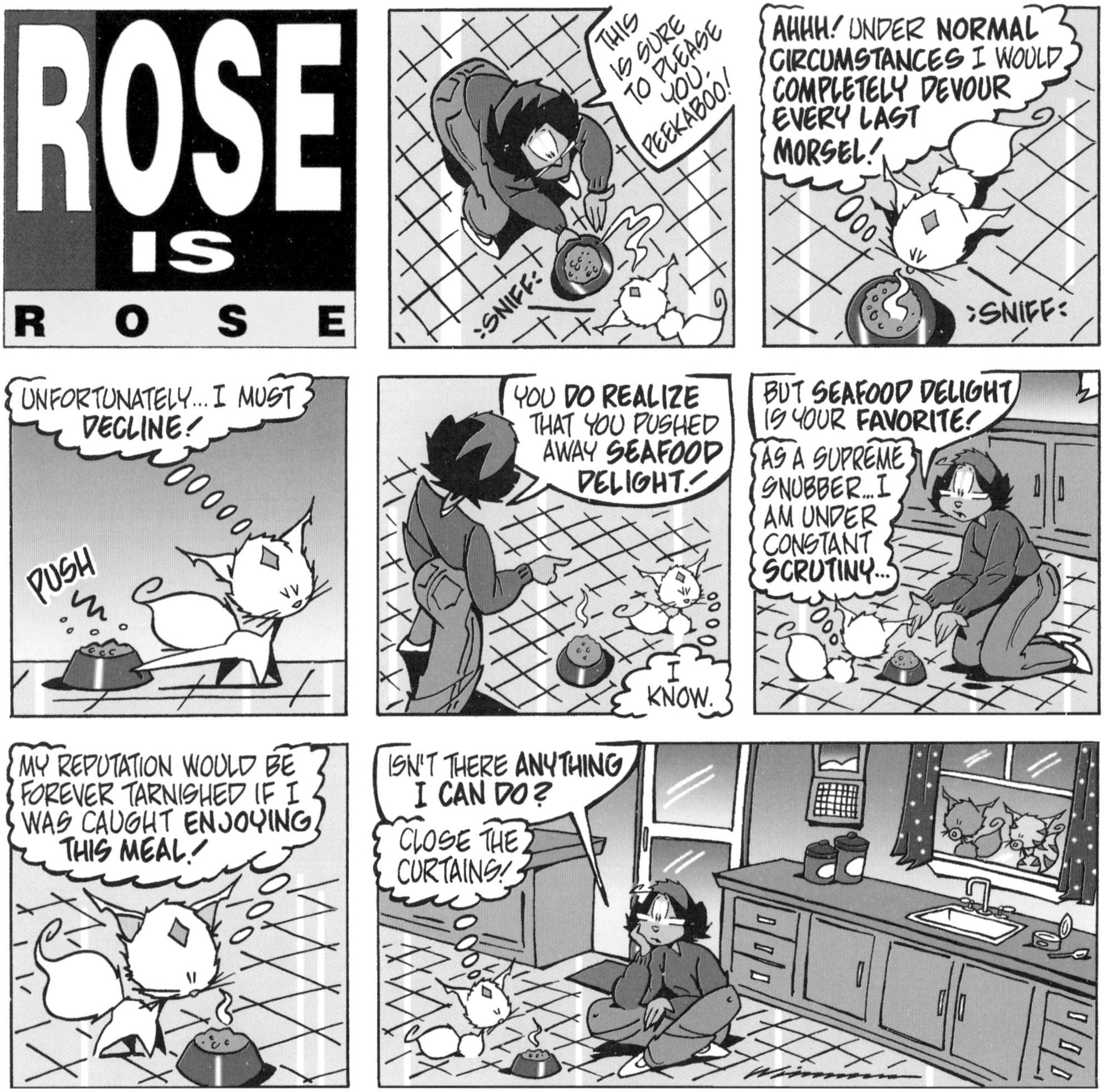
ROSE IS ROSE
THIS IS SURE TO PLEASE YOU, PEEKABOO!
:SNIFF:
AHHH! UNDER NORMAL CIRCUMSTANCES I WOULD COMPLETELY DEVOUR EVERY LAST MORSEL!
:SNIFF:
UNFORTUNATELY... I MUST DECLINE!
PUSH
YOU DO REALIZE THAT YOU PUSHED AWAY SEAFOOD DELIGHT.
I KNOW.
BUT SEAFOOD DELIGHT IS YOUR FAVORITE!
AS A SUPREME SNUBBER... I AM UNDER CONSTANT SCRUTINY...
MY REPUTATION WOULD BE FOREVER TARNISHED IF I WAS CAUGHT ENJOYING THIS MEAL!
ISN'T THERE ANYTHING I CAN DO?
CLOSE THE CURTAINS!

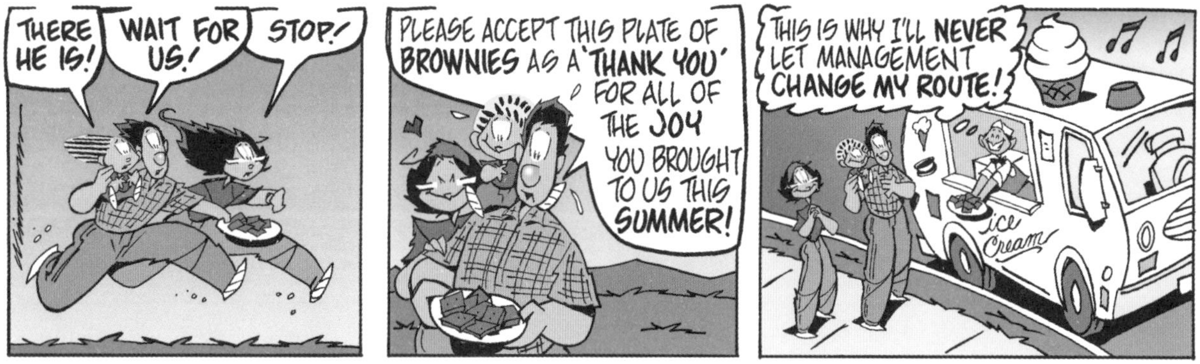
THERE HE IS!
WAIT FOR US!
STOP!
PLEASE ACCEPT THIS PLATE OF BROWNIES AS A 'THANK YOU' FOR ALL OF THE JOY YOU BROUGHT TO US THIS SUMMER!
THIS IS WHY I'LL NEVER LET MANAGEMENT CHANGE MY ROUTE!
ICE CREAM

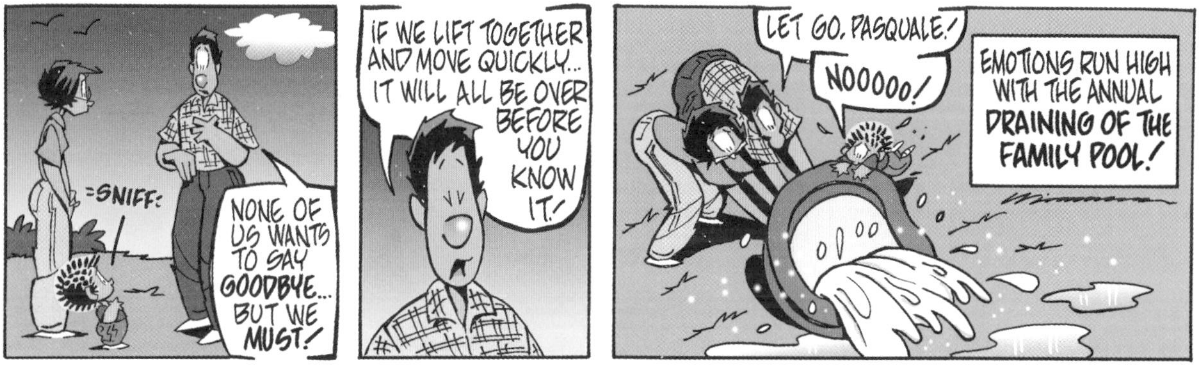
=SNIFF=
NONE OF US WANTS TO SAY GOODBYE... BUT WE MUST!
IF WE LIFT TOGETHER AND MOVE QUICKLY... IT WILL ALL BE OVER BEFORE YOU KNOW IT!
LET GO, PASQUALE!
NOOOOO!
EMOTIONS RUN HIGH WITH THE ANNUAL DRAINING OF THE FAMILY POOL!

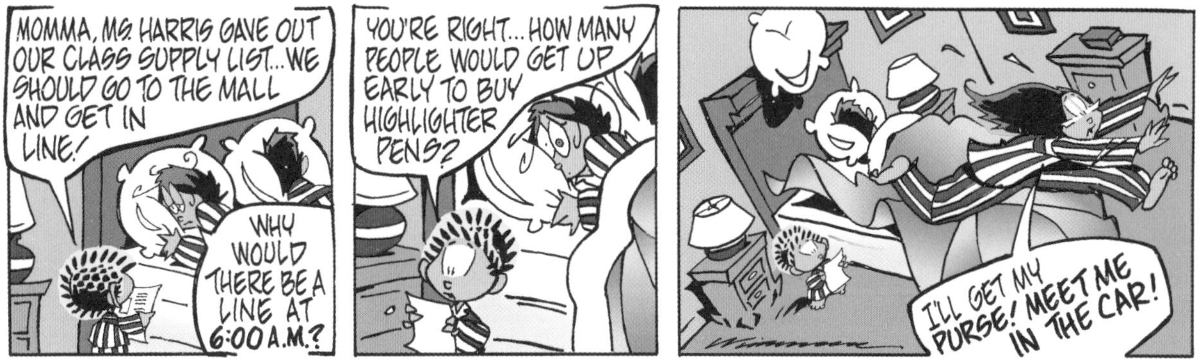
MOMMA, MS. HARRIS GAVE OUT OUR CLASS SUPPLY LIST... WE SHOULD GO TO THE MALL AND GET IN LINE!
WHY WOULD THERE BE A LINE AT 6:00 A.M.?
YOU'RE RIGHT... HOW MANY PEOPLE WOULD GET UP EARLY TO BUY HIGHLIGHTER PENS?
I'LL GET MY PURSE! MEET ME IN THE CAR!

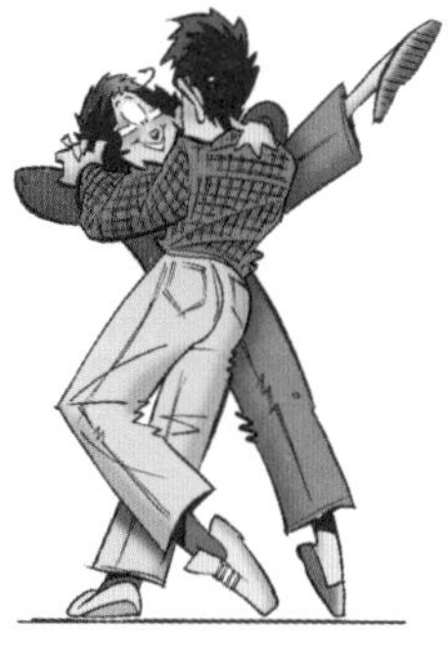

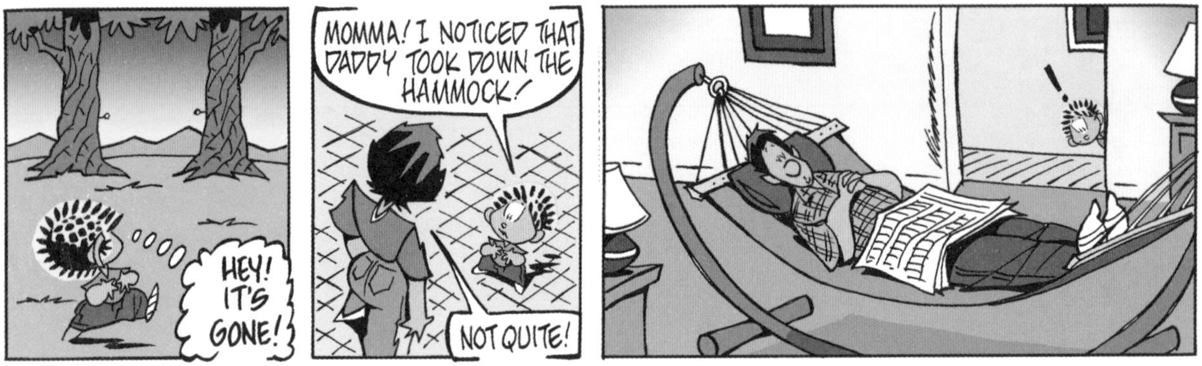
HEY! IT'S GONE!
MOMMA! I NOTICED THAT DADDY TOOK DOWN THE HAMMOCK!
NOT QUITE!
!

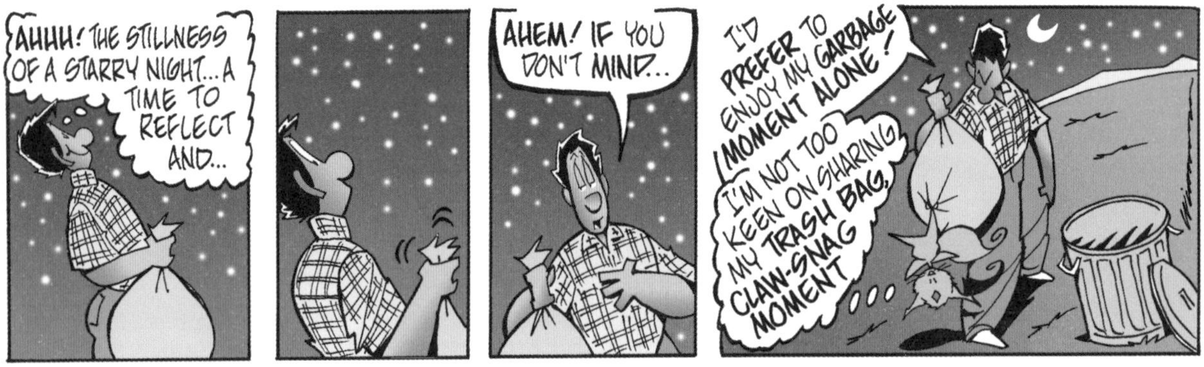
AHHH! THE STILLNESS OF A STARRY NIGHT... A TIME TO REFLECT AND...
AHEM! IF YOU DON'T MIND...
I'D PREFER TO ENJOY MY GARBAGE MOMENT ALONE!
I'M NOT TOO KEEN ON SHARING MY TRASH BAG CLAW-SNAG MOMENT

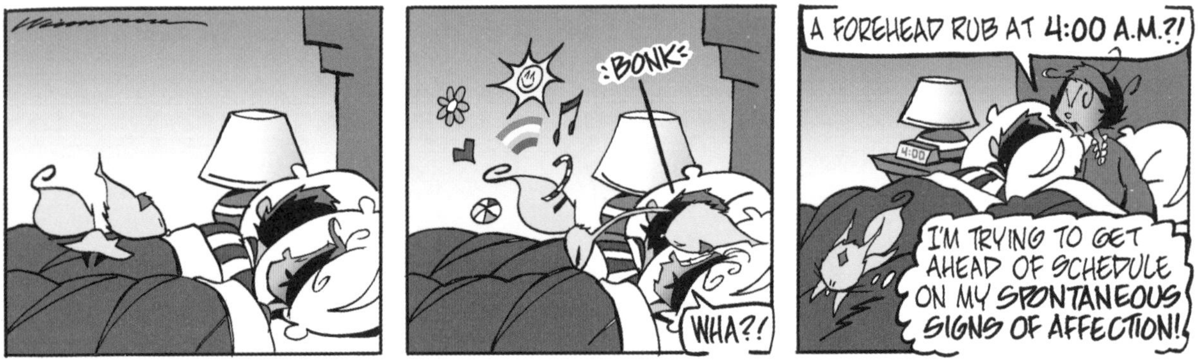
BONK
WHA?!
A FOREHEAD RUB AT 4:00 A.M.?!
4:00
I'M TRYING TO GET AHEAD OF SCHEDULE ON MY SPONTANEOUS SIGNS OF AFFECTION!

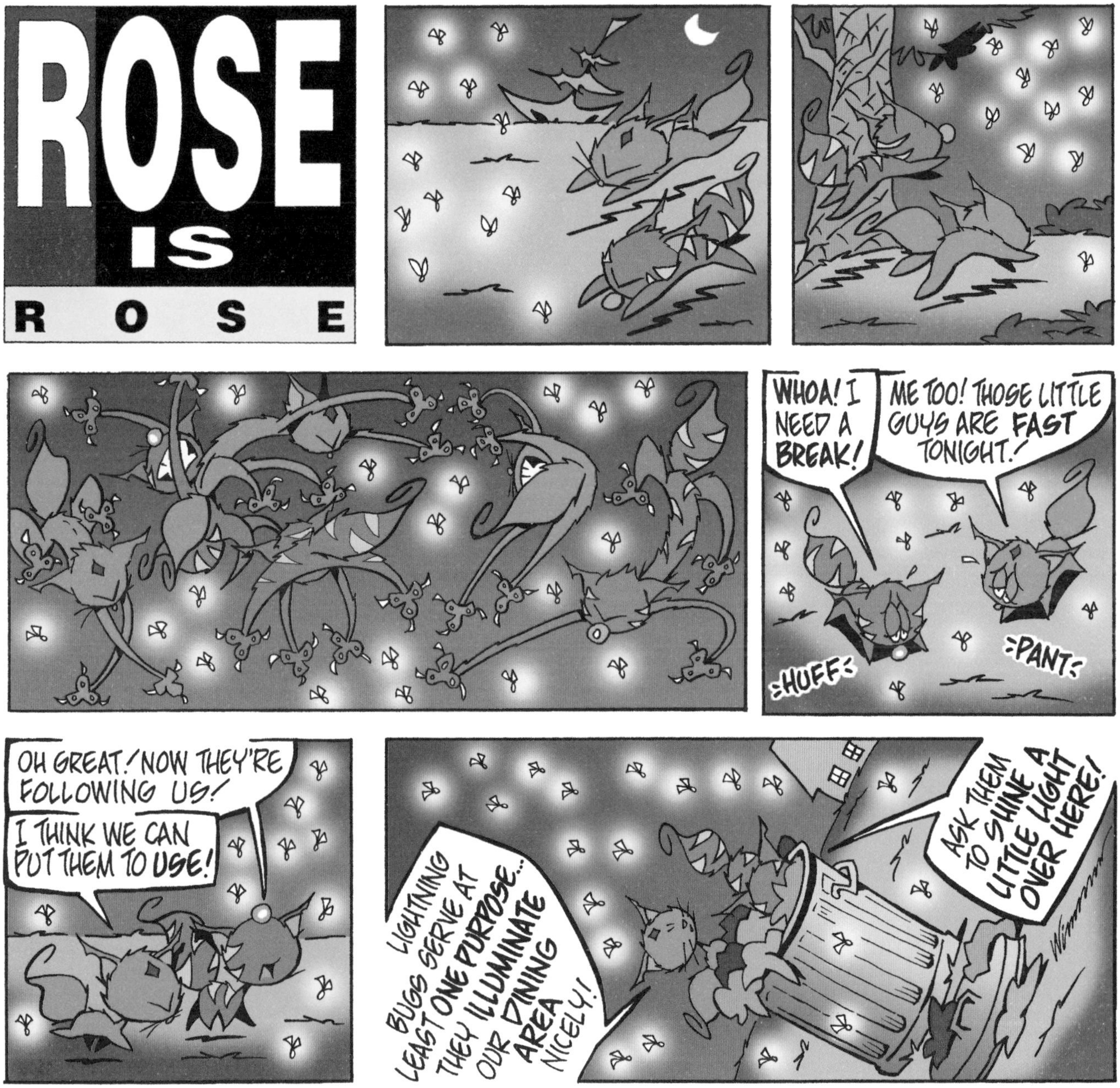
ROSE IS ROSE
WHOA! I NEED A BREAK!
ME TOO! THOSE LITTLE GUYS ARE FAST TONIGHT!
HUFF
PANT
OH GREAT! NOW THEY'RE FOLLOWING US!
I THINK WE CAN PUT THEM TO USE!
LIGHTNING BUGS SERVE AT LEAST ONE PURPOSE... THEY ILLUMINATE OUR DINING AREA NICELY!
ASK THEM TO SHINE A LITTLE LIGHT OVER HERE!

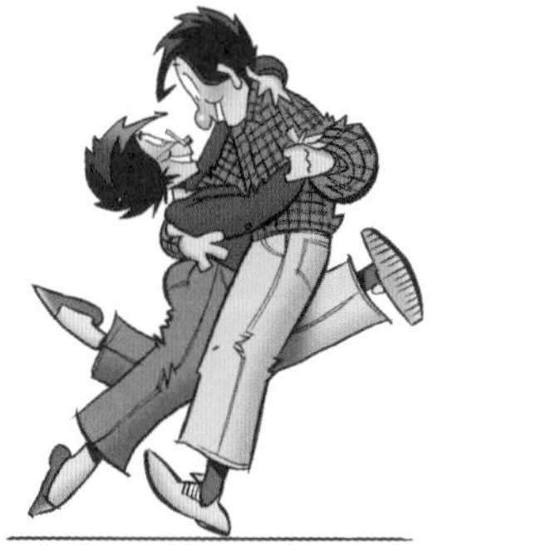

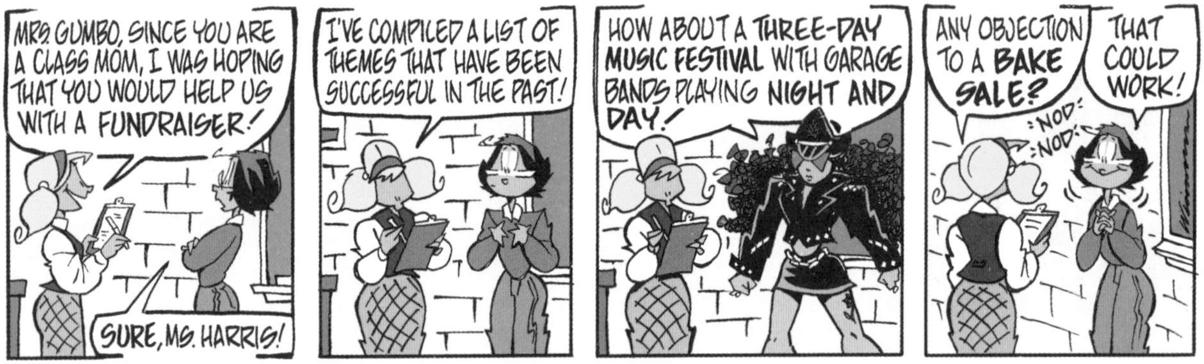
MRS. GUMBO, SINCE YOU ARE A CLASS MOM, I WAS HOPING THAT YOU WOULD HELP US WITH A **FUNDRAISER**!
SURE, MS. HARRIS!
I'VE COMPILED A LIST OF THEMES THAT HAVE BEEN SUCCESSFUL IN THE PAST!
HOW ABOUT A **THREE-DAY MUSIC FESTIVAL** WITH GARAGE BANDS PLAYING **NIGHT AND DAY**!
ANY OBJECTION TO A **BAKE SALE?**
NOD NOD
THAT COULD WORK!

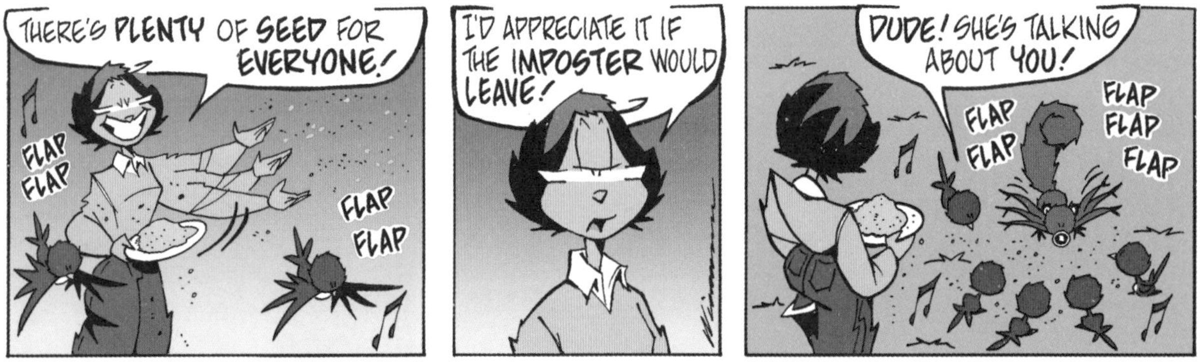
THERE'S **PLENTY** OF **SEED** FOR **EVERYONE**!
FLAP FLAP
FLAP FLAP
I'D APPRECIATE IT IF THE **IMPOSTER** WOULD **LEAVE**!
DUDE! SHE'S TALKING ABOUT **YOU**!
FLAP FLAP
FLAP FLAP FLAP

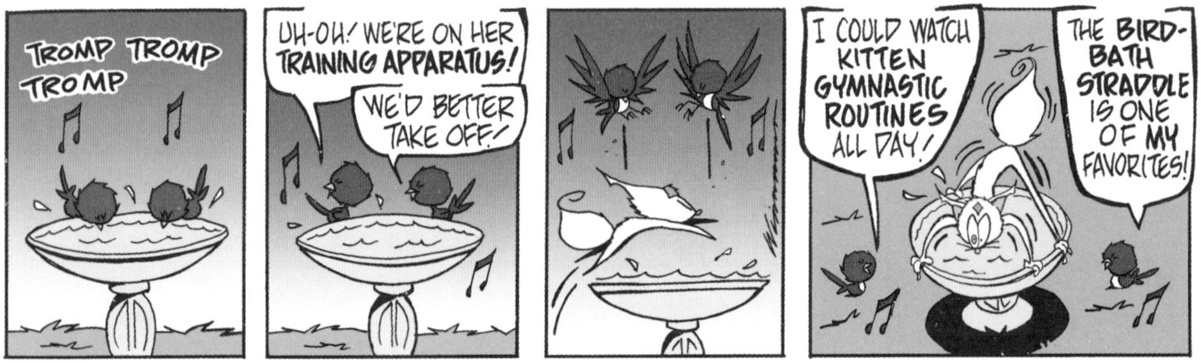
TROMP TROMP TROMP
UH-OH! WE'RE ON HER **TRAINING APPARATUS**!
WE'D BETTER TAKE OFF!
I COULD WATCH **KITTEN GYMNASTIC ROUTINES** ALL DAY!
THE **BIRD-BATH STRADDLE** IS ONE OF **MY** FAVORITES!

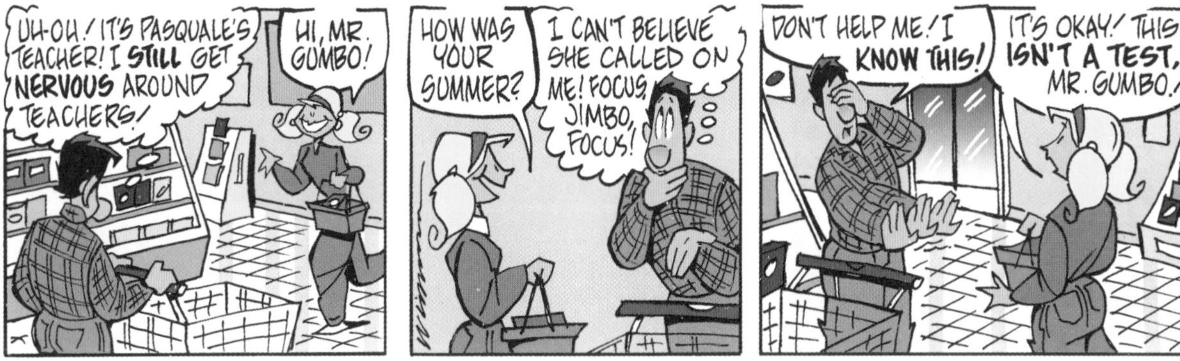
UH-OH! IT'S PASQUALE'S TEACHER! I **STILL** GET **NERVOUS** AROUND TEACHERS!
HI, MR. GUMBO!
HOW WAS YOUR SUMMER?
I CAN'T BELIEVE SHE CALLED ON ME! FOCUS, JIMBO, FOCUS!
DON'T HELP ME! I **KNOW THIS!**
IT'S OKAY! THIS **ISN'T A TEST,** MR. GUMBO!

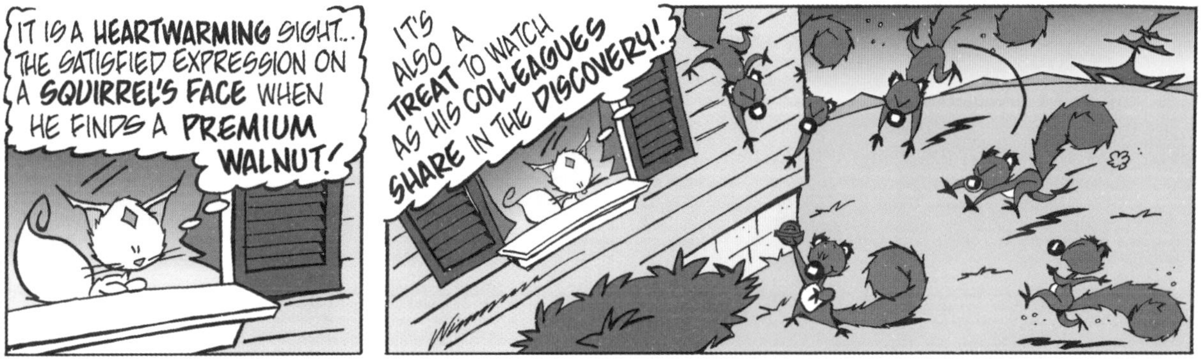
IT IS A **HEARTWARMING** SIGHT... THE SATISFIED EXPRESSION ON A **SQUIRREL'S FACE** WHEN HE FINDS A **PREMIUM WALNUT!**
IT'S ALSO A **TREAT** TO WATCH AS HIS **COLLEAGUES SHARE** IN THE **DISCOVERY!**

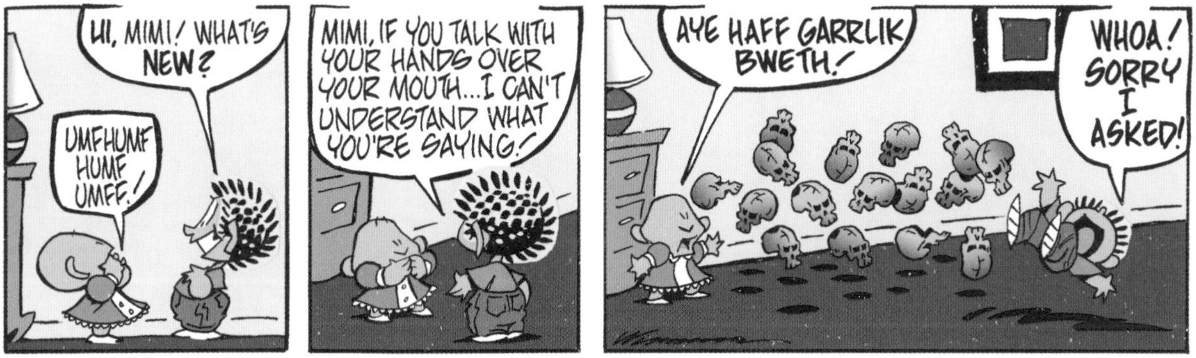
HI, MIMI! WHAT'S **NEW?**
UMFHUMF HUMF UMFF!
MIMI, IF YOU TALK WITH YOUR HANDS OVER YOUR MOUTH... I CAN'T UNDERSTAND WHAT YOU'RE SAYING!
AYE HAFF GARRLIK BWETH!
WHOA! SORRY I ASKED!

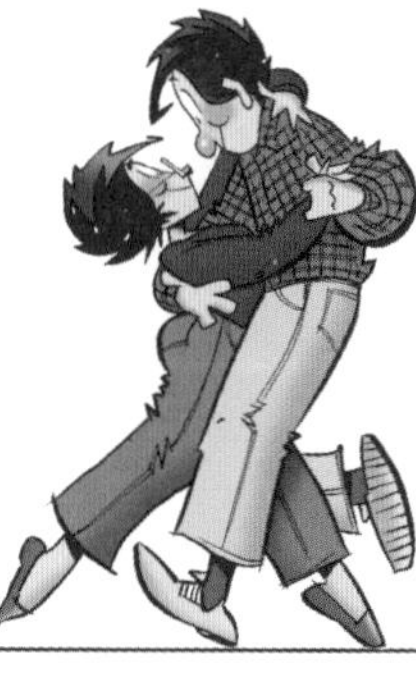

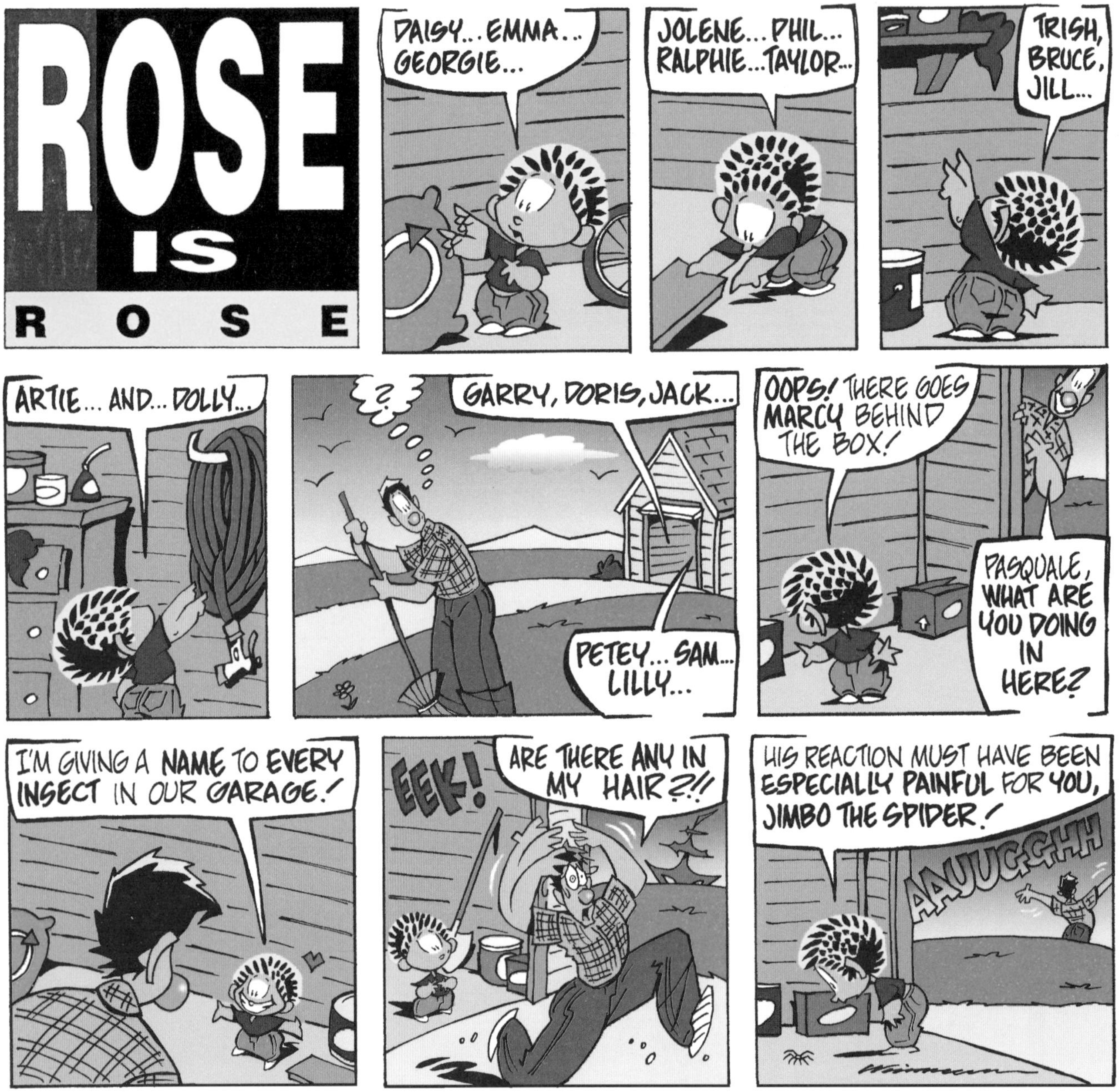
ROSE IS ROSE
DAISY... EMMA... GEORGIE...
JOLENE... PHIL... RALPHIE... TAYLOR...
TRISH, BRUCE, JILL...
ARTIE... AND... DOLLY...
?
GARRY, DORIS, JACK...
PETEY... SAM... LILLY...
OOPS! THERE GOES MARCY BEHIND THE BOX!
PASQUALE, WHAT ARE YOU DOING IN HERE?
I'M GIVING A NAME TO EVERY INSECT IN OUR GARAGE!
EEK!
ARE THERE ANY IN MY HAIR?!!
HIS REACTION MUST HAVE BEEN ESPECIALLY PAINFUL FOR YOU, JIMBO THE SPIDER!
AAUUGGHH

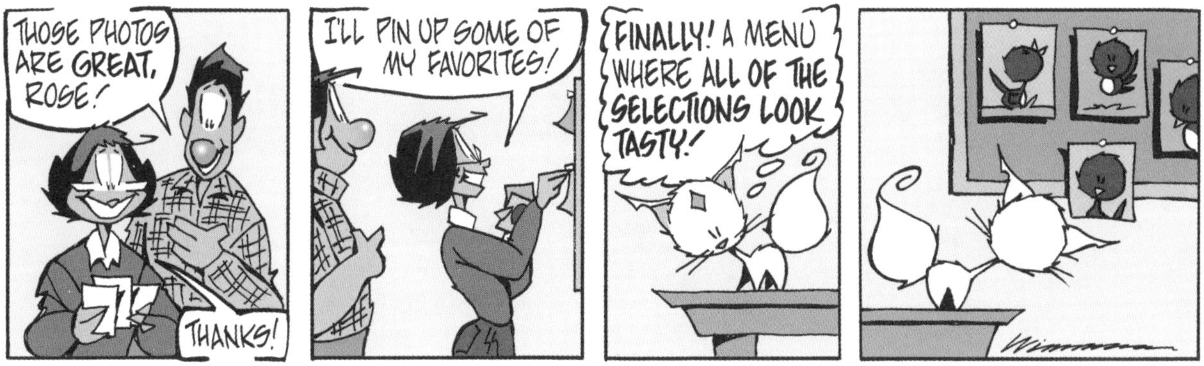
THOSE PHOTOS ARE GREAT, ROSE!
THANKS!
I'LL PIN UP SOME OF MY FAVORITES!
FINALLY! A MENU WHERE ALL OF THE SELECTIONS LOOK TASTY!

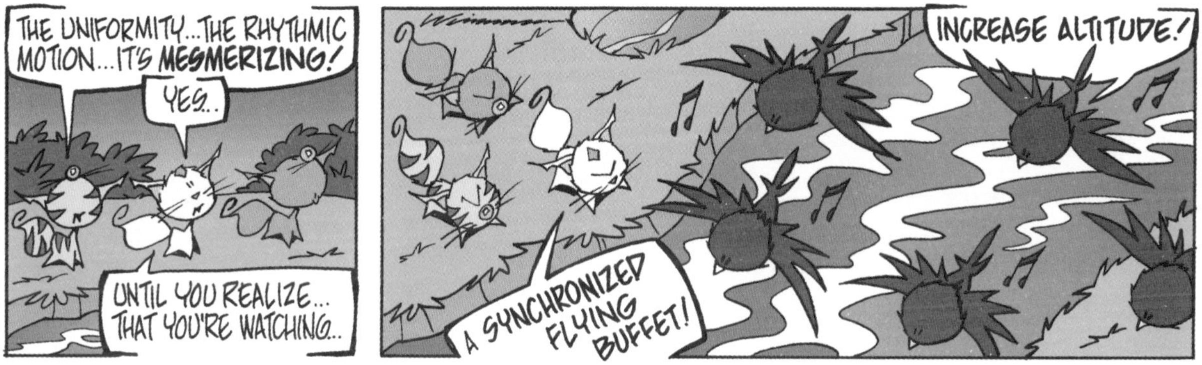
THE UNIFORMITY...THE RHYTHMIC MOTION...IT'S MESMERIZING!
YES...
UNTIL YOU REALIZE... THAT YOU'RE WATCHING...
A SYNCHRONIZED FLYING BUFFET!
INCREASE ALTITUDE!

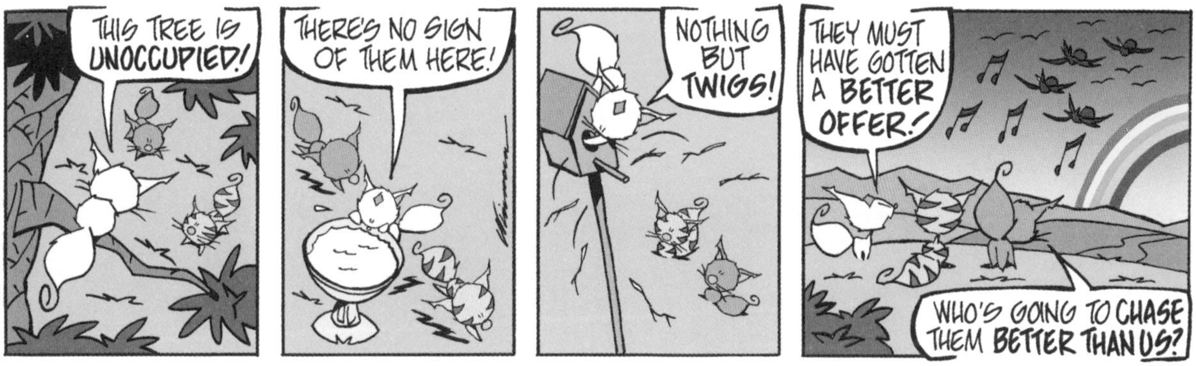
THIS TREE IS UNOCCUPIED!
THERE'S NO SIGN OF THEM HERE!
NOTHING BUT TWIGS!
THEY MUST HAVE GOTTEN A BETTER OFFER!
WHO'S GOING TO CHASE THEM BETTER THAN US?

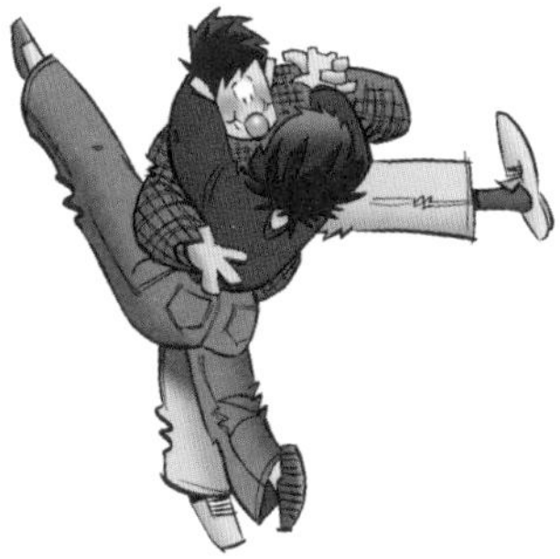

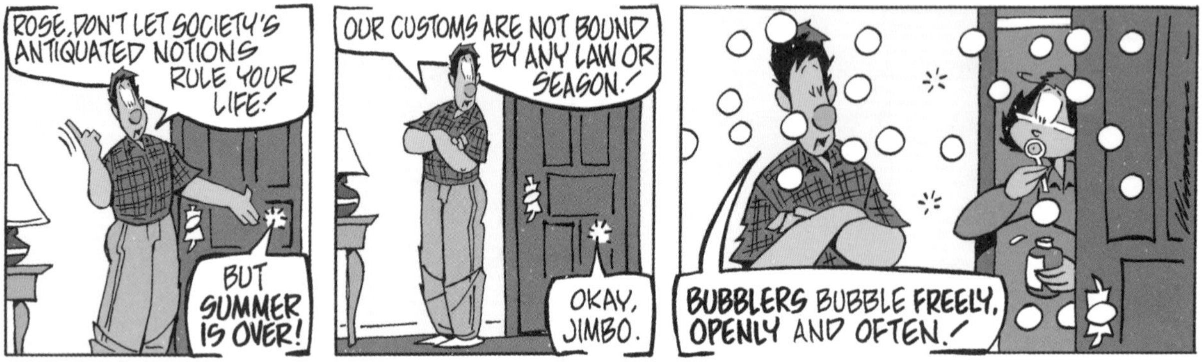
ROSE, DON'T LET SOCIETY'S ANTIQUATED NOTIONS RULE YOUR LIFE!
BUT SUMMER IS OVER!
OUR CUSTOMS ARE NOT BOUND BY ANY LAW OR SEASON!
OKAY, JIMBO.
BUBBLERS BUBBLE FREELY, OPENLY AND OFTEN!

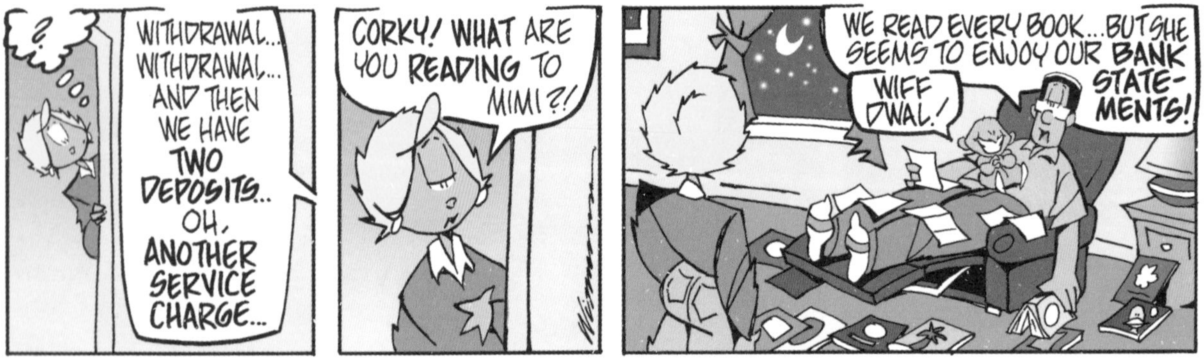
?
WITHDRAWAL... WITHDRAWAL... AND THEN WE HAVE TWO DEPOSITS... OH, ANOTHER SERVICE CHARGE...
CORKY! WHAT ARE YOU READING TO MIMI?!
WE READ EVERY BOOK... BUT SHE SEEMS TO ENJOY OUR BANK STATEMENTS!
WIFF DWAL!

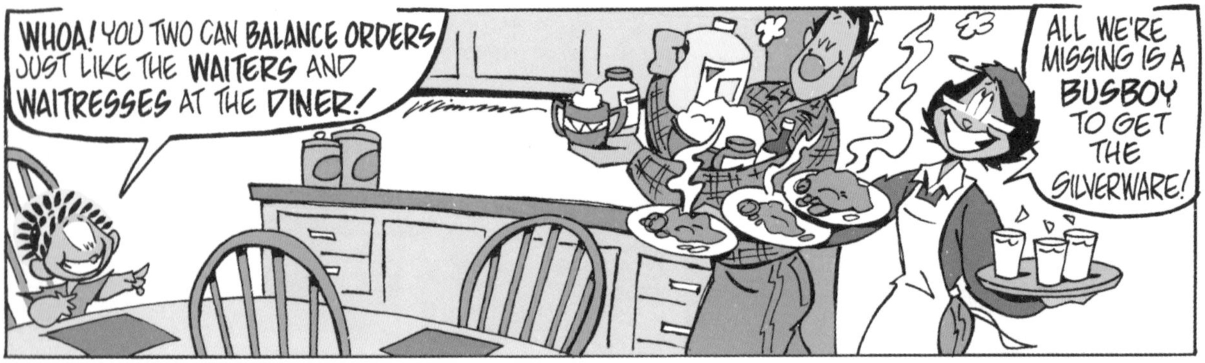
WHOA! YOU TWO CAN BALANCE ORDERS JUST LIKE THE WAITERS AND WAITRESSES AT THE DINER!
ALL WE'RE MISSING IS A BUSBOY TO GET THE SILVERWARE!

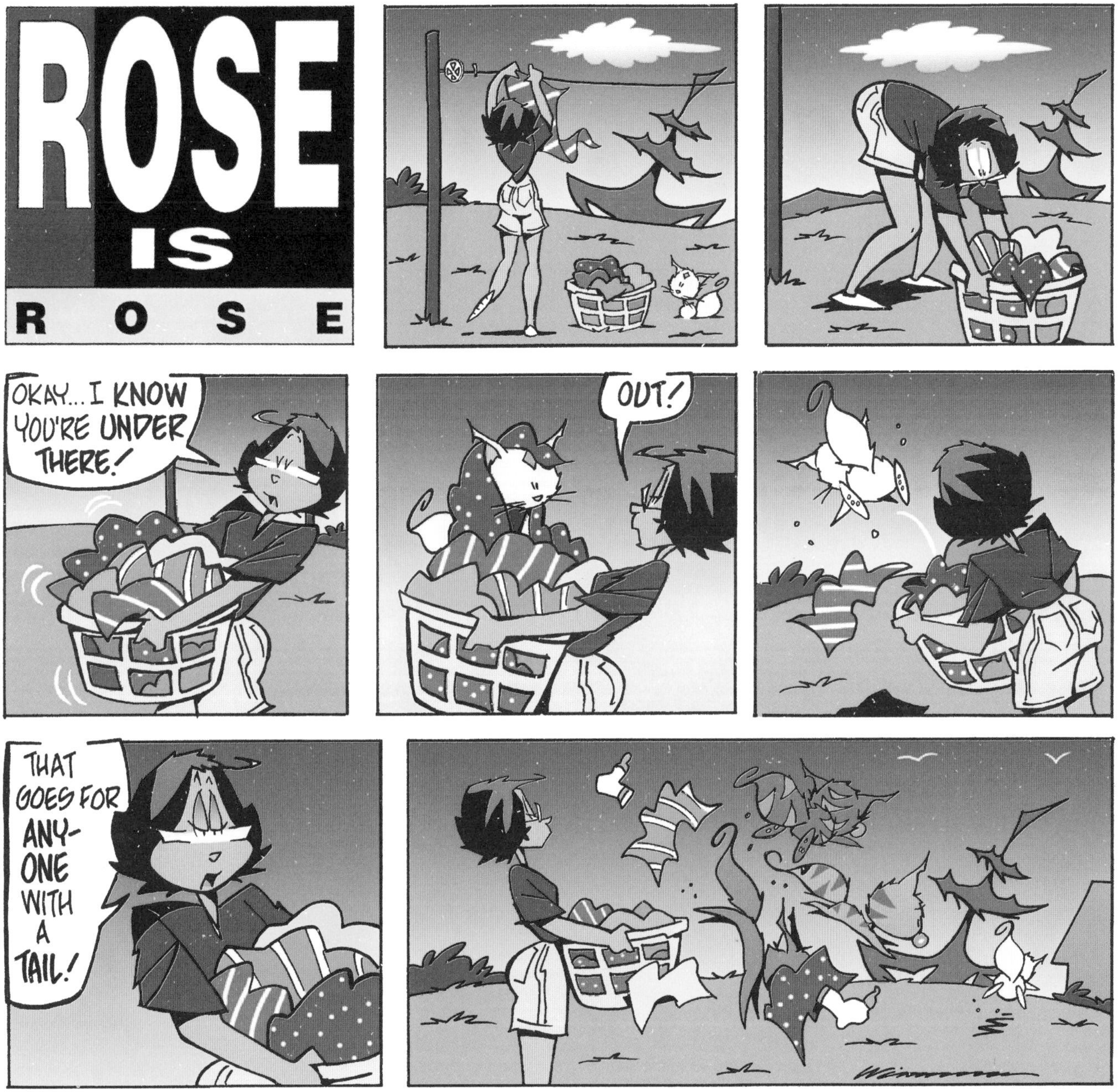
ROSE IS ROSE
OKAY... I KNOW YOU'RE UNDER THERE!
OUT!
THAT GOES FOR ANY-ONE WITH A TAIL!

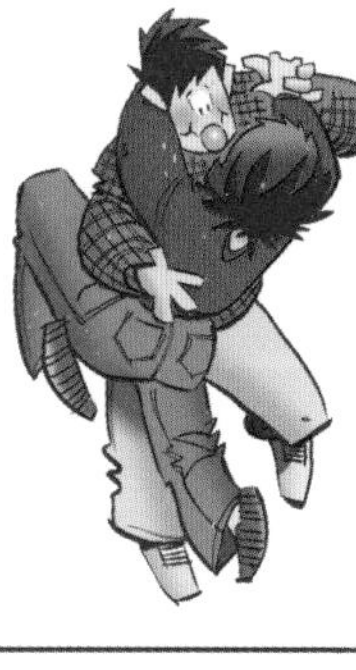

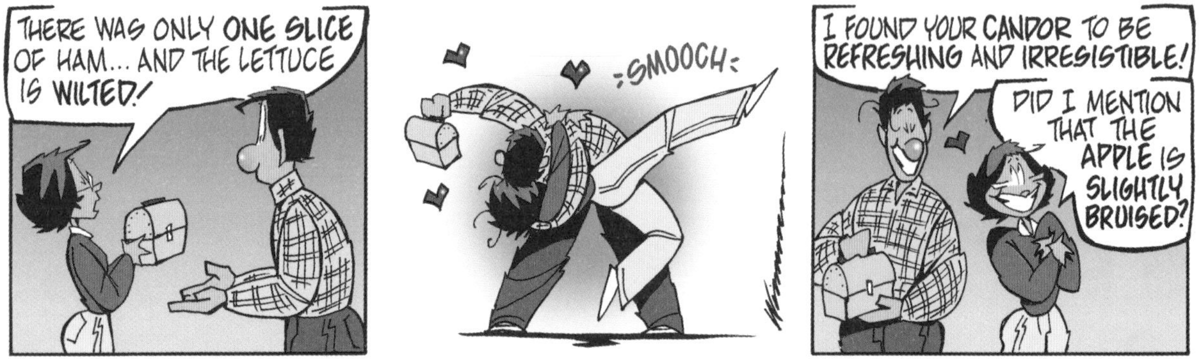
THERE WAS ONLY ONE SLICE OF HAM... AND THE LETTUCE IS WILTED!
:SMOOCH:
I FOUND YOUR CANDOR TO BE REFRESHING AND IRRESISTIBLE!
DID I MENTION THAT THE APPLE IS SLIGHTLY BRUISED?

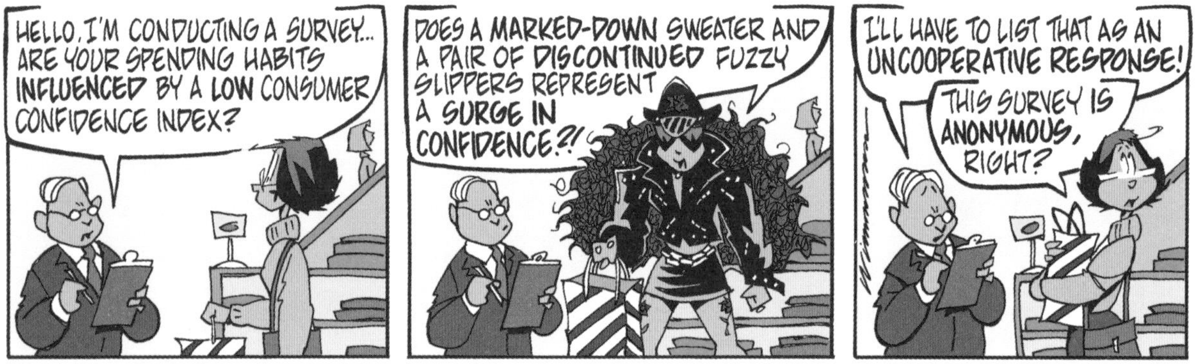
HELLO, I'M CONDUCTING A SURVEY... ARE YOUR SPENDING HABITS INFLUENCED BY A LOW CONSUMER CONFIDENCE INDEX?
DOES A MARKED-DOWN SWEATER AND A PAIR OF DISCONTINUED FUZZY SLIPPERS REPRESENT A SURGE IN CONFIDENCE?!
I'LL HAVE TO LIST THAT AS AN UNCOOPERATIVE RESPONSE!
THIS SURVEY IS ANONYMOUS, RIGHT?

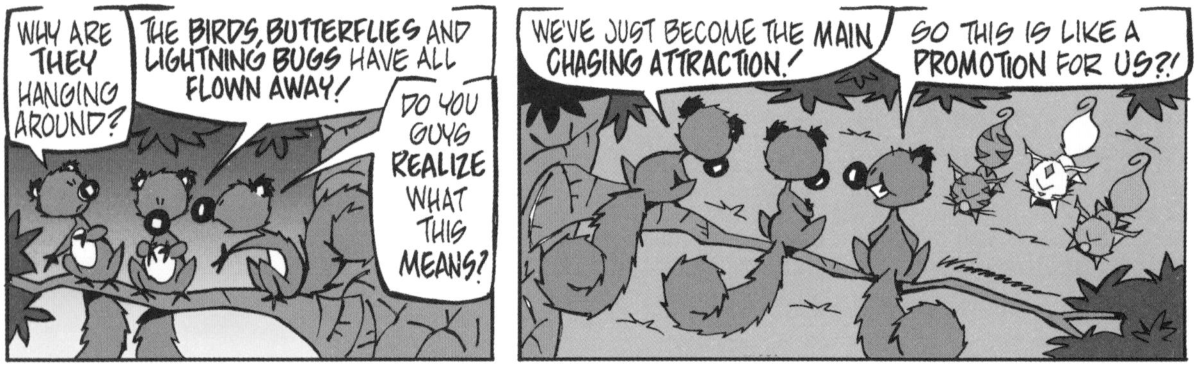
WHY ARE THEY HANGING AROUND?
THE BIRDS, BUTTERFLIES AND LIGHTNING BUGS HAVE ALL FLOWN AWAY!
DO YOU GUYS REALIZE WHAT THIS MEANS?
WE'VE JUST BECOME THE MAIN CHASING ATTRACTION!
SO THIS IS LIKE A PROMOTION FOR US?!

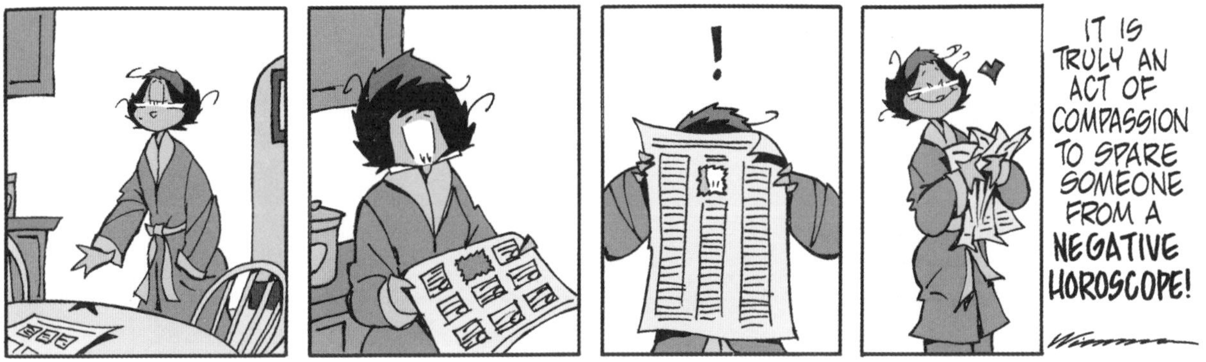
!
IT IS TRULY AN ACT OF COMPASSION TO SPARE SOMEONE FROM A NEGATIVE HOROSCOPE!

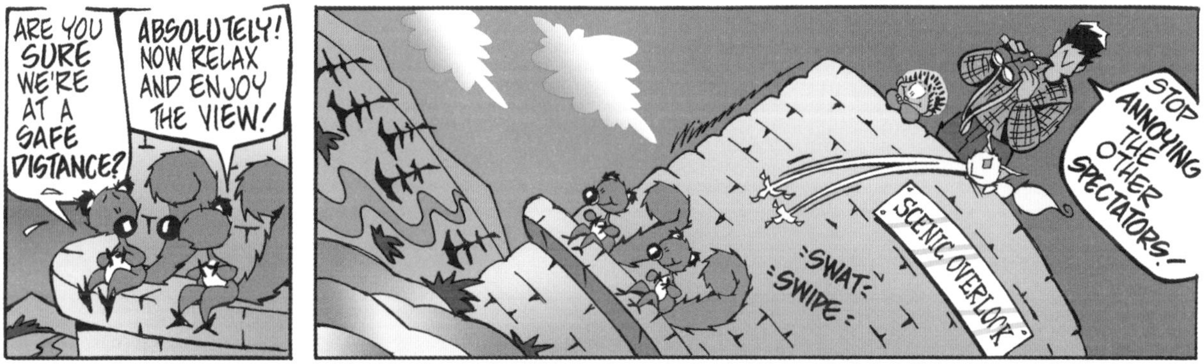
ARE YOU SURE WE'RE AT A SAFE DISTANCE?
ABSOLUTELY! NOW RELAX AND ENJOY THE VIEW!
STOP ANNOYING THE OTHER SPECTATORS!
SCENIC OVERLOOK
SWAT
SWIPE

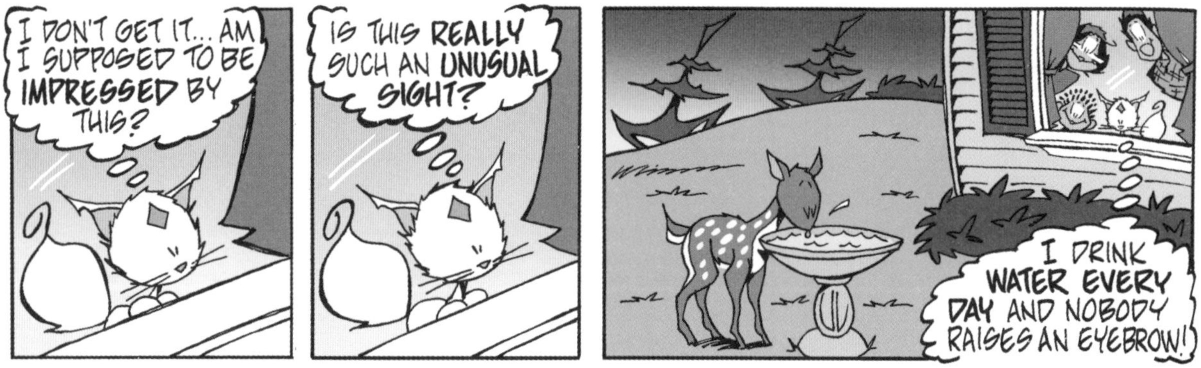
I DON'T GET IT... AM I SUPPOSED TO BE IMPRESSED BY THIS?
IS THIS REALLY SUCH AN UNUSUAL SIGHT?
I DRINK WATER EVERY DAY AND NOBODY RAISES AN EYEBROW!

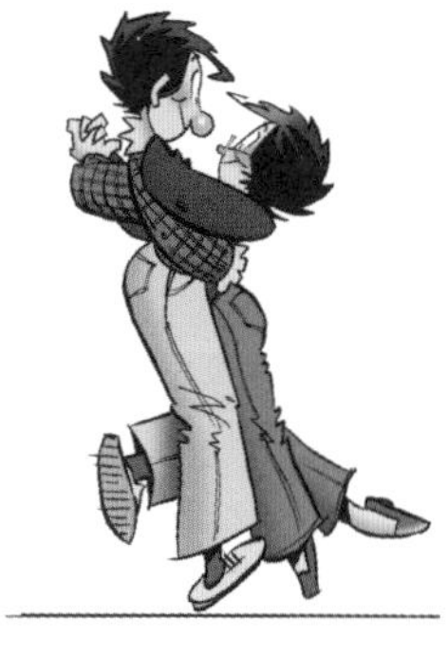

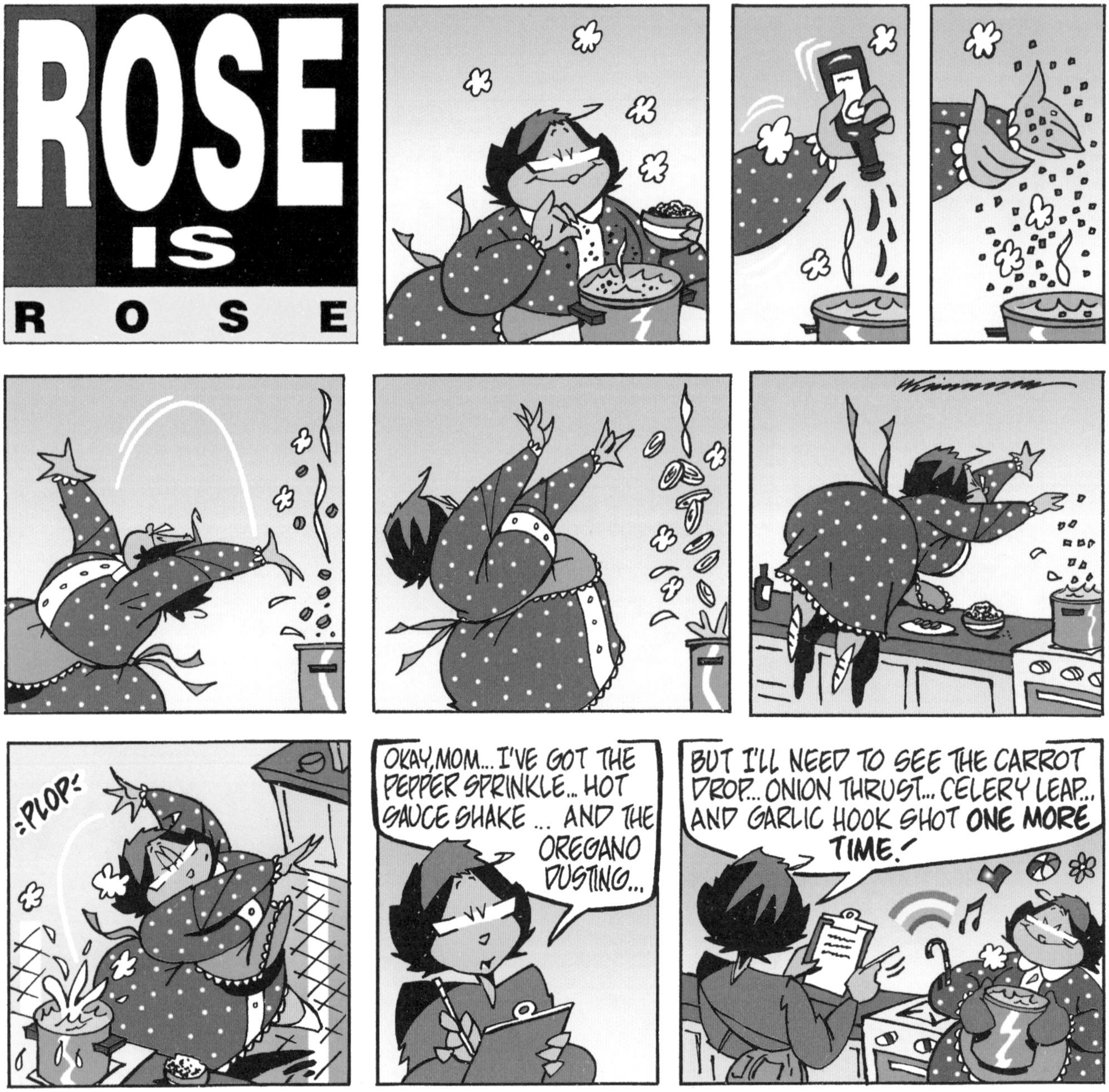
ROSE IS ROSE
PLOP!
OKAY, MOM... I'VE GOT THE PEPPER SPRINKLE... HOT SAUCE SHAKE ... AND THE OREGANO DUSTING...
BUT I'LL NEED TO SEE THE CARROT DROP... ONION THRUST... CELERY LEAP... AND GARLIC HOOK SHOT ONE MORE TIME!

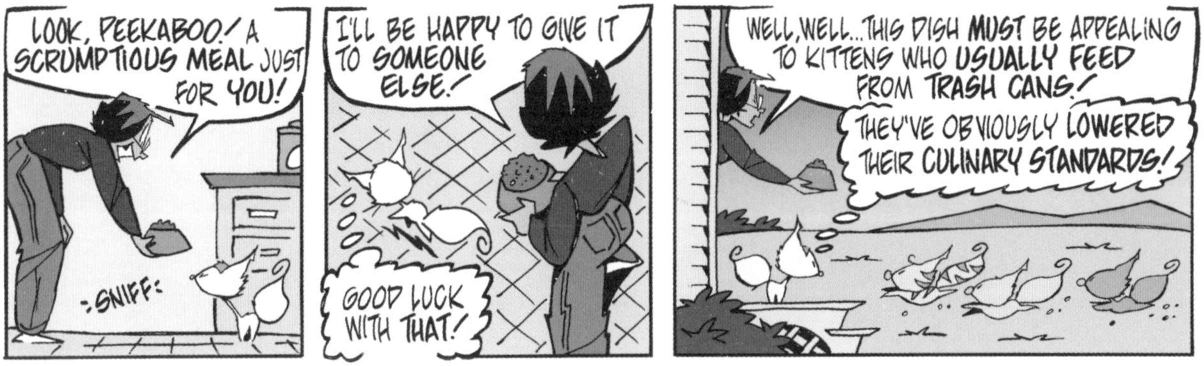
LOOK, PEEKABOO! A SCRUMPTIOUS MEAL JUST FOR YOU!
SNIFF
I'LL BE HAPPY TO GIVE IT TO SOMEONE ELSE!
GOOD LUCK WITH THAT!
WELL, WELL... THIS DISH MUST BE APPEALING TO KITTENS WHO USUALLY FEED FROM TRASH CANS!
THEY'VE OBVIOUSLY LOWERED THEIR CULINARY STANDARDS!

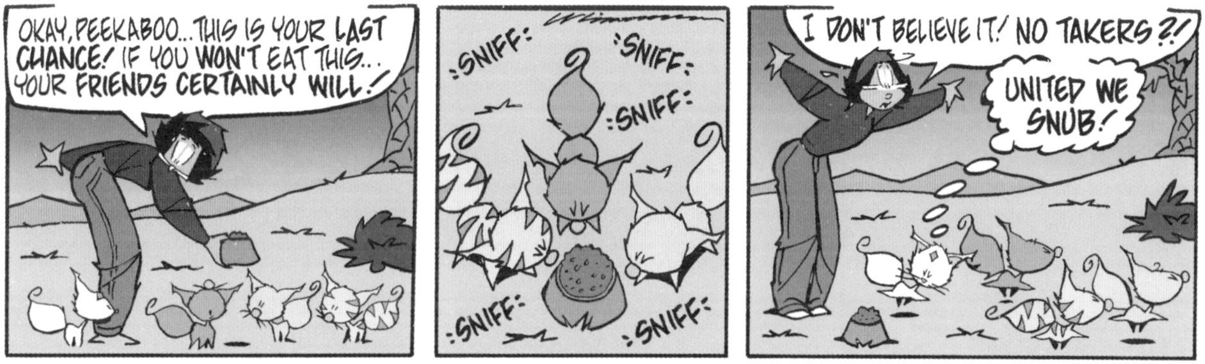
OKAY, PEEKABOO... THIS IS YOUR LAST CHANCE! IF YOU WON'T EAT THIS... YOUR FRIENDS CERTAINLY WILL!
SNIFF
SNIFF
SNIFF
SNIFF
SNIFF
I DON'T BELIEVE IT! NO TAKERS?!
UNITED WE SNUB!

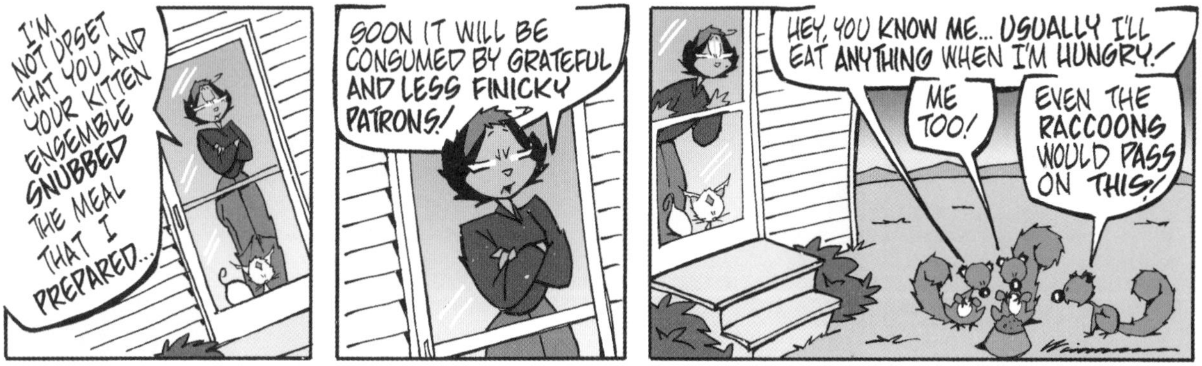
I'M NOT UPSET THAT YOU AND YOUR KITTEN ENSEMBLE SNUBBED THE MEAL THAT I PREPARED...
SOON IT WILL BE CONSUMED BY GRATEFUL AND LESS FINICKY PATRONS!
HEY, YOU KNOW ME... USUALLY I'LL EAT ANYTHING WHEN I'M HUNGRY!
ME TOO!
EVEN THE RACCOONS WOULD PASS ON THIS!

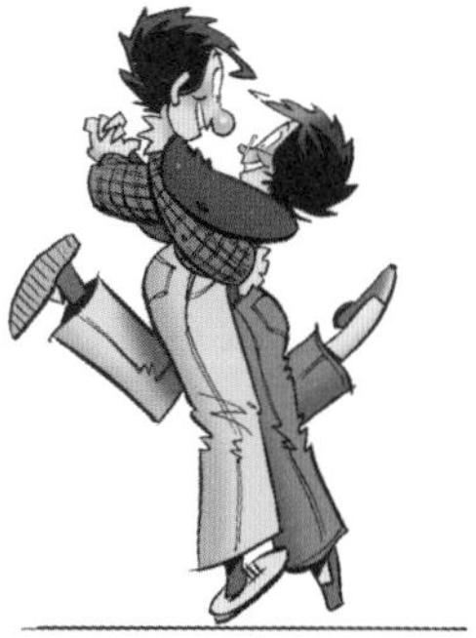

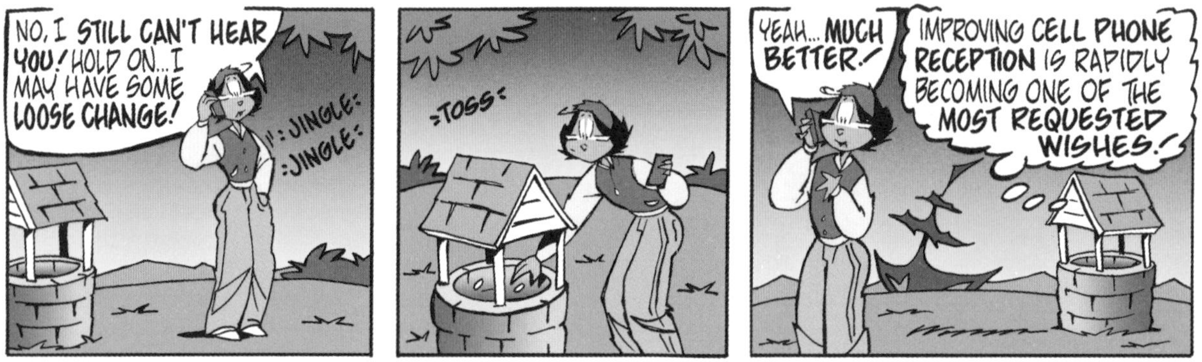
NO, I STILL CAN'T HEAR YOU! HOLD ON... I MAY HAVE SOME LOOSE CHANGE!
:JINGLE:
:JINGLE:
:TOSS:
YEAH... MUCH BETTER!
IMPROVING CELL PHONE RECEPTION IS RAPIDLY BECOMING ONE OF THE MOST REQUESTED WISHES!

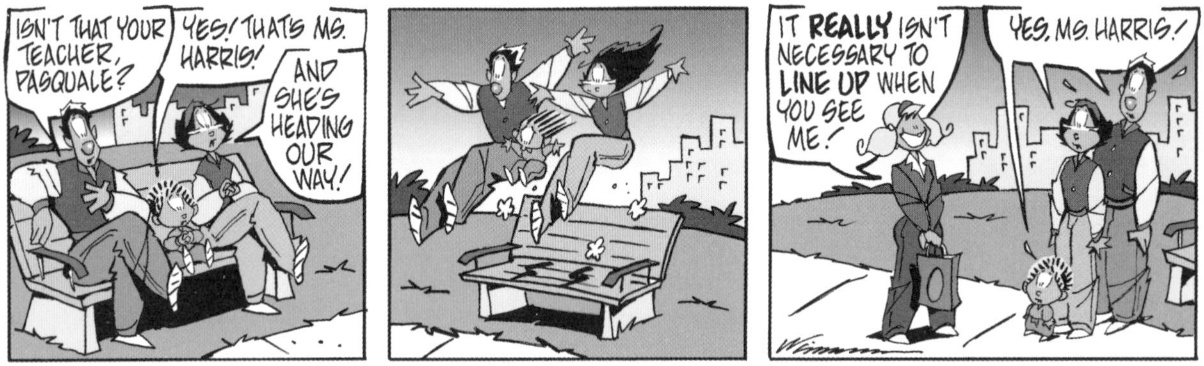
ISN'T THAT YOUR TEACHER, PASQUALE?
YES! THAT'S MS. HARRIS!
AND SHE'S HEADING OUR WAY!
IT REALLY ISN'T NECESSARY TO LINE UP WHEN YOU SEE ME!
YES, MS. HARRIS!

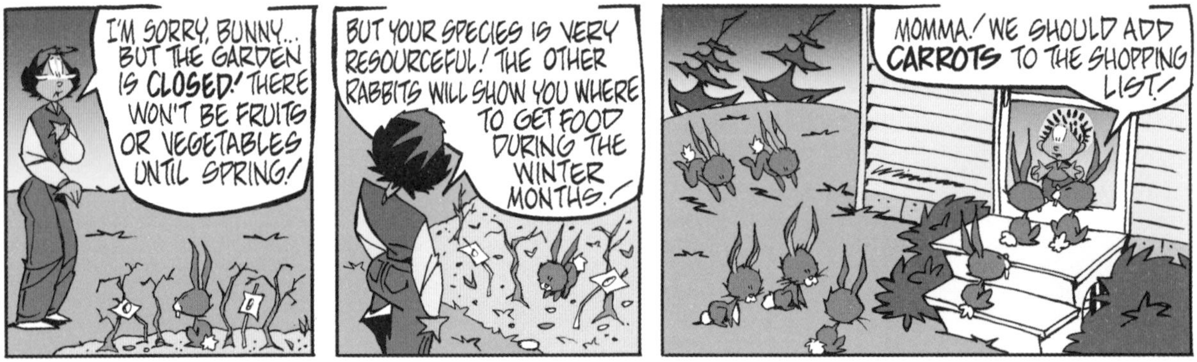
I'M SORRY, BUNNY... BUT THE GARDEN IS CLOSED! THERE WON'T BE FRUITS OR VEGETABLES UNTIL SPRING!
BUT YOUR SPECIES IS VERY RESOURCEFUL! THE OTHER RABBITS WILL SHOW YOU WHERE TO GET FOOD DURING THE WINTER MONTHS!
MOMMA! WE SHOULD ADD CARROTS TO THE SHOPPING LIST!

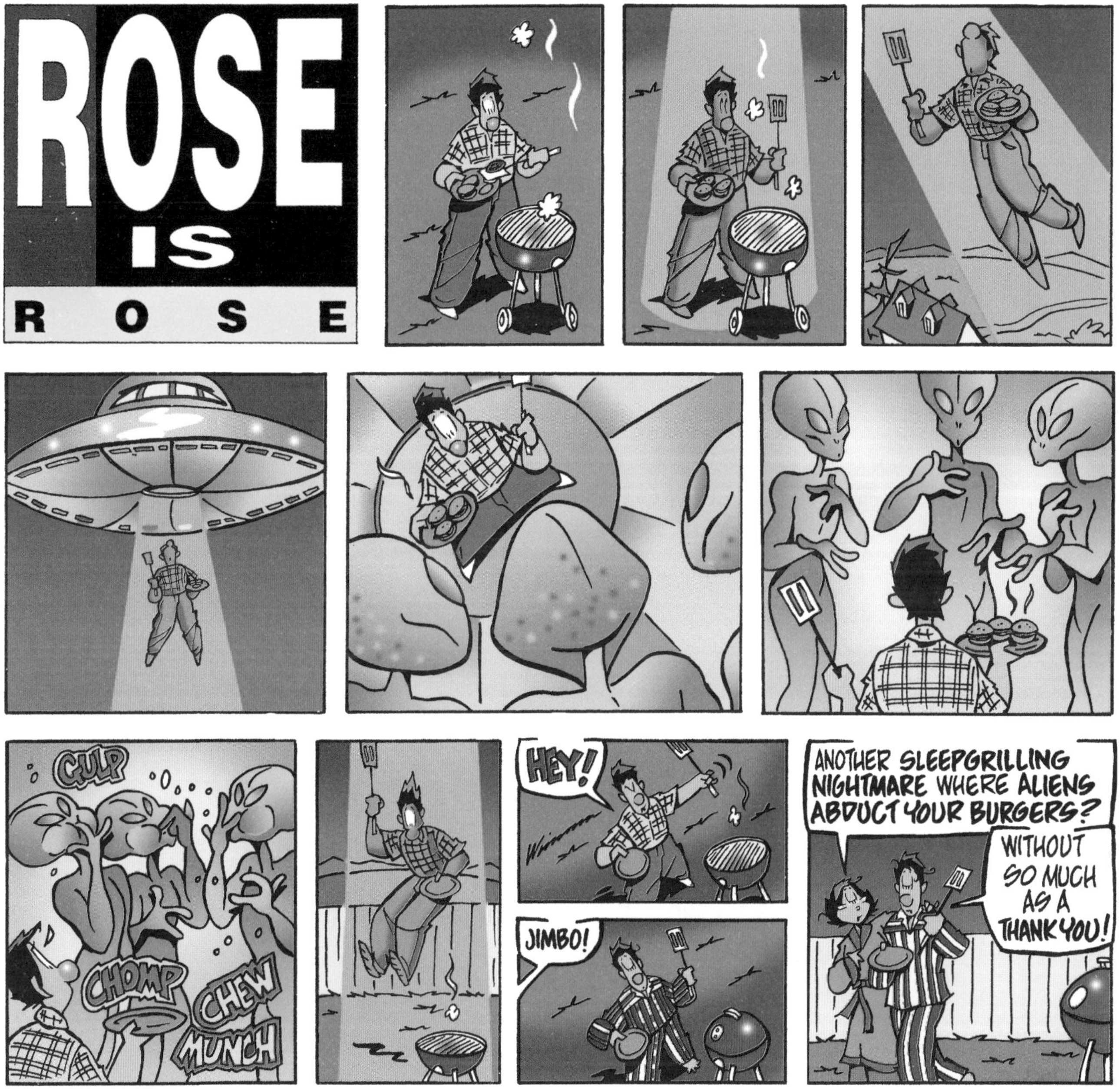
ROSE IS ROSE
GULP
CHOMP
CHEW
MUNCH
HEY!
JIMBO!
ANOTHER SLEEPGRILLING NIGHTMARE WHERE ALIENS ABDUCT YOUR BURGERS?
WITHOUT SO MUCH AS A THANK YOU!

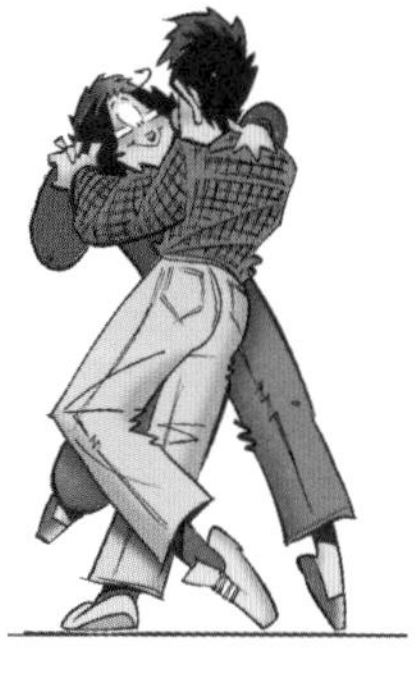

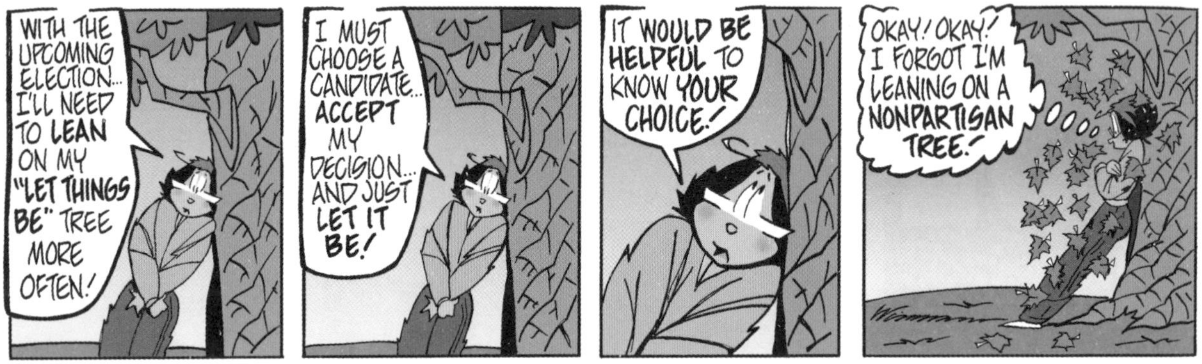
WITH THE UPCOMING ELECTION... I'LL NEED TO LEAN ON MY "LET THINGS BE" TREE MORE OFTEN!
I MUST CHOOSE A CANDIDATE... ACCEPT MY DECISION... AND JUST LET IT BE!
IT WOULD BE HELPFUL TO KNOW YOUR CHOICE!
OKAY! OKAY! I FORGOT I'M LEANING ON A NONPARTISAN TREE!

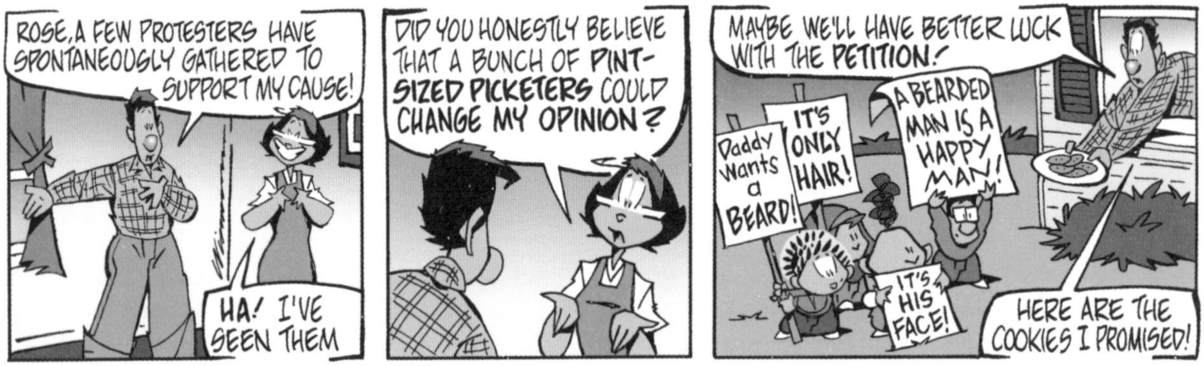
ROSE, A FEW PROTESTERS HAVE SPONTANEOUSLY GATHERED TO SUPPORT MY CAUSE!
HA! I'VE SEEN THEM
DID YOU HONESTLY BELIEVE THAT A BUNCH OF PINT-SIZED PICKETERS COULD CHANGE MY OPINION?
MAYBE WE'LL HAVE BETTER LUCK WITH THE PETITION!
Daddy Wants a BEARD!
IT'S ONLY HAIR!
A BEARDED MAN IS A HAPPY MAN!
IT'S HIS FACE!
HERE ARE THE COOKIES I PROMISED!

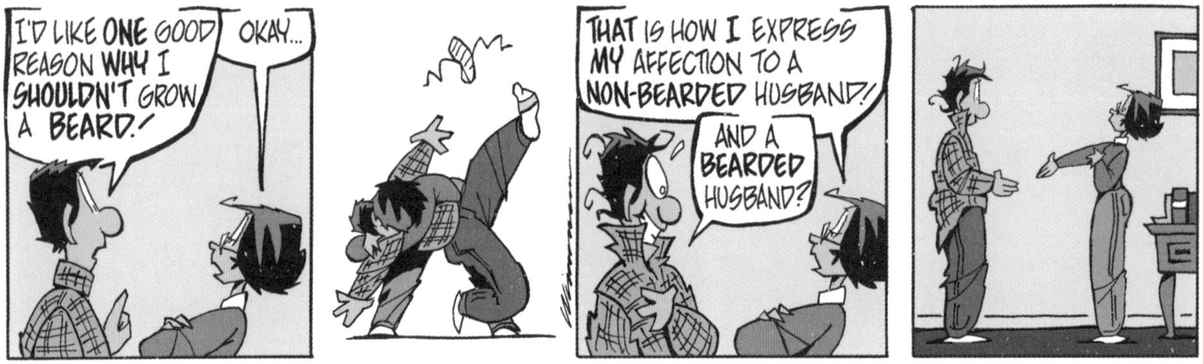
I'D LIKE ONE GOOD REASON WHY I SHOULDN'T GROW A BEARD!
OKAY...
THAT IS HOW I EXPRESS MY AFFECTION TO A NON-BEARDED HUSBAND!
AND A BEARDED HUSBAND?

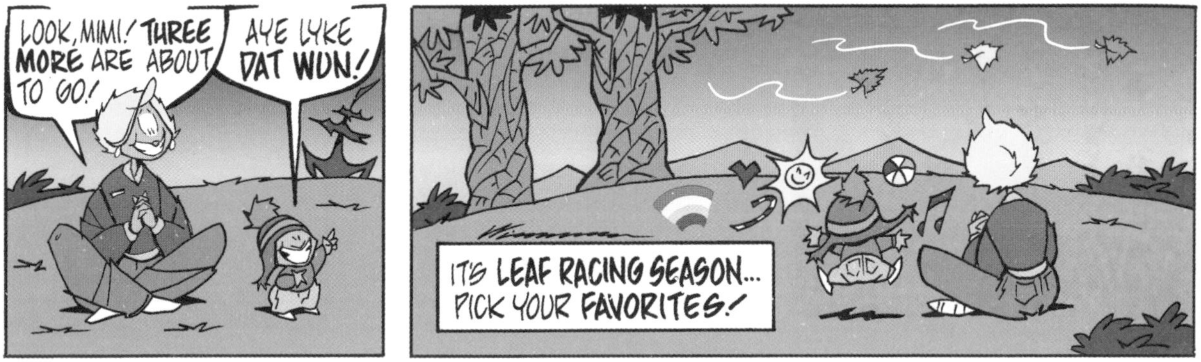
LOOK, MIMI! THREE MORE ARE ABOUT TO GO!
AYE LYKE DAT WUN!
IT'S LEAF RACING SEASON... PICK YOUR FAVORITES!

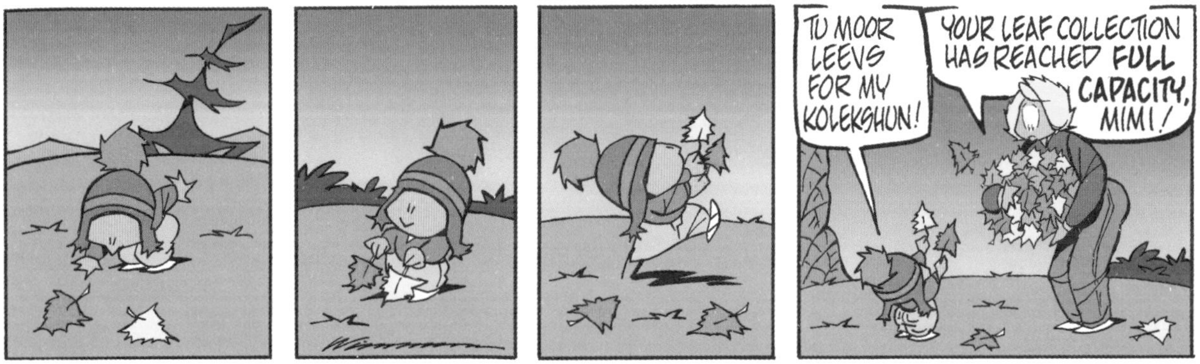
TU MOOR LEEVS FOR MY KOLEKSHUN!
YOUR LEAF COLLECTION HAS REACHED FULL CAPACITY, MIMI!

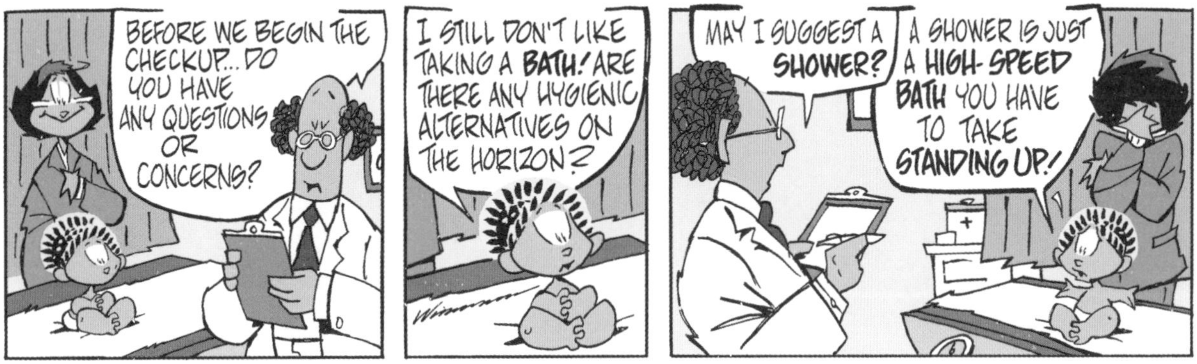
BEFORE WE BEGIN THE CHECKUP... DO YOU HAVE ANY QUESTIONS OR CONCERNS?
I STILL DON'T LIKE TAKING A BATH! ARE THERE ANY HYGIENIC ALTERNATIVES ON THE HORIZON?
MAY I SUGGEST A SHOWER?
A SHOWER IS JUST A HIGH-SPEED BATH YOU HAVE TO TAKE STANDING UP!

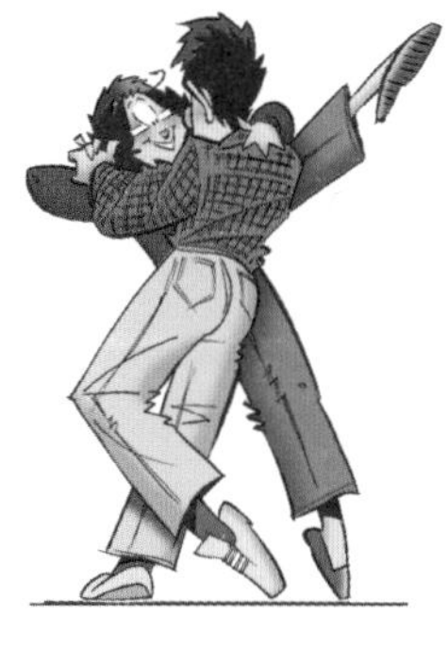

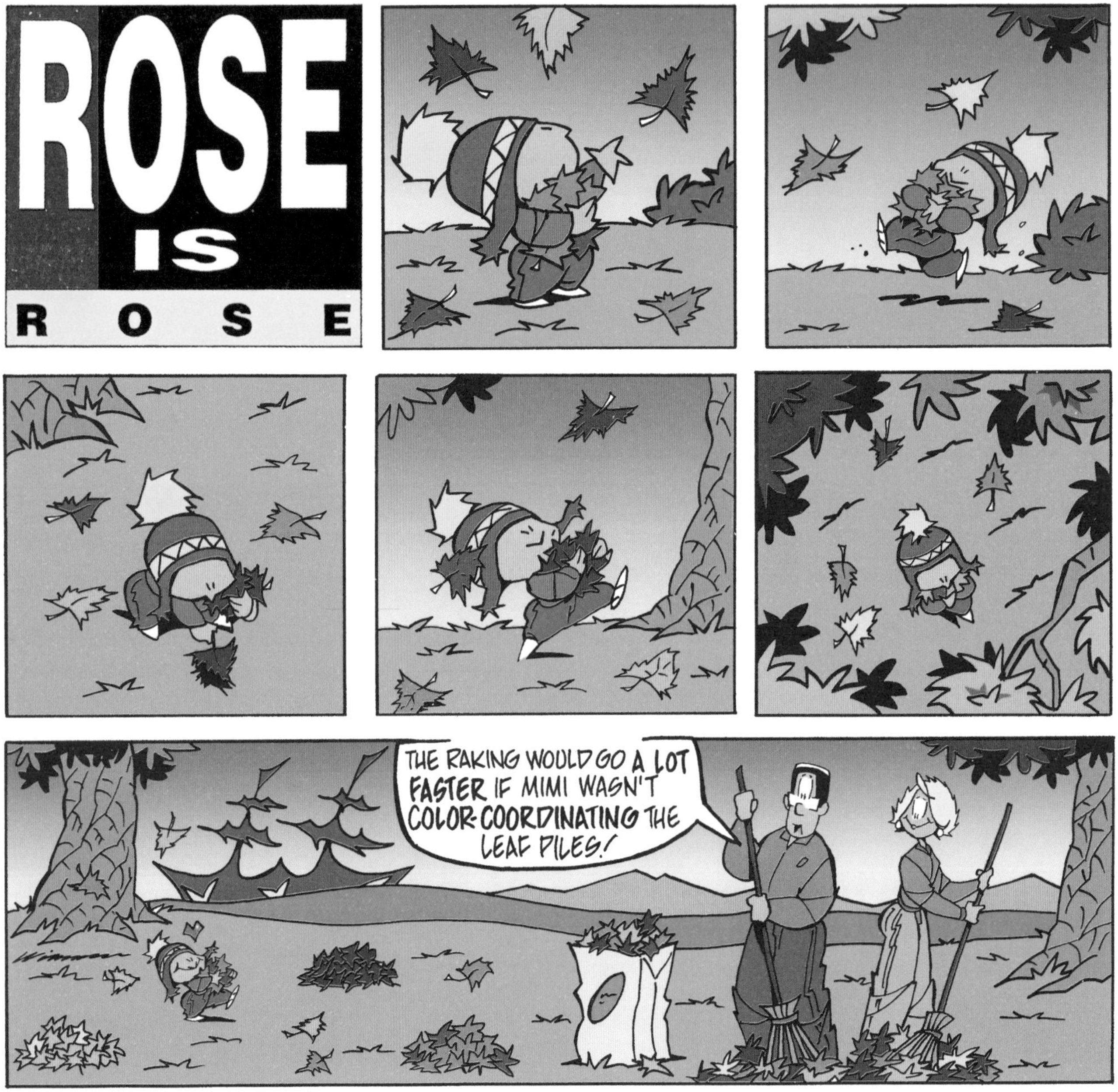
ROSE IS ROSE
THE RAKING WOULD GO A LOT FASTER IF MIMI WASN'T COLOR-COORDINATING THE LEAF PILES!

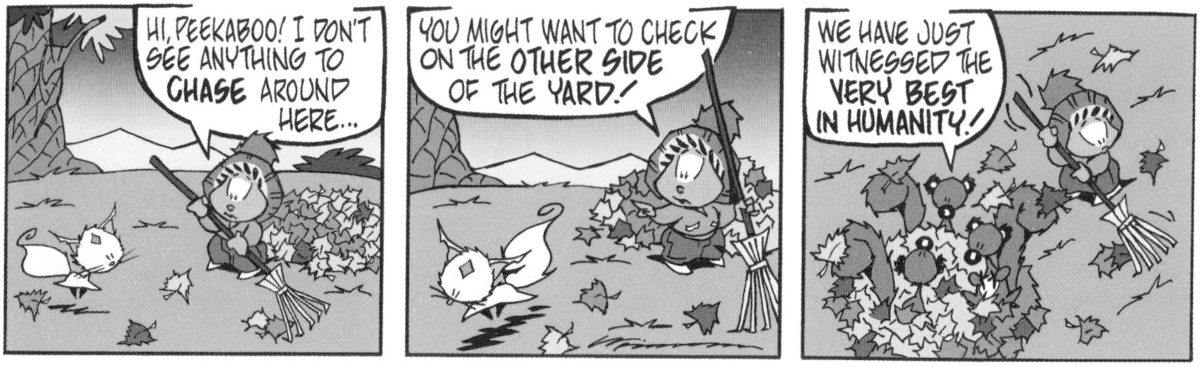
HI, PEEKABOO! I DON'T SEE ANYTHING TO CHASE AROUND HERE...
YOU MIGHT WANT TO CHECK ON THE OTHER SIDE OF THE YARD!
WE HAVE JUST WITNESSED THE VERY BEST IN HUMANITY!

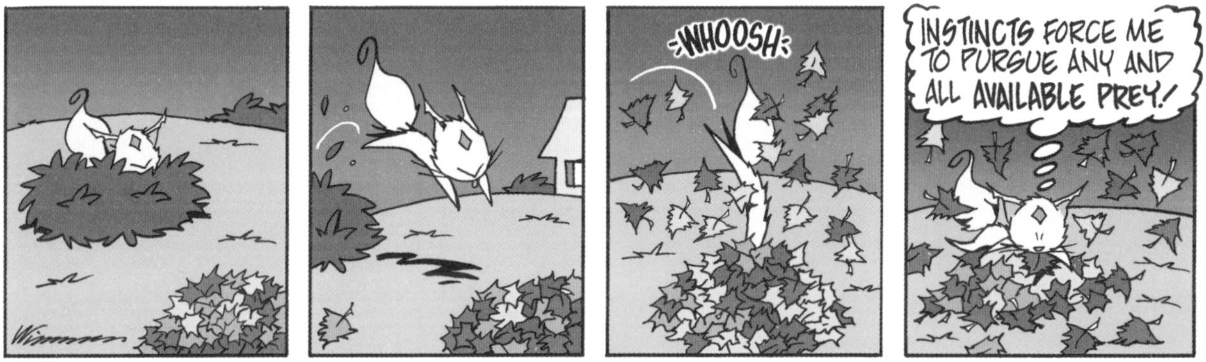
WHOOSH
INSTINCTS FORCE ME TO PURSUE ANY AND ALL AVAILABLE PREY!

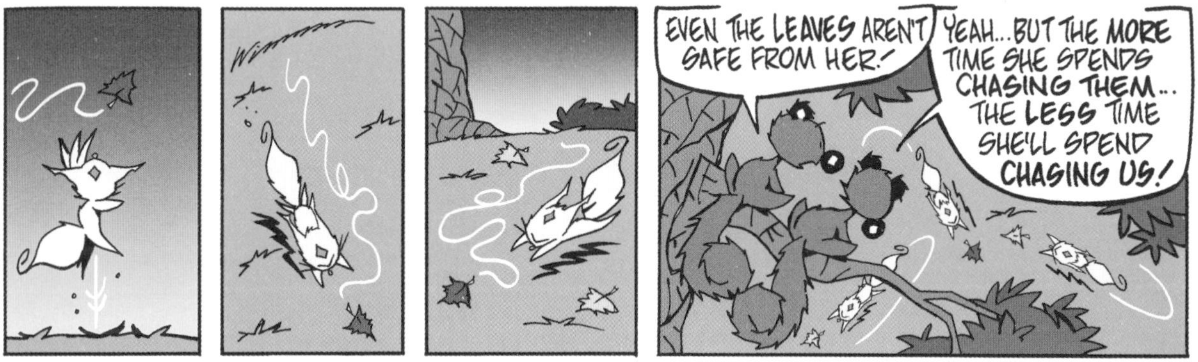
EVEN THE LEAVES AREN'T SAFE FROM HER!
YEAH...BUT THE MORE TIME SHE SPENDS CHASING THEM... THE LESS TIME SHE'LL SPEND CHASING US!

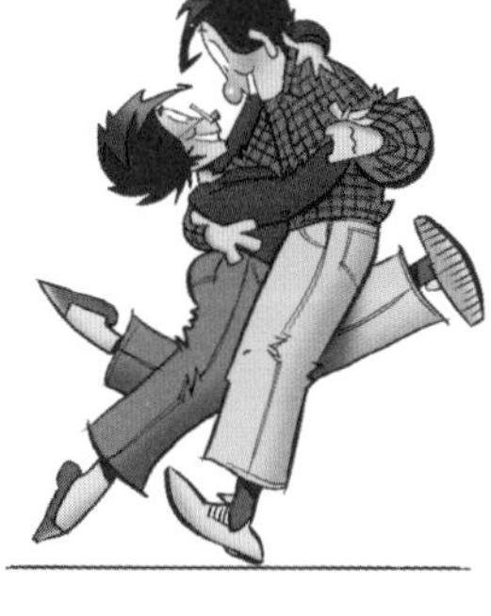

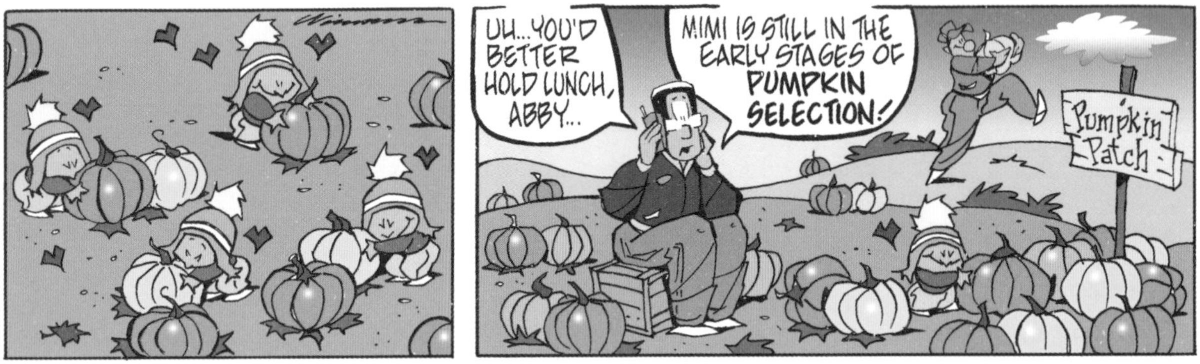
UH... YOU'D BETTER HOLD LUNCH, ABBY...
MIMI IS STILL IN THE EARLY STAGES OF PUMPKIN SELECTION!
Pumpkin Patch

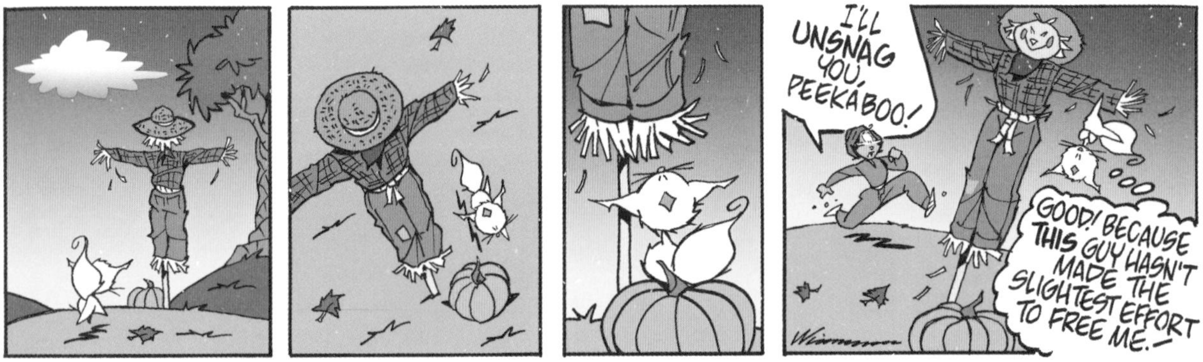
I'LL UNSNAG YOU, PEEKABOO!
GOOD! BECAUSE THIS GUY HASN'T MADE THE SLIGHTEST EFFORT TO FREE ME.

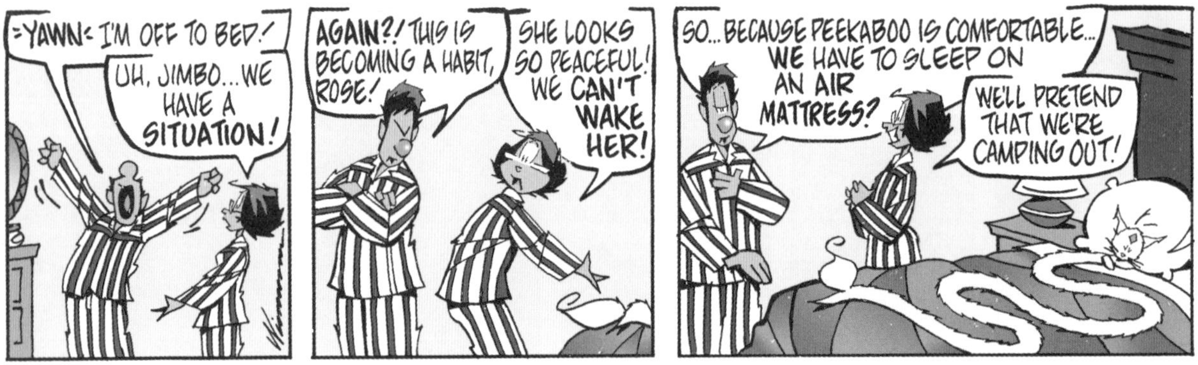
=YAWN= I'M OFF TO BED!
UH, JIMBO... WE HAVE A SITUATION!
AGAIN?! THIS IS BECOMING A HABIT, ROSE!
SHE LOOKS SO PEACEFUL! WE CAN'T WAKE HER!
SO... BECAUSE PEEKABOO IS COMFORTABLE... WE HAVE TO SLEEP ON AN AIR MATTRESS?
WE'LL PRETEND THAT WE'RE CAMPING OUT!

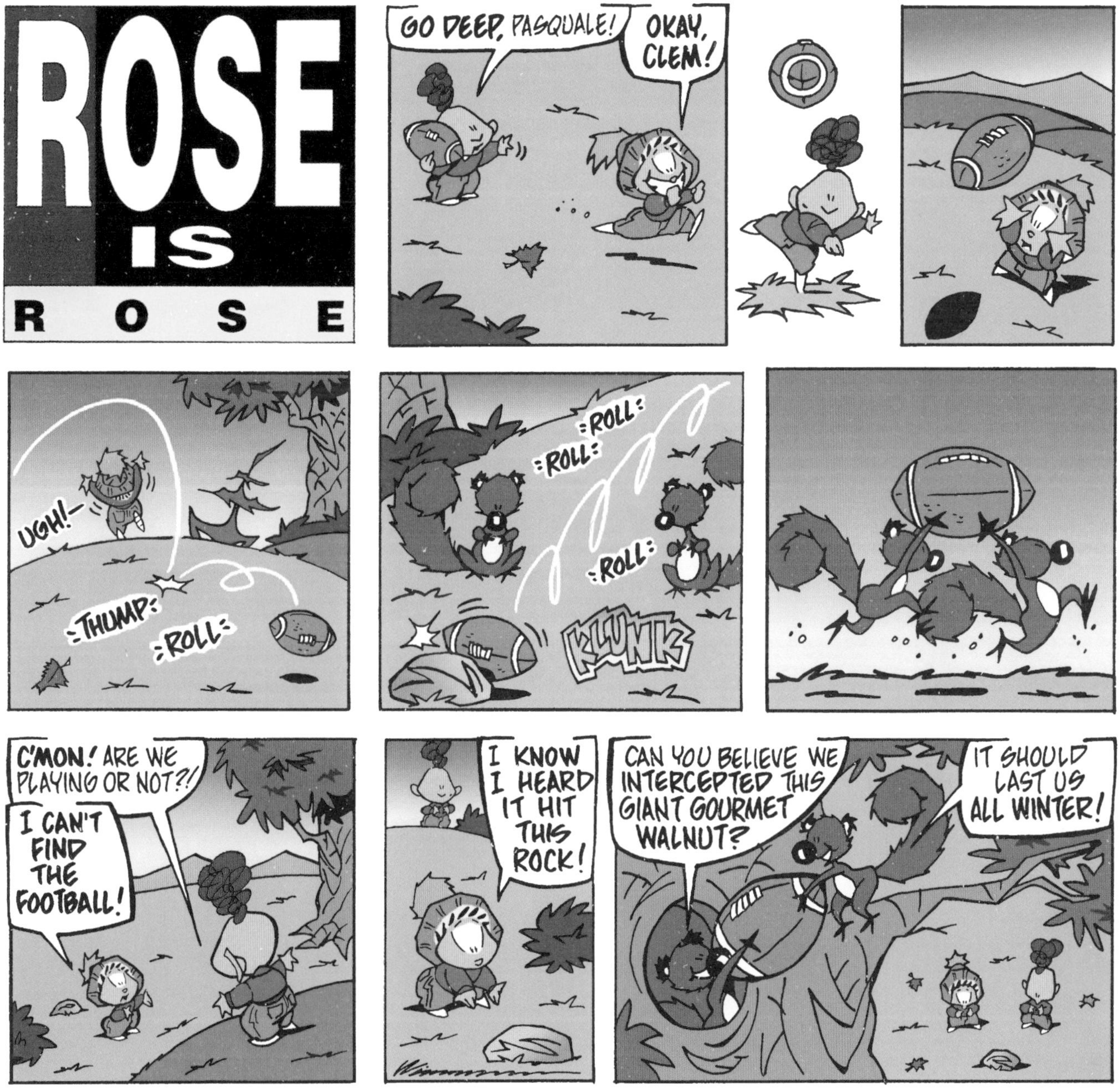
ROSE IS ROSE
GO DEEP, PASQUALE!
OKAY, CLEM!
UGH!
THUMP
ROLL
ROLL
ROLL
ROLL
KLUNK
C'MON! ARE WE PLAYING OR NOT?!
I CAN'T FIND THE FOOTBALL!
I KNOW I HEARD IT HIT THIS ROCK!
CAN YOU BELIEVE WE INTERCEPTED THIS GIANT GOURMET WALNUT?
IT SHOULD LAST US ALL WINTER!

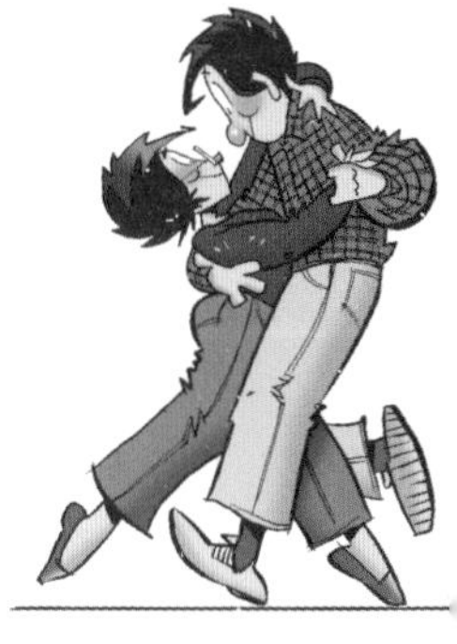

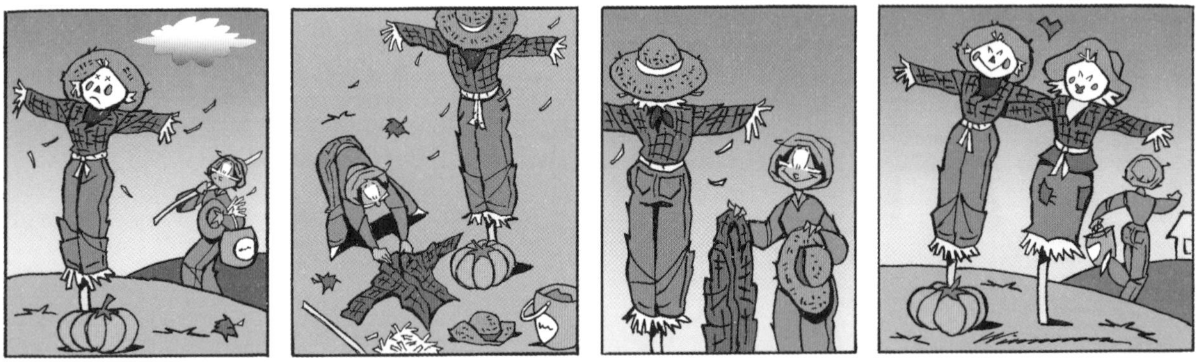

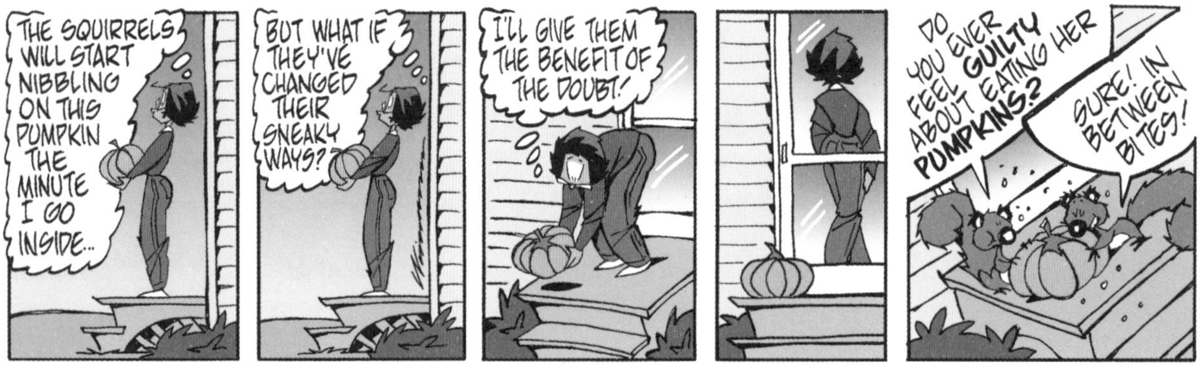
THE SQUIRRELS WILL START NIBBLING ON THIS PUMPKIN THE MINUTE I GO INSIDE...
BUT WHAT IF THEY'VE CHANGED THEIR SNEAKY WAYS?
I'LL GIVE THEM THE BENEFIT OF THE DOUBT!
DO YOU EVER FEEL GUILTY ABOUT EATING HER PUMPKINS?
SURE! IN BETWEEN BITES!

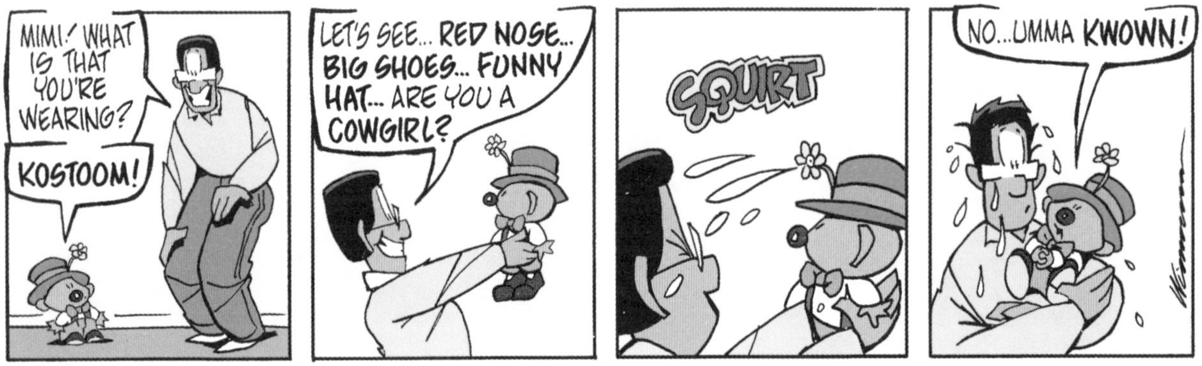
MIMI! WHAT IS THAT YOU'RE WEARING?
KOSTOOM!
LET'S SEE... RED NOSE... BIG SHOES... FUNNY HAT... ARE YOU A COWGIRL?
SQUIRT
NO...UMMA KWOWN!

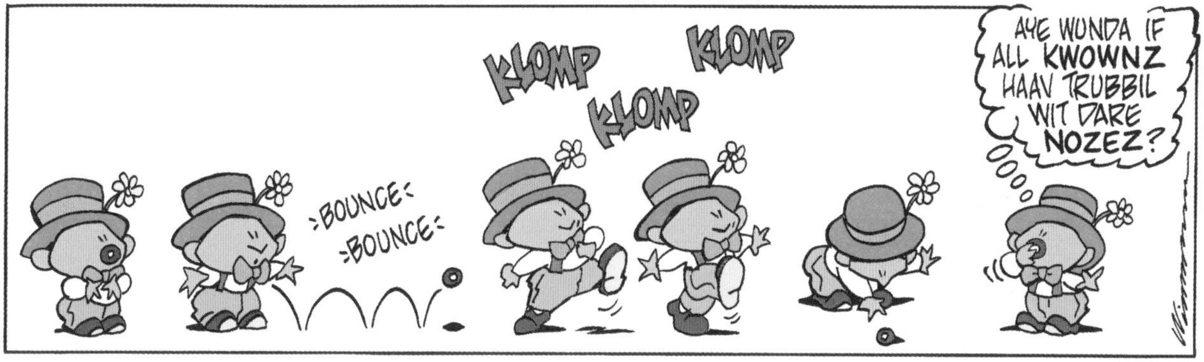

BOUNCE
BOUNCE
KLOMP
KLOMP
KLOMP
AYE WUNDA IF ALL KWOWNZ HAAV TRUBBIL WIT DARE NOZEZ?

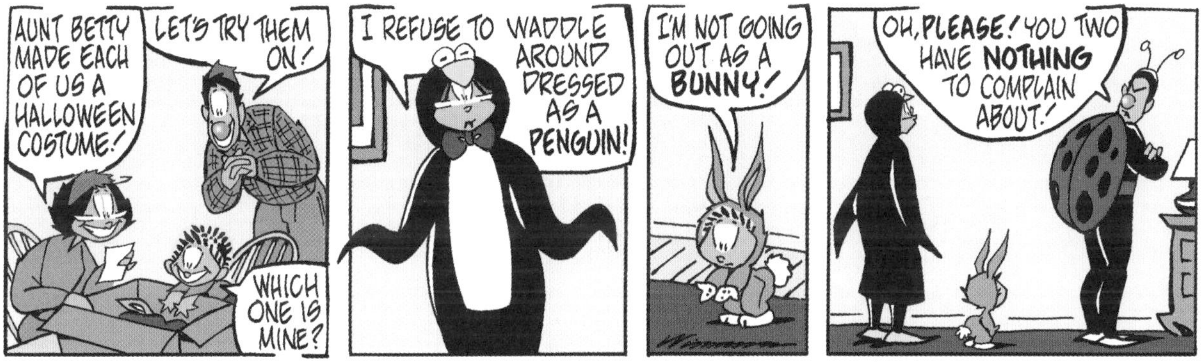

AUNT BETTY MADE EACH OF US A HALLOWEEN COSTUME!
LET'S TRY THEM ON!
WHICH ONE IS MINE?
I REFUSE TO WADDLE AROUND DRESSED AS A PENGUIN!
I'M NOT GOING OUT AS A BUNNY!
OH, PLEASE! YOU TWO HAVE NOTHING TO COMPLAIN ABOUT!

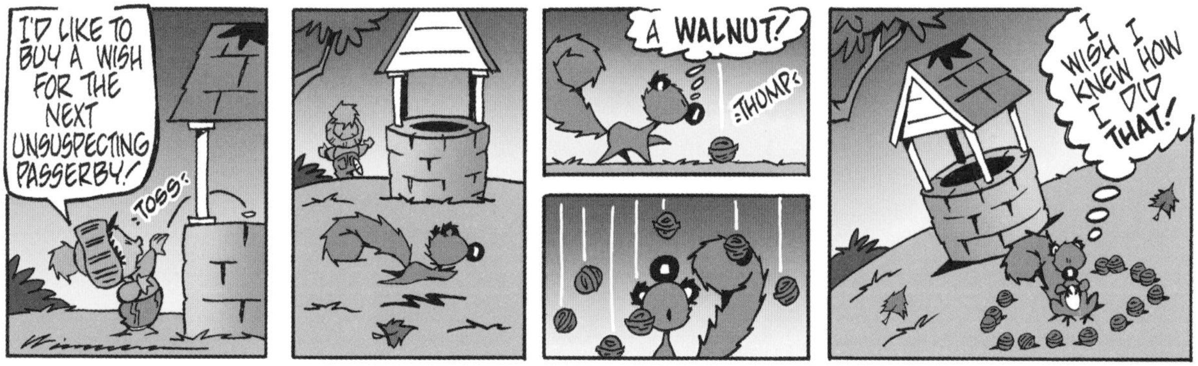

I'D LIKE TO BUY A WISH FOR THE NEXT UNSUSPECTING PASSERBY!
TOSS
A WALNUT!
THUMP
I WISH I KNEW HOW I DID THAT!

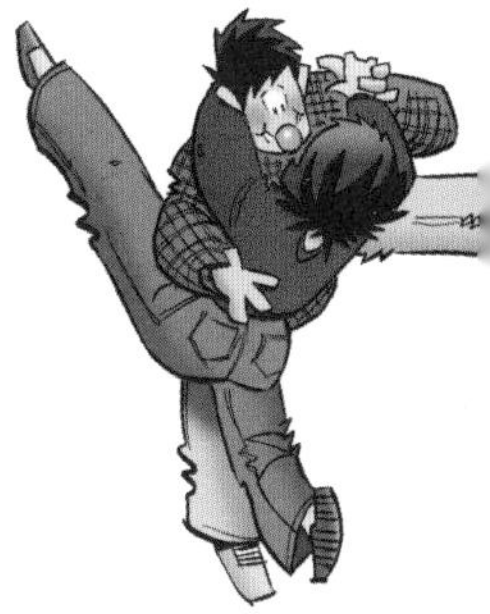

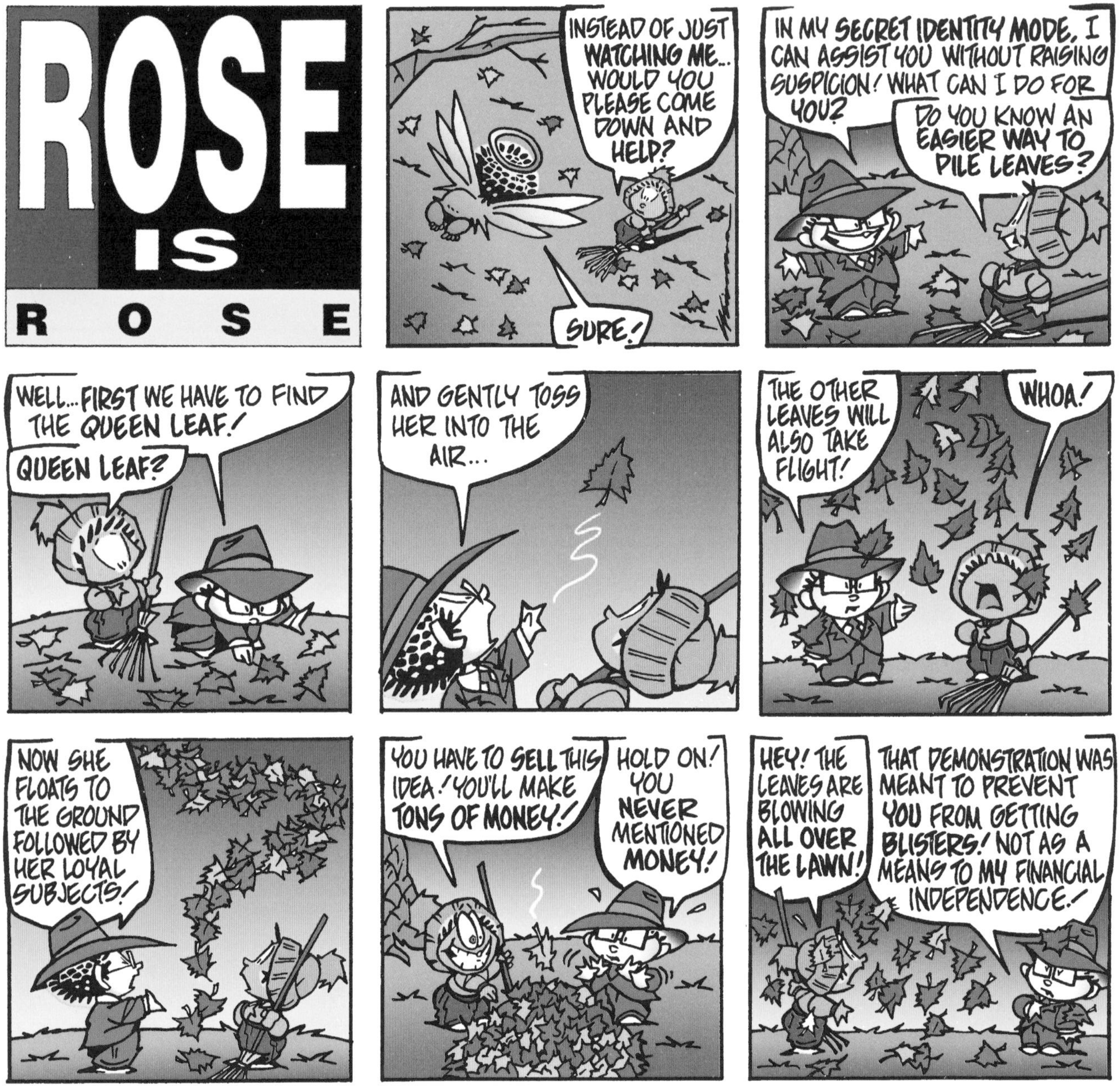
ROSE IS ROSE
INSTEAD OF JUST WATCHING ME... WOULD YOU PLEASE COME DOWN AND HELP?
SURE!
IN MY SECRET IDENTITY MODE, I CAN ASSIST YOU WITHOUT RAISING SUSPICION! WHAT CAN I DO FOR YOU?
DO YOU KNOW AN EASIER WAY TO PILE LEAVES?
WELL... FIRST WE HAVE TO FIND THE QUEEN LEAF!
QUEEN LEAF?
AND GENTLY TOSS HER INTO THE AIR...
THE OTHER LEAVES WILL ALSO TAKE FLIGHT!
WHOA!
NOW SHE FLOATS TO THE GROUND FOLLOWED BY HER LOYAL SUBJECTS!
YOU HAVE TO SELL THIS IDEA! YOU'LL MAKE TONS OF MONEY!
HOLD ON! YOU NEVER MENTIONED MONEY!
HEY! THE LEAVES ARE BLOWING ALL OVER THE LAWN!
THAT DEMONSTRATION WAS MEANT TO PREVENT YOU FROM GETTING BLISTERS! NOT AS A MEANS TO MY FINANCIAL INDEPENDENCE!

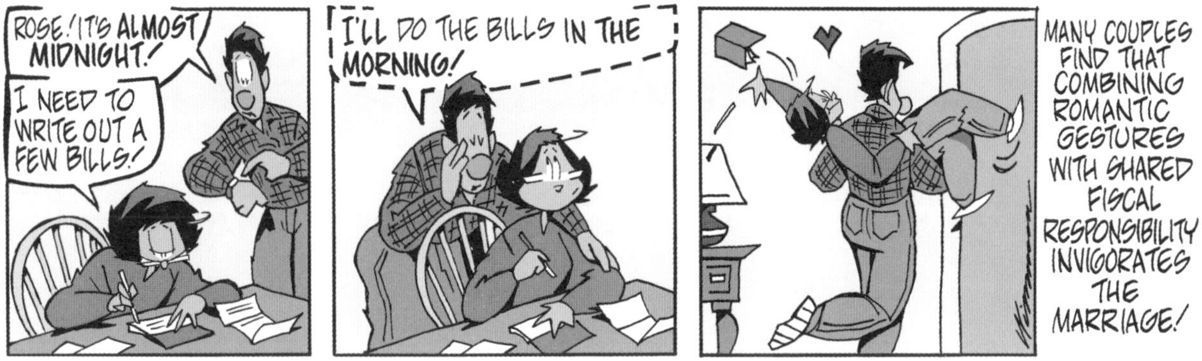
ROSE! IT'S ALMOST MIDNIGHT!
I NEED TO WRITE OUT A FEW BILLS!
I'LL DO THE BILLS IN THE MORNING!
MANY COUPLES FIND THAT COMBINING ROMANTIC GESTURES WITH SHARED FISCAL RESPONSIBILITY INVIGORATES THE MARRIAGE!

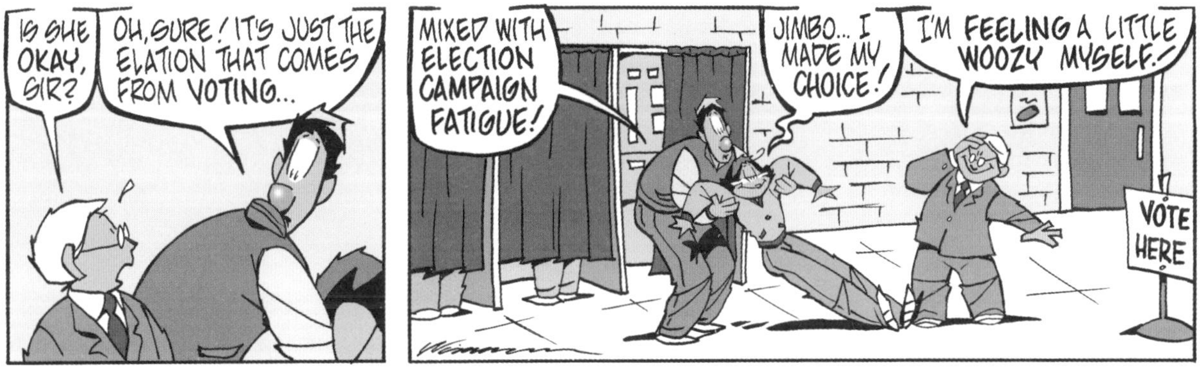
IS SHE OKAY, SIR?
OH, SURE! IT'S JUST THE ELATION THAT COMES FROM VOTING...
MIXED WITH ELECTION CAMPAIGN FATIGUE!
JIMBO... I MADE MY CHOICE!
I'M FEELING A LITTLE WOOZY MYSELF!
VOTE HERE

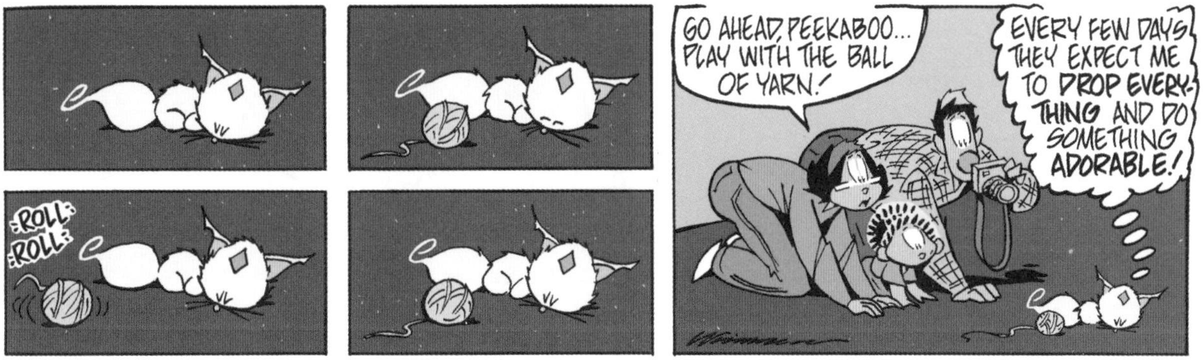
:ROLL:
:ROLL:
GO AHEAD, PEEKABOO... PLAY WITH THE BALL OF YARN!
EVERY FEW DAYS THEY EXPECT ME TO DROP EVERYTHING AND DO SOMETHING ADORABLE!

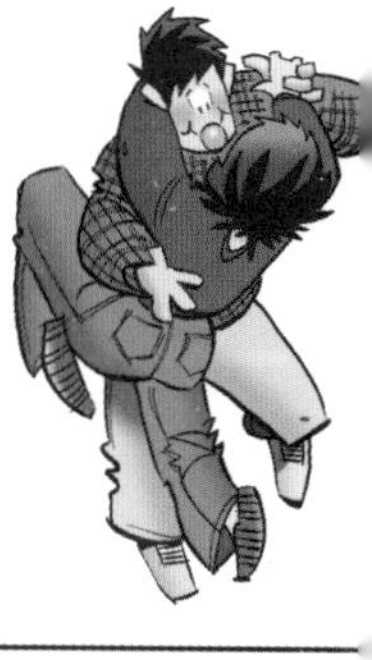

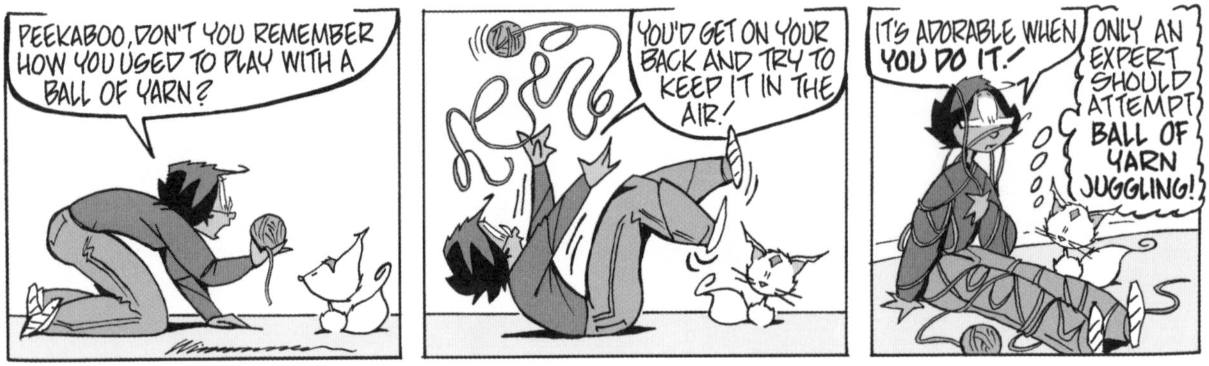
PEEKABOO, DON'T YOU REMEMBER HOW YOU USED TO PLAY WITH A BALL OF YARN?
YOU'D GET ON YOUR BACK AND TRY TO KEEP IT IN THE AIR!
IT'S ADORABLE WHEN **YOU DO IT!**
ONLY AN EXPERT SHOULD ATTEMPT **BALL OF YARN JUGGLING!**

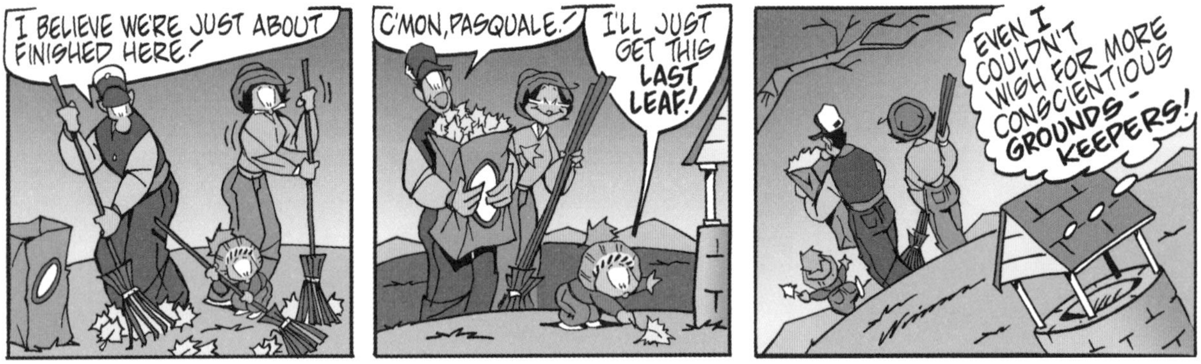
I BELIEVE WE'RE JUST ABOUT FINISHED HERE!
C'MON, PASQUALE!
I'LL JUST GET THIS **LAST LEAF!**
EVEN **I** COULDN'T WISH FOR MORE CONSCIENTIOUS **GROUNDS-KEEPERS!**

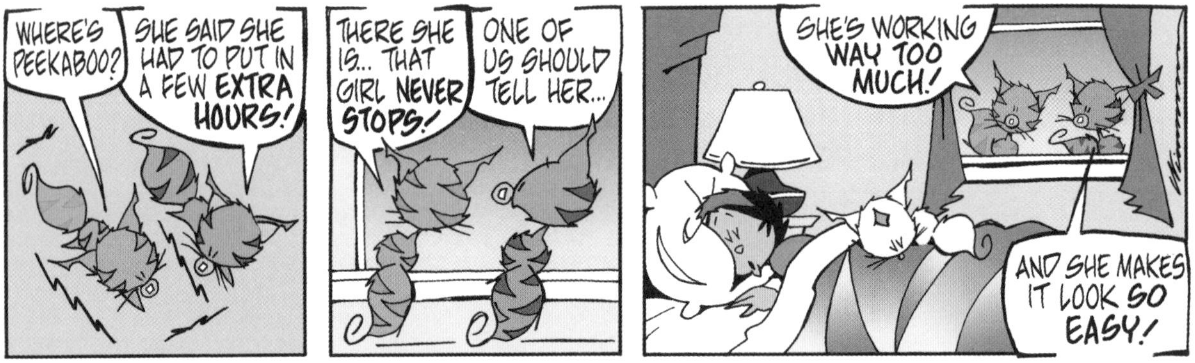
WHERE'S PEEKABOO?
SHE SAID SHE HAD TO PUT IN A FEW **EXTRA HOURS!**
THERE SHE IS... THAT GIRL **NEVER STOPS!**
ONE OF US SHOULD TELL HER...
SHE'S WORKING **WAY TOO MUCH!**
AND SHE MAKES IT LOOK **SO EASY!**

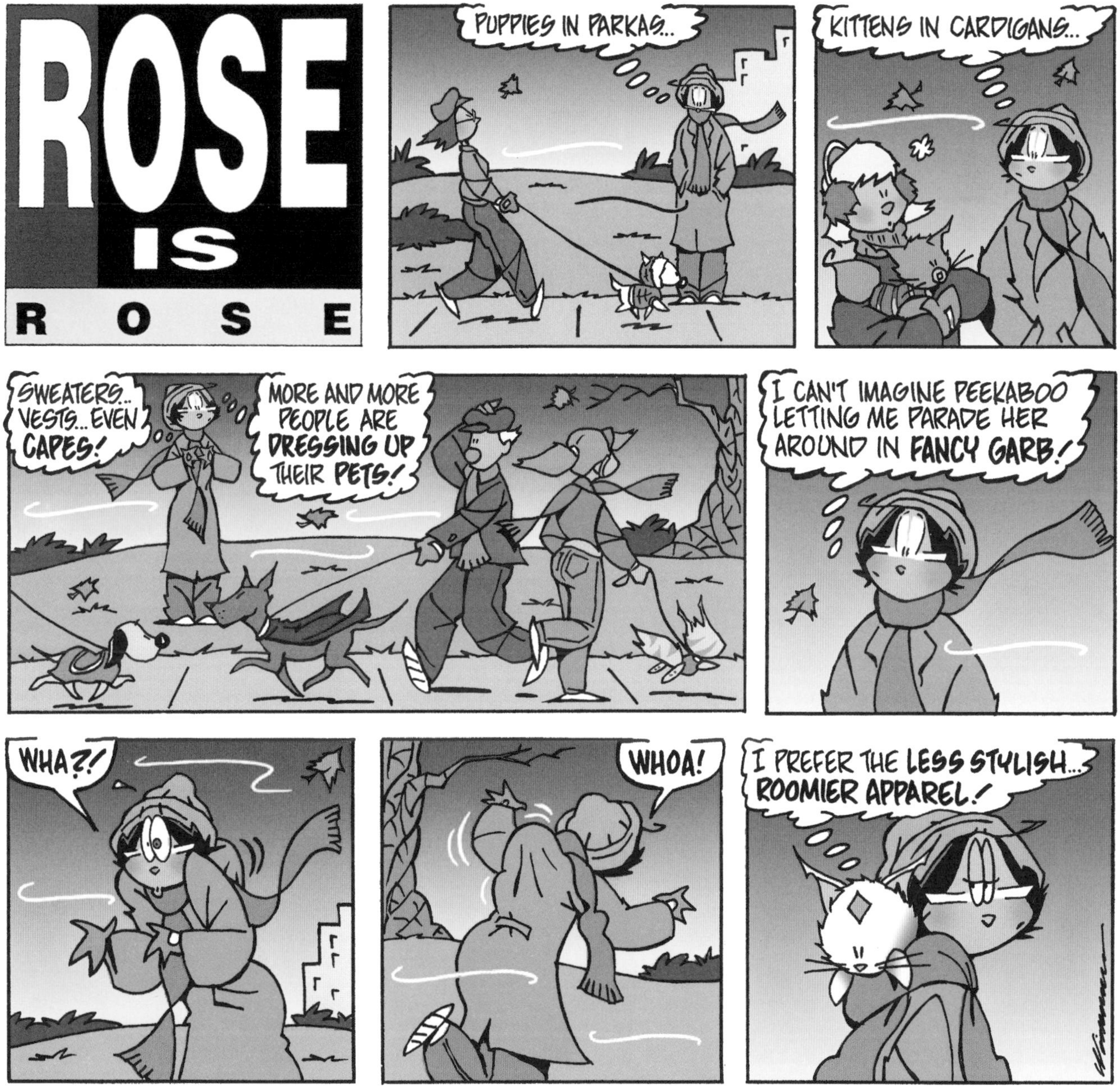
ROSE IS ROSE
PUPPIES IN PARKAS...
KITTENS IN CARDIGANS...
SWEATERS... VESTS... EVEN CAPES!
MORE AND MORE PEOPLE ARE DRESSING UP THEIR PETS!
I CAN'T IMAGINE PEEKABOO LETTING ME PARADE HER AROUND IN FANCY GARB!
WHA?!
WHOA!
I PREFER THE LESS STYLISH... ROOMIER APPAREL!

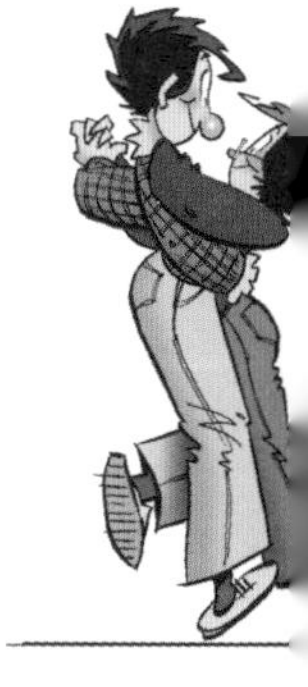

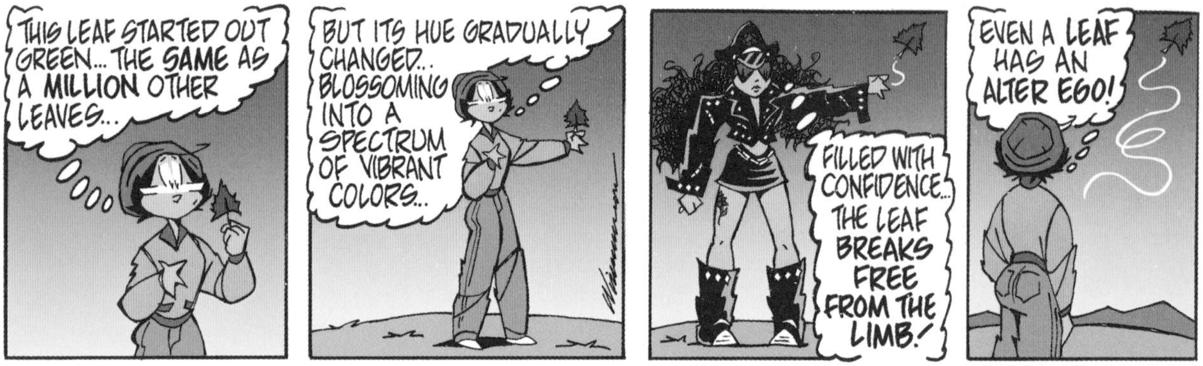
THIS LEAF STARTED OUT GREEN... THE SAME AS A MILLION OTHER LEAVES...
BUT ITS HUE GRADUALLY CHANGED.. BLOSSOMING INTO A SPECTRUM OF VIBRANT COLORS...
FILLED WITH CONFIDENCE... THE LEAF BREAKS FREE FROM THE LIMB!
EVEN A LEAF HAS AN ALTER EGO!

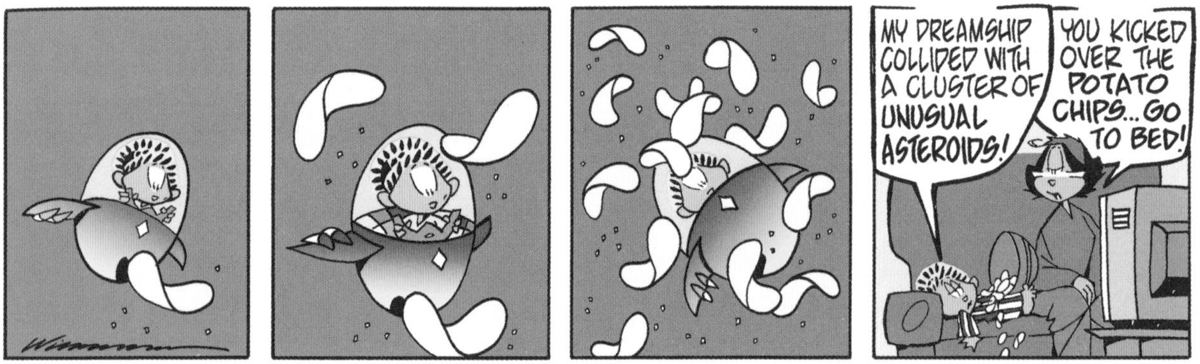
MY DREAMSHIP COLLIDED WITH A CLUSTER OF UNUSUAL ASTEROIDS!
YOU KICKED OVER THE POTATO CHIPS... GO TO BED!

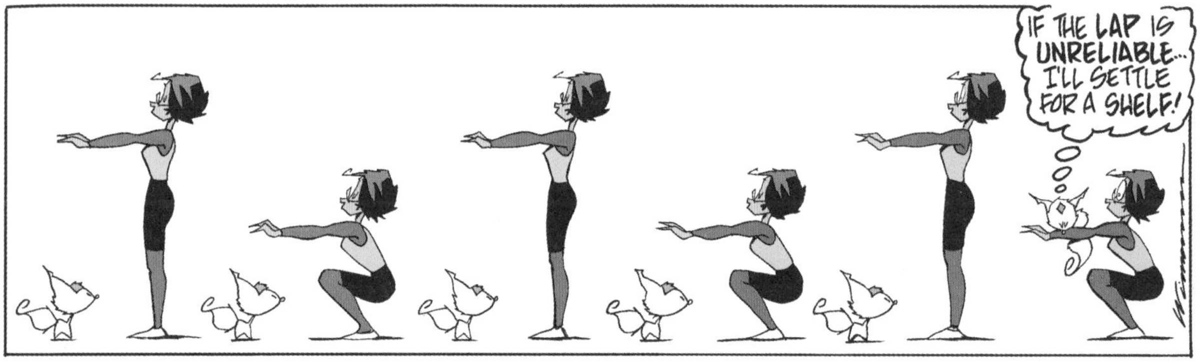
IF THE LAP IS UNRELIABLE... I'LL SETTLE FOR A SHELF!

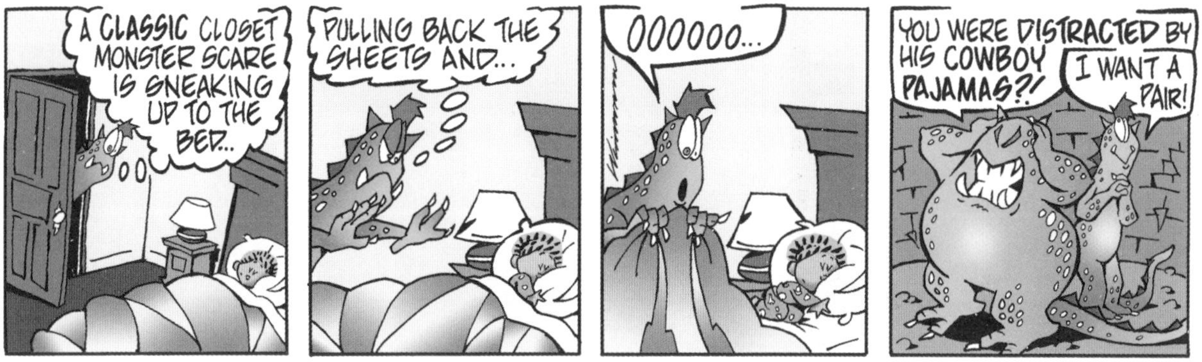
A CLASSIC CLOSET MONSTER SCARE IS SNEAKING UP TO THE BED...
PULLING BACK THE SHEETS AND...
OOOOOO...
YOU WERE DISTRACTED BY HIS COWBOY PAJAMAS?!
I WANT A PAIR!

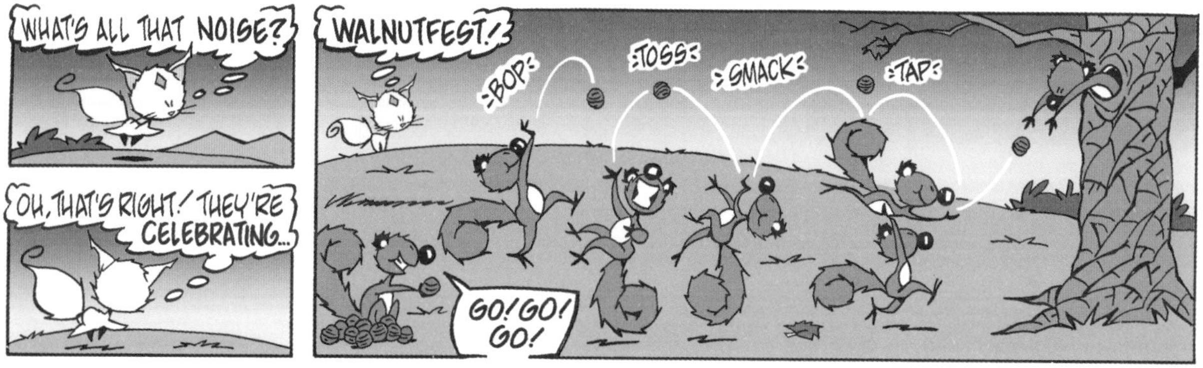
WHAT'S ALL THAT NOISE?
OH, THAT'S RIGHT! THEY'RE CELEBRATING...
WALNUTFEST!
BOP
TOSS
SMACK
TAP
GO! GO! GO!

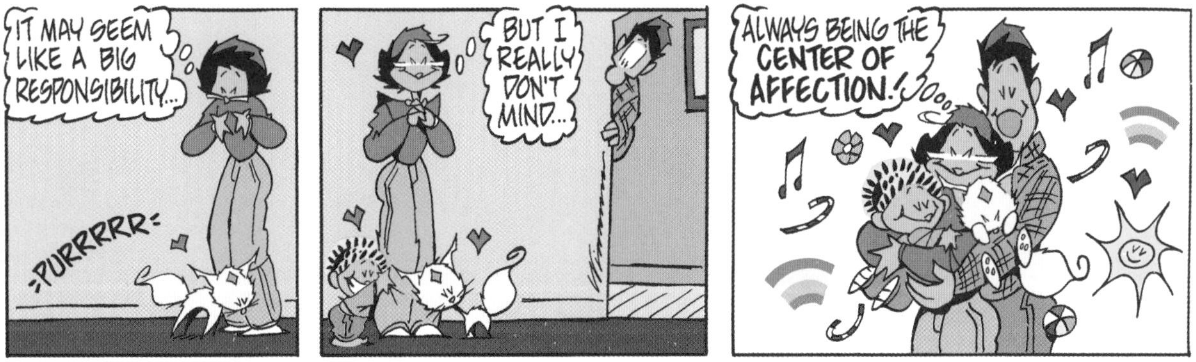
IT MAY SEEM LIKE A BIG RESPONSIBILITY...
PURRRRR
BUT I REALLY DON'T MIND...
ALWAYS BEING THE CENTER OF AFFECTION!

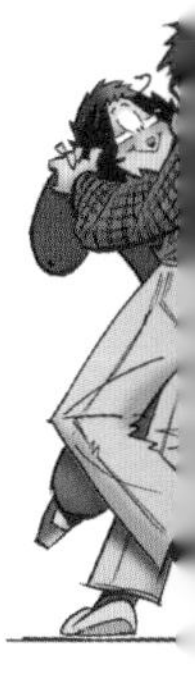

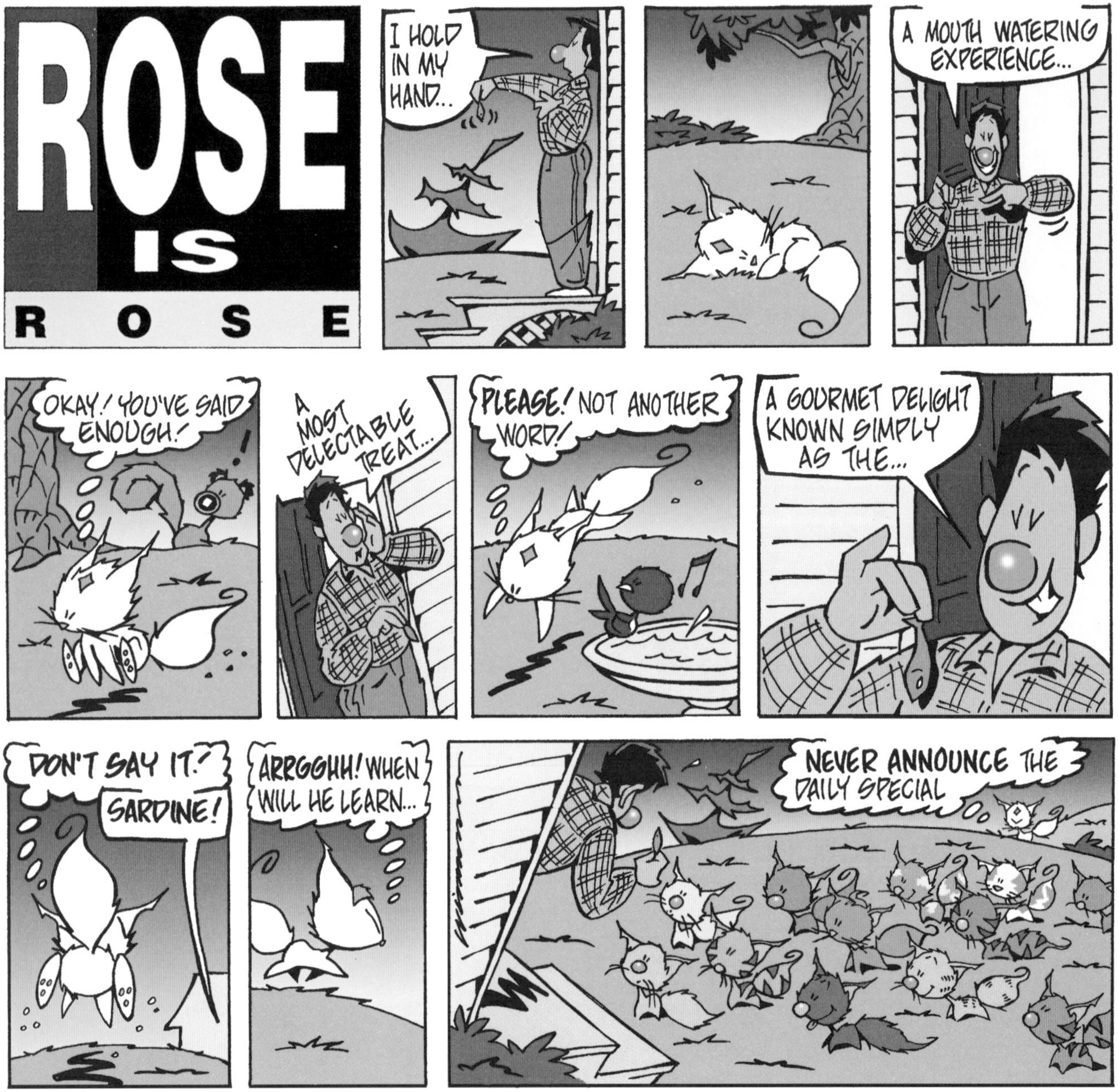
ROSE IS ROSE
I HOLD IN MY HAND...
A MOUTH WATERING EXPERIENCE...
OKAY! YOU'VE SAID ENOUGH!
A MOST DELECTABLE TREAT...
PLEASE! NOT ANOTHER WORD!
A GOURMET DELIGHT KNOWN SIMPLY AS THE...
DON'T SAY IT!
SARDINE!
ARRGGHH! WHEN WILL HE LEARN...
NEVER ANNOUNCE THE DAILY SPECIAL

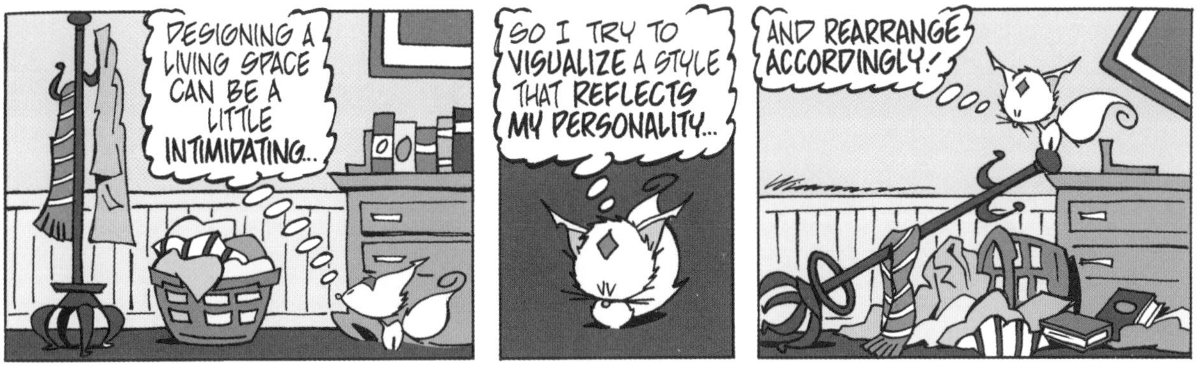
DESIGNING A LIVING SPACE CAN BE A LITTLE INTIMIDATING...
SO I TRY TO VISUALIZE A STYLE THAT REFLECTS MY PERSONALITY...
AND REARRANGE ACCORDINGLY!

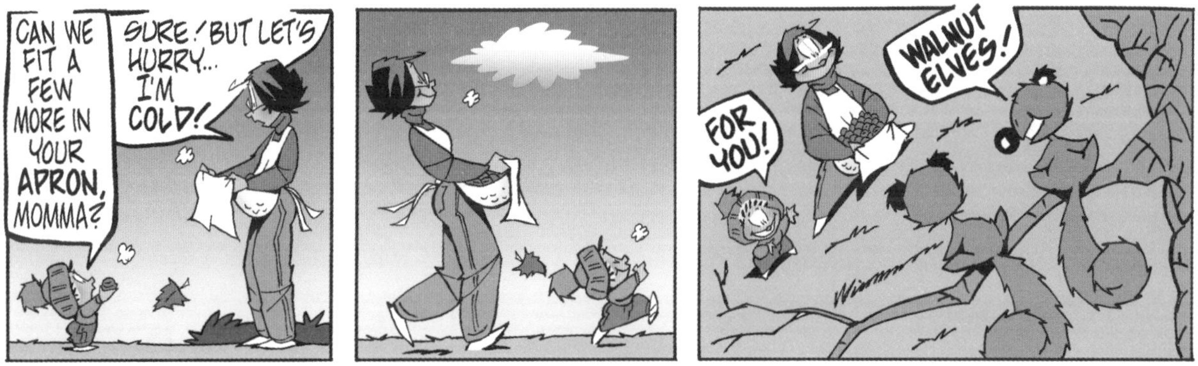
CAN WE FIT A FEW MORE IN YOUR APRON, MOMMA?
SURE! BUT LET'S HURRY... I'M COLD!
WALNUT ELVES!
FOR YOU!

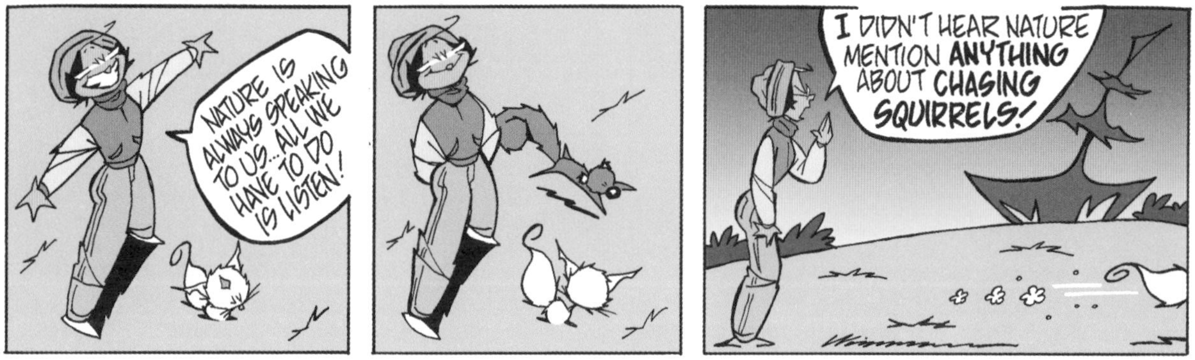
NATURE IS ALWAYS SPEAKING TO US...ALL WE HAVE TO DO IS LISTEN!
I DIDN'T HEAR NATURE MENTION ANYTHING ABOUT CHASING SQUIRRELS!

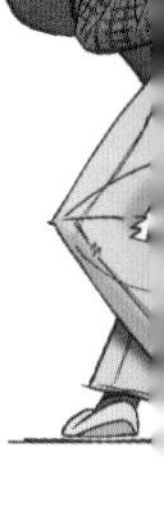

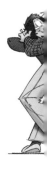

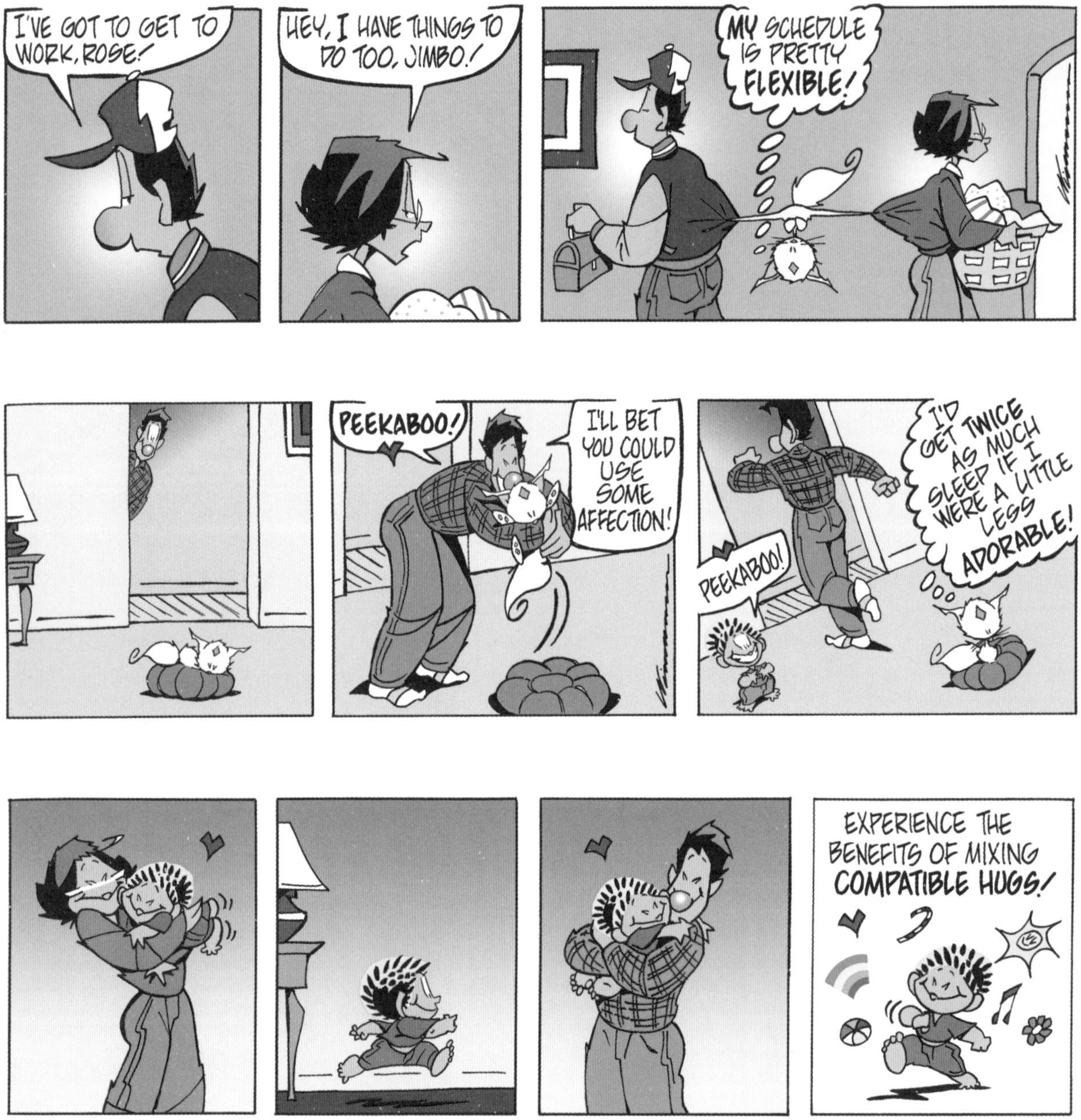
I'VE GOT TO GET TO WORK, ROSE!
HEY, I HAVE THINGS TO DO TOO, JIMBO!
MY SCHEDULE IS PRETTY FLEXIBLE!
PEEKABOO!
I'LL BET YOU COULD USE SOME AFFECTION!
PEEKABOO!
I'D GET TWICE AS MUCH SLEEP IF I WERE A LITTLE LESS ADORABLE!
EXPERIENCE THE BENEFITS OF MIXING COMPATIBLE HUGS!

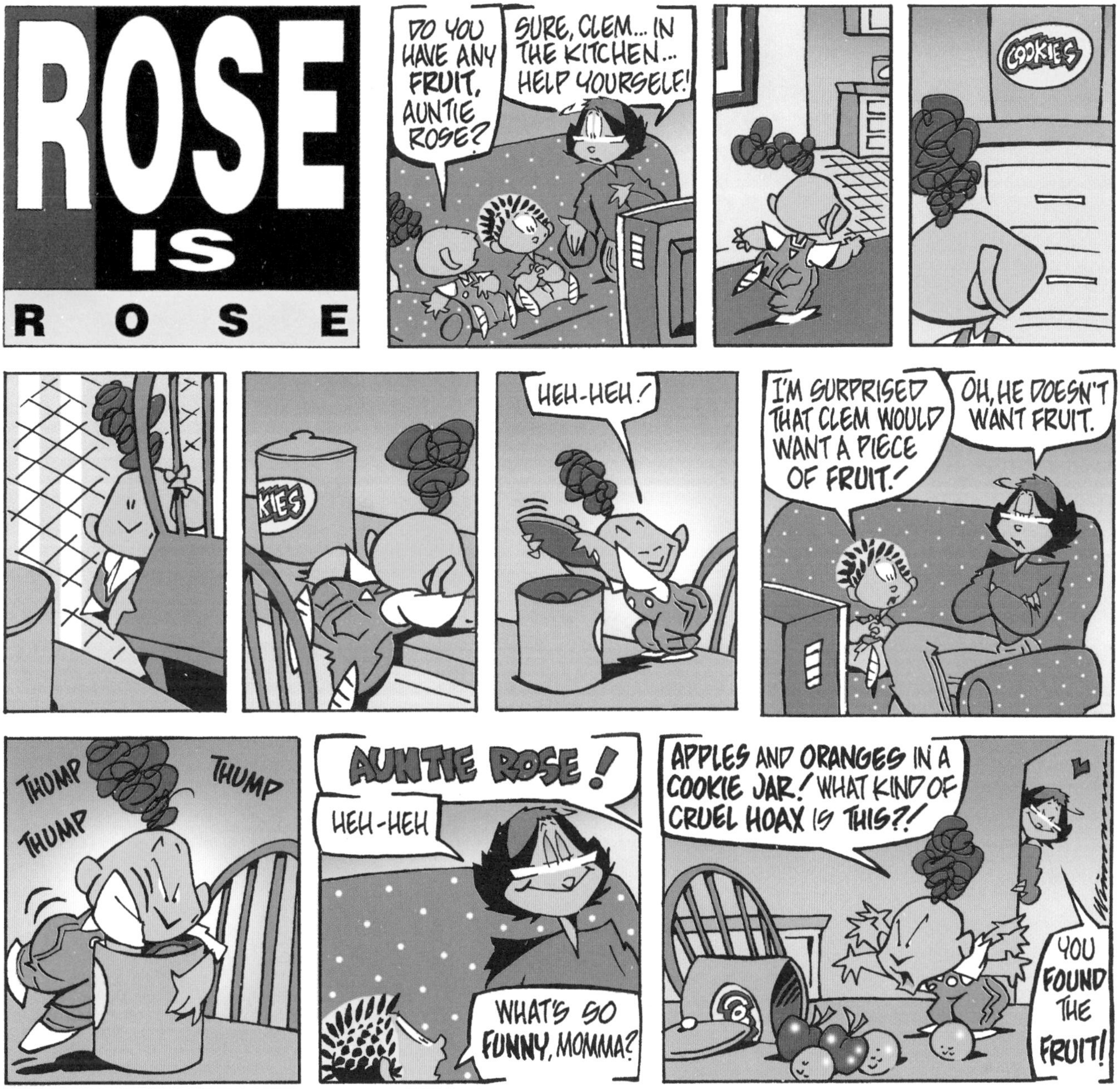
ROSE IS ROSE
DO YOU HAVE ANY FRUIT, AUNTIE ROSE?
SURE, CLEM... IN THE KITCHEN... HELP YOURSELF!
COOKIES
KIES
HEH-HEH!
I'M SURPRISED THAT CLEM WOULD WANT A PIECE OF FRUIT!
OH, HE DOESN'T WANT FRUIT.
THUMP
THUMP
THUMP
AUNTIE ROSE!
HEH-HEH
WHAT'S SO FUNNY, MOMMA?
APPLES AND ORANGES IN A COOKIE JAR! WHAT KIND OF CRUEL HOAX IS THIS?!
YOU FOUND THE FRUIT!

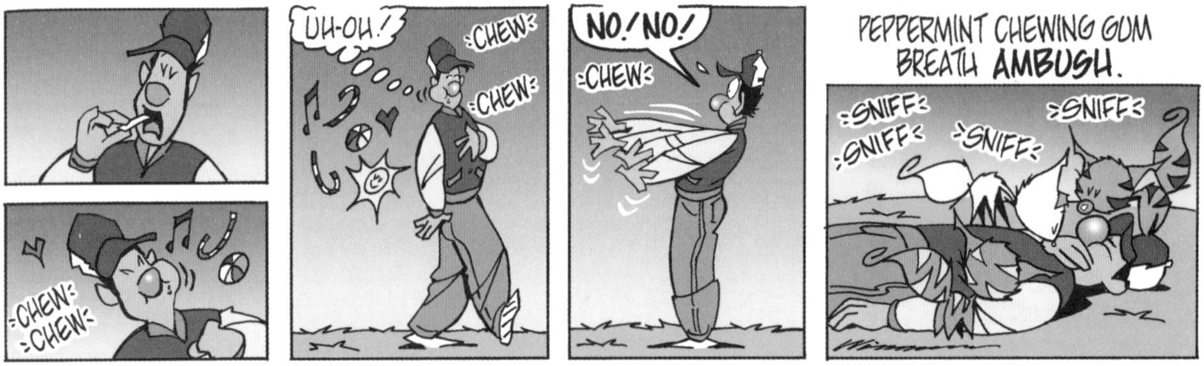
CHEW
CHEW
UH-OH!
CHEW
CHEW
NO! NO!
CHEW
PEPPERMINT CHEWING GUM BREATH AMBUSH.
SNIFF
SNIFF
SNIFF
SNIFF

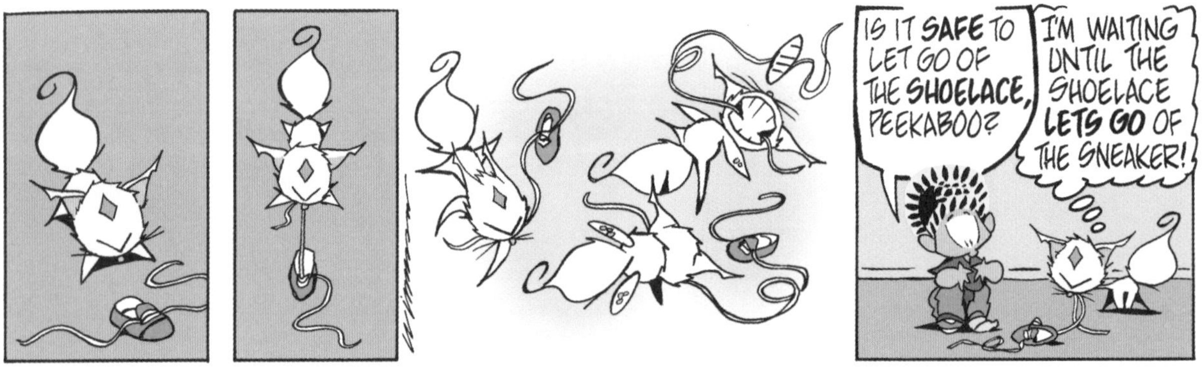
IS IT SAFE TO LET GO OF THE SHOELACE, PEEKABOO?
I'M WAITING UNTIL THE SHOELACE LETS GO OF THE SNEAKER!

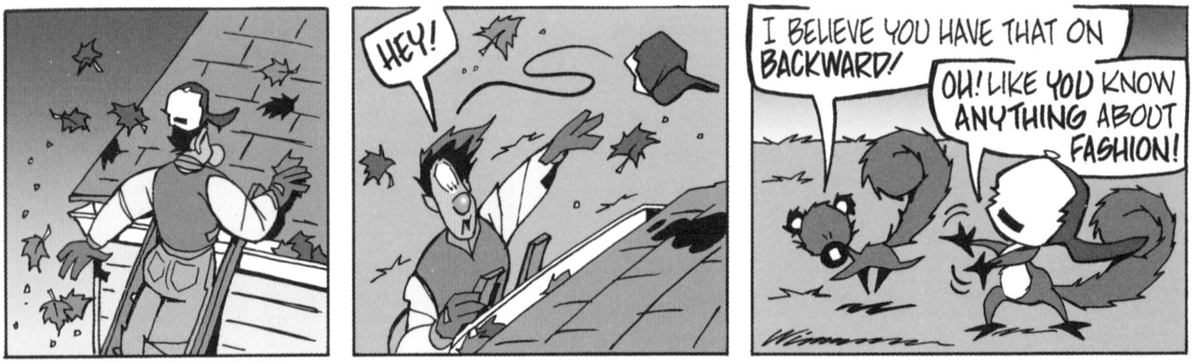
HEY!
I BELIEVE YOU HAVE THAT ON BACKWARD!
OH! LIKE YOU KNOW ANYTHING ABOUT FASHION!

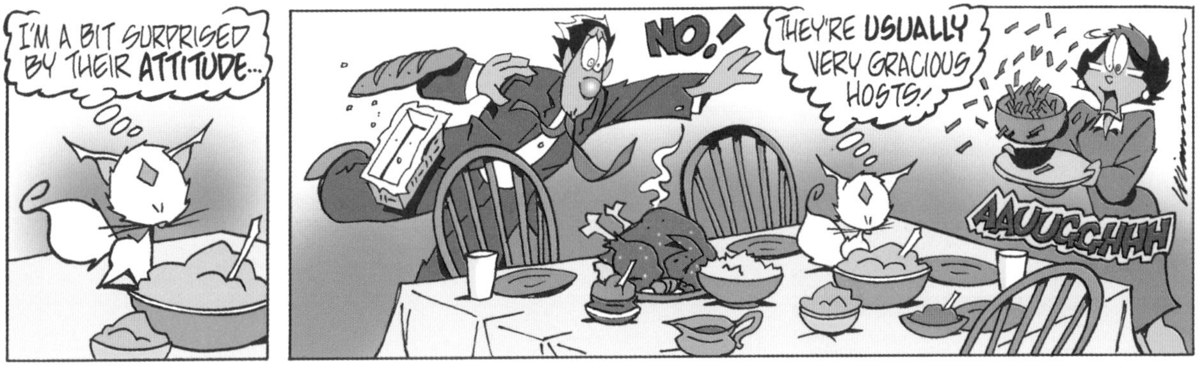
I'M A BIT SURPRISED BY THEIR ATTITUDE...
NO!
THEY'RE USUALLY VERY GRACIOUS HOSTS!
AAUUGGHHH

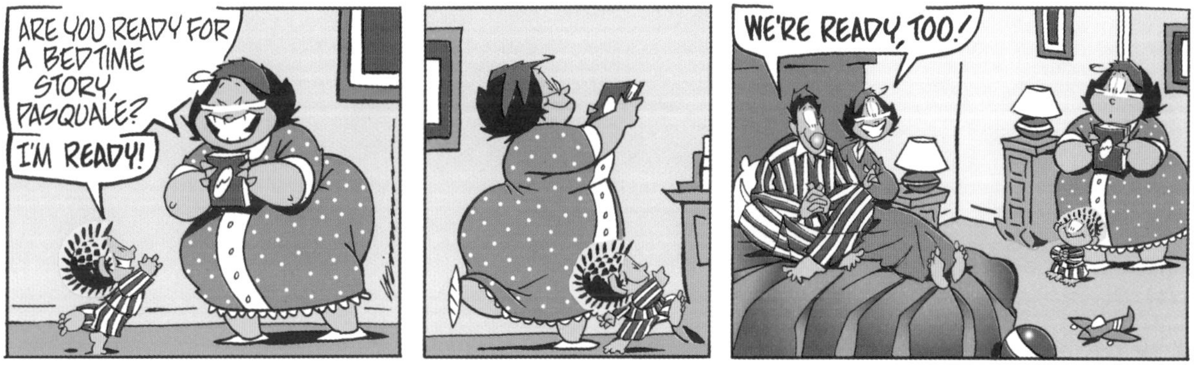
ARE YOU READY FOR A BEDTIME STORY, PASQUALE?
I'M READY!
WE'RE READY, TOO!

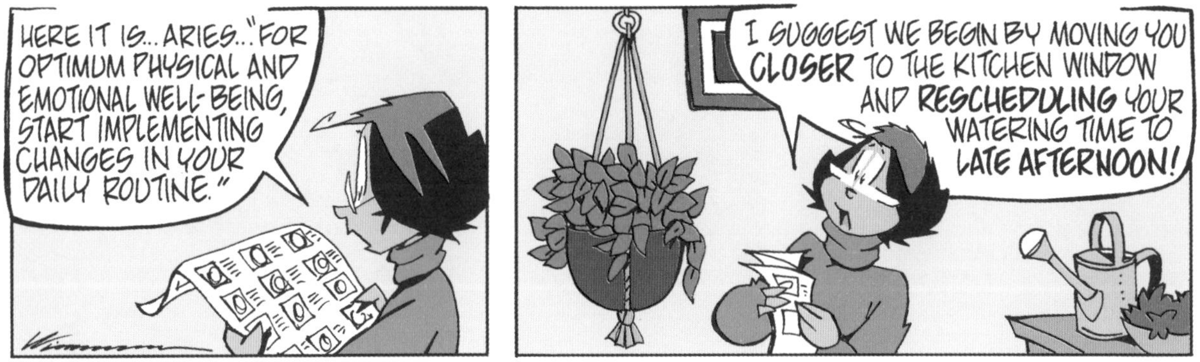
HERE IT IS... ARIES... "FOR OPTIMUM PHYSICAL AND EMOTIONAL WELL-BEING, START IMPLEMENTING CHANGES IN YOUR DAILY ROUTINE."
I SUGGEST WE BEGIN BY MOVING YOU CLOSER TO THE KITCHEN WINDOW AND RESCHEDULING YOUR WATERING TIME TO LATE AFTERNOON!

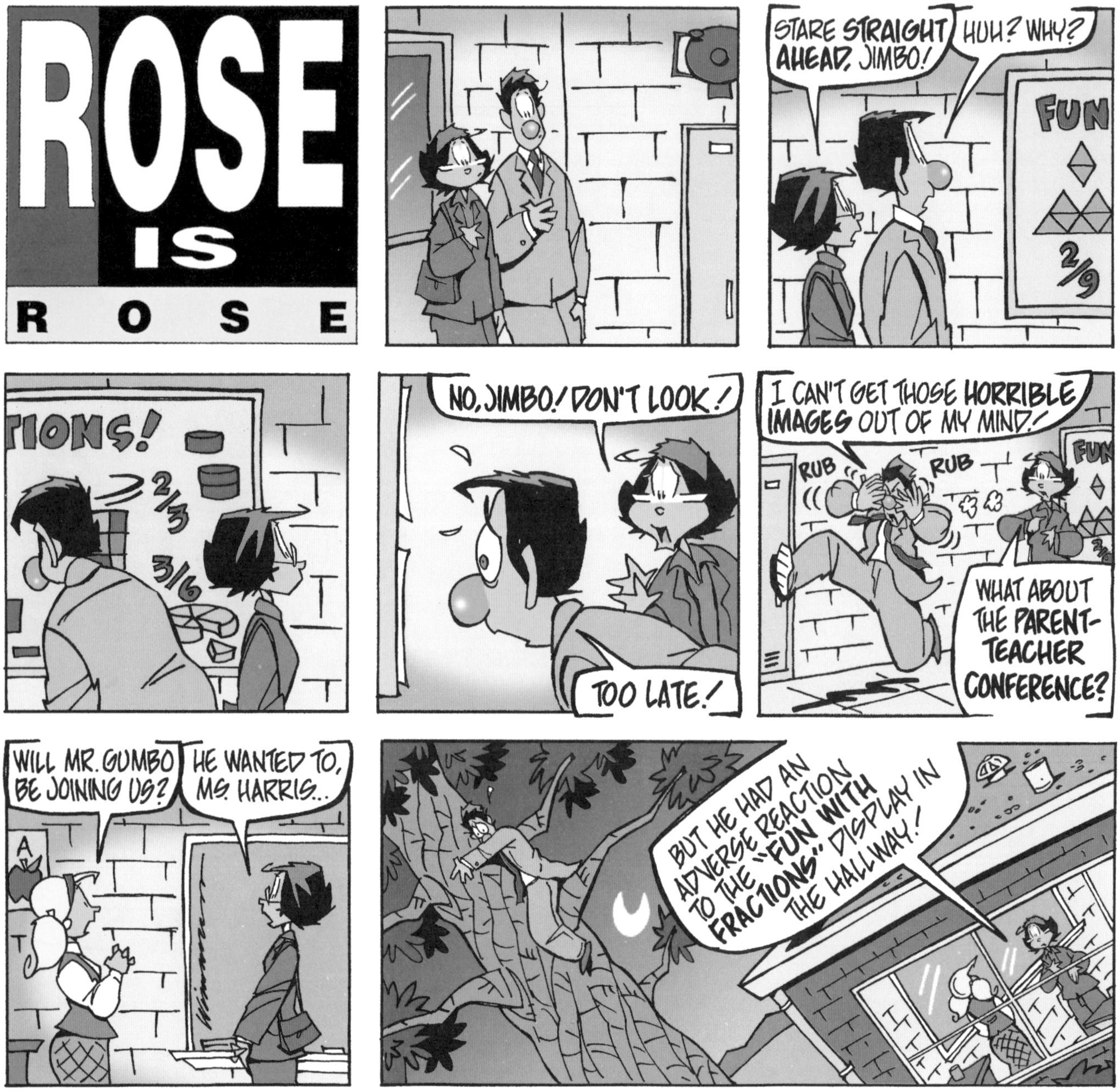
ROSE IS ROSE
STARE STRAIGHT AHEAD, JIMBO!
HUH? WHY?
FUN
2/9
TIONS!
2/3
3/6
NO, JIMBO! DON'T LOOK!
TOO LATE!
I CAN'T GET THOSE HORRIBLE IMAGES OUT OF MY MIND!
RUB
RUB
WHAT ABOUT THE PARENT-TEACHER CONFERENCE?
WILL MR. GUMBO BE JOINING US?
HE WANTED TO, MS. HARRIS...
BUT HE HAD AN ADVERSE REACTION TO THE "FUN WITH FRACTIONS" DISPLAY IN THE HALLWAY!

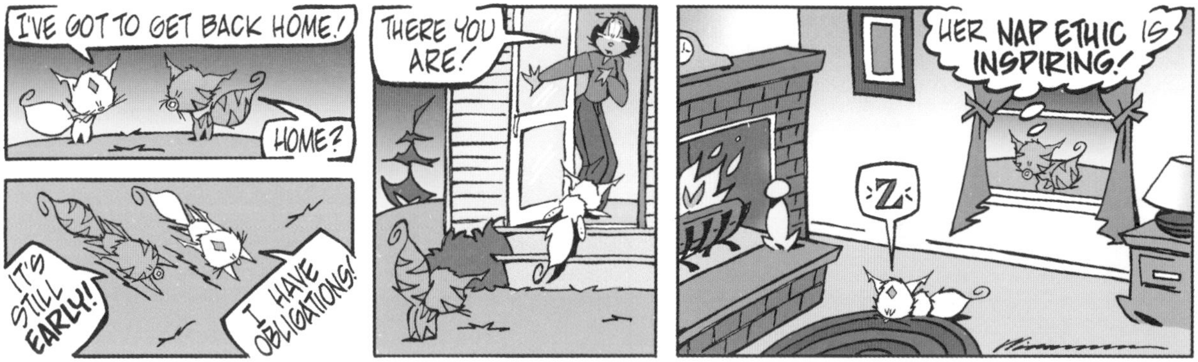
I'VE GOT TO GET BACK HOME!
HOME?
IT'S STILL EARLY!
I HAVE OBLIGATIONS!
THERE YOU ARE!
HER NAP ETHIC IS INSPIRING!
Z

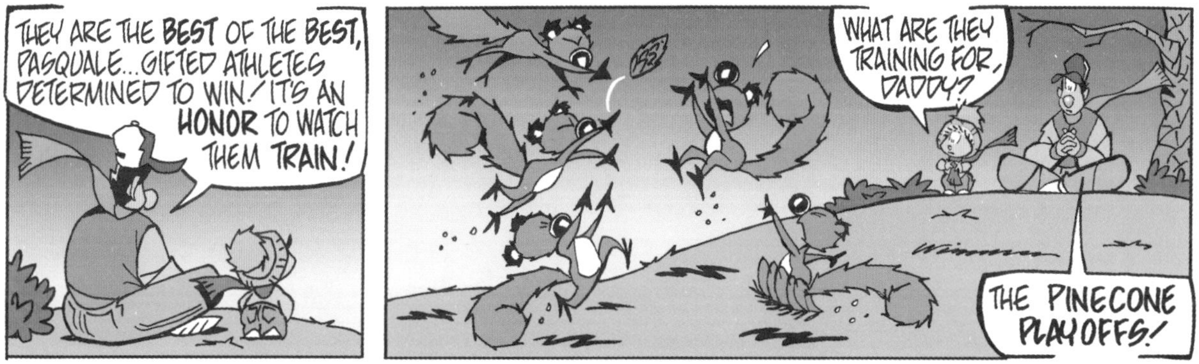
THEY ARE THE BEST OF THE BEST, PASQUALE...GIFTED ATHLETES DETERMINED TO WIN! IT'S AN HONOR TO WATCH THEM TRAIN!
WHAT ARE THEY TRAINING FOR, DADDY?
THE PINECONE PLAYOFFS!

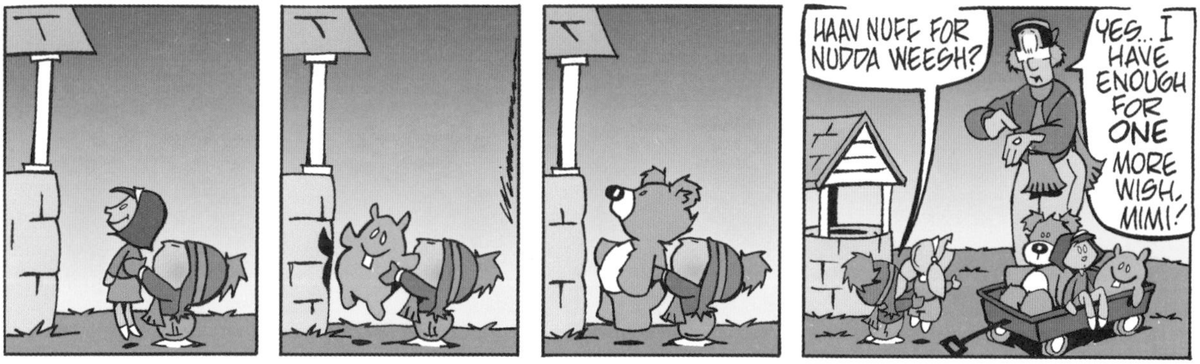
HAAV NUFF FOR NUDDA WEESH?
YES... I HAVE ENOUGH FOR ONE MORE WISH, MIMI!

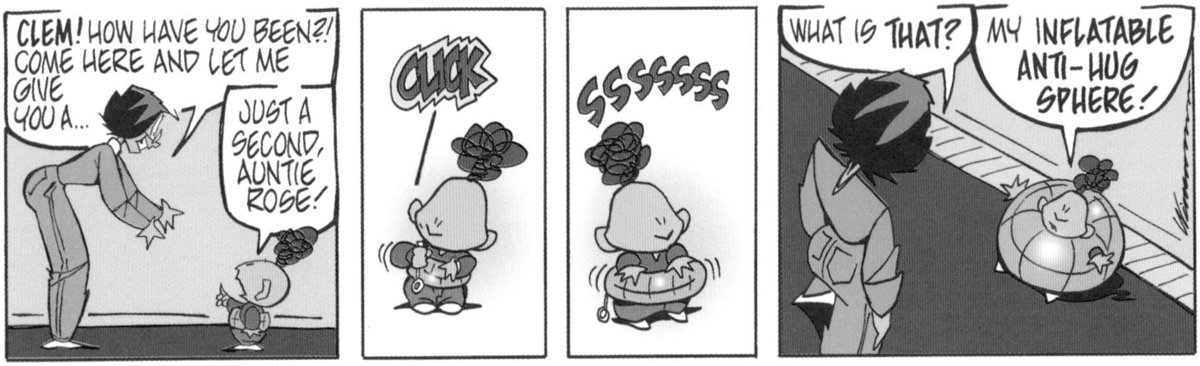
CLEM! HOW HAVE YOU BEEN?! COME HERE AND LET ME GIVE YOU A...
JUST A SECOND, AUNTIE ROSE!
CLICK
SSSSSSS
WHAT IS THAT?
MY INFLATABLE ANTI-HUG SPHERE!

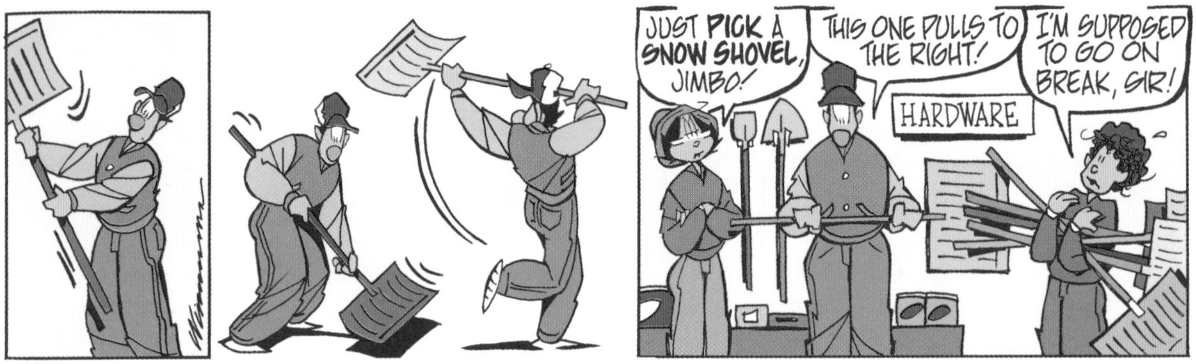
JUST PICK A SNOW SHOVEL, JIMBO!
THIS ONE PULLS TO THE RIGHT!
HARDWARE
I'M SUPPOSED TO GO ON BREAK, SIR!

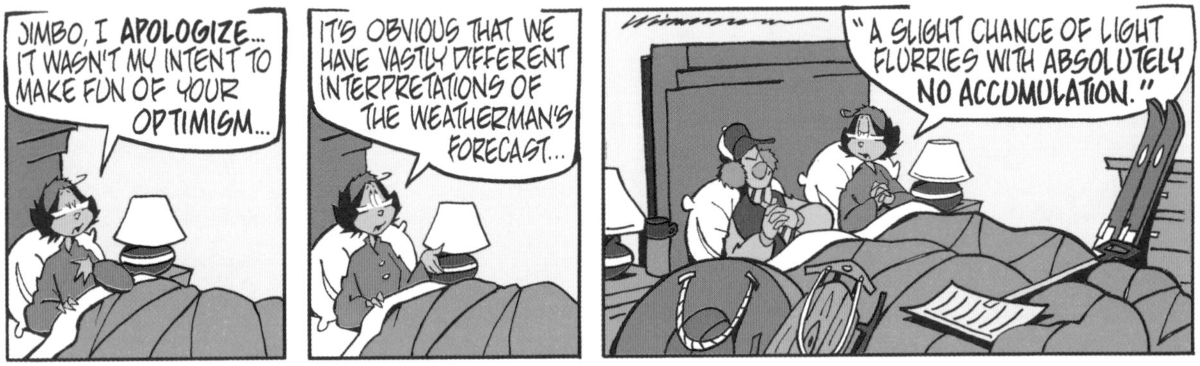
JIMBO, I APOLOGIZE... IT WASN'T MY INTENT TO MAKE FUN OF YOUR OPTIMISM...
IT'S OBVIOUS THAT WE HAVE VASTLY DIFFERENT INTERPRETATIONS OF THE WEATHERMAN'S FORECAST...
"A SLIGHT CHANCE OF LIGHT FLURRIES WITH ABSOLUTELY NO ACCUMULATION."

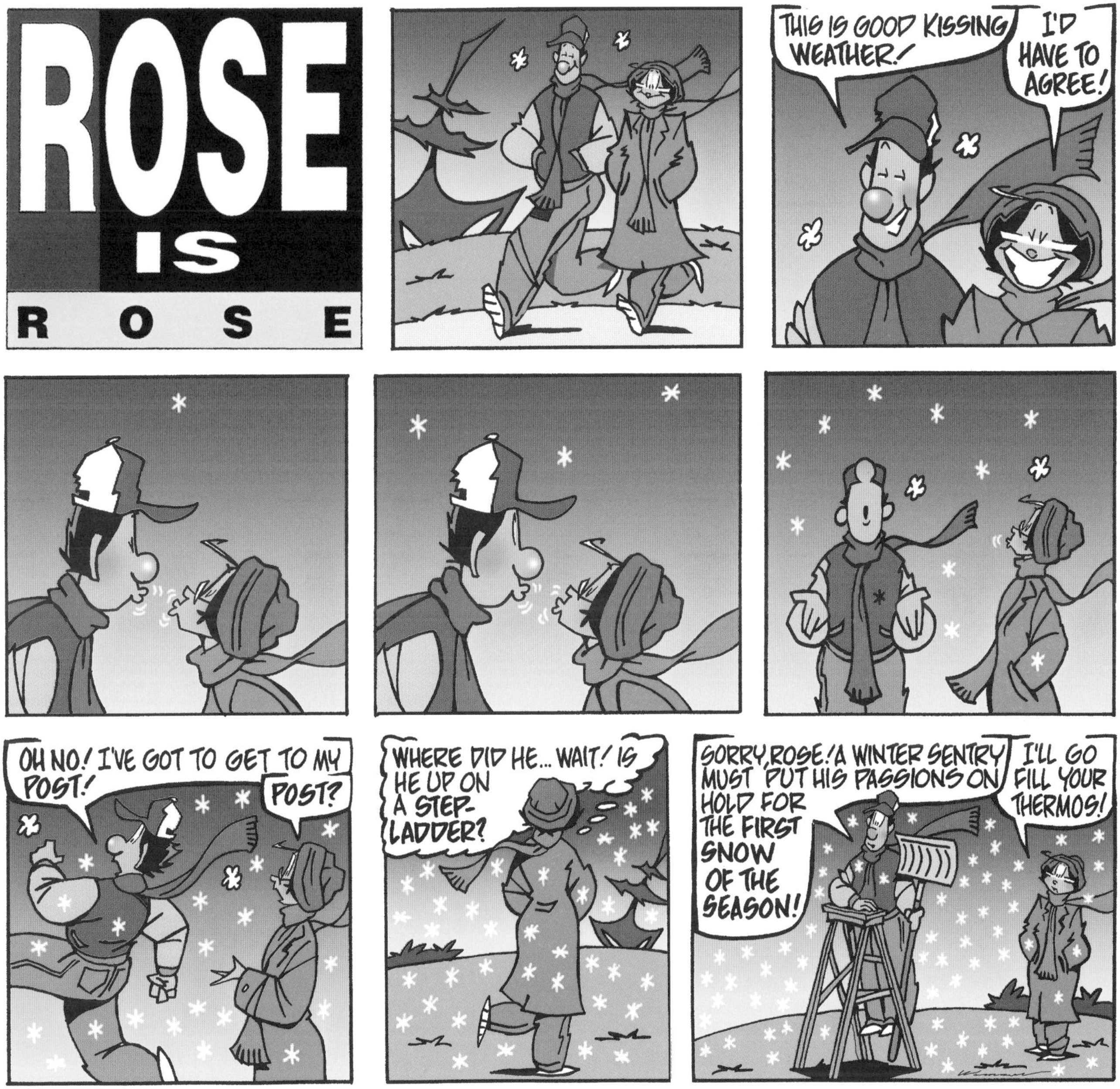
ROSE IS ROSE
THIS IS GOOD KISSING WEATHER!
I'D HAVE TO AGREE!
OH NO! I'VE GOT TO GET TO MY POST!
POST?
WHERE DID HE... WAIT! IS HE UP ON A STEP-LADDER?
SORRY, ROSE! A WINTER SENTRY MUST PUT HIS PASSIONS ON HOLD FOR THE FIRST SNOW OF THE SEASON!
I'LL GO FILL YOUR THERMOS!

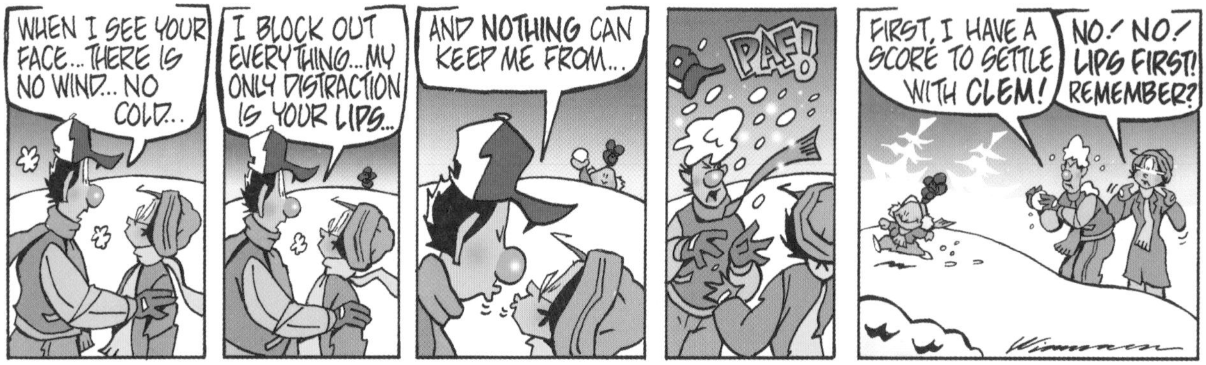

WHEN I SEE YOUR FACE... THERE IS NO WIND... NO COLD...
I BLOCK OUT EVERYTHING... MY ONLY DISTRACTION IS YOUR LIPS...
AND NOTHING CAN KEEP ME FROM...
PAF!
FIRST, I HAVE A SCORE TO SETTLE WITH CLEM!
NO! NO! LIPS FIRST! REMEMBER?

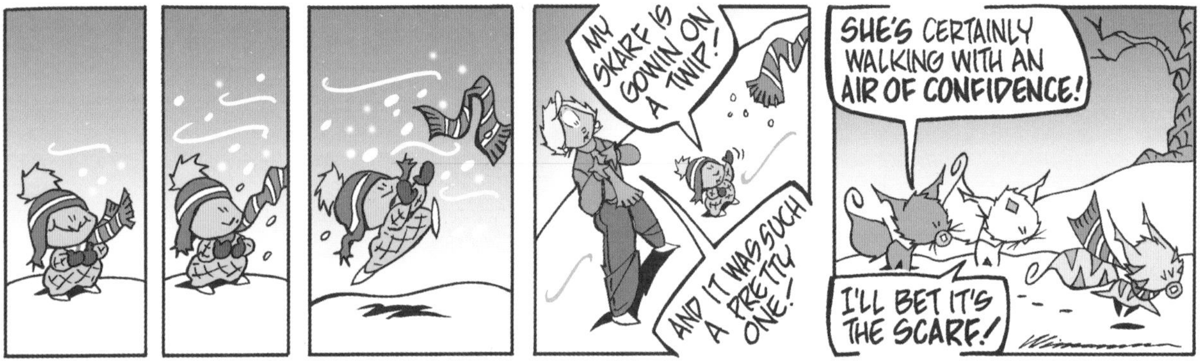

MY SKARF IS GOWIN ON A TWIP!
AND IT WAS SUCH A PRETTY ONE!
SHE'S CERTAINLY WALKING WITH AN AIR OF CONFIDENCE!
I'LL BET IT'S THE SCARF!

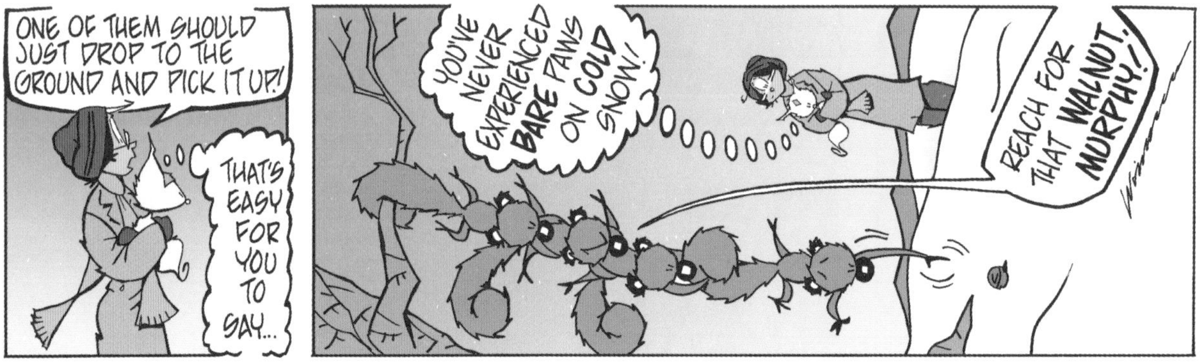

ONE OF THEM SHOULD JUST DROP TO THE GROUND AND PICK IT UP!
THAT'S EASY FOR YOU TO SAY...
YOU'VE NEVER EXPERIENCED BARE PAWS ON COLD SNOW!
REACH FOR THAT WALNUT, MURPHY!

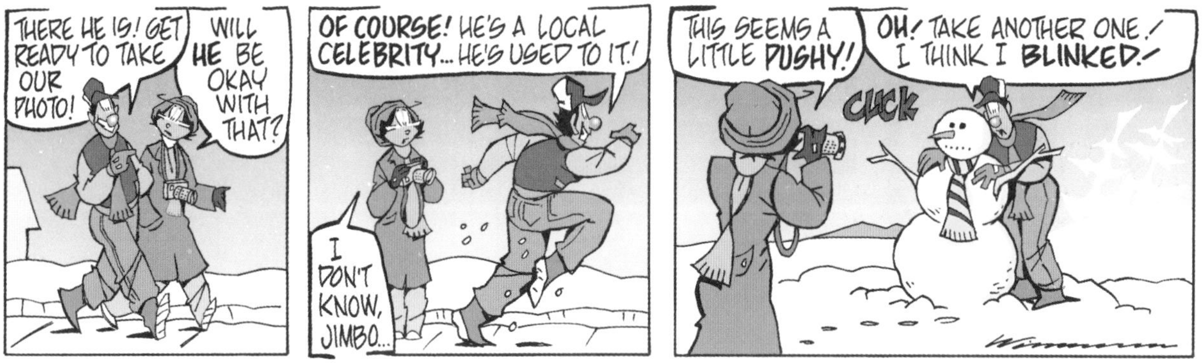
THERE HE IS! GET READY TO TAKE OUR PHOTO!
WILL HE BE OKAY WITH THAT?
OF COURSE! HE'S A LOCAL CELEBRITY... HE'S USED TO IT!
I DON'T KNOW, JIMBO...
THIS SEEMS A LITTLE PUSHY!
CLICK
OH! TAKE ANOTHER ONE! I THINK I BLINKED!

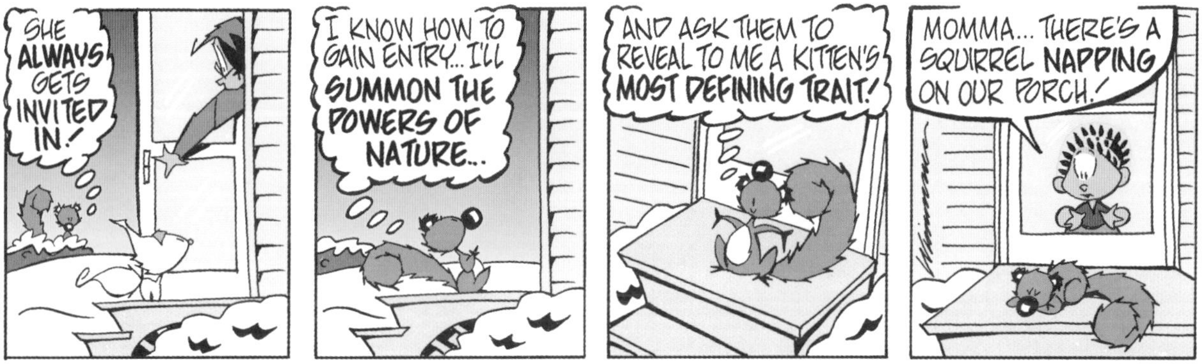
SHE ALWAYS GETS INVITED IN!
I KNOW HOW TO GAIN ENTRY... I'LL SUMMON THE POWERS OF NATURE...
AND ASK THEM TO REVEAL TO ME A KITTEN'S MOST DEFINING TRAIT!
MOMMA... THERE'S A SQUIRREL NAPPING ON OUR PORCH!

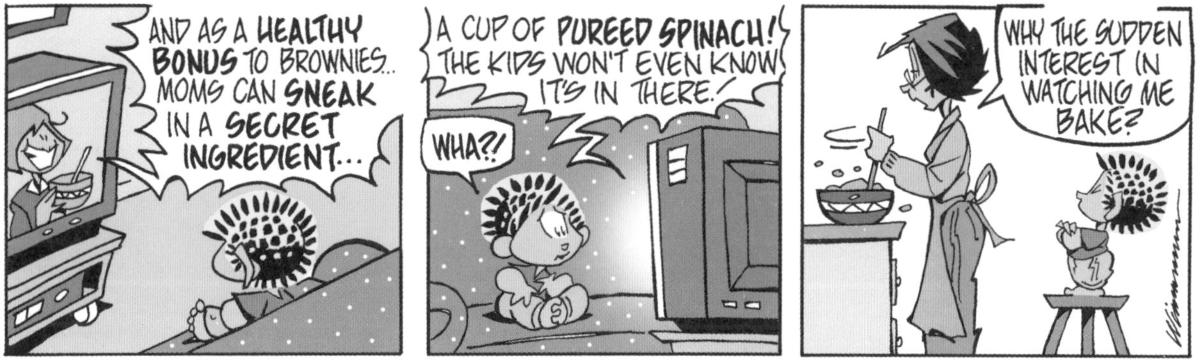
AND AS A HEALTHY BONUS TO BROWNIES... MOMS CAN SNEAK IN A SECRET INGREDIENT...
A CUP OF PUREED SPINACH! THE KIDS WON'T EVEN KNOW IT'S IN THERE!
WHA?!
WHY THE SUDDEN INTEREST IN WATCHING ME BAKE?

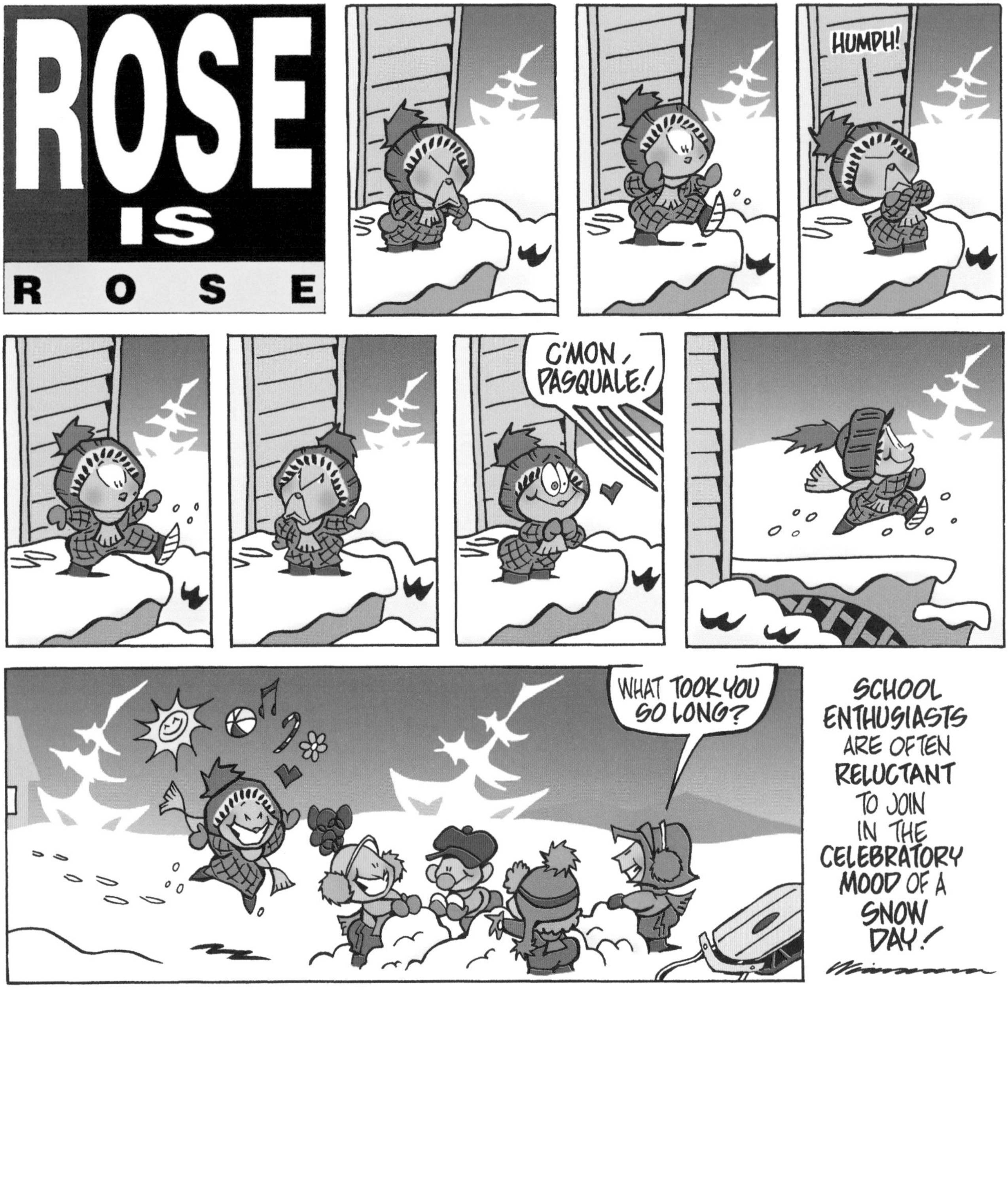
ROSE IS ROSE
HUMPH!
C'MON, PASQUALE!
WHAT TOOK YOU SO LONG?
SCHOOL ENTHUSIASTS ARE OFTEN RELUCTANT TO JOIN IN THE CELEBRATORY MOOD OF A SNOW DAY!

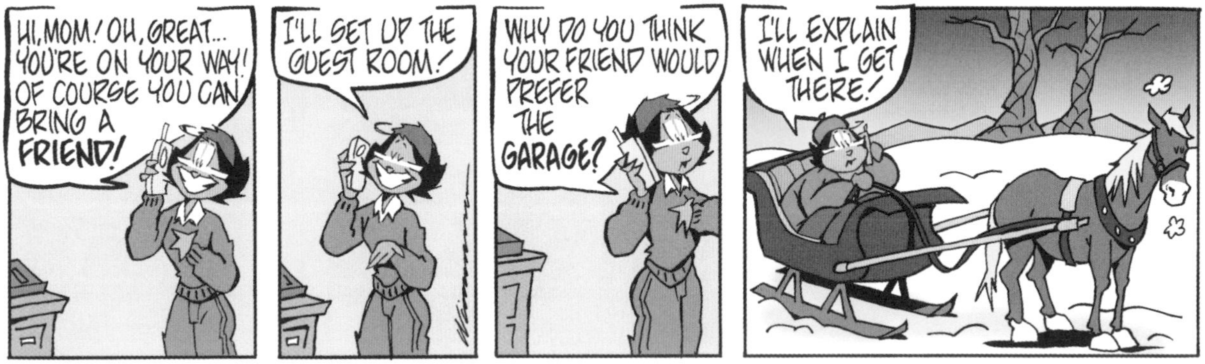
HI, MOM! OH, GREAT... YOU'RE ON YOUR WAY! OF COURSE YOU CAN BRING A **FRIEND!**
I'LL SET UP THE GUEST ROOM!
WHY DO YOU THINK YOUR FRIEND WOULD PREFER THE **GARAGE?**
I'LL EXPLAIN WHEN I GET THERE!

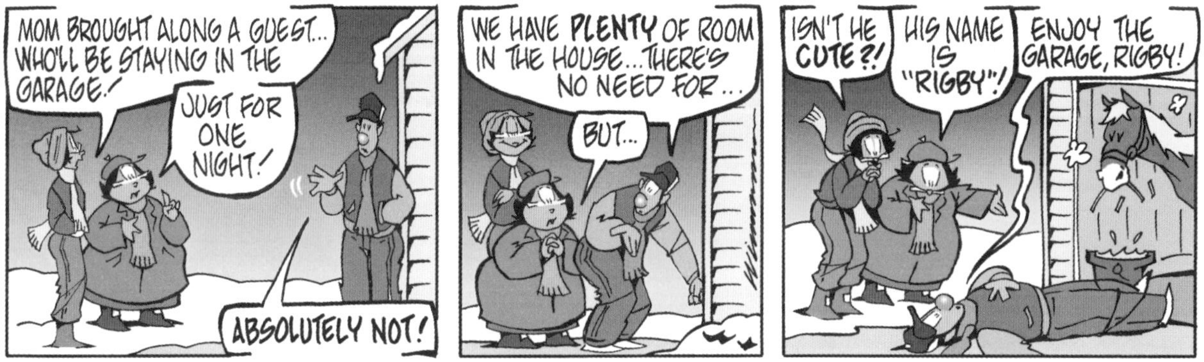
MOM BROUGHT ALONG A GUEST... WHO'LL BE STAYING IN THE GARAGE!
JUST FOR ONE NIGHT!
ABSOLUTELY NOT!
WE HAVE **PLENTY** OF ROOM IN THE HOUSE... THERE'S NO NEED FOR...
BUT...
ISN'T HE **CUTE?!**
HIS NAME IS **"RIGBY"!**
ENJOY THE GARAGE, RIGBY!

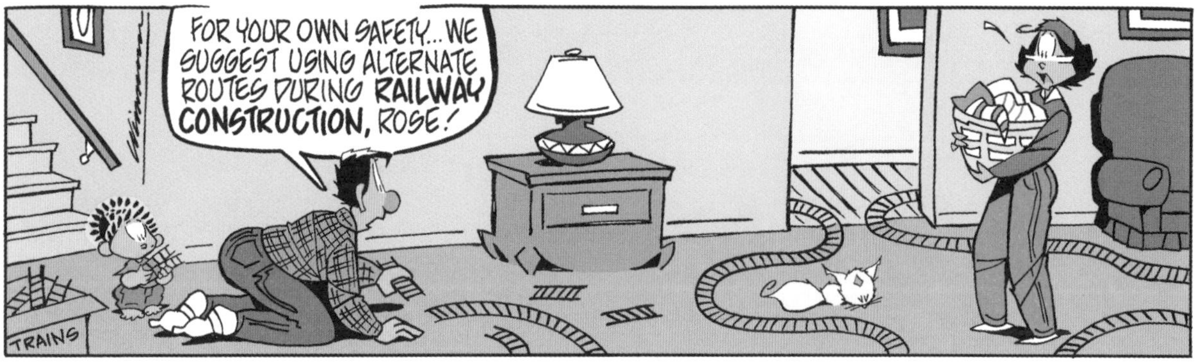
FOR YOUR OWN SAFETY... WE SUGGEST USING ALTERNATE ROUTES DURING **RAILWAY CONSTRUCTION**, ROSE!
TRAINS

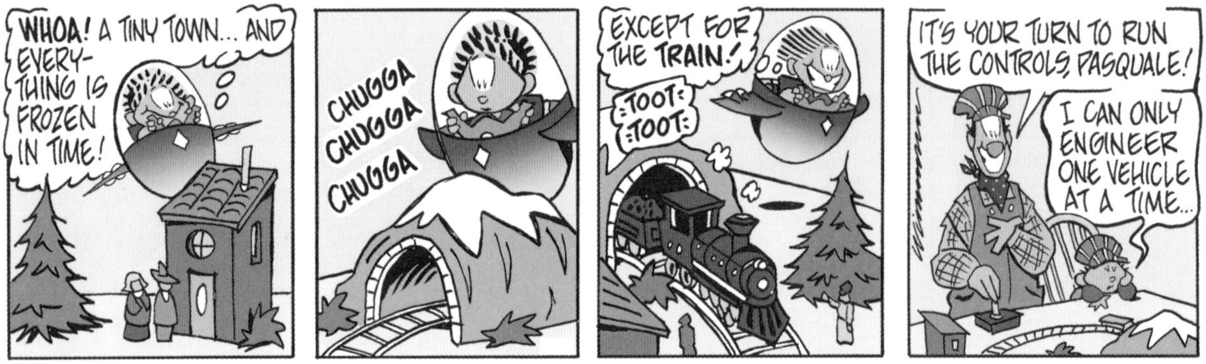
WHOA! A TINY TOWN... AND EVERY-THING IS FROZEN IN TIME!
CHUGGA CHUGGA CHUGGA
EXCEPT FOR THE TRAIN!
TOOT TOOT
IT'S YOUR TURN TO RUN THE CONTROLS, PASQUALE!
I CAN ONLY ENGINEER ONE VEHICLE AT A TIME...

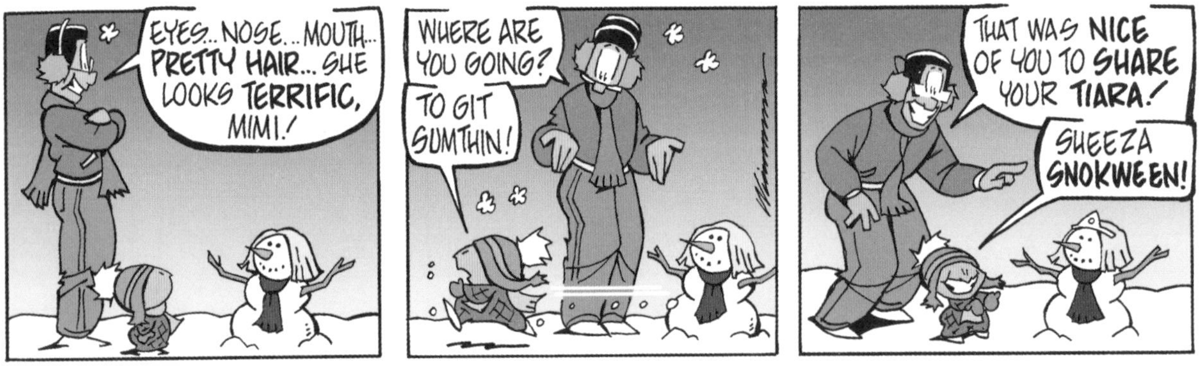
EYES... NOSE... MOUTH... PRETTY HAIR... SHE LOOKS TERRIFIC, MIMI!
WHERE ARE YOU GOING?
TO GIT SUMTHIN!
THAT WAS NICE OF YOU TO SHARE YOUR TIARA!
SHEEZA SNOKWEEN!

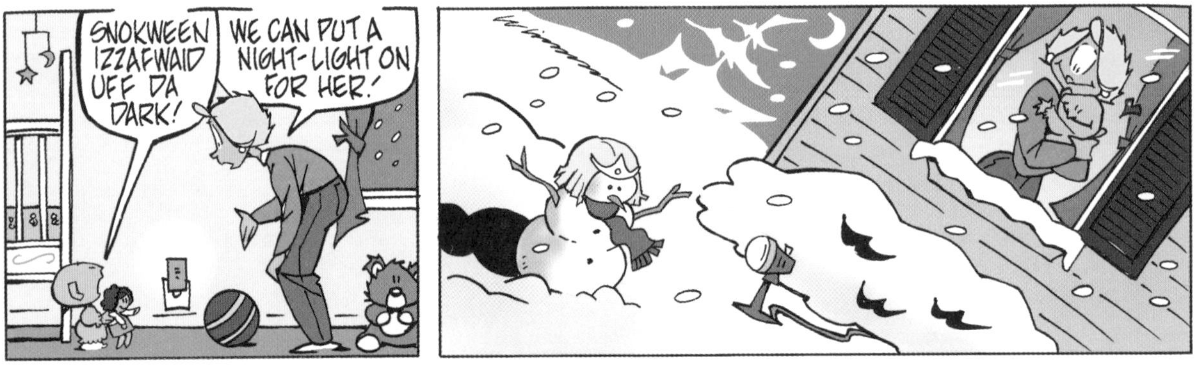
SNOKWEEN IZZAFWAID UFF DA DARK!
WE CAN PUT A NIGHT-LIGHT ON FOR HER!

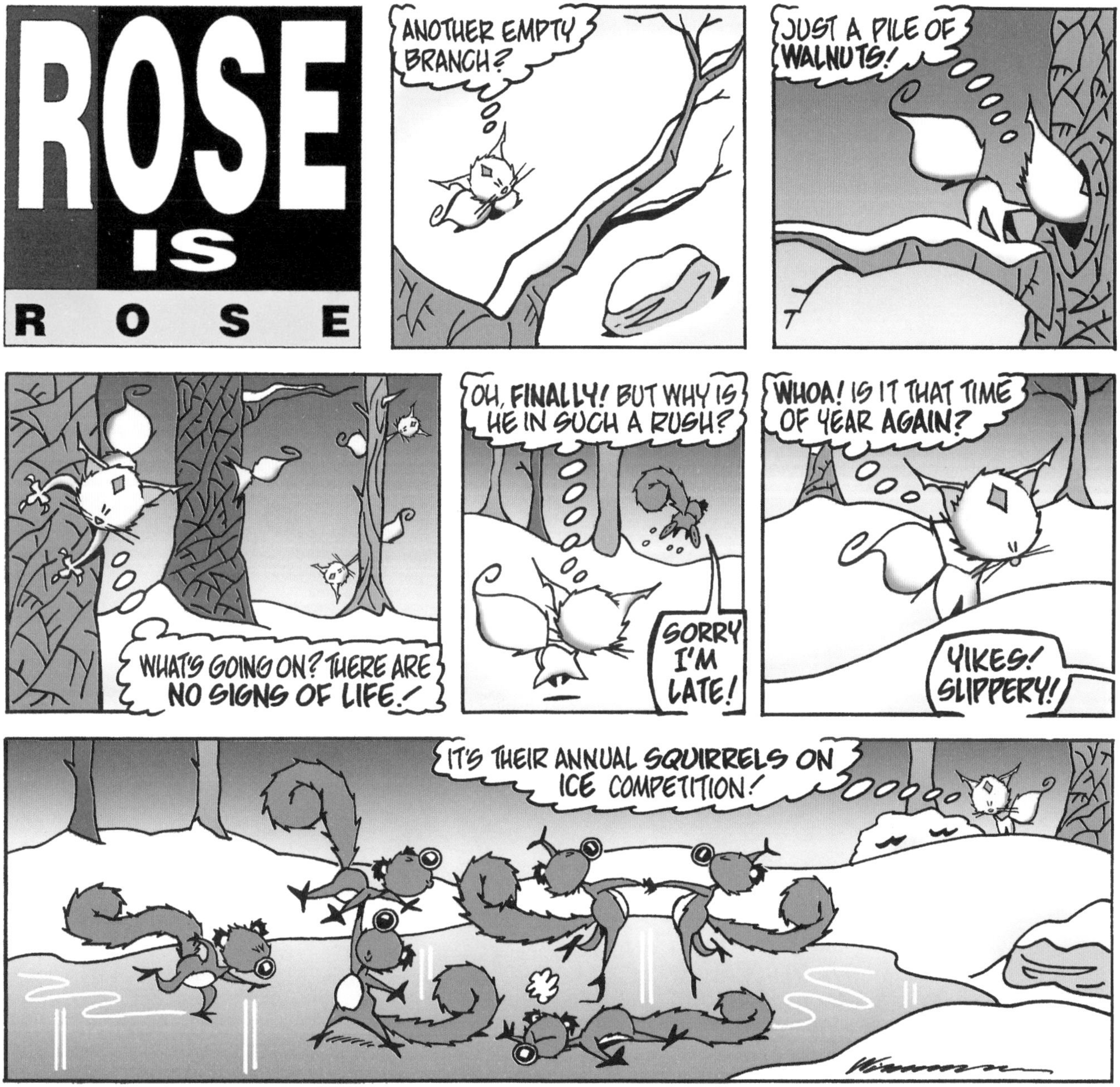
ROSE IS ROSE
ANOTHER EMPTY BRANCH?
JUST A PILE OF WALNUTS!
WHAT'S GOING ON? THERE ARE NO SIGNS OF LIFE!
OH, FINALLY! BUT WHY IS HE IN SUCH A RUSH?
SORRY I'M LATE!
WHOA! IS IT THAT TIME OF YEAR AGAIN?
YIKES! SLIPPERY!
IT'S THEIR ANNUAL SQUIRRELS ON ICE COMPETITION!

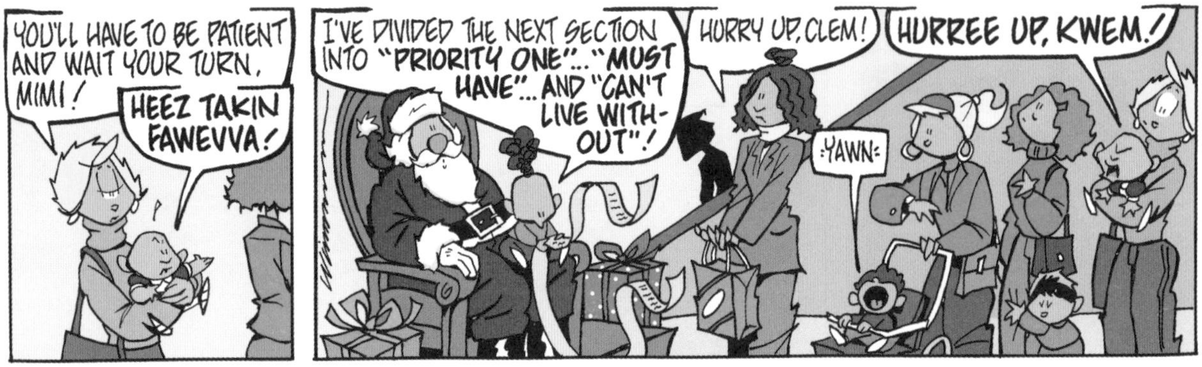
YOU'LL HAVE TO BE PATIENT AND WAIT YOUR TURN, MIMI!
HEEZ TAKIN FAWEVVA!
I'VE DIVIDED THE NEXT SECTION INTO "PRIORITY ONE"... "MUST HAVE"... AND "CAN'T LIVE WITH-OUT"!
HURRY UP, CLEM!
HURREE UP, KWEM!
:YAWN:

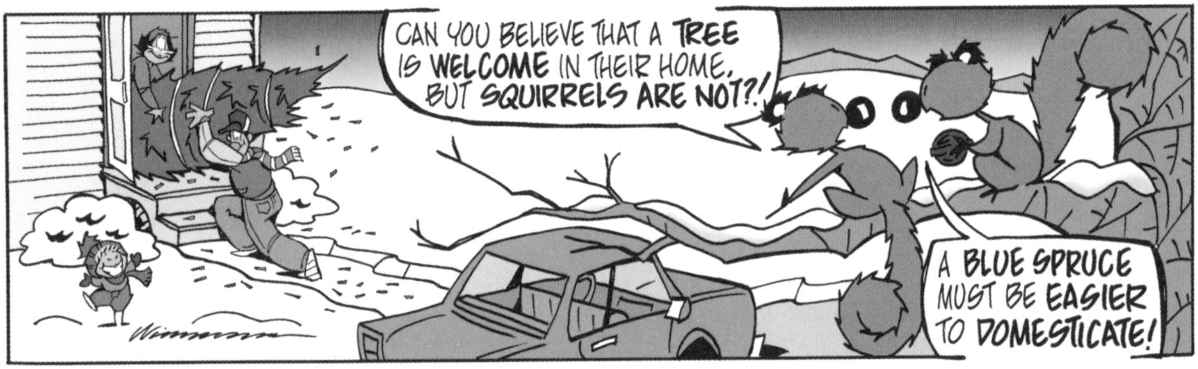
CAN YOU BELIEVE THAT A TREE IS WELCOME IN THEIR HOME, BUT SQUIRRELS ARE NOT?!
A BLUE SPRUCE MUST BE EASIER TO DOMESTICATE!

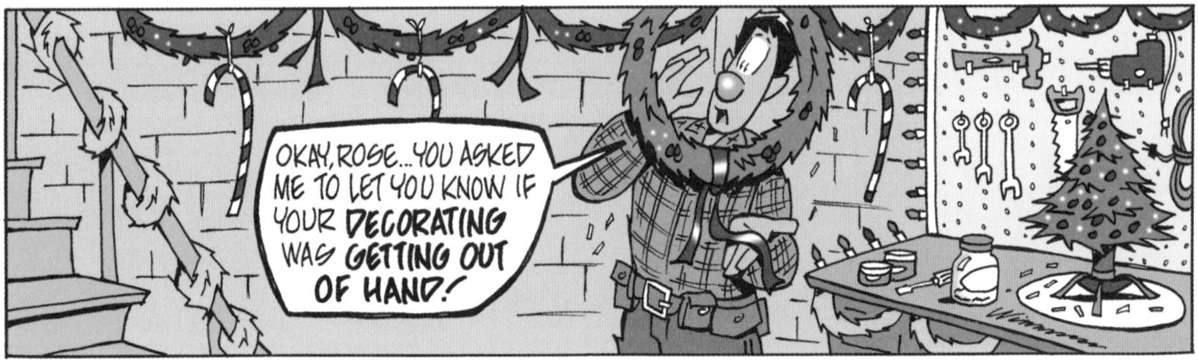
OKAY, ROSE... YOU ASKED ME TO LET YOU KNOW IF YOUR DECORATING WAS GETTING OUT OF HAND!

STOCKINGS AND CLAW SNAGS... A HOLIDAY TRADITION CONTINUES!

It must be a gift if it's wrapped with a bow!

CLEM GOT A NEW X1 SNOW RIPPER TOO! WE'RE GOING TO PLAY WITH THEM OUTSIDE!
OKAY, HAVE FUN!
VRROOOOM
YOU ARE SO LUCKY, PASQUALE! MY MOM WON'T LET ME KEEP MINE IN THE HOUSE!
VRROOM

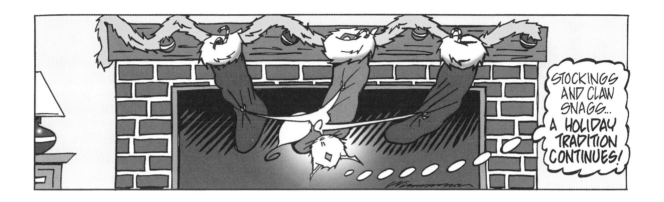

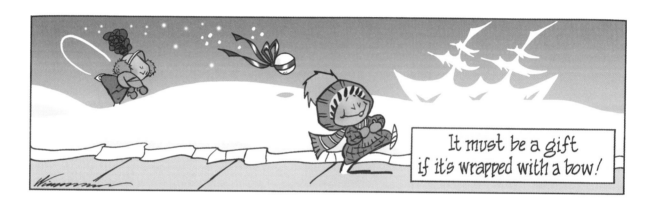

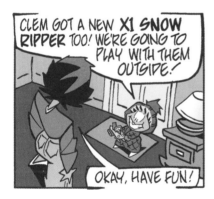

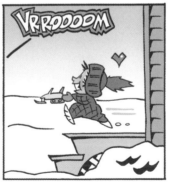

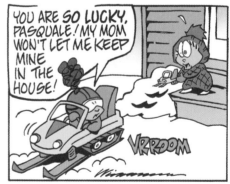

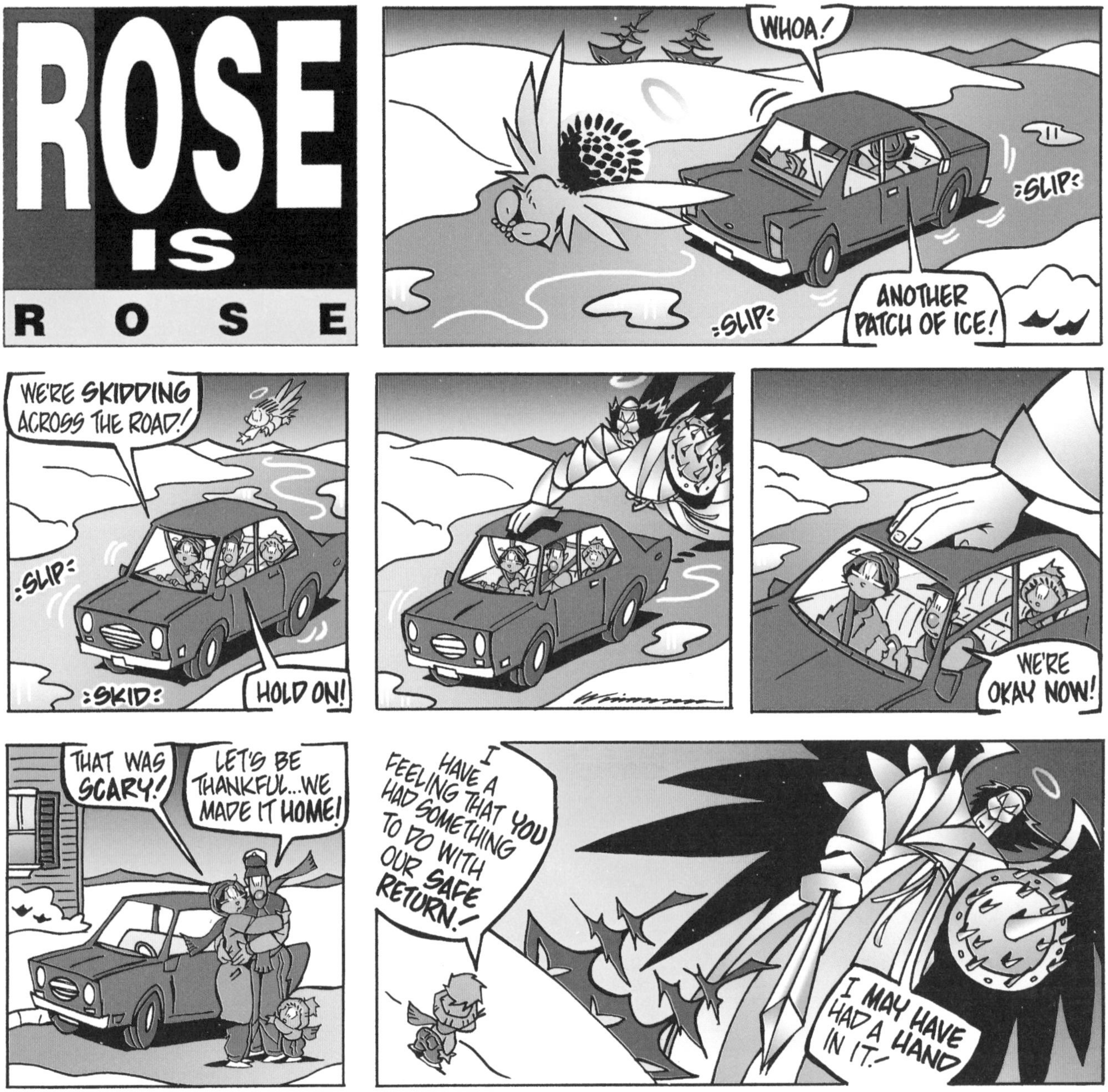
ROSE IS ROSE
WHOA!
ANOTHER PATCH OF ICE!
SLIP
SLIP
WE'RE SKIDDING ACROSS THE ROAD!
HOLD ON!
SLIP
SKID
WE'RE OKAY NOW!
THAT WAS SCARY!
LET'S BE THANKFUL...WE MADE IT HOME!
I HAVE A FEELING THAT YOU HAD SOMETHING TO DO WITH OUR SAFE RETURN!
I MAY HAVE HAD A HAND IN IT!

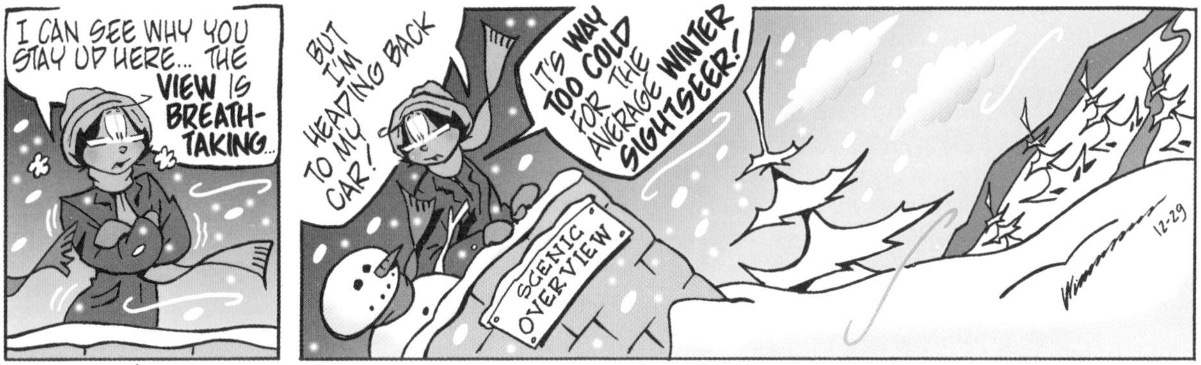
I CAN SEE WHY YOU STAY UP HERE... THE VIEW IS BREATH-TAKING...
BUT I'M HEADING BACK TO MY CAR!
IT'S WAY TOO COLD FOR THE AVERAGE WINTER SIGHTSEER!
SCENIC OVERVIEW
12-29

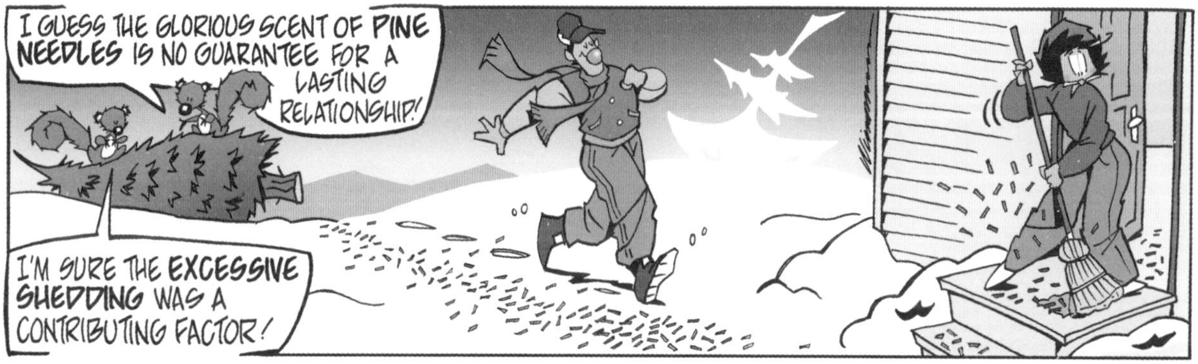
I GUESS THE GLORIOUS SCENT OF PINE NEEDLES IS NO GUARANTEE FOR A LASTING RELATIONSHIP!
I'M SURE THE EXCESSIVE SHEDDING WAS A CONTRIBUTING FACTOR!

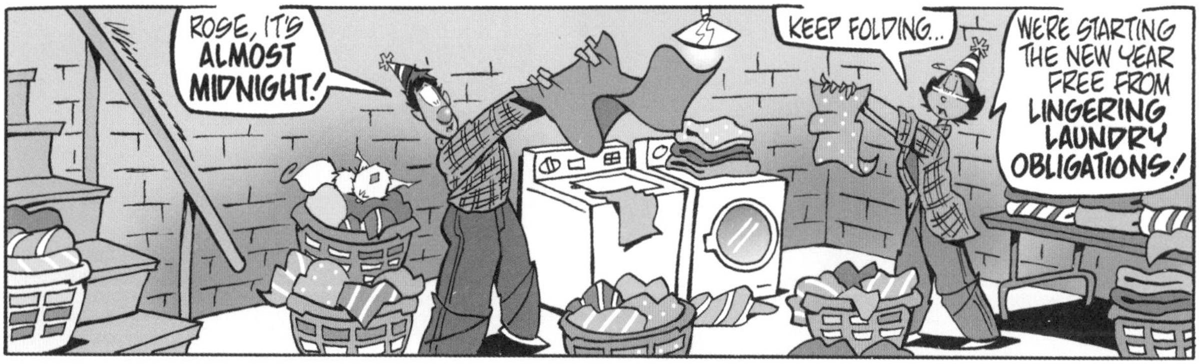
ROSE, IT'S ALMOST MIDNIGHT!
KEEP FOLDING...
WE'RE STARTING THE NEW YEAR FREE FROM LINGERING LAUNDRY OBLIGATIONS!

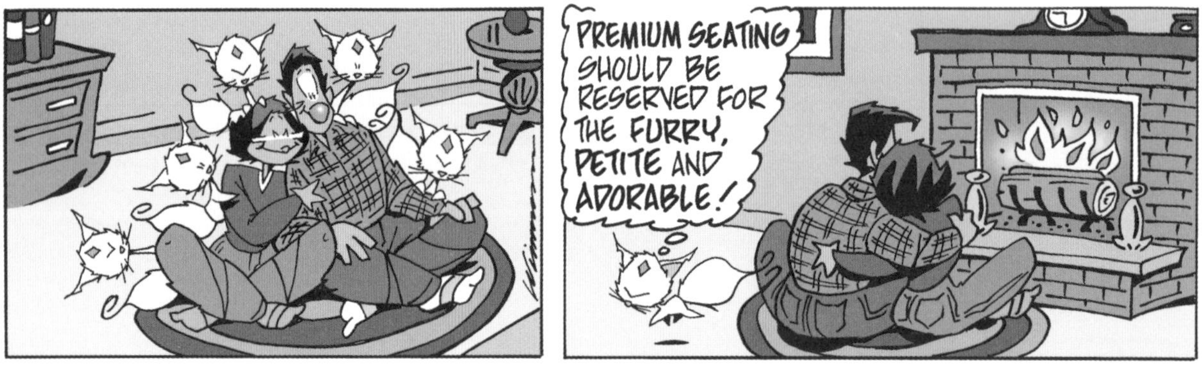
PREMIUM SEATING SHOULD BE RESERVED FOR THE FURRY, PETITE AND ADORABLE!

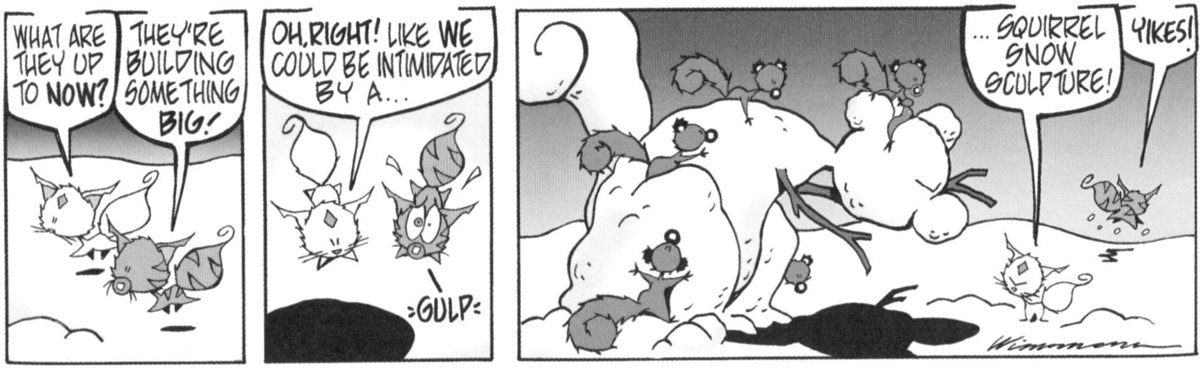
WHAT ARE THEY UP TO NOW?
THEY'RE BUILDING SOMETHING BIG!
OH, RIGHT! LIKE WE COULD BE INTIMIDATED BY A...
GULP
... SQUIRREL SNOW SCULPTURE!
YIKES!

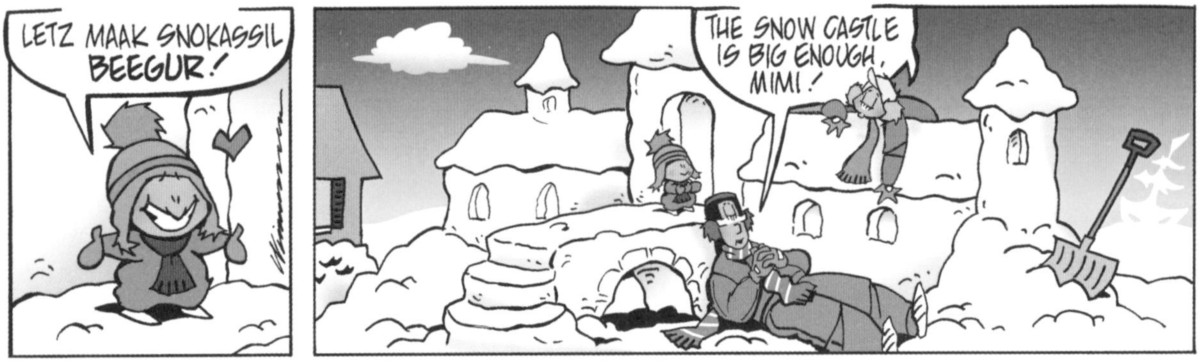
LETZ MAAK SNOKASSIL BEEGUR!
THE SNOW CASTLE IS BIG ENOUGH, MIMI!

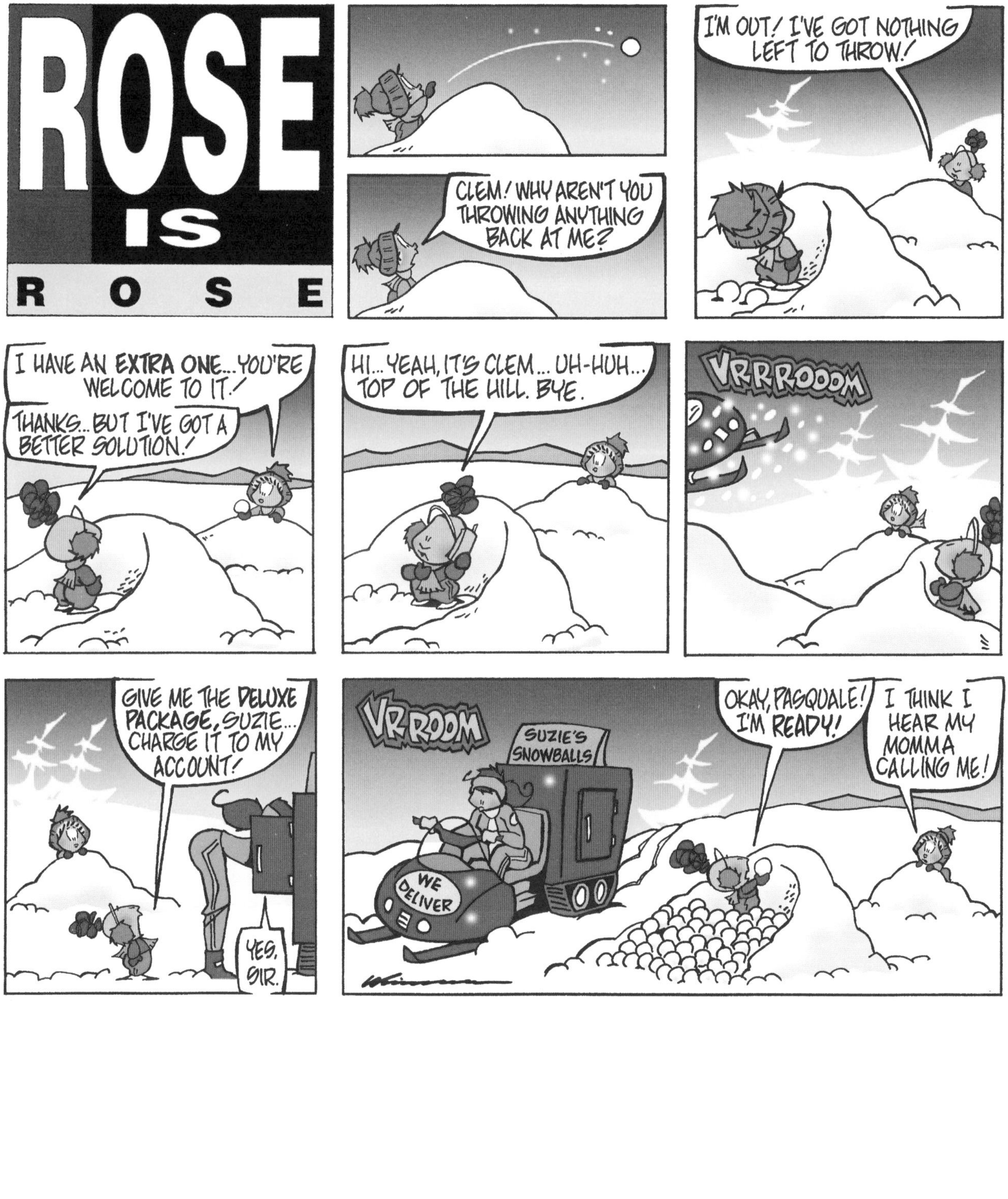
ROSE IS ROSE
CLEM! WHY AREN'T YOU THROWING ANYTHING BACK AT ME?
I'M OUT! I'VE GOT NOTHING LEFT TO THROW!
I HAVE AN EXTRA ONE...YOU'RE WELCOME TO IT!
THANKS...BUT I'VE GOT A BETTER SOLUTION!
HI...YEAH, IT'S CLEM... UH-HUH... TOP OF THE HILL. BYE.
VRRROOOM
GIVE ME THE DELUXE PACKAGE, SUZIE... CHARGE IT TO MY ACCOUNT!
YES, SIR.
VRROOM
SUZIE'S SNOWBALLS
WE DELIVER
OKAY, PASQUALE! I'M READY!
I THINK I HEAR MY MOMMA CALLING ME!

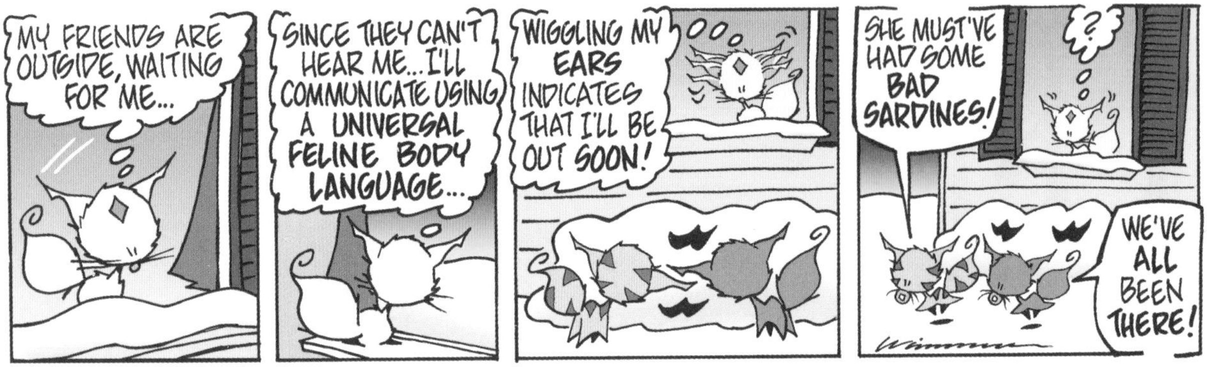
MY FRIENDS ARE OUTSIDE, WAITING FOR ME...
SINCE THEY CAN'T HEAR ME... I'LL COMMUNICATE USING A UNIVERSAL FELINE BODY LANGUAGE...
WIGGLING MY EARS INDICATES THAT I'LL BE OUT SOON!
SHE MUST'VE HAD SOME BAD SARDINES!
?
WE'VE ALL BEEN THERE!

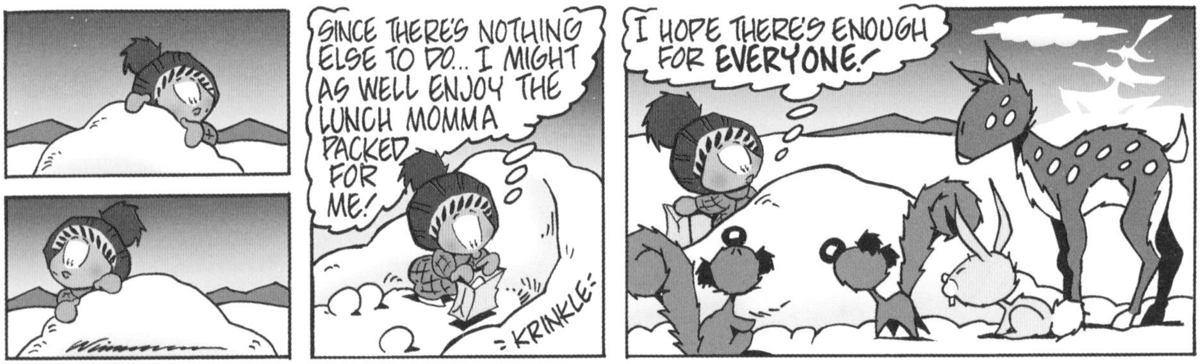
SINCE THERE'S NOTHING ELSE TO DO... I MIGHT AS WELL ENJOY THE LUNCH MOMMA PACKED FOR ME!
KRINKLE
I HOPE THERE'S ENOUGH FOR EVERYONE!

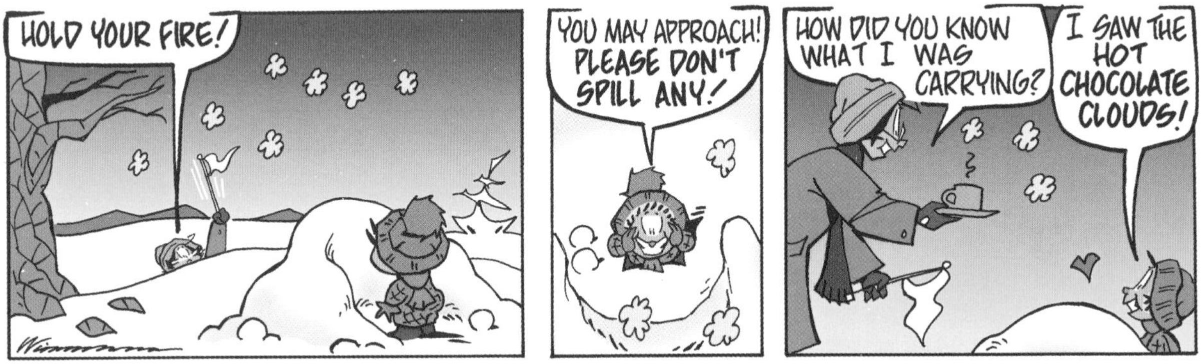
HOLD YOUR FIRE!
YOU MAY APPROACH! PLEASE DON'T SPILL ANY!
HOW DID YOU KNOW WHAT I WAS CARRYING?
I SAW THE HOT CHOCOLATE CLOUDS!

SITTING IN A SNOW FORT ALL DAY CAN BE VERY BORING...
THANK GOODNESS MOMMA LET ME BORROW HER RADIO!
CLICK
I COULD LISTEN TO THIS ALL DAY!
ONE MORE SONG AND THEN IT'S BACK TO GATHERING WALNUTS!

ROSE, EVEN YOU HAVE TO ADMIT THAT THIS IS OVER THE TOP!
I DISAGREE.
I SIMPLY WANT PASQUALE TO BE COMFORTABLE!
BUT SNOW FORTS SHOULDN'T HAVE CARPETING!
A TV WOULD BE NICE TOO!

FORTUNATELY... MEMBERS OF THE WINTER CLAW SNAG PATROL ARE ALWAYS ON DUTY!

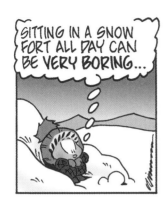

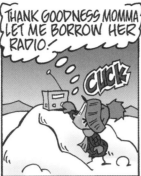

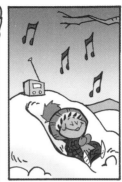

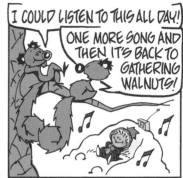

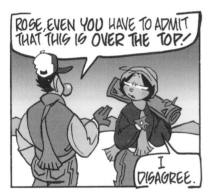

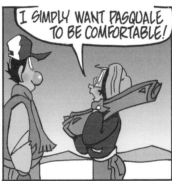

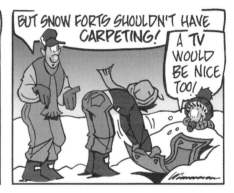

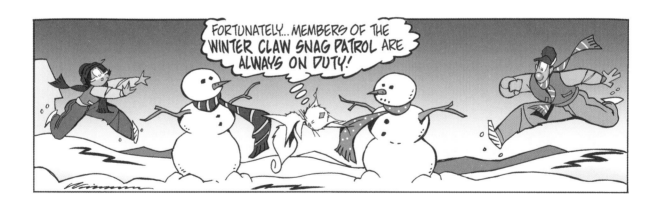

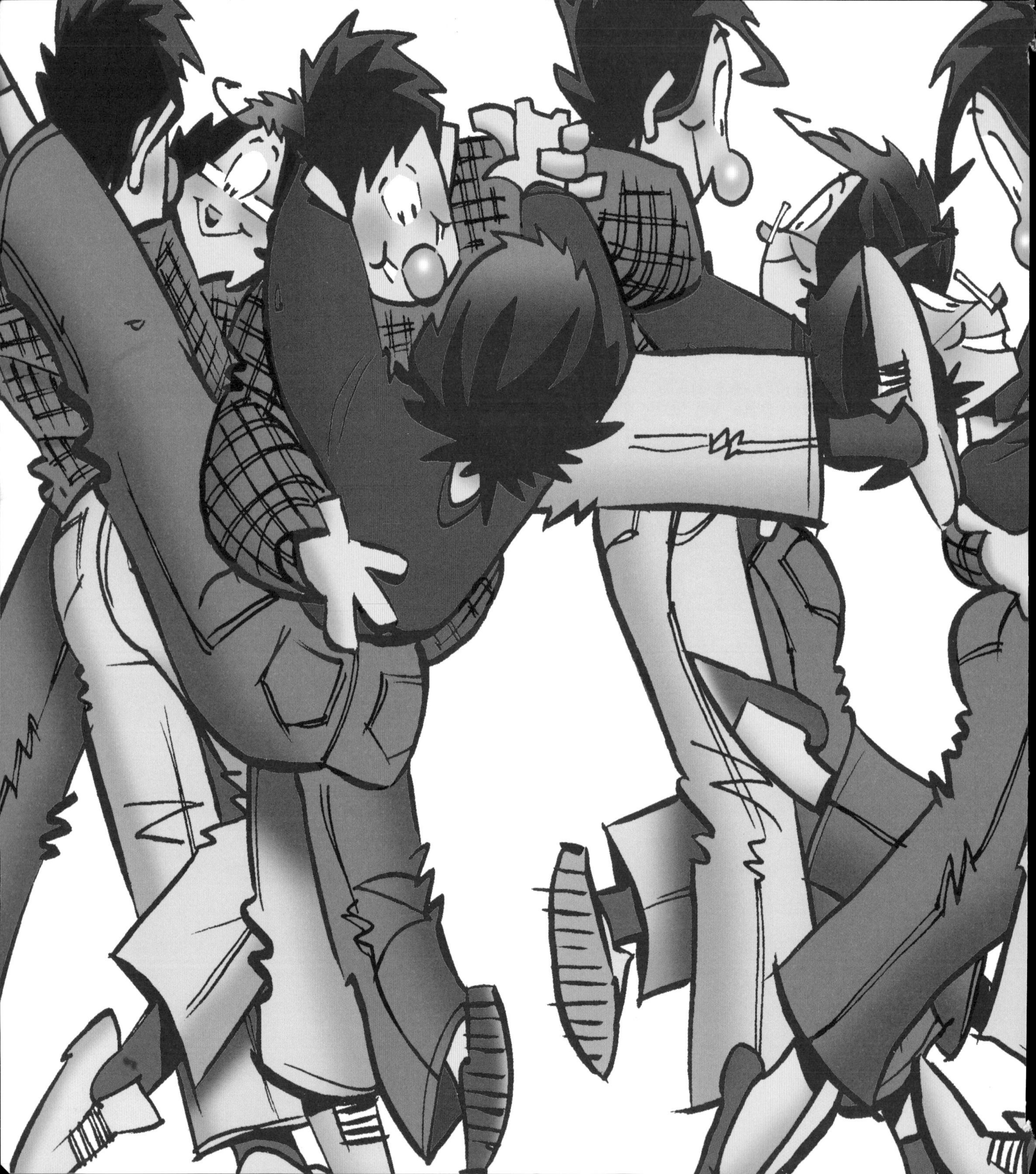